Current
Research
on
Instruction

Current Research on Instruction

Edited by

Richard C. Anderson
Gerald W. Faust
Marianne C. Roderick
Donald J. Cunningham
Thomas Andre

PRENTICE-HALL, INC., Englewood Cliffs, N.J.

© *1969 by PRENTICE-HALL, INC.*
ENGLEWOOD CLIFFS, NEW JERSEY

Current printing (last digit):
10 9 8 7 6 5 4 3 2 1

C-13-195610-8
P-13-195602-7

Library of Congress catalog card number:
69-17486

Printed in the United States of America

Prentice-Hall International, Inc., *London*
Prentice-Hall of Australia, Pty. Ltd., *Sydney*
Prentice-Hall of Canada, Ltd., *Toronto*
Prentice-Hall of India Private Ltd., *New Delhi*
Prentice-Hall of Japan, Inc., *Tokyo*

Preface

Traditionally educational psychology courses have aimed to give the student some exposure to virtually all of the aspects of psychology which could have relevance for the educational process and for an understanding of youth. Courses of study run the gamut from infant physiology to the sociology of institutions, from personality development to aptitude testing, and from classical conditioning to social psychology. While undeniably it would be good for the student to know something about each of these topics, the really essential issues are inevitably slighted with such broad coverage. We hold that learning and instruction are at the heart of educational psychology. It is our conviction that educational psychology and educational psychology courses should be directed mainly toward answering two questions: Under what conditions is student learning maximized? What features of instructional materials and teaching procedures facilitate student learning?

There does not exist a collection of papers on instructional research and development suitable for use in educational psychology classes. To be sure, some relevant papers appear in every reader, but nowhere is there a collection based on a systematic analysis of human learning and instruction. Herein lies the purpose of this book. The editors have tried to identify the important aspects of the instructional process about which something substantial is known and then to select the papers which best explicate and document the current state of knowledge. We have not shrunk from controversy; witness Section I on strategies of instructional research and Section II on instructional objectives. Nor have we avoided anomalies. For instance, as several of the studies reported in Section V illustrate, systematic use of reinforcement is a potent tool for modifying behavior. Yet, paradoxically, immediate knowledge of results in programed instruction—one of the most widely heralded applications of reinforcement principles—fails to facilitate student performance (see Chapter 24). Evidently knowledge of results is not a reinforcer, at least not a strong one, or there are interactions between knowledge of results and other features of programs which "short circuit" the instructional process. More research will be required to disentangle these issues and to engineer optimumly successful instruction.

With the exception of Sections I and VIII, the book is organized in terms of manipulable aspects of instructional materials and procedures. That is, it is organized in terms of independent or input variables instead of dependent or output variables. A section on problem solving and creativity, popular topics among educators, was not included. In addition to being poor research on the whole, studies dealing with problem solving and creativity have not clarified the features of instruction or conditions of learning which lead to the desired outcomes.

The criterion for choosing the themes upon which the sections are based was whether there was good reason to believe that implementation of the themes would result in better instruction. A section on classroom interaction was rejected because, in our opinion, research in this area has not led to warranted conclusions about features of instructional procedures that facilitate learning. A section on motivation was rejected for the same reason. Most of what is known about motivation that can be directly implemented in the classroom is better viewed in terms of reinforcement.

A case could be made for a collection of "classic" papers on instruction; however, as the title of the book suggests, we have chosen to emphasize recent papers. There are several justifications for an emphasis on current research. One is that such an emphasis may help give the student the sense that he is at the frontiers of knowledge, which indeed he is—or can be. Another is that research is generally cumulative: While fashion and other irrelevant forces control the behavior of researchers to some extent, recent studies do tend to be better designed and more pregnant in implications for classroom instruction than their precursors.

The last several years have seen an enormous increase in the quantity of instructional research. At least three new journals devoted to educational research have commenced publication. The number of papers read at the annual meetings of the American Educational Research Association has increased from 30 to 50 per cent in each of the last five years. In the face of the burgeoning number of reports, articles, and papers, it is difficult for the teacher of educational psychology—let alone the student—to keep abreast of important developments. Contributing to this difficulty is the fact that many significant papers are inaccessible because they were read at conventions, appeared in obscure government reports, or were published in now-defunct journals. "Classic" papers are likely to be well known and accessible. Some recent papers are less widely known and some are, practically speaking, inaccessible to most students in a course of more than 30 students.

This book is intended as a text or supplementary source for students of education and students of psychology concerned with its application to education. The editors hope that it will be used in undergraduate as well as graduate classes. To this end, every effort has been made to find readable papers which do not entail unnecessary technical complexity.

The editors gratefully acknowledge the assistance of Bonnie E. Anderson in preparing the manuscript for publication. We are indebted to the authors and publishers who permitted their papers to be reprinted.

RCA
GWF
MCR
DJC
TA

Contents

IV
The Student Response   115

V
Reinforcement and Feedback   179

VI   The Facilitation of Concept Learning   217

VII

Organization and Sequence 277

VIII

Evaluation of Instruction 343

Current
Research
on
Instruction

I

Approaches to Instructional Research and Development

The areas of instructional research and development are very broad. One goal of this first section is to give an indication of the scope of these areas. Another is to give some idea as to how educators view the current educational scene and how they feel education can be improved. It is our feeling that education today is facing a new frontier, a time of great change and great improvement. Some possible directions education in general and educational research and development in particular may take in the next few years are suggested in the pages following.

Gage and Unruh begin the section with a general review of current trends in research on teaching. Their chapter provides a glimpse of the many ways in which educational thinkers and researchers perceive the classroom situation. How these thinkers and researchers view the classroom and school learning determines to a great extent how they will answer the question which is central to this section—What research is worth doing?

In his chapter Ebel expresses the opinion that basic research—that is, research which has as its immediate goal the formulation of a small set of basic laws from which guides to educational practice can be derived—has little promise for education. Ebel argues that we should gather data which describe the present state of education and then let experience, reason, dialogue, and consensus—rather than controlled experimentation—guide us on the road to educational improvement.

Skinner's chapter provides a counterbalance to Ebel's position. Skinner reflects on a decade of teaching machines and the educational technology that has risen from his basic research on learning. He feels that great educational improvements will come from the application of the techniques of experimental analysis of behavior. Skinner considers many alternative ways of solving educational problems. Each of these he dismisses in favor of the alternative presented by the programed instruction movement. He feels that only through the development of an empirically based educational technology can we hope to bridge the gap between teaching theory and actual practice. Skinner goes on to explain some of the teaching principles developed under the aegis of the programed instruction movement and concludes by arguing that educational research directed toward the behavior of individual students holds the greatest promise. One of Skinner's main points is that educational researchers should get closer to live students. Through close contact with individual students, the researcher will learn which manipulations cause changes in student behavior and which do not. And thus, he will develop both an insight into education and a confidence in man's ability to improve it.

In the last chapter in this section J. M. Atkin attempts an in-depth analysis of the effects of educational research on one segment of the educational world, science education. In doing so he provides a commentary on the progress and promise of educational research and development work in general. Atkin speaks as one who has been deeply involved in the large curriculum reform projects. His position is somewhat similar to that of Ebel in that he feels there is little to be gained from basic psychological research. In fact, he believes that major changes in our educational system will most likely come from curriculum development projects like those with which he has been associated. Furthermore, he thinks that a new approach is needed if we are to develop a viable educational theory. And Atkin suggests that this approach be similar in form to that taken by ethologists: we should immerse great thinkers from a great variety of academic backgrounds in the classroom, and then see what explanations they give for what goes on there. Atkin's broad aesthetic approach clashes strongly with the highly structured analytic approach supported by Gage and Unruh and Skinner.

Theoretical Formulations for Research on Teaching

N. L. GAGE / *Stanford University*

W. R. UNRUH / *Stanford University*

What conceptualizations, formulations, and analyses of research on teaching have been set forth since 1962? Writing of this kind has appeared in some abundance, as befits a field of research that has not yet achieved the new paradigms that are the precursors of fruitful revolutions in science. The ideas in such discourse determine the research worker's answer to his first and crucial question: What research is worth doing?

The Proposed Revolution in Teaching

A revolution in teaching is being fomented. If successful, it will overthrow the hegemony of the centuries-old pattern whereby one teacher and 20 to 40 pupils engage for most kinds of instruction in a teacher-dominated discourse. The revolutionary force is programed instruction—broadly defined (Corey, 1967) as instruction in which objectives

are described with special care and explicitness, behaviors are analyzed with much psychological sophistication, sequencing is based on an experimental approach, revisions are made after empirical evidence, instructional stimuli are carefully developed and controlled, frequent and explicit responding by the learner is procured, and relatively quick knowledge of results is provided the learner. If the revolution succeeds, the teacher will spend much less time each day with groups of students in time-honored ways—discussing, lecturing, tutoring, demonstrating, and so on. And such traditional activities will need to be justified rather than taken for granted.

The gathering signs of the revolu-

Reprinted with the permission of the senior author and the publisher from *Review of Educational Research*, 1967, Vol. 37, 358–70.

tion have been noted in the mass media (e.g., Bowen, 1967), in *Fortune* (Silberman, 1966), in the *Scientific American* (Suppes, 1966), and in a yearbook of the National Society for the Study of Education (1967). Hanson and Komoski (1965) reported that the percentage of responding school administrators reporting some use of programed instruction increased from 11 percent in 1962 to 36 percent in 1963. In short, a spectre is haunting research on teaching—the spectre of programed instruction.

Educational research workers are divided on this possible transformation of the school. Some (e.g., Jackson, 1966b) regard it as neither desirable nor probable, while others hold that "there is every reason to suppose that good self-instructional programs are highly effective" (Gagné, 1965, p. 282) and, further, that "holding students together in a class is probably the greatest source of inefficiency in education" (Skinner, 1961, p. 387).

Whether the revolution is smoldering or well under way is a matter of perspective. But it cannot be ignored in the present review, since it threatens to render irrelevant much of the research on teaching that has been done, including much of that published since 1962. It is with this caveat in mind that the reader should consider what follows.

"DESCRIBING" VERSUS "IMPROVING" IN RESEARCH ON TEACHING

One cleavage in approaches to research on teaching is that between describing, or concern with the way teaching is (Jackson, 1966a), and improving, or concern with the way teaching ought to be (Stolurow, 1965). The first of these approaches regards teaching as a realm of phenomena worth studying simply because it exists and is fascinating. The second deals with teaching as something needing to be improved, because it is not as good as it ought to be. The first approach resembles that of the anthropologist studying cultures neutrally; the second, that of the inventor working on a better way to meet a practical need.

Protagonists of the two approaches have difficulty understanding one another. Describers see improvers as tampering with humanistic values and probably failing because of their poor understanding of the human condition. Improvers consider describers to be indifferent to the inadequacies of the conventional classroom or bent merely on improving our knowledge of obsolescent forms. Describers like Bellack and his co-workers (1966), Flanders (1964), Jackson (1966a), and Meux and Smith (1964) have produced detailed analyses of what goes on in present-day classrooms. Improvers like Glaser (1965), Skinner (1965), and Stolurow (1965) regard the present-day class as hopelessly inconsistent with known facts about individual differences among learners, the difficulties of appropriately structuring and sequencing subject matter in the heat of teacher-learner interaction, and the needs of learners for thousands of reinforcement contingencies.

The long-range assumption of describers is that once important correlates of teacher effectiveness in the present-day classroom have been ascertained, it will be possible to train teachers to be more effective. They take the conventional classroom as given and seek to improve the behavior of the teachers in it. To lay the bases for such improvements, they seek the correlates of teacher effectiveness in the classroom. They take what Stolurow (1965) called a "passive" approach in that they seek to "model the master teacher." The improvers, taking an "active" approach, attempt rather to "master the teaching model," i.e., to develop a new model of instruction that will make explicit the manipulable elements and relationships needed to optimize learning. Experimentation will correct and refine the model.

TWO CONVERGENCES ON CONCEPTIONS OF TEACHING

Despite their differences, describers and improvers have produced some strikingly similar formulations. First, consider how they analyze the teaching task. Jackson (1966a) distinguished between the "preactive" and the "interactive" phases of teaching. By preactive, he meant those aspects of teaching behavior that the teacher engages in prior to meeting pupils face-to-face. In this phase, the teacher selects objectives, plans the curriculum, arranges the classroom, and studies the readiness of pupils. In the interactive phase, the teacher provides pupils with verbal stimulation of various kinds, makes explanations, asks questions, listens to students' responses, and provides guidance.

This distinction parallels that made by Stolurow (1965) in formulating the model of programed instruction. He first distinguished the "pretutorial" phase, which is aimed at the selection of an initial teaching program intended to produce a given outcome; it takes into account the desired outcomes, or objectives, and the learner's entry behaviors. The "tutorial" phase, analogous to Jackson's interactive phase, consists in the ongoing programed instruction itself, in which the student is presented with instructional material and tasks in "frames," is required to respond to the tasks, and is given feedback as to the correctness of his response.

Second, consider their formulations of the instructional process. How different is this process in conventional classrooms from that in programed instruc-

tion? Bellack and his associates (1966) made an intensive study of typescripts of tape-recorded language in 15 social studies classes. They found that—

The fundamental pedagogical pattern of discourse consisted of a teacher's solicitation followed by a pupil's response; this sequence was frequently followed by a teacher's reaction. In other words, a typical pattern started with the teacher asking a question. . ., which a pupil answered . . ., followed by the teacher's reaction to or rating of the pupil's response. . . (p. 55).

At least in these classes, teachers typically followed a pattern similar to that of programed instruction.

Both live and programed instruction exhibit a repeated sequence of (a) structuring, (b) presentation of ideas, (c) solicitation of a response, (d) response by the learner, and (e) reaction to the response. This is the same model, in essence, as that explicated by Gage (1963) on the basis of formulations by B. O. Smith (the "cycle of giving and taking instruction"), Ryans (adapting the schema of dyadic units set forth by R. R. Sears), Stone and Leavitt, and Runkel. The carefully analyzed data of Bellack and his co-workers confirm what has long been suspected to be the predominant pattern of teacher-student interaction in the classroom. In short, live teaching and programed instruction seem to have in common a basic cycle or rhythm.

Models of the Domain of Research on Teaching

Attempts to schematize the domain of research on teaching continue to appear. Teacher behavior was formulated as information processing by Ryans (1963). The information processing was hypothesized to involve a five-phase sequence of activities: (a) sensing, identifying, and classifying inputs; (b) evaluation of possible courses of action; (c) the making of decisions by the teacher; (d) programing or logical-psychological ordering and arranging of information output; and (e) transmission of appropriate information to the pupil. The whole process was considered to be influenced by the teacher's information inputs and information processing capabilities, on the one hand, and by external information inputs, or interacting conditions external to the teacher, on the other.

The formulation seems to be all-embracing, and that is perhaps its major weakness; it seems to exclude nothing and to provide little guidance as to the entry points for fruitful research. As elaborated by Ryans's two complex charts, it includes almost every variable conceivably relevant to teaching.

A criticism of the formulation of teaching as information processing and decision making was made by Jackson (1966a) in his distinction between the preactive and interactive phases of teaching. Preactive behavior may indeed "resemble, albeit crudely, the stereotype of the problem solver, the decision maker, the hypothesis tester, the inquirer" (p. 13). But—

In the interactive setting the teacher's behavior is more or less spontaneous . . . lately it has become popular to think of the teacher's activity in terms that describe the problem solver or the hypothesis tester. . . . There may be some advantage in using these logical and highly rational models to describe the teacher's in-class activities, and there may even be some moments when the teacher feels like a decision maker in the interactive setting, but these moments, I would wager, are few and far between (pp. 13, 14).

The interactive phase was similarly characterized by Cronbach (1967). In adapting instructional method to the individual, the teacher—

Barely acknowledges the comment one pupil makes in class discussion, and stops to praise a lesser contribution from another who (he thinks) needs special encouragement. He turns away from one pupil who asks for help—"You can find the answer by yourself if you keep at it"—and walks the length of the classroom to offer help to another, because he has decided to encourage independence of the former pupil and minimize frustration of the latter. . . . The significant thing about these adaptations is their informality (pp. 28–29).

The uncontrived character, speed, and uncontrollability of teaching moves in the "interactive" phase make the formulation of teaching as information processing seem merely metaphorical, not to be taken literally.

Biddle (1964) offered a "seven-variable model" for the investigation of teacher effectiveness. In this model, (a) formative experiences, (b) teacher properties, (c) teacher behaviors, (d) immediate effects, and (e) long-term consequences serve as main sequence variables; (f) classroom situations and (g) school and community contexts serve as contextual variables. The main sequence variables form a casually linked chain, while the contextual variables provide the situations and environments which imbed and interact with the variables thus linked. Biddle's model, falling into the category of criterion-of-effectiveness paradigms, resembles those formulated by Mitzel and Ryans, as reviewed by Gage (1963).

After reviewing the forms of measurement available for the variables in his model, Biddle classified these methods as "recommended," "alternate," and "poor" for each of his seven categories of variables. Whether such evaluations of a given method—such as "objective instruments," "behavioral observation," or "rating forms"—should be made without regard to its specific form and purpose is questionable. In particular, rating methods have often been used in reliable and valid ways; Biddle's call for "the elimination of rating forms in serious research on teacher effectiveness until an understanding of the biases is available" seems much too strong. But his overall categorization of variables seems useful, in view of its similarity to previous attempts, in indicating an emerging consensus as to the major domains of research on teaching.

Another comprehensive model—one for school learning—was set forth by Carroll (1965) in terms that provided for (a) "quality of instruction" as one of five major variables, the others being (b) aptitude, expressed as the amount of time required by the learner to attain a specified criterion; (c) perseverance, measured by the amount of time the learner is willing to spend at learning; (d) opportunity to learn, defined as amount of time actually allowed for learning in the particular setting; and (e) ability to comprehend instruction, or perhaps verbal intelligence. Such a model, applied to the study of teaching, would require that the other four variables be controlled, held constant, or adjusted for. Statistical methods (e.g., analysis of covariance or factorial design), matching, or random assignment to experimental and control groups could be used to compare one instructional method with another. As determiners of the quality of teaching itself, Carroll sees such factors as listenability, readability, the structure and logic of the concepts presented, reinforcement schedules, and incentive systems.

Siegel and Siegel (1967) suggested a paradigm entailing multivariate analysis and provision for studying interaction among variables. Their "instructional gestalt" embraces four classes of independent variables (learning environments, instructors, learners, and courses) and their interactions; the dependent variables include both effectiveness and process criteria of achievement, thought, attitude, and extraclass behavior. As for methodology, they regard factorially designed analysis of variance as preferable to correlational methods. In any one investigation, it becomes necessary to exclude some classes of independent variables to prevent the number of combinations from becoming unmanageable. A separate analysis of variance is made for each of the criteria. The approach was illustrated with an investigation of factors affecting the outcomes of television instruction.

The substantive and methodological aspects of the approach need to be considered separately. The former determines the variables investigated and depends on the theories of teaching and learning implicit or explicit in the investigator's operational definitions. Whether the Siegels have chosen wisely in their general outline is hardly disputable, but whether their specific choices in their illustrative investigation will prove fruitful in future investigations remains, of course, to be seen. The methodological model, factorially designed analysis of variance, has long been available, but its uses have not previously been urged as convincingly and forcefully for the investigation of instructional variables. It deserves further trial to determine whether significant interaction patterns can be consistently obtained in successive investigations of the same independent variables, above and beyond main effects. Educational doctrine about the importance of such interactions can be tested in this way.

Relation of Theories of Teaching to Theories of Learning

Must theory of teaching depend on theory of learning? Scandura (1966) took a negative position: many learning principles may be of only incidental importance to a theory of teaching, some teaching concepts and laws have no direct counterparts in learning theory— technologies like task analysis and sequencing could form the subject matter of a teaching theory. Teaching theory operates at a molar level, and reductionism, i.e., reducing molar teacher behaviors to molecular learning principles, is unlikely to be fruitful.

A different position on this question was taken by Ausubel (1967), who held that the present irrelevance of learning theory (Gage, 1964) is not inevitable; it holds only for learning theory to date and not for "a truly realistic and scientifically viable theory of classroom learning" (p. 210). Ausubel similarly took exception to B. O. Smith's position that learning and teaching are different and that a theory of learning cannot tell one how to teach. Rather, "learning is still the only feasible measure of teaching merit . . . valid principles of teaching are necessarily based on relevant principles of learning, but are not simple and direct applications of these principles. . . . I would classify basic principles of teaching as special derivatives of school learning theory" (pp. 212, 213).

In his provocatively entitled *Toward a Theory of Instruction,* Bruner (1966a) presented one chapter bearing directly on theory of instruction. In his view, such a theory must differ from descriptive theories of learning by being prescriptive and normative; that is, such theory is "concerned with how what one wishes to teach can best be learned, with improving rather than describing learn-

ing" (p. 40). The theory should specify the experiences that predispose the individual toward learning, the ways in which a body of knowledge should be structured, the most effective sequences in which to present the materials, and the nature and pacing of rewards and punishments. The problem of "predispositions" refers to the activation, maintenance, and direction of the learner's exploration of alternatives. The structure and form of knowledge refer to the ways in which the mode of representation, economy, and power of the structure of any domain of knowledge affect the ability of the learner to master it. In discussing "sequence and its uses," Bruner proposed that the optimal sequence will proceed from "enactive" through "iconic" to "symbolic" representations. As to the form and pacing of reinforcement, he held that knowledge of results is useful at the right time and place. To "discern how the student grasps what has been presented, what his systematic errors are, and how these are overcome," Bruner suggested both "systematic observational studies—work close in spirit to that of Piaget and of ethologists like Tinbergen" (p. 54)— and the use of programs to obtain a detailed behavioral record for analysis.

In a "Discussion of Bruner's 'Theorems' " (Bruner, 1966b, pp. 245–52), participants in the Working Conference on Research on Children's Learning agreed that, whether or not learning theory can handle the problem of instruction, it is not doing so now. On the question of whether separate theories of instruction are needed for different subject matters and grade levels, it was urged that it is possible to concentrate on "general parameters, on transdisciplinary principles which could be concretely applied in different disciplines" (p. 246). Further, it was held that a theory of instruction must rest not only on a theory of learning but also on a theory of development.

Setting forth problems concerning the nature of theory that must be faced prior to any valid development of a theory of instruction, Travers (1966) objected to the position, implied by Bruner's term *prescriptive*, that such a theory must focus on "optimum conditions." That is,

Optimum conditions of various kinds derive from theories but are not the essence of scientific theories. . . . I would conceive of a theory of instruction as consisting of a set of propositions stating relationships between, on the one hand, measures of the outcomes of education and, on the other hand, measures of both the conditions to which the learner is exposed and the variables representing characteristics of the learner (p. 50).

Travers holds that a major obstacle to such theory development is that the technical language needed for such a task has not yet evolved. A theory of instruction has to be empirically based, and the data must be closely related to the phenomena of the classroom.

The dependent variables of the system, rather than being specified in terms of behavior, should be specified in terms of tasks or problem situations or task solutions; thus, a useful taxonomy of objectives would involve a taxonomy of tasks. The task characteristic should be directly observable rather than response-inferred. The tasks should be arranged into a system of scales such that, for a given outcome, all lower tasks can be successfully completed and all higher tasks cannot. The major independent variables can be classified as relating to pupils, pupil tasks, teachers, and teacher tasks. Pupil task variables include those that teachers can manipulate to optimize learning; examples are reading difficulty level, sequencing variables, perceptual complexity, and concreteness versus ab-

stractness. (Computer-based instruction seems objectionable to Travers because it cannot furnish the concrete objects and situations, manipulable by pupils, that are needed for effective learning in the elementary school.) As for research on teacher behavior variables, the difficulty is that hypothetical patterns can be concocted but not acted out by actual teachers. The proper distribution of teacher time over the various tasks could be determined by applying the methods that operations research has developed for solving the "transportation problem," or the problem of optimum use of shipping space to provide, say, maximum military effort at the final port.

No one would disagree with Travers' notions about the importance of empirical data and verification. But he may be wrong in objecting to data-free, or "armchair," analyses and formulations of the problem of theory of instruction, of which his own paper is an instance. Such analyses are helpful in making decisions about what kinds of data should be sought.

This kind of analysis was attempted by Gage (1964) in setting forth the need for specification in developing theories of teaching. He suggested distinctions in terms of teaching activities, objectives, families of learning theory, and components of the learning process. Then he went on to illustrate how certain combinations of these make better sense than others. For example, for one kind of teacher activity (explaining) and objective (comprehension), it makes better sense to draw upon one kind of theory of learning (cognitive) and focus upon one particular component of the learning process (perception). Learning theorists agree that there are many kinds of learning whose dissimilarities in terms of process and phenomena are "much more striking than the similarities" (Melton, 1964, p. 338). Similarly, there must be several kinds of theory of instruction, some better for one combination of objectives and learners and some for others.

A compilation of points of view and approaches to the study of teaching (Verduin, 1967) contained brief chapters on the ideas of various writers. The chapters on the ideas of Bellack, Broudy, Gage, Gallagher, Hickey, B. O. Smith, Suchman, Taba, and Woodruff dealt with cognitive aspects of teaching, or ways in which teachers' behaviors affect learners' achievement of cognitive objectives; the chapters on the ideas of Flanders and Getzels dealt with affective and social phenomena in the classroom.

The Need for Synthesis

Various writers use different conceptualizations of the variables and processes that enter into learning and teaching. This diversity becomes especially apparent in volumes like those assembled by Bellack (1963), Biddle and Ellena (1964), Siegel (1967), and Verduin (1967). Many of the same writers appear in several of these volumes, with only slight modifications of their ideas. Apart from that fact, the books impress one with the need for serious efforts to bring together the ideas that, despite differences in vocabulary and detail, seem to arise in two or more apparently disparate formulations. Successful efforts of this kind would reduce the disorder that arises from the way in which theorists of different persuasions talk past each other, each in seemingly autistic disregard of what the others say.

Item: the concepts of (a) "entry behaviors," as promulgated by the programed instruction school (e.g., Stolurow, 1965); (b) readiness, as advanced by educational psychologists in general; and (c) the pre-existing cognitive struc-ture under which new ideas are subsumed, as formulated by Ausubel (1967). These concepts deal with properties of the learner that affect what and how he will learn. Although they differ substantially in emphasis, detail, and hypothesized *modus operandi*, they have much in common and ought to be collated.

Item: the concepts of (a) cognitive structure, as formulated by Ausubel (1967) and Bruner (1966a); (b) learning structure (Gagné, 1965); and (c) logic tree (Hickey and Newton, 1964), among others. Again, whatever their variations in vocabulary and detail, these similar ideas ought to be assimilated to one another.

Item: the conceptions of the instructional process as (a) cyclical give-and-take (Runkel, Ryans, Smith, and Stone and Leavitt, as cited by Gage, 1963); (b) a pattern of structuring-soliciting-responding-reacting, as described by Bellack and his associates (1966); and (c) a sequence of stimulus (frame representation), response, and reinforcement (knowledge of results), as formulated by the programed instruction school (Stolurow, 1965). Except for reading and lecturing, most instances of instruction, whether programed or provided in the conventional classroom, seem to partake of repeated occurrences of a cycle of this kind. The common elements in these formulas ought to be recognized as such and brought together.

Item: the compilation of teacher behaving styles by Ryans (1963), based on an examination of a considerable literature on ratings, observations, students' evaluations, responses to inventories, and test results. Although Ryans's lists of variables are categorized in terms of his conception of teacher behavior as information processing, their usefulness does not depend on acceptance of that model. His clusters already make good sense of a roughly logical sort, but the lists can be used in formulating more systematic and coherent categorizations of teacher behaviors and characteristics.

Views on Promising Directions

Apart from those already mentioned, several writers have indicated what they regard as bases for hope that future research on teaching will yield significant advances. Cogan (1963), for example, saw a "new phase" as possible because of the availability of devices for recording classroom behavior in ways that make possible much more meticulous and repeated analyses of such behavior—devices such as sound film and videotape recorders. (Biddle makes the same point in the preceding chapter of this issue of the REVIEW.) Gage (1967) regarded as promising an analytic approach whereby much smaller time-segments of teacher behavior, such as those studied and manipulated in microteaching (Bush, 1966), will be examined for their relationships to much more finely discriminated aspects of learner behavior and achievement, i.e., to "micro-criteria" of effectiveness (Gage, 1963, p. 120).

But others see the main hope of progress in thoroughgoing efforts to individualize instruction. Thus, Ericksen (1967, pp. 156–57) hoped to "release and give greater freedom to individual-difference variables. . . . The student-linked factors . . . are the key factors that will open up new resources for making significant changes in the quality of the educational process." Related to this outlook is the conviction on the part of many psychologists (e.g., Skinner, Gagné) that instruction in graded classrooms is, in large part, a drawback. "Individually prescribed instruction"

(Lindvall and Bolvin, 1967) represents an attempt to do away with the teaching of whole classes at a time by permitting pupils to work at their own pace on tasks prescribed by teachers on the basis of frequently administered measures of learning on small, carefully planned units of instruction.

But even were this general position concerning classroom teaching to be accepted, few would deny that, for some objectives, the teaching of pupils in groups, even whole classes, is advantageous or essential. The question, What are these objectives? has not yet been subjected to rigorous analysis. At the least, of course, "ability to participate in group discussions" is such an objective at all levels of education. Similarly, various kinds of ability to explore ideas through intellectual interaction may require classroom teaching. Or, those things that can be learned best from observing the teacher's modeling of how an educated person behaves require live teachers in classrooms.

Yet much of the contemporary argument in favor of individualizing instruction, or adapting teaching to individual differences among learners, for many kinds of objectives, is extremely plausible. Learners do differ in ways relevant to their ability to profit from different kinds of instruction, content, incentives, and the like. Almost by definition, instruction adapted to these individual differences should be more effective.

If so, why has not the evidence from attempts to individualize instruction yielded more dramatic results? Why are not the mean scores on achievement measures of pupils taught with due respect for their individual needs and abilities substantially higher, in unmistakable ways, than those of students taught in the conventional classroom, where everyone reads the same book, listens to the same lecture, participates in the same classroom discussion, moves at the same pace, and works at the same problems? For the fact is that, despite several decades of concern with individualization, few if any striking results have been reported.

Perhaps the time is ripe for a reexamination of assumptions about what goes on in the conventional classroom. Despite the kinds of apparent uniformity noted above, pupils in the conventional classroom may somehow individualize instruction for themselves so that each takes from it what is fairly well suited to his needs. A search for explanations of this kind may be more fruitful than continued recourse to the plea that, so far, the individualization has not been good enough. Is it inconceivable that the kind of "spraying" of stimuli, ideas, questions, and answers that goes on in a relatively unplanned (unprogramed) way in the conventional classroom does succeed nonetheless, by virtue of its near randomness, in hitting most pupils where they are? Careful analysis of who gets what out of instruction in the conventional classroom may

reveal a much greater degree of appropriate individualization than has been thought possible, especially by proponents of explicitly individualized instruction.

But beyond such a possibility there lies the promise, at least in principle, that improved individualization will make a major difference. Such improved individualization could be based upon what Cronbach (1967) described as "aptitude-treatment" interactions. Similar to those outlined by Siegel and Siegel (1967), such interactions occur when "the regression line relating aptitude to payoff crosses the regression line for the competing treatment" (Cronbach, 1967, p. 30). "And it will be a long time before we have adequately validated rules of adaptation that take into account even a half-dozen differential variables" (p. 37). If so, instruction that is not explicitly individualized will not soon be shown to be unmistakably inferior to that which is. Research on teaching in the conventional classroom will not, in that event, be unrelated to educational needs.

References

Ausubel, David P. A cognitive-structure theory of school learning. In Laurence Siegal, ed., *Instruction: some contemporary viewpoints.* San Francisco: Chandler Publishing Co., 1967. Chapter 8, pp. 207–57.

Bellack, Arno A., ed. *Theory and research in teaching.* New York: Bureau of Publications, Teachers College, Columbia University, 1963. 122 pp.

Bellack, Arno A., and others. *The language of the classroom.* New York: Teachers College Press, 1966. 273 pp.

Biddle, Bruce J. The integration of teacher effectiveness research. In Bruce J. Biddle and William J. Ellena, eds., *Contemporary research on teacher effectiveness.* New York: Holt, Rinehart and Winston, 1964. Chapter 1, pp. 1–40.

Biddle, Bruce J., and Ellena, William J., eds. *Contemporary research on teacher effectiveness.* New York: Holt, Rinehart and Winston, 1964. 352 pp.

Bowen, Ezra. The computer as a tutor. *Life* **62,** No. 4: 68–69, 72, 74–76, 78, 81; January 27, 1967.

Bruner, Jerome S. *Toward a theory of instruction.* Cambridge: Harvard University Press, 1966. 176 pp. (a)

Bruner, Jerome S., ed. *Learning about learning: A conference report.* U.S. Department of Health, Education, and Welfare, Office of Education, Cooperative Research Monograph No. 15. Washington, D.C.: Government Printing Office, 1966. 276 pp. (b)

Bush, Robert N. The science and art of educating teachers. In Stanley Munson Elam, ed., *Improving teacher education in the United States.* Bloomington, Ind.: Phi Delta Kappa, 1966. Chapter 2, pp. 35–62.

Carroll, John B. School learning over the long haul. In John D. Krumboltz, ed., *Learning and the educational process.* Chicago: Rand McNally and Co., 1965. Chapter 10, pp. 249–69.

Cogan, Morris L. Research on the behavior of teachers: A new phase. *Journal of Teacher Education,* **14**: 238–43, September 1963.

Corey, Stephen M. The nature of instruction. *Programed instruction.* Sixty-Sixth Yearbook, Part II, National Society for the Study of Education. Chicago: University of Chicago Press, 1967. Chapter 1, pp. 5–27.

Cronbach, Lee J. How can instruction be adapted to individual differences? In Robert M. Gagné, ed., *Learning and individual differences.* Columbus, Ohio: Charles E. Merrill Books, 1967. Chapter 2, pp. 23–39.

Ericksen, Stanford C. The zigzag curve of learning. In Laurence Siegel, ed., *Instruction: some contemporary viewpoints.* San Francisco: Chandler Publishing Co., 1967. Chapter 6, pp. 141–79.

Flanders, Ned A. Some relationships among teacher influence, pupil attitudes, and achievement. In Bruce J. Biddle and William J. Ellena, eds., *Contemporary research on teacher effectiveness.* New York: Holt, Rinehart and Winston, 1964. Chapter 7, pp. 196–231.

Gage, N. L. Paradigms for research on teaching. In N. L. Gage, ed., *Handbook of research on teaching.* Chicago: Rand McNally and Co., 1963. Chapter 3, pp. 94–141.

Gage, N. L. Theories of teaching. *Theories of learning and instruction.* Sixty-Third Yearbook, Part I, National Society for the Study of Education. Chicago: University of Chicago Press, 1964. Chapter 11, pp. 268–85.

Gage, N. L. *An analytic approach to research on instructional methods.* Research Memorandum No. 2, 1967. Stanford, Calif.: Stanford Center for Research and Development in Teaching, March 1967. 16 pp. (Mimeo.)

Gagné, Robert M. *The conditions of learning.* New York: Holt, Rinehart and Winston, 1965. 308 pp.

Glaser, Robert. Toward a behavioral science base for instructional design. In Robert Glaser, ed., *Teaching machines and programed learning, II: Data and directions.* Washington, D.C.: National Education Association, Department of Audiovisual Instruction, 1965. Chapter 17, pp. 771–809.

Hanson, Lincoln F. and Komoski, P. Kenneth. School use of programed instruction. In Robert Glaser, ed., *Teaching machines and programed learning, II: Data and directions.* Washington, D.C.: National Education Association, Department of Audiovisual Instruction, 1965. Chapter 14, pp. 647–84.

Hickey, Albert E., and Newton, John M. *The logical basis of teaching: I. The effect of sub-concept sequence on learning.* Final Report to Office of Naval Research, Personnel and Training Branch, Contract Nonr-4215 (00), January 1964. 75 pp.

Jackson, Philip W. The way teaching is. *The way teaching is: Report of the seminar on teaching.* Association for Supervision and Curriculum Development and the Center for the Study of Instruction. Washington, D.C.: National Education Association, 1966. Pp. 7–27. (a)

Jackson, Philip W. *The teacher and the machine: Observations on the impact of educational technology.* Paper presented to the Committee on Economic Development, November 1966. Chicago: Department of Education, University of Chicago. 32 pp. (Mimeo.) (b)

Lindvall, C. M. and Bolvin, John O. Programed instruction in the schools: An application of programing principles in "individually prescribed instruction." *Programed instruction.* Sixty-Sixth Yearbook, Part II, National Society for the Study of Education. Chicago: University of Chicago Press, 1967. Chapter 8, pp. 217–54.

Melton, Arthur W. The taxonomy of human learning: Overview. In Arthur W. Melton, ed., *Categories of human learning.* New York: Academic Press, 1964. Pp. 325–39.

Meux, Milton and Smith, B. Othanel. Logical dimensions of teaching behavior. In Bruce J. Biddle and William J. Ellena, eds., *Contemporary research on teacher effectiveness.* New York: Holt, Rinehart and Winston, 1964. Chapter 5, pp. 127–64.

National Society for the Study of Education. *Programed instruction.* Sixty-Sixth Yearbook, Part II. Chicago: University of Chicago Press, 1967. 334 pp.

Ryans, David G. Teacher behavior theory and research: Implications for teacher education. *Journal of Teacher Education,* **14**: 274–93, September 1963.

Scandura, Joseph M. Teaching—technology or theory. *American Educational Research Journal,* **3**: 139–46, March 1966.

Siegel, Laurence, ed. *Instruction: Some contemporary viewpoints.* San Francisco: Chandler Publishing Co., 1967. 376 pp.

Siegel, Laurence and Siegel, Lila Corkland. The instructional gestalt. In Laurence Siegel, ed., *Instruction: Some contemporary viewpoints.* San Francisco: Chandler Publishing Co., 1967. Chapter 9, pp. 261–90.

Silberman, Charles E. Technology is knocking at the schoolhouse door. *Fortune,* **74**, No. 3: 120–25, 198, 203–205, August 1966.

Skinner, B. F. Why we need teaching machines. *Harvard Educational Review,* **31**: 377–98, Fall 1961.

Skinner, B. F. Reflections on a decade of teaching machines. In Robert Glaser, ed., *Teaching machines and programed learning, II: Data and directions.* Washington, D.C.: National Education Association, Department of Audiovisual Instruction, 1965. Chapter 1, pp. 5–20.

Stolurow, Lawrence M. Model the master teacher or master the teaching model. In John D. Krumboltz, ed., *Learning and the educational process.* Chicago: Rand McNally and Co., 1965. Chapter 9, pp. 223–47.

Suppes, Patrick. The uses of computers in education. *Scientific American,* **215**, No. 3: 206–20, September 1966.

Travers, Robert M. W. Towards taking the fun out of building a theory of instruction. *Teachers College Record,* **68**: 49–60, October 1966.

Verduin, John R., Jr. *Conceptual models in teacher education: An approach to teaching and learning.* Washington, D.C.: American Association of Colleges for Teacher Education, a department of the National Education Association, 1967. 140 pp.

2

Some Limitations of Basic Research in Education

ROBERT L. EBEL / *Michigan State University*

The thesis I will try to defend is this:

Basic research in education can promise very little improvement in the process of education, now or in the foreseeable future.

If this is true, and if the primary task of professional educators is to improve the process of education as much as possible, as rapidly as possible, they will do well to direct their efforts, not toward basic research on the conditions of learning or the processes of instruction, but instead toward applied research designed to yield information immediately useful in the solution of contemporary educational problems.

This view is almost diametrically opposed to that recently expressed by Cronbach (1966). He argued that efforts to improve education on the technological level would be largely futile, and that significant improvement could come only out of deep understanding of such basic elements of education as learning and motivation. He may be right. Obviously many educational research workers share the same opinion. But this opinion seems to rest more on faith and hope than on evidence and logic. Hence I invite you to examine its foundations critically. Perhaps they are no more substantial than the Emperor's new clothes.

To begin we must say clearly what the term *basic research* will mean in this discussion. We use it to refer to the activity whose immediate aim is the quantitative formulation of verifiable general laws, and whose ultimate aim is establishment of a system of concepts and relations (the so-called nomothetic net) in which all specific propositions are deducible from a few general principles. Basic research seeks eternal verities. Its hallmark is the carefully designed and well controlled experiment

Reprinted with the permission of the author and the publisher from *Phi Delta Kappan*, October, 1967, 81–84.

whose conclusions are rigorously tested for statistical significance.

Applied research, on the other hand, refers to the collection of data that promise help in the solution of some immediate practical problem. Experience, not experiment, is the source of most applied research data. The problems, the data, the solutions tend to be ephemeral, not eternal.

The foregoing definition of basic research is not the only one possible, and probably not the one that is currently most popular. Some research workers define basic research negatively, but very inclusively, as any research that does *not* seek to help solve a current problem, that does *not* promise results of practical value. These individuals almost seem to make a virtue of uselessness. No matter how insignificant a study may be, no matter how unrelated to any coherent theoretical structure of concepts and relations, they honor it as basic research so long as it is free from the taint of practical utility. Secure in the belief that whatever they do will add something to the store of human knowledge, they wash their hands of responsibility for showing that it is something of value. It is nice work if you can get it.

Some argue that the term *applied research* involves a contradiction, since all research, properly speaking, is concerned only with understanding and not at all with applications. What we are calling applied research they would call simply development, and distinguish it from research in the same way that technology is sometimes distinguished from science. Others point out that the distinction between basic and applied research is not categorical but rather a distinction between two poles of a continuum. What one man calls basic research another calls applied. An interesting illustration of this situation is that the amount the federal government re-

ported recently it was spending on basic research in the universities was only half the amount the universities reported they were receiving for basic research from the federal government (National Science Foundation, 1957).

But whatever terms we use to describe these activities, it is clear that they are different, if only in degree. What Mr. Cronbach favored is not the same thing that he deplored. Seeking to discover basic laws of learning or instruction is not the same as seeking to work out a solution to some immediate, specific educational problem. Cronbach and I are in full agreement that the difference between these two kinds of activities is real and important. What we do not agree on is which activity has more to offer toward the improvement of education.

There are three reasons why it seems to me that basic research in education can promise very little improvement in the process of education.

1. Its record of past performance is very poor.
2. The justifiable explanations of that poor performance call attention to serious basic difficulties that are unlikely to be overcome in the foreseeable future.
3. The process of education is not a natural phenomenon of the kind that has sometimes rewarded scientific study in astronomy, physics, chemistry, geology, and biology.

Let us consider each of these in turn. Almost everyone agrees that basic research in education has not produced many results that excite admiration. Years ago, when the first Encyclopedia of Educational Research appeared, Isaac Kandel (1950) recorded his doubts of the extent to which the mountain of material reviewed there would lead to improvement in educational practice. More recently Tom Lamke (1955) wrote, ". . . if the research in the previous three years in medicine, agriculture, physics, and chemistry were to be wiped out, our life would be changed materially, but if research in the area of teacher personnel in the same three years were to vanish, educators and education would continue much as usual" (p. 192).

For all his advocacy of basic research in education, Cronbach would be among the last to argue that confidence in it is justified by its past performance. If the educational programs of most schools are inadequate, as he thinks they are, it is not for failure to apply the principles of instruction that basic research has revealed, for he says, ". . . we professionals do not know enough about learning and instruction to design the desired reform." And again, "The tragedy is that there is so small a gap between what we know and what we do." It is revealing to note that in this article of his that urges the value of basic research in education so strongly, there is not even a single example of basic research that has yielded a valuable result. Where are the illustrations of the kinds of rigorous laws of learning, and of teaching, we are supposed to get from such basic research? Where are even the basic, operationally defined quantitative concepts which such laws might relate?

Again, in Mouly's (1963) list of 21 outstanding examples of significant educational research studies, which included Binet's study of the measurement of scholastic aptitude, the Eight-Year study of the Progressive Education Association, Hartshorn and May's studies of character, Morphett and Washburne's investigation of the best age to begin reading instruction, studies of reliability of grading examinations by Starch and Elliott, and Wickman's study of teachers' attitudes toward children's behavior problems, not one could be called

basic research in terms of the definition given earlier. Either we need a different definition of basic research, or a different perception of the importance of basic research in education.

A great many explanations are offered for the failure of basic research in education to produce many useful results. One is that educational research is much younger than research in other areas, so that it has not had time to develop equally impressive results. But this does not explain why educators should have been so slow to get started. Were not the problems of education apparent to mankind just as soon as the problems of planetary motion, or of the behavior of falling bodies?

Another group of excuses is based on criticism of previous research activities. Too little money was available for research in education. The studies undertaken were too small in scope, too brief in duration, too local in applicability. Too few of the research workers were well trained. But here again the excuses fail to explain why research in the physical and biological sciences has been so much more fortunate in escaping such limitations.

A more plausible set of explanations calls attention to the great complexity of human behavior and the consequent difficulty of doing productive research on it. Each behavioral act is the resultant of very many antecedent and concomitant factors which are complexly interrelated. To identify these factors and to discover their functional relations is an awesome task, whose probable payoff does not begin to promise returns sufficient to justify the efforts that would have to be expended. The very modest level at which basic research in education has usually been supported may be all that its past performance and future prospects warrant.

The "variables" we ordinarily work

with in education—such constructs as ability, motivation, success, environment, self-concept, etc.—are so global and encompass such a diversity of specifics as to defy precise definition and exact quantification. The same generality and inclusiveness that makes them useful as verbal concepts ruins them as quantitative scientific constructs. If we were to analyze them into precisely definable and quantifiable specific elements, two things would be likely to happen.

1. The number of concepts for us to deal with would be enormously increased.
2. The importance of each to us would be sharply reduced.

Nor is the behavior we are attempting to study a stable phenomenon that can be isolated without distortion for scientific study. The very experiment designed to study it changes it. What was true of the naïve subject may no longer be true of the sophisticated subject, and there is no assurance that what was discovered in the controlled conditions of an experiment will hold true under more natural nonexperimental conditions.

Controlled experiments on human behavior are difficult not only because of the great variety of factors that must be controlled, but also because human beings are involved. People are not always easy to manipulate. The experimenter must treat his subjects as fellow human beings, not as depersonalized objects of his scientific study. No experimental treatment that is or may be harmful or even disadvantageous is likely to be tolerated.

These and other difficulties of research on human behavior help to explain why little progress has been made in understanding human behavior via basic research. They are justifiable ex-

cuses. But since these difficulties are inherent in the situation and are likely to persist, they justify skepticism concerning future progress in this area.

Nomothetic science has been highly successful in some areas, such as mechanics, electromagnetic radiations, and atomic physics. It has been distinctly less successful in other areas, such as weather phenomena, acoustics, and human behavior. The difference seems to lie in the extent to which there is simple structure in the phenomena involved—few variables and simple (often linear) relations among them. If the structure is complex, if the variables are numerous, if they interact complexly, if the lines of relationship have critical regions of nonlinearity or discontinuity, then the nomothetic net is likely to be sketchy or nonexistent.

To question the power of basic research on human behavior it is not necessary to deny, and I do not deny, the predictability *in principle* of every human act. What I do question, in view of the manifold influences (variables) involved, the complexity of the relations, and the inherent plasticity of the response system involved, is the practical feasibility of such predictions. The game is just not worth the candle.

The third reason why basic research in education can promise little improvement in education is that the process of education is not a rewarding subject for scientific study. Science has been defined as the systematic study of natural phenomena for the purpose of understanding them. But formal education (i.e., purposeful instruction), which is what we are trying to improve, is not a natural phenomenon. It is a human invention, a construction, a cultural institution designed and built by men. It is not so much in need of analysis and understanding as one of the givens in our universe as it is in need of redesign and reconstruction to serve our human purposes better. And we make a grave mistake, I fear, if we believe that the best way to redesign and reconstruct it is to study its current forms scientifically with a view to understanding them. Is the case for a scientific study of education, as a means of improving education, any stronger than the case for a scientific study of poetry, as a means of improving poetry? Of course we can, if we wish, do what appears to be basic research on anything, from the distribution of word lengths in Robert Frost's poems to the symbolism in a particular kindergartner's finger painting. But how basic is it, and to what? Basic research is no more free than any other human activity from the necessity of being worthwhile.

What I have been saying about the limitations of basic research in education is intended to apply to formal education, to schooling, to instruction, not to the psycho-biology of learning. For learning *is* a natural phenomenon. What learning is biologically, how it occurs, what happens to the organism and why —these are fit subjects of scientific study. Here basic research may be rewarding. But an understanding of the psycho-biology of learning is unlikely to contribute much to the improvement of formal education. It will do little to answer either of the two basic educational questions: What shall we try to teach children? And how shall we go about getting them to learn it?

Some defenders of basic research in education, admitting its limitations and the difficulties attending it, still argue that it should be supported generously and pursued energetically because, in their view, there is no other way to improve education. If science can't do it, they seem to say, nothing can. The jig is up. We may as well toss in the sponge. In this they are quite wrong, I think. They greatly overestimate the scope and versatility of nomothetic, experimental

science. They greatly underestimate the variety and power of other techniques of gathering data and solving problems. Doing basic research is not the only way, and probably not the best way, for a man to use his head to solve an educational problem.

Human beings were solving problems and making progress in building their culture long ages before experimental science was ever invented or popularized. Even today, when the prestige of science is at its height, most of the world's problems are being solved and most of the progress is being achieved by methods which involve experience and reason and dialogue and consensus. Seldom if ever do the findings of basic research have significant impact on the decision reached. The alternative to basic scientific research is not just traditionalism or mysticism or speculation. There are also empiricism (i.e., experience) and discussion and reasoned decision.

Most of the knowledge with which we guide our lives and solve our problems has come, not from controlled experiments, but from practical experience. The notion that we don't really know a thing is true until basic research has verified its truth is quite unwarranted. The things that experience has taught us about education, the things that Plato, Quintilian, Comenius, Rousseau, Spencer, James, Dewey, and Conant have called to our attention, are far truer on the whole than most of the new things that one reads under the heading of "News from the Research Frontier."

Most of the problems we face in the world today, including our educational problems, involve questions of purposes and values. Hence the decisions we must make in our parliaments and councils, in our school boards and faculty meetings, in our families and private lives are decisions that science could not possibly make for us. The scientific understanding of what *is* sheds only a little light on what ought to be. To make the decisions that will solve our problems we need in addition to knowledge free exchanges of ideas, open discussions of values, and sympathetic, cooperative search for consensus.

But knowledge is necessary. Seldom do we have as much knowledge as we need to decide wisely the questions before us. Research can give us this knowledge, but it is the kind of research that educational scientists tend to disdain as mere data gathering. For example, should we launch an extensive program to improve the self-concepts of slum children? No doubt we should if slum children don't learn mainly because they think they can't learn. But is it true that they have poor self-concepts? Is it true that they tend to blame themselves, not society, for their difficulties? Is it true that many of them think of themselves as lacking in ability to learn? To find the answers to these questions would involve data gathering, not basic research. But it could contribute substantially to the wisdom of our decision on a serious problem.

Consider another example. Should colleges institute pass-or-fail grading for certain courses in order to encourage the students to broaden the range of their educational experience? It has often been said that even good students are reluctant to take courses outside of their major field, courses in which they would have to compete for grades with students who were majoring in that field. Now, is it in fact true that a significant proportion of good students who want to take a course outside their major, and who feel that they are prepared to study it profitably, are deterred by the prospect of a lower grade? Do they choose instead to take a less valuable course that may give them a higher grade? A well-designed questionnaire could provide solid answers to these questions and thus help the decision makers to act wisely.

This article has contended that basic research in education promises little improvement in the process of education because it has not done so in the past, because it is fraught with serious, inherent limitations, and because the process of education is not a natural phenomenon, and hence not a profitable object of scientific study. In its proper sphere, and for its limited purposes, pure science, with the basic research on which it rests, is a powerful tool. But the problems of the world, and of education, we have argued, require the application of other sources of information and other processes of decision than pure science provides.

Let me not take too much credit for the views expressed in this paper, nor assume too solitary a role as a defender of them. Others, among whom are Morris Cohen (1931), Harold Larrabee (1945), and Ernest van den Hoag (1959) seem to hold similar views. Psychologists from James (1913) to Estes (1960) have warned educators not to expect much help from psychology in the solution of educational problems.

Basic research in education seeks to discover a simple structure of concepts and causal relations that will permit effective control of the process of education and precise prediction of its results. One can hardly doubt that the discovery of such a simple theoretical structure would place a powerful tool in the hands of the educational scientist. But it must be discovered; it cannot be invented. And if it does not exist it cannot be discovered. That is, if a sparsity of relevant variables and a simplicity of their interrelations are inherent in the process of education, basic research might discover it. If not, no amount of basic research can create it.

The search for a simple structure of basic variables underlying the apparent complexities of human behavior has motivated much of the work in factor analysis for decades. So far the search has not been notably successful. No one can say with certainty that such a simple structure *does not* exist and await discovery, but as of the present moment there is little if any reason to believe that it *does* exist. To persist in searching for something that persists in not being found, and in giving no reason to believe that it even exists, is hardly a profitable way to spend one's time.

Herein, it seems to me, lies one of the reasons for the futility of some research in education. We have persisted in using the techniques of basic research despite persistent failure of those techniques to pay off. Of course there are other weaknesses. Some studies concern themselves with trivial problems, or are inadequate in design, or are incompetently executed. The room for improvement in educational research is, as many critics have pointed out, almost unlimited.

What are we then to do? Shall we abandon research in education? By no means. Let us even persist in basic research on those psycho-biological problems where basic research has a fighting chance to produce useful results. But let us also push, and rather more strongly, the kind of survey research that provides data crucial to the decisions we must make. Let us not worship pure science and basic research unrealistically and irrationally.

What I have been saying may sound anti-scientific. It may seem to have a mystical humanistic or theistic bias that glories in the limitations of science and fights to preserve some field of activity for the free, undetermined spirit of man, some sphere of influence for a mysterious, powerful God. But this is not my intent. I am a thorough-going rational empiricist. I believe in the power of knowledge, and in the wisdom of decisions solidly based on relevant knowledge. Where I differ from some of my colleagues is not in faith in science, broadly defined as human knowledge, verified and organized. It is rather in my doubts that basic research, as here defined, will ever provide the knowledge we need to solve the educational problems that perplex us.

References

Cohen, M. R. *Reason and nature.* New York: Harcourt, Brace, 1931. Pp. 250–63.

Cronbach, L. The role of the university in improving education. *Phi Delta Kappan,* June 1966, pp. 539–45.

Estes, W. K. Learning. In Chester W. Harris, ed., *Encyclopedia of educational research* (3rd ed.), New York: Macmillan, 1960. P. 752.

James, W. *Talks to teachers.* New York: Henry Holt, 1913. Pp. 7–8.

Kandel, I. L. Educational research. *School and Society,* October 7, 1950, p. 232.

Lamke, T. Introduction. *Review of Educational Research,* June 1955, p. 192.

Larrabee, H. *Reliable knowledge.* Cambridge, Mass.: Houghton Mifflin, 1945. Pp. 473–505.

Mouly, G. *The science of educational research.* New York: American Book Company, 1963. Pp. 429–76.

National Science Foundation. *Basic research, a national resource.* Washington, D.C., 1957. P. 25.

van den Hoag, E. Man as an object of science. *Science,* January 30, 1959, pp. 243–47.

3

Reflections on a Decade
of Teaching Machines

B. F. SKINNER / *Harvard University*

To the general public, and to many educators as well, the nature and scope of teaching machines are by no means clear. There is an extraordinary need for more and better teaching, and any enterprise which may help to meet it will not be left to develop normally. The demand for information about teaching machines has been excessive. Articles and books have been published and lectures given; symposia have been arranged, and conferences and workshops have been held and courses taught. Those who have had anything useful to say have said it far too often, and those who have had nothing to say have been no more reticent.

Education is big business. Teaching machines were soon heralded as a growth industry, and fantastic predictions of the sales of programed texts were circulated. Devices have been sold as teaching machines which were not well built or designed with any understanding of their function or the practical exigencies of their use. No author was ever more warmly received by a publisher than the author of a programed text. Many programs, to be used either with machines or in textbook form, have been marketed without adequate evaluation.

Teachers and Devices

The "mechanizing of education" has been taken literally in the sense of doing by machine what was formerly done by people. Some of the so-called computer-based teaching machines are designed simply to duplicate the behavior of teachers. To automate education with mechanical teachers is like automating

Reprinted with the permission of the author and the publisher from *Teachers College Record*, 1963, Vol. 65, pp. 168–77.

22

banking with mechanical tellers and bookkeepers. What is needed in both cases is an analysis of the functions to be served, followed by the design of appropriate equipment. Nothing we now know about the learning process calls for very elaborate instrumentation.

Educational specialists have added to the confusion by trying to assimilate the principles upon which teaching machines are based to older theories of learning and teaching.

In the broadest sense, teaching machines are simply devices which make it possible to apply our technical knowledge of human behavior to the practical field of education (Skinner, 1954). Teaching is the expediting of learning. Students learn without teaching, but the teacher arranges conditions under which they learn more rapidly and effectively. In recent years, the experimental analysis of behavior has revealed many new facts about relevant conditions. The growing effectiveness of an experimental analysis is still not widely recognized, even within the behavioral sciences themselves, but the implications of some of its achievements for education can no longer be ignored.

An important condition is the relation between behavior and its consequences; learning occurs when behavior is "reinforced." The power of reinforcement is not easily appreciated by those who have not had firsthand experience in its use or have not at least seen some sort of experimental demonstration. Extensive changes in behavior can be brought about by arranging so-called contingencies of reinforcement. Various kinds of contingencies are concealed in the teacher's discussions with his students, in the books he gives them to read, in the charts and other materials he shows them, in the questions he asks them, and in the comments he makes on their answers. An experimental analysis clarifies these contingencies and suggests many improvements.

Shaping by Program

An important contribution has been the so-called "programing" of knowledge and skills—the construction of carefully arranged sequences of contingencies leading to the terminal performances which are the object of education. The teacher begins with whatever behavior the student brings to the instructional situation; by selective reinforcement, he changes that behavior so that a given terminal performance is more and more closely approximated. Even with lower organisms, quite complex behaviors can be "shaped" in this way with surprising speed; the human organism is presumably far more sensitive. So important is the principle of programing that it is often regarded as the main contribution of the teaching machine movement, but the experimental analysis of behavior has much more to contribute to a technology of education.

The direct contact which often exists between teacher and student favors the construction of programed sequences, and the teacher who understands the process can profit from the opportunity to improvise programs as he goes. Programs can be constructed in advance, however, which will successfully shape the behavior of most students without local modifications, and many of them can conveniently be mediated by mechanical devices. Laboratory studies have shown that contingencies emphasizing subtle properties of behavior can often be arranged *only* through instrumentation. There are potentially as many different kinds of teaching machines as there are kinds of contingencies of reinforcement.

Teaching machines which present material to the student and differentially reinforce his responses in well constructed programs differ in several ways from self-testing devices and self-scoring test forms, as well as from the training devices which have long been used by industry and the armed services. As Pressey (1926) pointed out many years ago, a student will learn while taking a multiple-choice test if he is told immediately whether his answers are right or wrong. He learns not to give wrong answers again, and his right answers are strengthened. But testing has traditionally been distinguished from teaching for good reason. Before using a self-testing device, the student must already have studied the subject and, presumably, learned most of what he is to learn about it. Tests usually occupy only a small part of his time. Their main effect is motivational: A poor score induces him to study harder and possibly more effectively. Materials designed to be used in self-testing devices have recently been programed, but the contingencies which prevail during a test are not favorable to the shaping and maintaining of behavior.

Conventional training devices arrange conditions under which students learn, usually by simulating the conditions under which they eventually perform. Their original purpose was to prevent injury or waste during early stages of learning, but attention has recently been given to programing the actual behaviors they are designed to teach. To the extent that they expedite learning, they are teaching machines. Terminal performances have usually been selected for practical reasons, but a more promising possibility is the analysis and programing of basic motor and perceptual skills—a goal which should have an important place in any statement of educational policy.

In arranging contingencies of reinforcement, machines do many of the things teachers do; in that sense, they teach. The resulting instruction is not impersonal, however. A machine presents a program designed by someone who knew what was to be taught and could prepare an appropriate series of contingencies. It is most effective if used by a teacher who knows the student, has followed his progress, and can adapt available machines and materials to his needs. Instrumentation simply makes it possible for programer and teacher to provide conditions which maximally expedite learning. Instrumentation is thus secondary, but it is nevertheless inevitable if what is now known about behavior is to be used in an effective technology.

The New Pedagogy

Any practical application of basic knowledge about teaching and learning is, of course, pedagogy. In the United States at least, the term is now discredited, but by emphasizing an analysis of learning processes, teaching machines and programed instruction have been responsible for some improvement in its status. The significance of the teaching machine movement can be indicated by noting the astonishing lack of interest which other proposals for the improvement of education show in the teaching process.

FIND BETTER TEACHERS

In his *Talks to Teachers*, William James (1899) insisted that there was nothing wrong with the American school system which could not be corrected by "impregnating it with geniuses." It is an old formula: If you cannot solve a problem, find someone who can. If you do not know how to teach, find someone who knows or can find out for himself. But geniuses are in short supply, and good teachers do not come ready-made. Education would no doubt be improved if, as Conant (1963) has repeatedly pointed out, good teachers who know and like the subjects they teach could be attracted and retained. But something more is needed. It is not true that "the two essentials of a good teacher are (a) enthusiasm and (b) thorough knowledge of and interest in his subject" (Helwig, 1960, p. 845). A third essential is knowing how to teach. //

EMULATE MODEL SCHOOLS

Rickover's (1959) criticism of the present American school system is well known. His only important positive suggestion is to set up model schools, staffed by model teachers. The implication is that we already have, or at least can have for the asking, schools which need no improvement and whose methods can be widely copied. This is a dangerous assumption if it discourages further inquiry into instruction.

SIMPLIFY WHAT IS TO BE LEARNED

Unsuccessful instruction is often blamed on refractory subject matters. Difficulties in teaching the verbal arts are often attributed to the inconsistencies and unnecessary complexities of a language. The pupil is taught manuscript handwriting because it more closely resembles printed forms. He is taught to spell only those words he is likely to use. Phonetic alphabets are devised to help him learn to read. It may be easier to teach such materials, but teaching itself is not thereby improved. Effective teaching would correct these pessimistic estimates of available instructional power.

REORGANIZE WHAT IS TO BE LEARNED

The proper structuring of a subject matter is perhaps a part of pedagogy, but it can also serve as a mode of escape. Proposals for improving education by reorganizing what is to be learned usually contain an implicit assumption that students will automatically perceive and remember anything which has "good form"—a doctrine probably traceable to Gestalt psychology. Current revisions of high school curricula often seem to lean heavily on the belief that if what the student is to be taught has been "structured," he cannot help understanding and remembering it (Bruner, 1960). Other purposes of such revisions cannot be questioned: Materials should be up to date and well organized. But a high school presentation acceptable to a current physicist is no more easily taught or easily remembered than the out-of-date and erroneous material to be found in texts of a decade or more ago. Similarly, the accent of a native speaker encountered in a language laboratory is no more easily learned than a bad accent. No matter how well structured a subject matter may be, it must still be taught.

IMPROVE PRESENTATION

Pedagogy can also be avoided if what is to be learned can be made memorable. Audio-visual devices are often recommended for this purpose. Many of their other purposes are easily defended. It is not always easy to bring the student into contact with the things he is to learn about. Words are easily imported into the classroom, and books, lectures, and discussions are therefore staples of education; but this is often an unfortunate bias. Audio-visual devices can enlarge the student's nonverbal experience. They can also serve to present material clearly and conveniently. Their use in attracting and holding the student's attention and in dramatizing a subject matter in such a way that it is almost automatically remembered must be questioned, however. It is especially tempting to turn to them for these purposes when the teacher does not use punitive methods to "make students study." But the result is not the same. When a student observes or attends to something in order to see it more clearly or remember it more effectively, his behavior must have been shaped and maintained by reinforcement. The temporal order was important. Certain reinforcing events must have occurred *after* the student looked at, read, and perhaps tested himself on the material. But when colored displays, attractive objects, filmed episodes, and other potentially reinforcing materials are used to attract attention, they must occur *before* the student engages in these activities. Nothing can reinforce a student for *paying* attention if it has already been used to *attract* his attention. Material which attracts attention fails to prepare the student to attend to material which is not interesting on its face, and material which is naturally memorable fails to prepare him to study and recall things which are not, in themselves, unforgettable. A well prepared instructional film may appear to be successful in arousing interest in a given subject, and parts of it may be remembered without effort, but it has not taught the student that a subject may *become* interesting when more closely examined or that intensive study of something which is likely to be overlooked may have reinforcing consequences.

MULTIPLY CONTACTS BETWEEN
TEACHER AND STUDENT

Audio-visual devices, particularly when adapted to television, are also used to improve education by bringing one teacher into contact with an indefinitely large number of students. This can be done, of course, without analyzing how the teacher teaches, and it emphasizes a mode of communication which has two serious disadvantages: The teacher cannot see the effect he is having on his students, and large numbers of students must proceed at the same pace. Contributions to pedagogy may be made in designing programs for educational television, but the mere multiplication of contacts is not itself an improvement in teaching.

EXPAND THE EDUCATIONAL SYSTEM

Inadequate education may be corrected by building more schools and recruiting more teachers so that the total quantity of education is increased, even though there is no change in efficiency.

RAISE STANDARDS

Least effective in improving teaching are demands for higher standards. We may agree that students will be better educated when they learn more, but how are they to be induced to do so? Demands for higher standards usually come from critics who have least to offer in improving teaching itself.

The movement symbolized by the teaching machine differs from other proposals in two ways. It emphasizes the direct improvement of teaching on the principle that no enterprise can improve itself to the fullest extent without examining its basic processes. In the second place, it emphasizes the implementation of basic knowledge. If instructional practices violate many basic principles, it is only in part because these principles are not widely known. The teacher cannot put what he knows into practice in the classroom. Teaching machines and programed instruction constitute a direct attack on the problem of implementation. With appropriate administrative changes, they may bridge the gap between an effective pedagogical theory and actual practice.

Educational Goals

An effective technology of teaching calls for a re-examination of educational objectives. What is the teacher's actual assignment? Educational policy is usually stated in traditional terms: The teacher is to "impart knowledge," "improve skills," "develop rational faculties," and so on. That education is best, says Dr. Hutchins (1963), which develops "intellectual power." The task of the teacher is to change certain inner processes or states. He is to improve the mind.

The role of the teacher in fostering mental prowess has a certain prestige. It has always been held superior to the role of the trainer of motor skills. And it has the great advantage of being almost invulnerable to criticism. In reply to the complaint that he has not produced observable results, the teacher of the mind can lay claim to invisible achievements. His students may not be able to read, but he has only been trying to make sure they wanted to learn. They may not be able to solve problems, but he has been teaching them simply to think creatively. They may be ignorant of specific facts, but he has been primarily concerned with their general interest in a field.

Traditional specifications of the goals of education have never told the teacher what to do upon a given occasion. No one knows how to alter a mental process or strengthen a mental power, and no one can be sure that he has done so when he has tried. There have been many good teachers who have supposed themselves to be working on the minds of their students, but their actual practices and the results of those practices can be analyzed in other ways. The well educated student is distinguished by certain characteristics. What are they, and how can they be produced? Perhaps we could answer by redefining traditional goals: Instead of imparting knowledge, we could undertake to bring about those changes in behavior which are said to be the conspicuous manifestations of knowledge, or we could set up the behavior which is the mark of a man possessing well developed rational power. But mentalistic formulations are warped by irrelevant historical accidents. The behavior of the educated student is much more effectively analyzed directly as such.

Contrary to frequent assertions, a behavioristic formulation of human behavior is not a crude positivism which rejects mental processes because they are not accessible to the scientific public (Skinner, 1963). It does not emphasize the rote learning of verbal responses. It does not neglect the complex systems of verbal behavior which are said to show that a student has had an idea, or developed a concept, or entertained a proposition. It does not ignore the behavior involved in the intellectual and ethical problem solving called "thinking." It does not overlook the value judgments said to be invoked when we decide to teach one thing rather than another or when we defend the time and effort given to education. It is merely an effective formulation of those activities of teacher and student which have always been the concern of educational specialists (Skinner, 1961).

Not all behavioristic theories of learning are relevant, however. A distinction is commonly drawn between learning and performance. Learning is said to be a change in some special part of the organism, possibly the nervous system, of which behavior is merely the external and often erratic sign. With modern techniques, however, behavior can be much more successfully studied and manipulated than any such inner system, even when inferences about the latter are drawn from the behavior with the help of sophisticated statistics. An analysis of learning which concentrates on the behavior applies most directly to a technology, for the task of the teacher is to bring about changes in the student's behavior. His methods are equally conspicuous: He makes changes in the environment. A teaching method is simply a way of arranging an environment which expedites learning.

Managing Contingencies

Such a formulation is not easily assimilated to the traditional psychology of learning. The teacher may arrange contingencies of reinforcement to set up new *forms* of response, as in teaching handwriting and speech or nonverbal forms of behavior in the arts, crafts, and sports. He may arrange contingencies to bring responses under new kinds of *stimulus control,* as in teaching the student to read or draw from copy, or to behave effectively upon other kinds of occasions. Current instructional programs designed to fulfill such assignments are mainly verbal, but comparable contingencies generate nonverbal behavior, including perceptual and motor skills and various kinds of intellectual and ethical self-management.

A second kind of programing maintains the student's behavior in strength. The form of the response and the stimulus control may not change; the student is simply more likely to respond. Some relevant methods are traditionally discussed under the heading of motivation. For example, we can strengthen behavior by introducing new reinforcers or making old ones more effective, as in giving the student better reasons for getting an education. The experimental analysis of behavior suggests another important possibility: Schedule available reinforcers more effectively. Appropriate terminal schedules of reinforcement will maintain the student's interest, make him industrious and persevering, stimulate his curiosity, and so on; but less demanding schedules, carefully designed to maintain the behavior at every stage, must come first. The programing of schedules of reinforcement is a promising alternative to the aversive control which, in spite of repeated reforms, still prevails in educational practice.

In neglecting programing, teaching methods have merely followed the lead of the experimental psychology of learning, where the almost universal practice has been to submit an organism immediately to terminal contingencies of reinforcement (Skinner, 1963b). A maze or a discrimination problem, for example, is learned only if the subject acquires appropriate behavior before the behavior he brings to the experiment has extinguished. The intermediate contingencies are largely accidental. The differences in behavior and in rate of learning which appear under these conditions are often attributed to inherited differences in ability.

In maximizing the student's success, programed instruction differs from so-called trial-and-error learning where the student is said to learn from his mistakes. At best, he learns not to make mistakes again. A successful response may survive, but trial-and-error teaching makes little provision for actually strengthening it. The method seems inevitably committed to aversive control. For the same reason, programed instruction does not closely resemble teaching patterned on everyday communication. It is usually not enough simply to tell the student something or induce him to read a book; he must be told or must read and then be questioned. In this "tell-and-test" pattern, the test is not given to measure what he has learned, but to show him what he has not learned and thus induce him to listen and read more carefully in the future. A similar basically aversive pattern is widespread at the college level, where the instructor assigns material and then examines on it. The student may learn to read carefully, to make notes, to discover for' himself how to study, and so on, because in doing so he avoids aversive consequences, but he has not necessarily been taught. Assigning-and-testing is not teaching. The aversive by-products, familiar to everyone in the field of education, can be avoided through the use of programed positive reinforcement.

Many facts and principles derived from the experimental analysis of behavior are relevant to the construction of effective programs leading to terminal contingencies. The facts and principles are often difficult, but they make up an indispensable armamentarium of the effective teacher and educational specialist. We have long since passed the point at which our basic knowledge of human behavior can be applied to education through the use of a few general principles.

Principle and Practice

The difference between general principles and an effective technology can be seen in certain efforts to assimilate the principles of programed instruction to earlier theories. Programed instruction has, for example, been called "Socratic." It is true that Socrates proceeded by small steps and often led his students through an argument with a series of verbal prompts, but the ex-

ample often cited to illustrate his method suggests that he was unaware of an important detail—namely, that prompts must eventually be "vanished" in order to put the student on his own. In the famous scene in the *Meno*, Socrates demonstrates his theory that learning is simply recollection by leading an uneducated slave boy through Pythagoras's Golden Theorem. The boy responds with the rather timid compliance to be expected under the circumstances and never without help. Although Socrates himself and some of those among his listeners who were already familiar with the theorem may have understood the proof better at the end of the scene, there is no evidence whatsoever that the boy understood it or could reconstruct it. In this example of Socratic instruction, at least, the student almost certainly learned nothing.[1]

A seventeenth-century anticipation of programed instruction has also been found in the work of Comenius, who advocated teaching in small steps, no step being too great for the student who was about to take it. Programing is sometimes described simply as breaking material into a large number of small pieces, arranged in a plausible genetic order. But size of step is not enough. Something must happen to help the student take each step, and something must happen as he takes it. An effective program is usually composed of small steps, but the whole story is not to be found in Comenius's philosophy of education.

Another venerable principle is that the student should not proceed until he has fully understood what he is to learn at a given stage. Several writers have

---

[1] The program of the *Meno* episode constructed by Cohen (1962) is an improvement in that the student responds with less prompting.

quoted E. L. Thorndike to this effect, who wrote in 1912,

> If, by a miracle of mechanical ingenuity, a book could be so arranged that only to him who had done what was directed on page one would page two become visible, and so on, much that now requires personal instruction could be managed by print.

In commenting on this passage, Finn and Perrin (1962) have written, ". . . Here are the insights of a genius. History can very often teach us a lesson in humility—and it does here. The interesting question is: Why couldn't we see it then?" We might also ask, why couldn't Thorndike see it then? He remained active in education for at least 30 years, but he turned from this extraordinarily promising principle to another and—as it proved—less profitable approach to educational psychology.

It is always tempting to argue that earlier ideas would have been effective if people had only paid attention to them. But a good idea must be more than right. It must command attention; it must make its own way because of what it does. Education does not need principles which will improve education as soon as people observe them; it needs a technology so powerful that it cannot be ignored. No matter how insightful the anticipation of modern principles in earlier writers may seem to have been, something was lacking or education would be much further advanced. We are on the threshold of a technology which will be not only right but effective (Skinner, in preparation).

Criteria of Research

A science of behavior makes its principal contribution to a technology of education through the analysis of useful contingencies of reinforcement. It also suggests a new kind of educational research. Thorndike never realized the potentialities of his early work on learning because he turned to the measurement of mental abilities and to matched-group comparisons of teaching practices. He pioneered in a kind of research which, with the encouragement offered by promising new statistical techniques, was to dominate educational psychology for decades. It led to a serious neglect of the process of instruction.

There are practical reasons why we want to know whether a given method of instruction is successful or whether it is more successful than another. We may want to know what changes it brings about in the student, possibly in addition to those it was designed to effect. The more reliable our answers to such questions, the better. But reliability is not enough. Correlations between test scores and significant differences between group means tell us less about the behavior of the student in the act of learning than results obtained when the investigator can manipulate variables and assess their effects in a manner characteristic of laboratory research. The practices evaluated in studies of groups of students have usually not been suggested by earlier research of a similar nature, but have been drawn from tradition, from the improvisations of skillful teachers, or from suggestions made by theorists working intuitively or with other kinds of facts. No matter how much they may have stimulated the insightful or inventive researcher, the evaluations have seldom led directly to the design of improved practices.

The contrast between statistical evaluation and the experimental analysis of teaching has an illuminating parallel in the field of medicine. Various drugs, regimens, surgical procedures, and so on must be examined with respect to a very practical question: Does the health of the patient improve? But "health" is only a general description of specific physiological processes, and "improvement" is, so to speak, merely a by-product of the changes in these processes induced by a given treatment. Medicine has reached the point where research on specific processes is a much more fertile source of new kinds of therapy than evaluations in terms of improvement in health. Similarly, in education, no matter how important improvement in the student's performance may be, it remains a by-product of specific changes in behavior resulting from the specific changes in the environment wrought by the teacher. Educational research patterned on an experimental analysis of behavior leads to a much better understanding of these basic processes. Research directed toward the behavior of the individual student has, of course, a long history, but it can still profit greatly from the support supplied by an experimental analysis of behavior.

This distinction explains why those concerned with experimental analyses of learning are not likely to take matched-group evaluations of teaching machines and programed instruction very seriously. It is not possible, of course, to evaluate either machines or programs *in general* because only specific instances can be tested, and available examples by no means represent all the possibilities; but even the evaluation of a given machine or program in the traditional manner may not give an accurate account of its effects. For example, those who are concerned with improvement are likely to test the student's capacity to give right answers. Being right has, of course, practical importance, but it is only one result of instruction. It is a doubtful measure of "knowledge" in any useful sense. We say that a student "knows the answer" if he can select it from an array of choices, but this does not mean that he could have given it

without help. The right answer to one question does not imply right answers to all questions said to show the "possession of the same fact." Instructional programs are often criticized as repetitious or redundant when they are actually designed to put the student in possession of a number of different responses "expressing the same proposition." Whether such instruction is successful is not shown by any one right answer.

Correct or Educated?

A preoccupation with correct answers has led to a common misunderstanding of programed materials. Since a sentence with a blank to be filled in by the student resembles a test item, it is often supposed that the response demanded by the blank is what is learned. In that case, a student could not be learning much because he may respond correctly in 19 out of 20 frames and must therefore already have known 95 per cent of the answers. The instruction which occurs as he completes an item comes from having responded to other parts of it. The extent of this instruction cannot be estimated from the fact that he is right 19 out of 20 times, either while pursuing a program *or on a subsequent test.* Nor will this statistic tell us whether other conditions are important. Is it most profitable for the student to execute the response by writing it out, by speaking it aloud, by speaking it silently, or by reading it in some other way? These procedures may or may not have different effects on a selected "right-answer" statistic, but no one statistic will cover all their effects.

Research in teaching must not, of course, lose sight of its main objective— to make education more effective. But improvement as such is a questionable dimension of the behavior of either teacher or student. Dimensions which are much more intimately related to the conditions the teacher arranges to expedite learning must be studied even though they do not contribute to improvement or contribute to it in a way which is not immediately obvious.

The changes in the behavior of the individual student brought about by manipulating the environment are usually immediate and specific. The results of statistical comparisons of group performances usually are not. From his study of the behavior of the individual student, the investigator gains a special kind of confidence. He usually knows what he has done to get one effect and what he must do to get another.

Confidence *in* education is another possible result of an effective technology of teaching. Competition between the various cultures of the world, warlike or friendly, is now an accepted fact, and the role played by education in strengthening and perpetuating a given way of life is clear. No field is in greater need of our most powerful intellectual resources. An effective educational technology based upon an experimental analysis will bring it support commensurate with its importance in the world today.

References

Bruner, J. S. *The process of education.* Cambridge: Harvard Univer. Press, 1960.

Cohen, I. S. Programed learning and the Socratic dialogue. *Amer. Psychologist*, 1962, **17**, 772–75.

Conant, J. B. *The education of American teachers.* New York: McGraw-Hill, 1963.

Finn, J. D. and Perrin, D. G. *Teaching machines and programmed learning: A survey of the industry, 1962.* Washington, D.C.: U.S. Office of Education, 1962.

Helwig, J. Training of college teachers. *Sci.*, 1960, **132**, 845.

Hutchins, R. M. *On education.* Santa Barbara: Center for the Study of Democratic Institutions, 1963.

James, W. *Talks to teachers.* New York: Holt, 1899.

Pressey, S. J. A simple device for teaching, testing, and research in learning. *Sch. & Soc.*, 1926, **23**, 373–76.

Rickover, H. G. *Education and freedom.* New York: Dutton, 1959.

Skinner, B. F. The science of learning and the art of teaching. *Harvard Educ. Rev.*, 1954, **24**, 86–97.

Skinner, B. F. Why we need teaching machines. *Harvard Educ. Rev.*, 1961, **31**, 377–98.

Skinner, B. F. Behaviorism at fifty. *Sci.*, 1963 a, **140**, 951–58.

Skinner, B. F. Operant behavior. *Amer. Psychologist*, 1963 b, **18**, 503–15.

Skinner, B. F. *The technology of teaching* (in preparation).

Thorndike, E. L. *Education.* New York: Macmillan, 1912.

4

Research Styles in Science Education

J. MYRON ATKIN / *University of Illinois*

Research in science education is a branch of educational research, rather than of research in the so-called natural sciences, or research in history, or research in agriculture, or research in some other discipline or profession. It usually is conducted by people whose models are derived most directly from the styles of research utilized in investigations of other *educational* phenomena. The same strengths and weaknesses which characterize the broad field of educational research also characterize research in science education.

This prelude is by way of stressing that the perspectives revealed in this paper stem as much from what appears to be happening in the total educational research community as from what is happening in the science education subset.

One focus of this paper is also directed toward the problem of improvement of educational practice, insofar as such practice is and can be affected by the activity we call "research." Presumably educational research is undertaken partly because of its potential influence on what goes on in the institution we call "school." Such mission-oriented activity of a scholarly nature, undertaken to change practice by producing a new product or program, sometimes travels under the label "development."

My subject, then, ranges over considerable territory. The aim here is not to analyze some discrete segment of research methodology in depth; I have no particular competence for such analysis. Rather, in coping with a broader range of issues and policies, it is my intention to concentrate on identifiable general trends. The goal is the better examina-

Reprinted with the permission of the author and the publisher from *Journal of Research in Science Teaching,* 1967–68, 5, 338–45.

tion of the effects of such trends. This task will be undertaken prior to the suggestion of an alternative mode for educational research, a mode that will be developed in outline form in this paper.

At the outset, one bias should be made clear: I consider that the most important substantive changes in the schools over the past two decades have been a direct result of the recent wave of curriculum development projects supported primarily by the National Science Foundation. It follows somewhat from this position that if a sharp distinction were maintained between "research" and "development," I would have to conclude that only a very small fraction of research seems to have made a major impact on the schools. (There are two major studies under way right now to counter this point, one by the National Academy of Education and the other by the American Educational Research Association. But until those reports are completed and released, I will proceed with the assumptions already stated.) One thesis that undergirds this paper is that it is artificial to separate educational research from educational development, without damaging both the research and the development. In a professional field, or in a craft, or in a skilled practice, research and development are so intertwined as to be inseparable.

Let me take a stab at identifying a major reason for the fact that educational research seems to have had little impact on the classroom—especially if we consider "research" apart from "development." The models of educational research currently in vogue are rooted in "scientific" approaches—inquiry modes that are based strongly on empirical, hypothesis-testing techniques. The overwhelming number of investigators using this model are either psychologists or individuals influenced primarily by psychology or another behavioral science. Doctoral programs at my own institution, and I imagine at yours, stress behavioral science techniques almost to the exclusion of any other in the preparation of educational researchers. As a direct result of this research bias, we usually find that problems in education that are investigated turn out to be either trivial, or they bear little relevance to classroom practice.

The triviality often results from the strong reliance in much psychological experimentation on "hard" measures of behavioral change. Inasmuch as we have not yet learned to assess behaviorally some of the most important educational changes for which we strive, the sophisticated research models that are used often manipulate insignificant variables. The researchers keep refining their procedures, largely but not exclusively statistical procedures, seemingly unaware of where the crucial problems lie. An elaborate research methodology has evolved around the investigation of inconsequential events.

The lack of relevance to educational practice often occurs because some of the best researchers operate from a theory base not rooted in education, but in some other discipline—again usually psychology. The problems they investigate explicate behavioral science theory, not necessarily educational theory. Most of these researchers, the better ones, are usually writing for colleagues in their parent disciplines. They think, I fear, that teachers should be able to work out the classroom implications of the research.

There is little doubt that the school is an excellent setting for the conduct of certain research in psychology, sociology, anthropology, and other behavioral sciences. Surely, it is well to encourage investigators from these fields to continue to work in classrooms. But it is naïve to expect that a significant amount of such research, considered in isolation, discipline by discipline, will affect educational practice. There is little in the history of educational research, largely psychological research, to warrant optimism about classroom payoff.

Activity in a classroom is complex and subtle. Any one of the traditional perspectives from which investigators have viewed the educational process has been extremely narrow in relation to that process. It may be true that these perspectives that have been used from the behavioral sciences are all that we have had. Perhaps it is best to work with what is available. However, the end result has been a view so simplified, or so segmented, as to have little relation to the total educational process.

For the moment let us call teaching a craft to enable the construction of an analogy, an analogy with the craft of metallurgy. For centuries, and continuing today, skilled craftsmen have been making metals. They have learned to add a little of this substance and a little of that, then to heat the batch for a certain length of time until it reaches a certain color, then to let it cool at a certain rate. The craft has been continually developed through the centuries, apprentices learning from masters. Meanwhile "scientific" approaches to metallurgy have not succeeded in fully explaining all that the master craftsman does. Physicists and chemists who study metallurgy recognize that the craftsman uses certain processes that scientists do not yet understand. Scientists study the metallurgists at work in the hope that this analysis will give them clues to better understand physics or chemistry.

To restate the argument, physicists don't feel that they can use their theories of the nature of matter to deduce very much about the fabrication of new metals. New metals are fabricated by superb craftsmen; then the physicist and chemist try to find out what happened.

Isn't it possible that teaching is at least as complex as metallurgy? The theories of psychologists, anthropologists, and sociologists—taken singly—do not permit us to deduce an educational program any more than a physicist's theories lead directly to fabrication of new metals. It doesn't seem unreasonable to follow the route of metallurgy. Let's see how superb craftsmen operate, in this case teachers in the classroom. We might then learn more about the behavioral sciences.

A second model has been developed for educational research within recent years to supplement the model drawn from the behavioral sciences. And it is a model that has been received with considerable favor in the educational R & D community. It is an approach that seems to be eminently compatible with models derived from the behavioral sciences, although it has some special attributes. I am referring to the engineering model for educational research and development. This particular approach is being fostered currently in many areas of human activity other than education. We see it used in the poverty programs, in health fields, in population control, and in penology. The engineering model is found under labels like "systems analysis," "operations analysis," "planning-programing-budgeting systems," and "cost-benefit approaches."

The engineering model is being pushed aggressively these days by many officials who control federal appropriations for civilian enterprises. For our purposes, it is perhaps sufficient to note that most bureaus at the U.S. Office of Education, including the Bureau of Research, seem committed to such styles.

This particular model has been used with apparent success in the space program and in the Department of Defense.

As the Government envisions broad expenditures in the civil sector, it seems attractive to utilize techniques that have been used to such apparently good effect in the military and in space.

I understand that when a space ship is to be designed one of the first steps entails the delineation of performance specifications. There first must be general agreement about what the ship is expected to do. The next job is to prepare the designs and engage a manufacturer who will most economically achieve the objective.

On the surface this seems a most appealing model for educational research and development activities. First, identify the performance objectives toward which the system should be aimed. Then design the system so that these objectives will be achieved economically. In the application of this model to the field of education, equate "performance objectives" with "pupil behaviors." (Parenthetically, it is relevant to note that those who have most conscientiously used the engineering model for educational research and development have seemed to assume that the only effects of the school system are on the children who attend, and that these effects are exclusively a result of the subjects that are taught.)

The engineering model seems to have been followed very rigorously by its most vocal enthusiasts in education. Performance objectives are identified early. Then the subsystem is designed. I have written elsewhere and at greater length about the shortcomings of this approach in the design of curriculum. . . .[1]

One of the major shortcomings of the engineering model when it is applied to the field of education centers on the

question of societal values. In the military and space spheres, responsibility for decision-making is relatively centralized. While many pressures are exerted before a decision is reached about a missile defense system, the final decision carries all of the authority of a Presidential decree. Industrial efforts are then mobilized toward a single end product. And there is a single buyer: the Federal Government.

Decision-making in education is more diffuse—as it is in poverty programs, health programs, and other domestic activities. Educational research and development models that are based strongly on engineering approaches don't sufficiently recognize the competition among diverse value systems and power groups. Difficulties are compounded by the relatively heavy involvement of private industry in educational affairs. The product mix in education is a broad one, and there is no consensus on specific ends.

Systems approaches also bog down when there is no agreement among competing users and sellers on basic objectives. Let me take an example outside the field of education, forest management, to make the point in a relatively uncontroversial manner. We can recognize probably that grazers, lumbermen, recreationalists, and conservationists—to name just a few groups—bring competing values to the issues associated with forest management.

Another difficulty inherent to the systems approach is the fact that values and social outcomes are difficult to quantify. How does one determine quantitatively the usefulness of five hours per week of physical education in grade four in limiting crime? Make no mistake. Precisely this type of calculation must be made to utilize the engineering model.

Still another difficulty with the engineering model is the lack of recogni-

---

[1] The reader is directed to Atkin's paper in Section II (Chapter 7).

tion of the fact that we cannot discard existing systems in education as readily as they can be discarded in the military and in space programs. We don't throw away old school buildings, nor do we retire fifty percent of the present teaching staff. Obsolescent systems in defense and in space are disposed of more readily than they are in education. Therefore the opportunity to inaugurate a radical new approach is limited.

It must be pointed out that the new entrants into the education industry, the large electronically oriented firms, have been some of the staunchest supporters of systems approaches to education. One reason is the fact that personnel in these companies are being redirected from defense and space enterprises to education, and the skills of operations analysis are the skills that have been nurtured most assiduously in these corporations. It is only natural for them to emphasize their strengths.

Also it is always easier to take a simplified view of phenomena being studied when one is unhampered about knowledge of the phenomenon. There is a certain appeal in entering the situation with a certain set of blinders in which one is alert to only a few of the relevant observables. It has been revealing to note that early enthusiasm displayed by the industrial giants for education has been now somewhat tempered after the second look and the initial blush of excitement. I think that some of the current disenchantment is due to the fact that the market place is confused, much more so than in space and in the military. One creates a market for an instructional system in a different way than he creates a market for a rocket.

I have puzzled long over possible reasons why the engineering model has been adopted so uncritically by the educational community, but it is doubtful that any of my speculation has been productive. It would be unkind perhaps

to jump to a conclusion that educational researchers are using the style broadly solely because that is where the Federal Government is placing its money. But I suppose that federal grants still do represent prestige in the research community, and a certain number of investigators, given a choice, would rather operate in fields where they can be handsomely subsidized, instead of in less popular fields.

I don't question that another reason for the popularity of the engineering model in education is the apparent logic. It seems appealing to delineate objectives, then design programs; though one would think that this argument would be less attractive than it seems to be to those who are well aware through experience of the subtleties inherent in the teaching situation. But these subtleties are difficult to talk about in operational terms, and so they lack power in modifying the engineering approaches.

There is no denying the fact that the engineering model plus approaches based on psychological theory (and it has been noted earlier that these styles are not incompatible) are the prevalent forms of research in science education today, as indeed they are in all of education. But a case has been made here that the psychologically based approach is often trivial or irrelevant. The engineering approach is simplistic, and it gives insufficient attention to questions of competing objectives and values.

It would be an error to interpret this statement as advocacy of a position in which psychologically based research or engineering modes are not supported. Systems approaches certainly should be utilized and examined critically. Research based on engineering models will surely result in improvement of certain of our instructional missions, particularly those that involve utilization of sophisticated technology. Psychologically based research entails the study of many interesting topics of concern to scholars. Possibly some of this research, in the long term, will change the schools.[2]

. . .

All of the foregoing carries the implication that there is a style of educational research and development that holds promise of greater payoff in the long term than the behavioral science and engineering models mentioned so far. Here, as you might suspect, it is difficult to offer well-defined remedies. However a broad domain for educational inquiry can indeed be staked out, and if you will accept the fact that this domain will be outlined here in only a rough fashion, and even possibly with inconsistencies, an attempt will be made to point to some possibly productive avenues for our developmental and research activities.

My underlying plea, as has been anticipated in this paper already, is that we develop a style of educational research based on *educational* theory and rooted in classroom events. The most potent innovators in education seem to have been individuals or groups with a penchant for initiating new curriculum programs—"development" if we use the R and D dichotomy. However these innovators, if broadly influential, have also had a strong taste for theory construction (e.g., Rousseau, Froebel, Herbart, and Dewey). I would stress that curriculum development alone, educational research alone, without concomitant articulation of educational theory, seems to lack power in affecting practice over a long period of time.

The model of educational research I am proposing here, and that may have considerable promise for influence on practice, places classroom analysis and developmental work at the core. It is possible to obtain agreement from a wide range of individuals that given innovations are tasteful and effective. On this point, chemists, biologists, educationists, novelists, psychologists, anthropologists, lawyers, philosophers, administrators, and historians will usually agree. An effective teacher is generally recognized as such. A job of the educational researcher is to begin examining the work of effective teachers, teachers working intelligently with appealing content, in an attempt to validate generalizations that may be made about the elements which make the teaching strong. I believe that a promising beginning may result if individuals from various disciplines, such as those listed above, immerse themselves in classrooms for a relatively long period of time and attempt to generate conversations across their special fields to describe the classroom activities and validate the quality of the judgments being made. I am suggesting a direct onslaught on the total educational picture as a substitute for the fragmentary approach that presently characterizes most educational research. Research undertaken in such a context has a strong likelihood of major and broad impact on the schools.

If we foster such research, initially we will be relying strongly, in all probability, on the perceptions of certain philosophers. But we must avoid substituting philosophical blinders for psychological ones. If we are aware of this possible danger and if we recognize that theory development in education will come slowly, progress may result.

All of this suggests that there is a need for educational investigation which places greater reliance on an intuitive and aesthetic dimension for making decisions than we have become familiar with in the educational research litera-

---

[2] Editor's note: A paragraph regarding the possible influence of Piaget on curriculum development has been omitted here.

ture of the last few decades. Of course, in ordinary discussions about education conducted by professionals or nonprofessionals, the aesthetic and anecdotal elements usually are strong. People frequently talk about teachers who make the subject "alive," about the "verve" characteristic of some teacher's approach, about the "satisfactions" children get through doing certain types of investigation, about the superb timing that a specific second grade teacher displays in teaching reading. But in currently acceptable styles of educational research and development, it is usually deemed "unscientific" to talk in such language. There is a continuing pressure for hard measures of educational change, a pressure and tradition that derives from the courses already described.

A case might be made that in the history of many sciences there have been oscillations between global perspectives of the field under study and microperspectives. In at least two contemporary science fields—physics and biology—we find much of the exciting research is taking place simultaneously at both ends of the scale. Major biologists today are working at the molecular level, while other biologists are rediscovering the importance of work in naturalistic settings. Some physicists are deep in the nucleus. Others are at the fringes of the universe.

In the field of educational research and development, we need a swing of this micro-macro pendulum—a swing toward the macro. We seem now to be laboring with a type of reductionism in which it is very difficult to put the various pieces together.

What we may need in the field of educational research and development in order to create a research community that focuses on the important problems, and not solely on the readily solvable

ones, is the evolution of a disciplinary approach that may be akin to the relatively recent development of the field of ethology. The conventional biological approaches—physiology, biochemistry, taxonomy, and embryology—were all useful, but they reinforced a fragmentary view of the interesting events in animal behavior. It was necessary to enunciate a new perspective. To understand classroom events, we also need new perspectives. Existing disciplines are helpful, but they all miss the classroom mark somewhat.

Because of the variety of talents required to do educational research in naturalistic settings, I think that universities will continue to be at the center of such activities. We don't find the necessary mix of philosophers, historians, novelists, chemists, journalists, and anthropologists in the public schools, or anywhere else. Just as importantly, academicians must participate heavily in content identification and story line delineation for the school subjects—as they have done in the recent round of curriculum revision projects supported primarily by the National Science Foundation. The task requires senior scholars, men found primarily at universities. Heavy R and D investments in public schools, regional laboratories, or private industry simply will not result in the level of innovativeness that is desirable and possible—although such agencies may serve admirably to reach teachers far removed from the sources of new, substantive ideas.

In short, and to reiterate, my view of a productive style of educational research still places strong reliance on individuals from the traditional academic disciplines as well as on educationists. These people are supplemented by writers of fiction, by journalists, perhaps by playwrights. All of them are encouraged to focus on classroom events. I don't think we have had enough trials that exemplify this style of educational research to have yet made me pessimistic about the outcome. In fact, the few attempts in which I have engaged in such tentative explorations seem to me to have been productive. It is revealing, what scholars of different backgrounds will say is important as they all watch the same math teacher for the same forty-five minute period. A mathematician is impressed with the superb sequencing of content. One psychologist is amazed at the amount of emotional support the teacher is able to give various children. A sociologist is impressed with the contributions made by a child who has been in the class for only one week as this child works in the neutral territory of mathematics.

It should be reiterated also that this research style, in order to work, requires the talents of senior scholars in the various disciplines. Junior men are prone to operate within the closely defined boundaries of the field in which they have recently been trained. It seems that the only people who can afford professionally to go beyond the boundaries of their own formal education are individuals who have already earned a reputation for scholarship within the field as the field is conventionally conceived. I don't think that this phenomenological approach to educational research stands a chance unless we can enlist the aid of well-established academicians.

Of course, the approach also requires the close attention of educationists who also are free to operate outside the boundaries of their own training. And, in view of the psychologically based training that most of our educationists now receive, it isn't clear how optimistic one can be about finding a sufficiently large cadre of such people. In any field it is extremely difficult to find individuals who are venturesome enough to

abandon a puzzle-solving type of approach in which the results can be largely anticipated in favor of one that may have great relevance but in which the form of the outcome is highly problematic and even the style of investigation is uncertain. And to compound the difficulty, the investment of time required may be enormous. Considerable immersion may be required before frameworks will begin to emerge that exemplify the point of view that I am attempting to develop here.

It is possible that my plea for research in naturalistic settings, my plea for putting aside our psychologically based and engineering models for a time, my plea for phenomenological approaches, my plea for the involvement of a broad array of academicians who will focus on classroom events—it is possible that all of these pleas have relatively little merit. But it is probably more likely that they have some merit—though not as much as I might claim for them—yet they will not be tried broadly because it is difficult to create an appropriate atmosphere at a university that will foster such a research style. Universities are extremely tradition-bound. It is true that we were successful in involving scholars from the sciences and from mathematics about ten years ago in the development of new curriculum programs below the college level. But it seems to have been an unusually opportune time. Such recruitment is more difficult today. And, as I have indicated, I don't think that much hope lies outside the university because private industry and regional laboratories have more difficulty recruiting the kind of people I am talking about than the universities. It will remain for some imaginative university to create a setting for a research style of this type. Where it will happen, I am not sure. But it will be at a place where relatively high risk ventures are encouraged if they have the support of productive people.

You recognize by now that these thoughts about research styles in education that have been characteristic of the past few years and that might be appropriate for the future are fragmentary and exploratory. I realize that detail is skimpy, and there are probably flaws in the rationale. But the field is a confusing one, and it may be more productive to explore in relatively uncharted territory than to attempt to refine our perspectives within well-worn boundaries, particularly if those boundaries seem with the passage of time to lack the relevance required to improve educational practice as much as it must be modified to meet the challenges of the next few decades.

II   Instructional Objectives

Instructional objectives have been closely identified with the programed instruction movement. Actually the need for instructional objectives was noted as long ago as the 1930's. Ralph W. Tyler (1934) stressed the need for instructional objectives as a prerequisite for test construction. Tyler's reasoning was compellingly clear: In order to construct a test to measure the outcomes of some sort of instruction, one first has to identify what is being taught. One has to have something to measure. Tyler was also one of the first to realize the importance of stating instructional objectives in behavioral terms, that is, in terms of observable behavior. Only when objectives are so stated is it possible to objectively evaluate the outcomes of instruction.

Instructional objectives have several important characteristics. First, they specify in observable behavioral terms what the student will be able to do at the end of a lesson. Consider the following two objectives:

1. The student will know the capitals of every state in the U.S.A.
2. Given a list of the states in the U.S.A. in an order he has never seen, the student will be able to write the state capitals for each of the states without making any errors.

The first objective says that the student will "know" the state capitals. What does this mean? Does it mean that he will be able to list the state capitals? If so, does this imply that the student knows that the capital of Illinois is Springfield? Not at all. The student may simply have memorized a list of names without having any idea of which capital goes with which state. In short, when an objective is stated in such general terms as "know" one is forced to guess at what the student will be able to *do* when he is said to "know" something.

Now consider the second objective. Here the terminal behavior—that is, the behavior expected of the student after instruction—is explicitly stated in objective behavioral terms. Anyone coming into the classroom would be able to ascertain if the students really "know" the state capitals by observing this student behavior. It should be noted also that the second objective states only one possible behavioral interpretation. Because an objective is stated behaviorally does not automatically insure that it is a good or desirable one. One could easily state in behavioral terms the objective of having students list the capitals in alphabetical order; but, as indicated above, this might not be the type of behavior most teachers would expect of students who "know" the state capitals. We shall return shortly to this question of the worth of objectives and the relationship between educational goals and educational objectives.

Objective 2 also demonstrates the second characteristic of instructional objectives. Objective 2 contains a statement of the conditions under which the terminal behavior is expected. Thus, the phrase "Given a list of the states in the U.S.A. in an order he has never seen . . ." defines the conditions under which the student should be able to name the state capitals. No such statement appears in Objective 1, and one does not know whether the student should be able to list the capitals, to mark them correctly on a map, or to match capital names with state names. Objective 2 is clear and precise about these conditions.

The third characteristic of instructional objectives is that they contain a standard of performance below which student performance is unacceptable. In Objective 2 the words "without making any errors" specify the standard. The first objective makes no such statement of standards and once again is ambiguous. Good instructional objectives (in the Tylerian sense) clearly state the criteria against which student performance is to be assessed.

One might well ask the question, Does the practice of formulating instructional objectives in behavioral terms pay off in better lessons? Little evidence exists on this matter, but what there is seems to suggest an affirmative answer. The first chapter in this section describes a study demonstrating that an emphasis on clarifying and then achieving instructional objectives has a rather strong and direct effect on instruction. Student teachers who were told that they would be graded on their ability to select appropriate behavioral changes in their students and then to bring about these changes produced greater gains in punctuation skills from the pre-test to the post-test than teachers who were told they would be graded on such things as "professional characteristics and teaching methods." Thus, McNeil's chapter suggests that teachers who construct and use instructional objectives are more effective teachers.

What of the individual learner, however? Mager and Clark (Chapter 6) address themselves to the problem of entering behavior; that is, the behavior the student is capable of emitting at the beginning of instruction. Mager and Clark note that students typically enter a learning situation with varying amounts of relevant knowledge or entering behavior. If the student is old enough to profit from independent instruction, then one method of dealing with initial student differences in entering behavior is to present the student with a list of instructional objectives. The student himself will be able to determine the areas in which he is strong (those areas in which he can already meet or nearly meet the objectives) as well as the areas in which he is weak (those in which he cannot meet the objectives). If the student is given control over his curriculum, he may then concentrate his learning efforts in those areas in which he is weak. Such a procedure would save much time for the student and would avoid submitting him to some possibly boring review of areas he already knows. It should be emphasized, however, that a procedure such as this can be used only with students who are capable of diagnosing their own strengths and weaknesses and who are capable of independent study.

These first two chapters illustrate well the advantages of stating and attaining instructional objectives. Such objectives state clearly what is expected of the student after instruction. One obvious advantage of this procedure is that by stating instructional objectives, one is also stating the criterion behavior against which students are to be evaluated. Second, instructional objectives can aid immeasurably in the planning of instruction. When one says that his students will "know" the state capitals, one hardly knows where to begin. This type of objective gives little help in deciding *what* to teach, let alone *how* to teach it. By stating objectives in precise behavioral terms, one gets a clear picture of the final desired result—where instruction is leading. Such a picture can aid in the development of lesson materials designed to reach that objective.

Despite these beneficial effects, the practice of defining educational objectives in terms of student behavior has been vigorously criticized, particularly by those involved in curriculum development. In order to understand these criticisms, it is necessary to distinguish between educational goals and instructional objectives. An *educational goal* is a broad general purpose which most of us feel is important to education. For example, one of the major functions of the school is to transmit the culture of our society to the young. How would one go about behaviorally stating this objective? What behaviors would a person who achieved such a goal possess? These are difficult questions to answer. Goals such as these are difficult to specify behaviorally and perhaps this is one of their advantages. These goals are stated in so general a form that few people disagree with them. Let someone try to operationalize them, however, and disagreements are numerous.

The point of this discussion is that there are many goals of education which seem to transcend the rather specific, day-to-day instructional objectives discussed earlier. One objection to instructional objectives is that by focusing attention on objectives which are rather easy to specify behaviorally, less attention may be given to long-term, general goals. The attaining of objectives in punctuation skills might be of little value to a child if he is not also taught some of the social skills necessary for a successful adjustment in the society. A second objection to instructional objectives is that it is very difficult to anticipate all of the possible outcomes of instruction. Atkin's "meal worm" example is a good one. The child may be learning far more than just the movements of the meal worm. Is it possible that by stating instructional objectives, other outcomes will go unnoticed? Third, some subject matters do not lend themselves well to specifying objectives behaviorally. Art is an example. What are the desired terminal behaviors in a subject matter such as this, where the emphasis is on style and sensitivity? Again, by concentrating on some rather short-term goals, such as paint mixing or brush work, important long-term goals could be slighted. Atkin (1963), Eisner (1967), and Atkin in Chapter 7 have raised objections such as these to instructional objectives. Popham has answered some of the more unreasonable objections in Chapter 8, but the fact remains that some of the objections are well taken.

The issue itself has become unreasonably polarized, with camps forming on both sides of "The Objectives Controversy." Moderation is needed by all concerned. The stating and attaining of instructional objectives have many beneficial effects on instruction. However, a rigid adherence to prespecified objectives would be foolish indeed. A teacher who slavishly follows her objectives will miss some golden opportunities to teach citizenship during a mathematics class, for instance. The effective teacher will be a flexible one.

References

Atkin, J. M. Some evaluation problems in a course content improvement project. *J. Res. Science Teaching*, 1963, **1**, 129–32.

Eisner, Elliot W. Educational objectives: Help or hindrance? *The School Review*, 1967, **75**, 250–76.

Tyler, R. W. *Constructing achievement tests*. Columbus: Ohio State University, 1934.

5

Concomitants of Using Behavioral Objectives in the Assessment of Teacher Effectiveness

JOHN D. McNEIL / *University of California, Los Angeles*

There has long been resistance to the basal proposition that the effectiveness of methods and teachers must be measured in terms of the results secured (Ayers, 1912). Those responsible for evaluating teachers have exalted procedures in teaching and have seldom examined the products, i.e., the efficiency of the teacher as indicated by what his pupils can do following instruction. However, we are beginning to see an increasing number of bold proposals founded on the assumption that the American public expects results from schooling. As public support of education increases, there will be greater insistence on judging a teacher in the light of his ability to enhance the learning of pupils. One way to do this is for a supervisor and a teacher to agree as to what behavioral objectives are to be sought for particular pupils and what will be accepted as evidence that the teacher has or has not been successful in obtaining the desired gain. An agreement is drawn in advance of the teacher's actions and is designed to counter the prevailing practice of making an ex post facto judgment.

Hypotheses

Logically, one might assume that supervision by objectives (i.e., focus upon results) would have these consequences:

1. Supervisors will perceive teachers as more effective in classroom instruction. It is likely that there have been many instances in the past where teachers have been successful in producing changes in learning, i.e., have been successful teachers, but have failed on their ratings as teachers because the supervisor did not concur in advance on the desirability of the results produced.

Reprinted with the permission of the author and the publisher from *The Journal of Experimental Education*, 1967, *36*, 69–74.

2. Pupils will show greater gain in the desired directions when the teacher's reinforcement is contingent upon such gains.

3. Teachers will perceive supervisors' suggestions as more relevant and helpful. When supervising by objectives, suggestions are viewed as means rather than ends. Definition of teaching goals in terms of specified pupil change excludes the making of the broad range of comments that might have occurred were the tasks less defined, e.g., arbitrary judgment and restriction—"You are trying to make that man into another you. One's enough."

Experimental evidence in support of the above is meager. There have been some industrial and social psychological studies of individual and group goals which tended to show that one functions better if he is clear as to the expected goals (Mager, 1962; Raven, 1959). Also, there is a single instance of an educational psychological study of set applied to student teaching (Wittrock, 1962) which provides data that teaching for pupil gain produces greater achievement than a comparable procedure that does not have results as the criterion of teacher effectiveness.

The following three studies were designed to collect evidence as to whether or not supervision by objectives produced predicted consequences.

Experiment I: Supervision by Objectives and Supervisors' Perception of Teacher Effectiveness

Seventy-seven university students from a single course "Principles of Instruction" were told they were to teach in public secondary schools for two consecutive days. The regular teachers were advised that the student teachers would be expected to assume major instructional responsibilities for the class during the two days and that subsequently the regular teachers would complete a rating form evaluating the student teachers in terms of:

(a) success in teaching as evidenced by pupil achievement (7 point rating scale)

(b) poise and personality (7 point rating scale)

(c) application of the principles of learning taught in the course (letter grade A, B, C, D, F).

The student teachers were randomly assigned either to an experimental or a control group. Both groups received printed instructions to report to particular schools and teachers. The instruction sheet also included the rating form to be completed by the training teacher.

The experimental variable was the difference in written instructions for the two groups. The experimental group was told to obtain agreement in advance from the training teacher as to what would constitute evidence of success in terms of pupil change, i.e., "Indicate the act, problem, or situation to be presented and the pupil responses that evidence success." The training teacher was asked to initial the agreement 1) that evidence to be collected would indicate that "pupils have learned something of significance" and 2) that "if the student teacher achieves these objectives with most pupils, he should be rated excellent; if he achieves only a few objectives and with only a few pupils, he should be rated good; if pupils do not respond as stipulated, the student teacher should get credit for trying."

In lieu of the above instructions, each individual in the control group was told to meet in advance with the training teacher in order to familiarize himself with the on-going activities of the class and to prepare and submit lesson plans to the regular teacher for the two-day teaching.

After the instruction had been completed, the completed rating scales and recommended grades were returned by the supervisory teachers with either (a) a copy of a "contract" (experimental group) or (b) a copy of the lesson plans (control group).

RESULTS OF THE FIRST EXPERIMENT

Consistent with the hypothesis, more of the experimental group were perceived by supervising teachers as achieving greater success in teaching as evidenced by pupil achievement ($t = 3.0, p < .01$). Also, those who were instructed to negotiate agreements regarding criteria for success in terms of pupil gain tended to be perceived by supervisors as more successful in the principles of learning (71% A's to 59% A's in the respective experimental and control groups). With respect to perceptions of poise and personality, no significant differences between the two groups were found. It should be noted that two members of the experimental group failed to negotiate a contract in advance of their teaching and that their subsequent ratings were among the lowest received. Their scores, however, are reflected in the total score for the experimental group.

Experiment II: Supervision by Objectives and Pupil Achievement

Forty-four elementary student teachers in inner-city elementary schools were required to administer an activity labeled as "an exercise in creative writing." This exercise was, in fact, an opportunity to collect a sample of the writing of third, fourth, and sixth grade pupils and to note proficiency in five skills of punctuation. The exercise consisted of the teacher reading an incomplete story and then asking each pupil to write his ending to the story. The teachers were told not to suggest ideas or change the written expressions of the pupils in any way.

Subsequently, the papers were scored for punctuation errors at the university and those pupils who made 70 percent or more errors on attempts within any one of the five classified skills were defined as "deficient." Matched experimental and control groups of pupils were drawn from the population of learners so declared deficient in one or more skills of punctuation.

FOCUS UPON PROCEDURES VERSUS FOCUS UPON RESULTS

Teachers were randomly assigned as "control" or "experimental." Teachers of the controls were advised in writing that their grade in student teaching would be determined by their "professional characteristics and teaching methods." Factors to be considered were listed on an attached rating scale and included items such as: appearance, maturity, classroom arrangement, and teaching procedures. In a letter to each of these teachers, they were told: "In a major way, you will be judged by your ability to follow the course of study and use appropriately the materials authorized for your class (i.e., textbook). Specifically, we will want a description (evaluation) of *how* you taught punctuation during the period January 3–14." Copies of the lesson plans used during this period were to be submitted as an indicator of the nature of the lessons.

Teachers of the experimental group were advised in writing that their grade in student teaching would be determined by their ability to select appropriate behavioral changes to be sought in learners and to effect those changes without undesirable by-products. In a letter to each of these teachers, they were told: "In a major way, you will be judged by your ability to get results. Specifically, we will want evidence of changes in pupil ability to use punctuation as a result of your activities during the period January 3–14." In addition, the teachers of the experimental group were advised as to which children had been identified as deficient in a particular punctuation skill and were asked to stipulate prior to instruction what they would provide as evidence that they had helped these pupils improve.

In short, whereas the teachers in the control group submitted detailed *plans* for lessons in punctuation, the teachers of the experimental group submitted their *criteria* for evaluating pupil change in punctuation.

Two post-tests were designed for measuring pupil achievement and willingness to use a skill of punctuation. One was another open-ended "creative-writing" exercise. A second was a standard printed composition, one page in length, which contained 67 errors in punctuation (five types of errors). Children were to correct the errors. The standard test was an instance of the class of instructional exercises common in the textbooks used by the control group. The test was similar in form but

did not include the same items selected as criteria by the teachers in the experimental group. In other words, the standard test was consistent with activities available in materials which teachers of the control group were directed to use and also generally consistent with the objectives selected by teachers of the experimental group.

The second open-ended post-test was administered one day; the standard test was given the next. The tests were preceded by ten days of classroom instruction in punctuation in accordance with the previously mentioned directions.

RESULTS OF THE SECOND EXPERIMENT

The difference in pupil scores between those taught by teachers in the experimental and the control groups was significant in terms of achievement on both the overall range of punctuation skills and the particular skill in which the learners had been labeled deficient. Tables 1–5 show both relative gain in overcoming the original deficiencies and

Table 1

FINAL MEAN SCORES EARNED BY PUPILS ORIGINALLY DEFICIENT IN SKILL OF USING INITIAL CAPITALIZATION

	Scores on initial capitalization (18 possible errors)		Scores on overall range of punctuation skills (67 possible errors)	
	Exp. condition	*Control condition*	*Exp. condition*	*Control condition*
Third grade				
Experimental N = 24	M = 8.9	M = 12.3	M = 45	M = 53.4
Control N = 24	SD = 4.4	SD = 3.5	SD = 7.6	SD = 8.5
	$t = 3.1, p < .01$		$t = 3.6, p < .01$	
Fourth grade				
Experimental N = 35	M = 5.7	M = 7.8	M = 34.3	M = 44.3
Control N = 35	SD = 3.2	SD = 2.7	SD = 9.7	SD = 7.2
	$t = 3.5, p < .01$		$t = 5.0, p < .01$	
Sixth grade				
Experimental N = 39	M = 4.1	M = 6.9	M = 29.4	M = 36.4
Control N = 39	SD = 3.1	SD = 2.6	SD = 11	SD = 8.9
	$t = 4.2, p < .01$		$t = 3.18, p < .01$	

Table 2

FINAL MEAN SCORES EARNED BY PUPILS ORIGINALLY DEFICIENT
IN SKILL OF USING PERIODS AT THE END OF A SENTENCE

	Scores on period at end of sentence (14 possible errors)		*Scores on overall range of punctuation skills (67 possible errors)*	
	Exp. condition	*Control condition*	*Exp. condition*	*Control condition*
Third grade				
Experimental N = 41	M = 6.8	M = 9.8	M = 42	M = 50.8
Control N = 41	SD = 3.6	SD = 2.8	SD = 13.2	SD = 9.5
	$t = 4.7, p < .01$		$t = 3.52, p < .01$	
Fourth grade				
Experimental N = 42	M = 5.7	M = 8.3	M = 38	M = 45
Control N = 42	SD = 4.1	SD = 2.2	SD = 15.8	SD = 8.3
	$t = 3.8, p < .01$		$t = 2.59, p < .05$	
Sixth grade				
Experimental N = 47	M = 3.9	M = 6.2	M = 26.9	M = 34.9
Control N = 47	SD = 3.3	SD = 1.7	SD = 13.4	SD = 12.5
	$t = 4.3, p < .01$		$t = 3.08, p < .01$	

the relative gain in all punctuation skills. Pupils taught by teachers in the experimental group (emphasis on results) achieved more than those taught by teachers in the control group (emphasis on procedures) with respect to their previously identified area of deficiency. More than that, pupils whose teachers were told to emphasize results tended to show greater achievement than their matched peers in the remaining types of punctuation skills as measured by the standard test. In other words, the focus of instruction upon overcoming a specific deficiency did not preclude desirable outcomes in other related areas.

Study 3: Supervision by Objectives and Perception by Student Teachers of the Supervisory Process

A questionnaire was completed by the 44 elementary teachers who participated in the second experimental study. This questionnaire called for responses regarding the amount of time spent in teaching punctuation skills during the period of evaluation, the extent of pres-sure, the amount of freedom to select own teaching procedures, and the amount of time given to individual pupils as opposed to the class as a whole. The teachers were also asked: "How would you prefer to be evaluated as a teacher—(a) by progress evidenced by my pupils (equating for their initial ability to learn), (b) by my ability to follow recommended procedures, (c) by my character, the extent to which I am a model for pupils, (d) by my ability to plan, (e) by my ability to work well with the faculty?"

Contrary to what was expected, teachers who had been exposed to supervision by objectives did not respond differently to the questionnaire items than those who had been subjected to conventional methods. Both groups tended to report the same amount of time given to the punctuation task (one half hour daily), felt very free to select their teaching procedures, found supervisor suggestions helpful, and centered most of their time on the class as a whole as opposed to focusing on individual pupils and their needs.

Table 3

FINAL MEAN SCORES EARNED BY PUPILS ORIGINALLY DEFICIENT
IN SKILL OF CAPITALIZATION OF PROPER NAMES

		Scores on capitalization of names (10 possible errors)		Scores on overall range of punctuation skills (67 possible errors)	
		Exp. condition	Control condition	Exp. condition	Control condition
Third grade					
Experimental	N = 21	M = 5.1	M = 7.9	M = 47	M = 52.2
Control	N = 21	SD = 2.4	SD = 2	SD = 8.5	SD = 8.0
		$t = 4.6, p < .01$		$t = 2.04, p < .05$	

The teachers were almost unanimous (98 percent) in their preference for the use of pupil progress (results) as the criterion for evaluation of teaching.

Conclusion

The data in the studies reported herein provide evidence that the emphasis and use of operational definitions of instructional goals, including specification of criterion measures, in the supervisory process is accompanied by more favorable assessment of teachers by supervisors and greater gain in desired directions on the part of learners. The practice of supervision by objectives with its emphasis upon obtaining results with pupils does not appear to produce undue pressures upon teachers. This is true at least under the conditions of this study where teachers determined the appropriateness of results in terms of the deficiencies of their own pupils and were not compared with other teachers on an absolute scale of pupil gain. Further, the focus upon specific objectives for particular learners does not appear to restrict pupil advancement to only the objectives stated but leads to increased achievement in a range of desirable directions.

Although teachers tend to see their supervisors' suggestions as helpful, both when results are the criterion and when teaching method, personality and other evaluative bases are operative, teachers are almost unanimous in believing that the criterion "results in terms of pupil gain" is the best of five bases for evaluating instructional effectiveness.

Table 4

FINAL MEAN SCORES EARNED BY PUPILS ORIGINALLY DEFICIENT
IN SKILL OF USING AN APOSTROPHE

		Scores on using an apostrophe (7 possible errors)		Scores on overall range of punctuation skills (67 possible errors)	
		Exp. condition	Control condition	Exp. condition	Control condition
Sixth grade					
Experimental	N = 20	M = 4.7	M = 6.3	M = 30.7	M = 36.6
Control	N = 20	SD = 2.4	SD = 1.3	SD = 8.3	SD = 9.7
		$t = 2.76, p < .01$		$t = 2.11, p < .05$	

Table 5

FINAL MEAN SCORES EARNED BY PUPILS ORIGINALLY DEFICIENT
IN SKILL OF USING A QUESTION MARK

	Scores on using a question mark (18 possible errors)		Scores on overall range of punctuation skills (67 possible errors)	
	Exp. condition	*Control condition*	*Exp. condition*	*Control condition*
Sixth grade				
Experimental N = 23	M = 7	M = 12.8	M = 16.9	M = 32
Control N = 23	SD = 6.6	SD = 5.0	SD = 12	SD = 8.8
	$t = 3.2, p < .01$		$t = 4.7, p < .01$	

References

Ayers, Leonard P. Measuring educational processes through educational results. *School Review*, Vol. XX (1912), 300–309.

Mager, R. F. and McCann, J. *Learner controlled instruction*. Palo Alto, California: Varian Associates, 1962.

Raven, B. H. The dynamics of groups. *Review of Educational Research*, Vol.
XXX, No. 4 (October 1959).

Wittrock, M. C. Set applied to student teaching. *Journal of Educational Psychology*, Vol. LIII, No. 4 (August 1962), 175–80.

6

Explorations in Student-Controlled Instruction

ROBERT F. MAGER / *RFM Associates, Los Altos Hills, California*

CECIL CLARK / *University of Washington*

The development of programmed instruction is, or certainly should be, a dynamic undertaking. While we may differ widely and even wildly on what programming will ultimately be like, few would question that we have some distance to go before we attain the ultimate. In short, some changes are indicated. The interesting thing about this is that, although most of us will acknowledge that change is necessary, we are ignoring some of the facts that indicate where changes should be made.

In this paper, we want to suggest an area in which program design can be improved. We shall try to accomplish our purpose by briefly describing a few studies, identifying some common features and suggesting what course of action is indicated. As our discussion proceeds you will undoubtedly be struck by the fact that there appears to be little, if any, new information. Even the conclusions we draw from the data have been

known and talked about by educators for years. What would be new (and what we advocate) would be the widespread application of these well-known facts; what would be novel would be for us to practice what we preach.

Most of the studies we will describe are those in which the learners were given a good deal of control over the learning experience. As a matter of fact, it was this feature in these experiments that led us to rediscover the astonishing phenomenon that adult learners enter a formal learning situation with previously gained knowledge relevant to the learning at hand.

The first study was undertaken about four years ago by Mager (1961) to discover whether a learner would sequence

---

Reprinted with the permission of the senior author and the publisher from *Psychological Reports*, 1963, Vol. 13, pp 71–76.

instruction in the same way in which an instructor typically sequences it. If the sequence of information called for by a learner was radically different from that prescribed by an instructor, it might be inferred that a course sequence generated exclusively by the instructor or the expert was less meaningful to the student than it might be. To explore this problem, one student at a time was given complete control over a curriculum in electronics. The instructor tried to behave like a mechanism that would respond to the student's questions, but which would offer no unsolicited information or explanation. The learner was encouraged to indicate which subjects he wanted to discuss, how deeply he wanted to have them explained, the kinds of equipment or demonstrations he felt would be useful, and the frequency and nature of reviews. The learner also controlled the length of each instructional session. Results of this study indicated that the sequence of information called for by the learner was considerably different from that of the traditional electronics curriculum. Also, the fact that the student had a good bit to say about the procedure seemed to exert a strong and favorable influence upon his motivation. These results were indeed interesting and provocative, and have led to further studies and to applied programming. In the programming department of Varian Associates, for example, as least two Ss are now run before any program frames are written so that guidance relative to information sequencing can be obtained from members of the target population.

In addition to the results just described a rather nagging phenomenon was repeatedly observed. No matter how ignorant the learners appeared to be, no matter how slowly they appeared to learn, no matter how naive they claimed to be, male or female, Ss all entered the experiment with some relevant knowledge about electronics. Some Ss knew more than others, of course, and one or two had developed some rather interesting misinformation about the subject. Nonetheless, no S started with zero relevant knowledge.

The second study (Mager & McCann, 1961) was an applied industrial experiment conducted in one of the manufacturing divisions of Varian Associates. The study involved an engineering course, 6 months long, given newly graduated engineers before they were permanently assigned to their positions. Training included theory, machine and instrument operation, manufacturing processes, and company procedures. The first 6 weeks of the course were devoted primarily to formal lectures. During the second 6 weeks each trainee was rotated through the various departments. During the last 3 months of the course the student was assigned as an assistant to an experienced engineer. Because of the small classes involved (4 to 8 students), each student received what amounted to 6 months of individual instruction.

Our experiment again called for a good deal of control on the part of the student. All classes were cancelled and the instructor was asked to "speak only when spoken to." Students were told that they would have complete control over what they learned, when they learned it, and how they learned it. They were told that they could ask for instruction from anyone in the division, but that they were not to accept instruction they did not want. One important difference between this study and the previous one was that this time the students were given 24 pages of detailed course objectives which specified the desired terminal behavior. The total effect was that the students had to decide what they needed to learn, in addition to what they already knew, in order to reach the objectives.

Some of the results of this study were as follows: (a) Training time was reduced 65%. All students were permanently assigned 6 to 8 weeks after training began. (b) The graduates of this program appeared better equipped than those of previous cycles, demonstrating more confidence and knowledge about manufacturing processes and microwave theory. The manager of the division considered these engineers "better trained" at the time they assumed their permanent responsibility than previously hired engineers. (c) Considerably less time was devoted to training by the instructor, administrators, and technical experts. (d) Content selected for study varied considerably from student to student. (e) The sequence of information studied varied from student to student, but in no case coincided with the sequence used previously.

Although no instructional programs were used in this study, it still appeared possible to reduce the length of a formal training program significantly, while at the same time improving the competence and confidence of the student. This result was obtained primarily by providing the student with a detailed description of the desired terminal behavior and by allowing him to fill in the knowledge gap between what he knew and what was required. Put another way, he was not required to relearn what he already knew. Since some of these students had been trained previously as electrical engineers, some as industrial or mechanical engineers, it was known that they entered the course with a considerable amount of relevant knowledge which would help account for their rapid progress. It was noted, however, that students in previous cycles also came in as trained engineers.

A third study (as yet unpublished)

that we would like to mention also investigated content sequencing. This study used the skill of electrical meter reading as the vehicle. During the early phases of the study we wanted to determine empirically the meter reading skill of several kinds of experts. An automated meter reading examination was thus administered to a group of physicists, a group of engineers, and a group of technicians. The final score for each of these groups was approximately 80%. When housewives were given the same examination without any prior training, their average score on the examination was 40%. Again, although these Ss all claimed ignorance in this area of electronics and meter reading, and although they had no formal training in this or related areas, their performances were significantly better than zero and half as good as those of the experts. Unlike the previous study, here is an example of a group of students entering a training situation supposedly with a minimal amount of relevant information; obviously, however, these housewives possessed a considerable amount of relevant knowledge.

Still another experiment (Mager & Clark, 1963) provided results indicating that the expert was no better than the naive S. The object of this particular study was to determine whether a qualitative knowledge of results could be used to teach information for which there was no right or wrong answer. Specifically, the object was to determine whether Ss could learn to discriminate different smoothnesses of metal surfaces when their responses were confirmed by the percentage of expert agreement with the response rather than by an indication of correctness or incorrectness. To complete the device used in the experiment it was necessary to obtain expert judgments. The stimulus items were therefore judged by 36 experts and their average judgment wired into the machine. For this experiment an "expert" was defined as a person who had final authority over the disposition of the metal materials in question, rather than in terms of skill.

The relevant result of this study is that the performance of the experts turned out to be identical in every respect to that of the control group receiving no training whatsoever.

While the previous experiments we described suggest that students frequently know more than we give them credit for, the results of the smoothness experiment suggest that some experts know a good deal *less* than we give them credit for. In other words, the behavior of the expert, or should we say instructor, may not be as different from that of the layman as we and he would like to believe. But while it may be more comfortable to talk about engineers in this way than about ourselves, we have similar problems closer to home. There have been many studies, for example, in which the ability to predict human behavior was studied as a function of training and experience level. The ego-deflating results have uniformly demonstrated that the predictions of those naive organisms commonly referred to as "college sophomores" and "underpaid secretaries" were essentially as accurate as judgments made by highly trained and experienced clinical psychologists. The expert, in other words, didn't make judgments any better than the novice. We also suspect that the judgments of "experts" in other disciplines, if subjected to a reality test, might not justify the confidence or the credibility attributed to their pronouncements.

In an experiment conducted at Stanford last spring (Allen & McDonald, 1963), Ss were required to learn the pieces, rules, and strategies of a new game. One group learned from a linear program, while each member of another group was provided with objectives and an instructor that he could turn on and off at will. The members of the group which had control of the curriculum performed almost as well as those learning from the linear program, but they required only *half* the instruction time required by those using the program. A peculiar observation made during this study was that, while Ss of the experiment were bright students, those in the group which had control of the curriculum exhibited little skill at systematic information collection. In other words, had you watched these Ss you would probably have predicted poor terminal performance because of the chaotic way in which they asked questions of their information source. Nonetheless, this group performed almost as well as the program group, in half the time.

The general conclusion we draw from these studies is that adult students are likely to enter a learning situation with a significant amount of relevant knowledge; in other words, they are likely already to know something about that which is to be taught.

Let us examine some possible implications of such a conclusion. Is this new information? Certainly not! One of the oldest rules of teaching exhorts the teacher to "take the student from where he is to where you want him to be." Presumably this means that one should start instruction at the edge of the student's knowledge; to start beyond the edge of his knowledge is to construct unnecessary obstacles in the path of his learning, and to start within his knowledge is to bore him. The incredible thing is that we are well aware of the existence of differences in student knowledge and experience. At the same time, however, we behave as though we wished this difference would go away. We are willing to recognize that students enter instruction in various stages of *un*-preparation, and we apply remedial procedures to the learner to minimize his lack of preparation. But the questions to be raised are, why don't we also recognize that students may enter instruction in various stages of *over*-preparation, and why don't we apply remedial procedures to the curriculum? Certainly we admit the existence of "over-preparation" every time we decide to "control" an experiment by using a pre-test. Yet in programming, the overwhelming tendency is to force each learner to work his way through exactly the same sequence of information; this is true for both linear and branching programs, even though the branching program allows students to omit a good many remedial discussions. What we seem to have overlooked is the possible advantage to be gained by subtracting from his curriculum that which the learner already knows. There is, after all, no reason to believe that the only way to obtain further improvements in instructional efficiency is through the improvements of programs and teaching machines. We submit that it is timely to begin thinking about curriculum-generating machines. These devices would be designed to detect what the student already knows, compare this body of knowledge with that required by the objectives of the program, and then generate a curriculum for the student. The result would be a saving in student time equal to the time it would take to teach him what he already knows relating to the instructional objectives, minus the time required to detect the state of his knowledge; boredom would also be reduced.

There is another possible implication which can be drawn from our conclusion. In the absence of a curriculum-generating machine the adult learner himself might be a better judge of what he needs to add to his current knowledge in order to reach some given set of objectives than is a textbook writer, instructor, or programmer. Given half a chance and a set of reasonable objectives, he will probably generate for himself a curriculum that will lead him to achieve these objectives. Interestingly, this implication is not without support. There are several studies (Duke, 1959; Milton, 1959; Weitman & Gruber, 1960) wherein one college class attended all lectures while another group was prohibited from any lecture attendance. Even in the absence of carefully specified objectives, students of the group who were not allowed to come to class performed just as well as those in attendance. While this is not conclusive evidence that teachers aren't necessary, the data do suggest that we might improve the efficiency of instruction by making better use of the intelligence and background which the adult student brings to the formal instructional experience.

Thus, the new frontiers in program design that may be fruitful are these: (1) the development of effective methods for detecting the relevant background level of the incoming student, and for adjusting the curriculum accordingly; (2) the development of techniques which the learner himself can use to efficiently generate a curriculum which will lead him as economically as possible to the objectives.

To summarize, while we feel that further improvement in programming can be achieved by continued research with variables having to do with subject matter *presentation*, we suggest that greater improvements can be attained by focusing on variables relating to subject matter *selection*.

References

Allen, D. W. and McDonald, F. J. The effects of self-selection on learning in programmed instruction. Paper read at annual meeting of Amer. Educ. Res. Assn., Chicago, February, 1963.

Duke, B. C., Jr. An analysis of the learning effect of differential treatment upon above and below average college students enrolled in a closed-circuit television course. Unpublished doctoral dissertation, Penn State Univer., 1959.

Mager, R. F. On the sequencing of instructional content. *Psychol. Rep.*, 1961, **9,** 405–13.

Mager, R. F. and Clark, C. *The effects of qualitative feedback in automated instruction.* Palo Alto: Varian Assoc., 1963.

Mager, R. F. and McCann, J. *Learner-controlled instruction.* Palo Alto: Varian Assoc., 1961.

Milton, O. Learning without class instruction. Unpublished manuscript, Univer. of Tennessee, 1959.

Weitman, M. and Gruber, H. E. Experiments in self-directed study: effects on immediate achievement, permanence of achievement and educational values. Paper read at Western Psychol. Assn., San Jose, April, 1960.

7

Behavioral Objectives in Curriculum Design: A Cautionary Note

J. MYRON ATKIN / *University of Illinois*

In certain influential circles, anyone who confesses to reservations about the use of behaviorally stated objectives for curriculum planning runs the risk of being labeled as the type of individual who would attack the virtues of motherhood. Bumper stickers have appeared at my own institution, and probably at yours, reading, STAMP OUT NONBEHAVIORAL OBJECTIVES. I trust that the person who prepared the stickers had humor as his primary aim; nevertheless, the crusade for specificity of educational outcome has become intense and evangelical. The worthiness of this particular approach has come to be accepted as self-evident by ardent proponents, proponents who sometimes sound like the true believers who cluster about a new social or religious movement.

Behavioral objectives enthusiasts are warmly endorsed and embraced by the systems and operations analysis advocates, most educational technologists,

the cost-benefit economists, the planning-programing-budgeting system stylists, and many others. In fact, the behavioral objectives people are now near the center of curriculum decision making. Make no mistake. They have replaced the academicians and the general curriculum theorists—especially in the new electronically based education industries and in governmental planning agencies. The engineering model for educational research and development represents a powerful tide today. Those who have a few doubts about effects of the tide had better be prepared to be considered uninitiated and naive, if not slightly addlepated and antiquarian.

To utilize the techniques for long-term planning and rational decision

Reprinted with the permission of the author and the publisher from *The Science Teacher*, May 1968, pp. 27–30.

making that have been developed with such apparent success in the Department of Defense, and that are now being applied to a range of domestic and civilian problems, it is essential that hard data be secured. Otherwise these modes for developmental work and planning are severely limited. Fuzzy and tentative statements of possible achievement and questions of conflict with respect to underlying values are not compatible with the new instructional systems management approaches—at least not with the present state of the art. In fact, delineating instructional objectives in terms of identifiable pupil behaviors or performances seems essential in 1968 for assessing the output of the educational system. Currently accepted wisdom does not seem to admit an alternative.

There are overwhelmingly useful purposes served by attempting to identify educational goals in non-ambiguous terms. To plan rationally for a growing educational system, and to continue to justify relatively high public expenditures for education, it seems that we do need a firmer basis for making assessments and decisions than now exists. Current attention to specification of curriculum objectives in terms of pupil performance represents an attempt to provide direction for collection of data that will result in more informed choice among competing alternatives.

Efforts to identify educational outcomes in behavioral terms also provide a fertile ground for coping with interesting research problems and challenging technical puzzles. A world of educational research opens to the investigator when he has reliable measures of educational output (even when their validity for educational purposes is low). Pressures from researchers are difficult to resist since they do carry influence in the educational community, particularly

in academic settings and in educational development laboratories.

Hence I am not unmindful of some of the possible benefits to be derived from attempts to rationalize our decision-making processes through the use of behaviorally stated objectives. Schools need a basis for informed choice. And the care and feeding of educational researchers is a central part of my job at Illinois. However, many of the enthusiasts have given insufficient attention to underlying assumptions and broad questions of educational policy. I intend in this brief paper to highlight a few of these issues in the hope that the exercise might be productive of further and deeper discussion.

Several reservations about the use of behaviorally stated objectives for curriculum design will be catalogued here. But perhaps the fundamental problem, as I see it, lies in the easy assumption that we either know or can readily identify the educational objectives for which we strive, and thereafter the educational outcomes that result from our programs. One contention basic to my argument is that we presently are making progress toward thousands of goals in any existing educational program—progress of which we are perhaps dimly aware, can articulate only with great difficulty, and that contribute toward goals which are incompletely stated (or unrecognized), but which are often worthy.

For example, a child who is learning about meal worm behavior by blowing against the animal through a straw is probably learning much more than how this insect responds to a gentle stream of warm air. Let's assume for the moment that we can specify "behaviorally" all that he might learn about meal worm *behavior* (an arduous and never-ending task). In addition, in this "simple" activity, he is probably finding out something about interaction of objects, forces, humane treatment of animals, his own ability to manipulate the environment, structural characteristics of the larval form of certain insects, equilibrium, the results of doing an experiment at the suggestion of the teacher, the rewards of independent experimentation, the judgment of the curriculum developers in suggesting that children engage in such an exercise, possible uses of a plastic straw, and the length of time for which one individual might be engaged in a learning activity and still display a high degree of interest. I am sure there are many additional learnings, literally too numerous to mention in fewer than eight or ten pages. When any piece of curriculum is used with real people, there are important learning outcomes that cannot have been anticipated when the objectives were formulated. And of the relatively few outcomes that can be identified at all, a smaller number still are translatable readily in terms of student behavior. There is a possibility that the cumulative side effects are at least as important as the intended main effects.

Multiply learning outcomes from the meal worm activity by all the various curriculum elements we attempt to build into a school day. Then multiply this by the number of days in a school year, and you have some indication of the oversimplification that *always* occurs when curriculum intents or outcomes are articulated in any form that is considered manageable.

If my argument has validity to this point, the possible implications are potentially dangerous. If identification of all worthwhile outcomes in behavioral terms comes to be commonly accepted and expected, then it is inevitable that, over time, the curriculum will tend to emphasize those elements which have been thus identified. Important outcomes which are detected only with great difficulty and which are translated only rarely into behavioral terms tend to atrophy. They disappear from the curriculum because we spend all the time allotted to us in teaching explicitly for the more readily specifiable learnings to which we have been directed.

We have a rough analogy in the use of tests. Prestigious examinations that are widely accepted and broadly used, such as the New York State Regents examinations, tend over time to determine the curriculum. Whether or not these examinations indeed measure all outcomes that are worth achieving, the curriculum regresses toward the objectives reflected by the test items. Delineation of lists of behavioral objectives, like broadly used testing programs, may admirably serve the educational researcher because it gives him indices of gross achievement as well as details of particular achievement; it may also provide input for cost-benefit analysts and governmental planners at all levels because it gives them hard data with which to work; but the program in the schools may be affected detrimentally by the gradual disappearance of worthwhile learning activities for which we have not succeeded in establishing a one-to-one correspondence between the curriculum elements and rather difficult-to-measure educational results.

Among the learning activities most readily lost are those that are long term and private in effect and those for which a single course provides only a small increment. If even that increment cannot be identified, it tends to lose out in the teacher's priority scheme because it is competing with other objectives which have been elaborately stated and to which he has been alerted. But I will get to the question of priority of objectives a bit later.

The second point I would like to develop relates to the effect of demands for behavioral specification on innovation. My claim here is that certain types of innovation, highly desirable ones, are hampered and frustrated by early demands for behavioral statements of objectives.

Let's focus on the curriculum reform movement of the past fifteen years, the movement initiated by Max Beberman in 1952 when he began to design a mathematics program in order that the high school curriculum reflect concepts central to modern mathematics. We have now seen curriculum development efforts, with this basic flavor, in many science fields, the social sciences, English, aesthetics, etc. When one talks with the initiators of such projects, particularly at the beginning of their efforts, one finds that they do not begin by talking about the manner in which they would like to change pupils' behavior. Rather they are dissatisfied with existing curricula in their respective subject fields, and they want to build something new. If pressed, they might indicate that existing programs stress concepts considered trivial by those who practice the discipline. They might also say that the curriculum poorly reflects styles of intellectual inquiry in the various fields. Press them further, and they might say that they want to build a new program that more accurately displays the "essence" of history, or physics, or economics, or whatever. Or a program that better transmits a comprehension of the elaborate and elegant interconnections among various concepts within the discipline.

If they are asked at an early stage just how they want pupils to behave differently, they are likely to look quite blank. Academicians in the varous cognate fields do not speak the language of short-term or long-term behavioral change, as do many psychologists. In fact, if a hard-driving behaviorist attempts to force the issue and succeeds, one finds that the disciplinarians can come up with a list of behavioral goals that looks like a caricature of the subject field in question. (Witness the AAAS elementary-school science program directed toward teaching "process.")

Further, early articulation of behavioral objectives by the curriculum developer inevitably tends to limit the range of his exploration. He becomes committed to designing programs that achieve these goals. Thus if specific objectives in behavioral terms are identified early, there tends to be a limiting element built into the new curriculum. The innovator is less alert to potentially productive tangents.

The effective curriculum developer typically begins with *general* objectives. He then refines the program through a series of successive approximations. He doesn't start with a blueprint, and he isn't in much of a hurry to see his ideas represented by a blueprint.

A situation is created in the newer curriculum design procedures based on behaviorally stated objectives in which scholars who do not talk a behavioral-change language are expected to describe their goals at a time when the intricate intellectual subtleties of their work may not be clear, even in the disciplinary language with which they are familiar. At the other end, the educational evaluator, the behavioral specifier, typically has very little understanding of the curriculum that is being designed—understanding with respect to the new view of the subject field that it affords. It is too much to expect that the behavioral analyst, or anyone else, recognize the shadings of meaning in various evolving economic theories, the complex applications of the intricacies of wave motion, or the richness of nuance reflected in a Stravinsky composition.

Yet despite this two-culture problem —finding a match between the behavioral analysts and the disciplinary scholars—we still find an expectation being created for early behavioral identification of essential outcomes.

(Individuals who are concerned with producing hard data reflecting educational outputs would run less risk of dampening innovation if they were to enter the curriculum development scene in a more unobtrusive fashion—and later—than is sometimes the case. The curriculum developer goes into the classroom with only a poorly articulated view of the changes he wants to make. Then he begins working with children to see what he can do. He revises. He develops new ideas. He continually modifies as he develops. *After* he has produced a program that seems pleasing, it might then be a productive exercise for the behavioral analyst to attempt with the curriculum developer to identify *some* of the ways in which children seem to be behaving differently. If this approach is taken, I would caution, however, that observers be alert for long-term as well as short-term effects, subtle as well as obvious inputs.)

A third basic point to be emphasized relates to the question of instructional priorities, mentioned earlier. I think I have indicated that there is a vast library of goals that represent possible outcomes for any instructional program. A key educational task, and a task that is well handled by the effective teacher, is that of relating educational goals to the situation at hand—as well as relating the situation at hand to educational goals. It is impractical to pursue all goals thoroughly. And it does make a difference *when* you try to teach something. Considerable educational potential is lost when certain concepts are taught didactically. Let's assume that some third grade teacher considers it important to develop concepts related to sportsmanship. It would be a rather naive teacher who decided that she would undertake this task at 1:40 P.M. on Friday of next week. The experienced teacher has always realized that learnings related to such an area must be stressed in an appropriate context, and the context often cannot be planned.

Perhaps there is no problem in accepting this view with respect to a concept like sportsmanship, but I submit that a similar case can be made for a range of crucial cognitive outcomes that are basic to various subject matter fields. I use science for my examples because I know more about this field than others. But equilibrium, successive approximation, symmetry, entropy, and conservation are pervasive ideas with a broad range of application. These ideas are taught with the richest meaning only when they are emphasized repeatedly in appropriate and varied contexts. Many of these contexts arise in classroom situations that are unplanned, but that have powerful potential. It is detrimental to learning not to capitalize on the opportune moments for effectively teaching one idea or another. Riveting the teacher's attention to a few behavioral goals provides him with blinders that may limit his range. Directing him to hundreds of goals leads to a confusing, mechanical pedagogic style with a concomitant loss of desirable spontaneity.

A final point to be made in this paper relates to values, and it deals with a primary flaw in the consumption of much educational research. It is difficult to resist the assumption that those attributes which we can measure are the elements which we consider most important. This point relates to my first, but I feel that it is essential to emphasize the problem. The behavioral analyst seems to assume that for an objective to be worthwhile, we must have methods of observing progress. But worthwhile goals come first, not our methods for assessing progress toward these goals. Goals are derived from our needs and from our philosophies. They are not and should not be derived primarily from our measures. It borders on the irresponsible for those who exhort us to state objectives in behavioral terms to avoid the issue of determining worth. Inevitably there is an implication of worth behind any act of measurement. What the educational community poorly realizes at the moment is that behavioral goals may or may not be worthwhile. They are articulated from among the vast library of goals because they are stated relatively easily. Again, let's not assume that what we can presently measure necessarily represents our most important activity.

I hope that in this paper I have increased rather than decreased the possibilities for constructive discourse about the use of behavioral objectives for curriculum design. The issues raised here represent a few of the basic questions that seem crucial enough to be examined in an open forum that admits the possibility of fresh perspectives. Too much of the debate related to the use of behavioral objectives has been conducted in an argumentative style that characterizes discussions of fundamental religious views among adherents who are poorly informed. A constructive effort might be centered on identification of those issues which seem to be amenable to resolution by empirical means and those which do not. At any rate, I feel confident that efforts of the next few years will better inform us about the positive as well as negative potential inherent in a view of curriculum design that places the identification of behavioral objectives at the core.

8

Probing the Validity of Arguments
Against Behavioral Goals

W. JAMES POPHAM / *University of California, Los Angeles*

Within the last few years a rather intense debate has developed in the field of curriculum and instruction regarding the merits of stating instructional objectives in terms of measurable learner behaviors. Because I am thoroughly committed, both rationally and viscerally, to the proposition that instructional goals should be stated behaviorally, I view this debate with some ambivalence. It is, however, probably desirable to have a dialogue of this sort among specialists in our field. We test the respective worth of opposing positions.

I am committed to the point of view that those who discourage educators from precisely explicating their instructional objectives are often permitting, if not promoting, the same kind of unclear thinking that has led in part to the generally abysmal quality of instruction in this country.

In the remainder of this paper I shall examine eleven reasons given by my colleagues in opposition to objectives stated in terms of measurable learner behaviors. I believe each of these reasons is, for the most part, invalid. There may be minor elements of truth in some, but in essence none of these reasons should be considered strong enough to deter educators from specifying all of their instructional goals in the precise form advocated by the "good guys" in this argument.

Reason one: Trivial learner behaviors are the easiest to operationalize; hence the really important outcomes of education will be underemphasized.

This particular objection to the use of precise goals is frequently voiced by

A symposium presentation at the Annual American Educational Research Association Meeting, Chicago, February, 1968. Reprinted with the permission of the author.

educators who have recently become acquainted with the procedures for stating explicit, behavioral objectives. Since even behavioral objectives enthusiasts admit that the easiest kinds of pupil behaviors to operationalize are usually the most pedestrian, it is not surprising to find so many examples of behavioral objectives which deal with the picayune. In spite of its overall beneficial influence, the programmed booklet by Robert Mager (1962) dealing with the preparation of instructional objectives has probably suggested to many that precise objectives are usually trivial. Almost all of Mager's examples deal with cognitive behaviors which, according to Bloom's taxonomy, would be identified at the very lowest level.

Contrary to the objection raised in reason one, however, the truth is that explicit objectives make it far *easier* for educators to attend to *important* instructional outcomes. To illustrate, if you were to ask a social science teacher what his objectives were for his government class and he responded as follows, "I want to make my students better citizens so that they can function effectively in our nation's dynamic democracy," you would probably find little reason to fault him. His objective sounds so profound and eminently worthwhile that few could criticize it. Yet, beneath such facades of profundity, many teachers really are aiming at extremely trivial kinds of pupil behavior changes. How often, for example, do we find "good citizenship" measured by a trifling true-false test? Now if we'd asked for the teacher's objectives in operational terms and had discovered that, indeed, all the teacher was attempting to do was promote the learner's achievement on a true-false test, we might have rejected the aim as being unimportant. But this is possible *only* with the precision of explicitly stated goals.

In other words, there is the danger that because of their ready translation to operational statements, teachers will tend to identify too many trivial behaviors as goals. But the very fact that we can make these behaviors explicit permits the teacher and his colleagues to scrutinize them carefully and thus eliminate them as unworthy of our educational efforts. Instead of encouraging unimportant outcomes in education, the use of explicit instructional objectives makes it possible to identify and reject those objectives which are unimportant.

Reason two: Prespecification of explicit goals prevents the teacher from taking advantage of instructional opportunities unexpectedly occurring in the classroom.

When one specifies explicit *ends* for an instructional program there is no necessary implication that the *means* to achieve those ends are also specified. Serendipity in the classroom is always welcome but, and here is the important point, *it should always be justified in terms of its contribution to the learner's attainment of worthwhile objectives.* Too often teachers may believe they are capitalizing on unexpected instructional opportunities in the classroom, whereas measurement of pupil growth toward any defensible criterion would demonstrate that what has happened is merely ephemeral entertainment for the pupils, temporary diversion, or some other irrelevant classroom event.

Prespecification of explicit goals does not prevent the teacher from taking advantage of unexpectedly occurring instructional opportunities in the classroom, it only tends to make the teacher justify these spontaneous learning activities in terms of worthwhile instructional ends. There are undoubtedly gifted teachers who can capitalize mag-

nificently on the most unexpected classroom events. These teachers should not
be restricted from doing so. But the
teacher who prefers to probe instructional periphery, just for the sake of its
spontaneity, should be deterred by the
prespecification of explicit goals.

*Reason three: Besides pupil behavior
changes, there are other types of educational outcomes which are important,
such as changes in parental attitudes,
the professional staff, community values,
etc.*

There are undoubtedly some fairly
strong philosophic considerations associated with this particular reason. It
seems reasonable that there are desirable changes to be made in our society
which might be undertaken by the
schools. Certainly, we would like to
bring about desirable modifications in
such realms as the attitudes of parents.
But as a number of educational philosophers have reminded us, the schools
cannot be all things to all segments of
society. It seems that the primary responsibility of the schools should be to
educate effectively the youth of the society. And to the extent that this is so,
all modifications of parental attitudes,
professional staff attitudes, etc., should
be weighed in terms of a later measurable impact on the learner himself. For
example, the school administrator who
tells us that he wishes to bring about
new kinds of attitudes on the part of his
teachers should ultimately have to
demonstrate that these modified attitudes result in some kind of desirable
learner changes. To stop at merely
modifying the behavior of teachers
without demonstrating further effects
upon the learner would be insufficient.

So while we can see that there are
other types of important social outcomes
to bring about, it seems that the school's

primary responsibility is to its pupils.
Hence, all modifications in personnel or
external agencies should be justified in
terms of their contribution toward the
promotion of desired pupil behavior
changes.

*Reason four: Measurability implies be-
havior which can be objectively, mecha-
nistically measured; hence there must be
something dehumanizing about the approach.*

This fourth reason is drawn from a
long history of resistance to measurement on the grounds that it must, of
necessity, reduce human learners to
quantifiable bits of data. This resistance
probably is most strong regarding earlier forms of measurement which were
almost exclusively examination-based,
and were frequently multiple-choice test
measures at that. But a broadened conception of evaluation suggests that there
are diverse and extremely sophisticated
ways of securing qualitative as well as
quantitative indices of learner performance.

One is constantly amazed to note the
incredible agreement among a group of
judges assigned to evaluate the complicated gyrations of skilled springboard
divers in the televised reports of national aquatic championships. One of
these athletes will perform an exotic,
twisting dive, and a few seconds after he
has hit the water, five or more judges
raise cards reflecting their independent
evaluations which can range from 0 to
10. The five ratings very frequently run
as follows: 7.8, 7.6, 7.7, 7.8, and 7.5.
The possibility of reliably judging something as qualitatively complicated as a
springboard dive does suggest that our
measurement procedures do not have to
be based on a theory of reductionism. It
is currently possible to assess many
complicated human behaviors in a re-

fined fashion. Developmental work is underway in those areas where we now must rely on primitive measures.

Reason five: It is somehow undemocratic to plan in advance precisely how the learner should behave after instruction.

This particular reason was raised a few years ago in a professional journal (Arnstine, 1964), suggesting that the programmed instruction movement was basically undemocratic because it spelled out in advance how the learner was supposed to behave after instruction. A brilliant refutation (Komisar and McClellan, 1965) appeared several months later, in which the rebutting authors responded that instruction is by its very nature undemocratic and to imply that freewheeling democracy is always present in the classroom would be untruthful. Teachers generally have an idea of how they wish learners to behave, and they promote these goals with more or less efficiency. Society knows what it wants its young to become, perhaps not with the precision that we would desire, but certainly in general. And if the schools were allowing students to "democratically" deviate from societally mandated goals, one can be sure that the institutions would cease to receive society's approbation and support.

Reason six: That isn't really the way teaching is; teachers rarely specify their goals in terms of measurable learner behaviors; so let's set realistic expectations of teachers.

Jackson (1966) recently offered this argument. He observed that teachers just don't specify their objectives in terms of measurable learner behavior and implied that, since this is the way

the real world is, we ought to recognize it and live with it. Perhaps.

There is obviously a difference between identifying the *status quo* and applauding it. Most of us would readily concede that few teachers specify their instructional aims in terms of measurable learner behaviors, *but they ought to*. What we have to do is to mount a widespread campaign to modify this aspect of teacher behavior. Instructors must begin to identify their instructional intentions in terms of measurable learner behaviors. The way teaching really is at the moment just isn't good enough.

Reason seven: In certain subject areas, e.g., fine arts and the humanities, it is more difficult to identify measurable pupil behaviors.

Sure it's tough. Yet, because it is difficult in certain subject fields to identify measurable pupil behaviors, those subject specialists should not be allowed to escape this responsibility. Teachers in the fields of art and music often claim that it is next to impossible to identify acceptable works of art in precise terms —but they do it all the time. In instance after instance the art teacher does make a judgment regarding the acceptability of pupil-produced artwork. What the art teacher is reluctant to do is put his evaluative criteria on the line. He has such criteria. He must have to make his judgments. But he is loath to describe them in terms that anyone can see.

Any English teacher, for example, will tell you how difficult it is to make a valid judgment of a pupil's essay response. Yet criteria lurk whenever this teacher does make a judgment, and these criteria must be made explicit. No one who really understands education has ever argued that instruction is a simple task. It is even more difficult in such areas as the arts and humanities. As a noted art educator observed several years ago, art educators must quickly get to the business of specifying "tentative, but clearly defined criteria" by which they can judge their learners' artistic efforts (Munro, 1960).

Reason eight: While loose general statements of objectives may appear worthwhile to an outsider, if most educational goals were stated precisely, they would be revealed as generally innocuous.

This eighth reason contains a great deal of potential threat for school people. The unfortunate truth is that much of what is going on in the schools today is indefensible. Merely to reveal the nature of some behavior changes we are bringing about in our schools would be embarrassing. As long as general objectives are the rule, our goals may appear worthwhile to external observers. But once we start to describe precisely what kinds of changes we are bringing about in the learner, there is the danger that the public will reject our intentions as unworthy. Yet, if what we are doing is trivial, educators would know it and those who support the educational institution should also know it. To the extent that we are achieving innocuous behavior changes in learners, we are guilty. We must abandon the ploy of "obfuscation by generality" and make clear exactly what we are doing. Then we are obliged to defend our choices.

Reason nine: Measurability implies accountability; teachers might be judged on their ability to produce results in learners rather than on the many bases now used as indices of competence.

This is a particularly threatening reason and serves to produce much

teacher resistance to precisely stated objectives. It doesn't take too much insight on the part of the teacher to realize that if objectives are specified in terms of measurable learner behavior, there exists the possibility that the instructor will have to become *accountable* for securing such behavior changes. Teachers might actually be judged on their ability to bring about desirable changes in learners. They should be.

But a teacher should not be judged on the particular instructional *means* he uses to bring about desirable *ends*. At present many teachers are judged adversely simply because the instructional procedures they use do not coincide with those once used by an evaluator when "he was a teacher." In other words, if I'm a supervisor who has had considerable success with open-ended discussion, I may tend to view with disfavor any teachers who cleave to more directive methods. Yet, if the teacher using the more direct methods can secure learner behavior changes which are desirable, I have no right to judge that teacher as inadequate. The possibility of assessing instructional competence in terms of the teacher's ability to bring about specified behavior changes in learners brings with it far more assets than liabilities to the teacher. He will no longer be judged on the idiosyncratic whims of a visiting supervisor. Rather, he can amass evidence that, in terms of his pupils' actual attainments, he is able to teach efficiently.

Even though this is a striking departure from the current state of affairs, and a departure that may be threatening to the less competent, the educator must promote this kind of accountability rather than the maze of folklore and mysticism which exists at the moment regarding teacher evaluation.

Reason ten: It is far more difficult to generate such precise objectives than to talk about objectives in our customarily vague terms.

Here is a very significant objection to the development of precise goals. Teachers are, for the most part, far too busy to spend the necessary hours in stating their objectives and measurement procedures with the kind of precision implied by this discussion. It is said that we are soon nearing a time when we will have more teachers than jobs. This is the time to reduce the teacher's load to the point where he can become a professional decision maker rather than a custodian. We must reduce public school teaching loads to those of college professors. This is the time when we must give the teacher immense help in specifying his objectives. Perhaps we should *give* him objectives from which to choose, rather than force him to generate his own. Many of the federal dollars currently being used to support education would be better spent on agencies which would produce alternative behavioral objectives for all fields at all grade levels. At any rate, the difficulty of the task should not preclude its accomplishment. We can recognize how hard the job is and still allocate the necessary resources to do it.

Reason eleven: In evaluating the worth of instructional schemes, it is often the unanticipated results which are really important, but prespecified goals may make the evaluator inattentive to the unforeseen.

Some fear that if we cleave to behaviorally stated objectives which must be specified prior to designing an instructional program, we will overlook certain outcomes of the program which were not anticipated yet which may be extremely important. They point out that some of the relatively recent "new curricula" in the sciences have had the unanticipated effect of sharply reducing pupil enrollments in those fields. In view of the possibility of such outcomes, both unexpectedly good and bad, it is suggested that we really ought not spell out objectives in advance, but should evaluate the adequacy of the instructional program after it has been implemented.

Such reasoning, while compelling at first glance, weakens under close scrutiny. In the first place, really dramatic unanticipated outcomes cannot be overlooked by curriculum evaluators. They certainly should not be. We should judge an instructional sequence not only by whether it attains its prespecified objectives but also by any unforeseen consequences it produces. But what can you tell the would-be curriculum evaluator regarding this problem? "Keep your eyes open," doesn't seem to pack the desired punch. Yet, it's about all you can say. For if there is reason to believe that a particular outcome may result from an instructional sequence, it should be built into the set of objectives for the sequence. To illustrate, if the curriculum designers fear that certain negative attitudes will be acquired by the learner as he interacts with an instructional sequence, then behavioral objectives can be devised which reveal whether the instructional sequence has effectively counteracted this affective outcome. It is probably always a good idea, for example, to identify behavioral indices of the pupil's "subject-approaching tendencies." We don't want to teach youngsters how to perform mathematical exercises, for example, but to learn to hate math in the process.

Yet, it is indefensible to let an awareness of the importance of unanticipated outcomes in evaluating instructional programs lead one to the rejection of rigorous pre-planning of instructional objectives. Such objectives should be the primary, but not exclusive, focus in evaluating instruction.

While these eleven reasons are not exhaustive, they represent most of the arguments used to resist the implementation of precise instructional objectives. In spite of the very favorable overall reaction to explicit objectives during the past five to ten years, a small collection of dissident educators has arisen to oppose the quest for goal specificity. The trouble with criticisms of precise objectives isn't that they are completely without foundation. As conceded earlier, there are probably elements of truth in all of them. Yet, when we are attempting to promote the wide-scale adoption of precision in the classroom, there is the danger that many instructors will use the comments and objections of these few critics as an excuse for not thinking clearly about their goals. Any risks we run by moving to behavioral goals are miniscule in contrast with our current state of confusion regarding instructional intentions. The objections against behaviorally stated goals are not strong enough. To secure a dramatic increase in instructional effectiveness, we must abandon our customary practices of goal-stating and turn to a framework of precision.

References

Arnstine, D. G. The language and values of programmed instruction: Part 2. *The Educational Forum*, XXVIII, 1964.

Jackson, P. W. *The way teaching is.* Washington, D.C.: National Education Association, 1966.

Komisar, P. B. and McClellan, J. E. Professor Arnstine and programmed instruction. Reprint from *The Educational Forum*, 1965.

Mager, R. F. *Preparing objectives for programmed instruction.* San Francisco: Fearon Press, 1962.

Munro, T. The interrelation of the arts in secondary education. In T. Munro and H. Read, eds., *The creative arts in American education.* Cambridge, Mass.: Harvard University Press, 1960.

III

Prompting and Fading Techniques

Much of the learning that is done in the classroom can be considered a form of discrimination learning. The student learns to make a specific response in the presence of one stimulus (the discriminative stimulus or S^D) and not in the presence of other stimuli (S^Δs). For example, the first grader learns to respond "boy" when asked to read the letters 'BOY,' and at the same time he learns that this response is not appropriate to a host of other letter combinations. Traditionally discriminations have been taught by reinforcing the desired response in the presence of the S^D and not reinforcing the response when it is made in the presence of an S^Δ. Much of the difficulty in using this procedure results from the fact that it is hard to eliminate errors; that is, it is hard to extinguish responses to an S^Δ. William James (1890) was one of the first to suggest that the teaching of discriminations might proceed more efficiently if, in the early stages of training, the difference between S^D and S^Δ was quite great and if this difference was gradually reduced as training proceeded. Recent research on discrimination training has proven the wisdom of James's words and has resulted in the development of two rather different techniques for increasing S^D-S^Δ differences; both these techniques include the gradual reduction (fading, or vanishing) of these initial differences.

One of the procedures involves changing the to-be-discriminated stimuli so that critical features (i.e., features which can be used to differentiate them) are exaggerated. This technique has been extensively investigated by Bijou (1965) and has been shown to be extremely successful, especially in the teaching of visual discriminations. The other technique uses the addition of a supplementary, or prompting, stimulus to the to-be-differentiated stimuli in order to make it easier for the student to differentiate between them.

Most of the research in the areas of prompting and fading techniques has been done since 1961, when H. S. Terrace first demonstrated that these techniques could be employed to teach pigeons a visual discrimination without errors (see Terrace, 1965). He found that he could teach a red-green discrimination without errors if the S^D and S^Δ initially differed with respect to brightness and duration, as well as color, and if these prompting stimuli were gradually removed as training proceeded. Moore and Goldiamond, in the first chapter in this section, report on an adaptation of Terrace's procedure to the teaching of visual discriminations to preschool children. They briefly presented their subjects with a sample triangle. When it was withdrawn the child was presented with an array of three triangles—the sample and two others that differed from it in degree of rotation. The child's task was to locate the triangle which was identical with the sample. By illuminating the correct triangle, the discrimination was readily established. This brightness prompt was then gradually faded until the student was responding solely on the basis of the form of the stimuli.

The second chapter serves as an example of how errorless discrimination training and fading techniques can be of direct practical value. Holland and Matthews report on their success in teaching discrimination of the [s] phoneme to children with [s] articulation disorders. One of their programs included four phases, with each succeeding phase requiring more difficult discriminations. Within each phase the discriminations required evolved gradually from simple to complex. In addition, early presentations of [s] were longer and louder than non-[s] sounds. These prompting stimuli were faded as each phase of the program progressed. The authors' enthusiasm for the "programed" approach is obvious throughout the chapter.

It is clear that errorless discrimination training and fading techniques like those employed by Moore and Goldiamond, and Holland and Matthews, are potentially of great practical value. Their applicability seems to be most obvious in cases in which the students cannot understand verbal instructions—such as with the very young, the deaf, or the retarded—and in cases in which the stimulus materials do not lend themselves to verbal descriptions. It is hard, for example, to see how much could have been accomplished with Holland and Matthews's subjects by explaining to them the differences between properly articulated and misarticulated [s] sounds.

In both Moore and Goldiamond's and Holland and Matthews's studies, it should be noted that initially it was the prompting stimuli which controlled the students' responses. The instructional problem in both cases was to transfer control of the response from the prompt to the cue, a stimulus which should control the response in the future. For example, Holland and Matthews had to transfer control of the identifying response from loudness or duration prompts to the phonetic cue, the [s] sound. This transfer was accomplished by gradually fading the prompt. There seems to be some critical stage at which the student is no longer able to make discriminations on the basis of the prompt and must shift to responding on the basis of the cue. If the fading sequence is not gradual enough, student performance deteriorates.

Lumsdaine, Sulzer, and Kopstein demonstrate a somewhat different use of prompting stimuli. They also use prompts to insure correct responding during training. However, the correct responding which their prompts insure is in the form of observing responses. They show that animation prompts in the form of pop-in labels and arrows can function to direct students' attention to critical aspects of a filmed instructional sequence. Their research would seem to indicate that a pointer can and should be put to good instructional use in the classroom.

John Oliver Cook presents a humorous comment on what he feels is superstitious behavior on the part of the programed instruction movement. After a short attack on the overt response requirement (see Section IV of this text for a discussion of this issue), Cook presents data which, he feels, indicate the value of *prompted instruction;* that is, instruction in which the student is told the answer before he is required to respond. Cook's paper was met with a prompt rebuttal by James Holland, entitled "Cook's Tour de Farce" (1964). However, since Cook's proposal of prompted instruction must be taken as a serious attempt to generalize from basic learning research to educational practice, we believe it is essential to point out some of the dangers of giving the student the correct answer before he is required to respond. The Anderson and Faust chapter does just that. They demonstrate that in actual practice, prompting can be detrimental to performance. Heavy-handed use of prompts may result in incomplete inspection of the stimulus material, since students may respond on the basis of the prompt alone, and, therefore, stimulus control will not be transferred from the prompt to the cue. In subsequent research Anderson and Faust have demonstrated that (1) overuse of a variety of prompts in actual lesson materials can result in decreased performance (Anderson, Faust, and Roderick, 1968); (2) that the effect of overprompting is especially detrimental under conditions of low motivation, fatigue, or time pressure (Faust, 1967); and (3) that thematic prompts, as well as formal prompts, can be misused in such a way that they result in inferior achievement (Faust and Bernstein, 1968).

In general, prompting and fading techniques have great potential as aids to instruction. However, as is the case with any technique of instruction, prompting and fading have their limiting conditions and most effective areas of application. Hopefully, future research will help to clarify these for us.

References

Anderson, R. C., Faust, G. W., and Roderick, M. C. Overprompting in programed instruction. *Journal of Educational Psychology*, 1968, **59,** 88–93.

Bijou, S. W. Systematic instruction in the attainment of right-left form concepts in young and retarded children. In J. G. Holland and B. F. Skinner, eds., *An analysis of the behavioral processes involved in self-instruction.* Final Report, USOE, NDEA Title VII, Project No. 191, 1965.

Faust, G. W. The effects of prompting in programed instruction as a function of motivation and instruction. Unpublished doctoral dissertation, University of Illinois, 1967.

Faust, G. W. and Bernstein, J. Motivation and the spatial arrangement of thematic prompts as factors in learning from programed instruction. Training Research Laboratory, Urbana, Ill., 1968.

Holland, J. G. Cook's tour de farce. *American Psychologist*, 1964, **19,** 683–84.

James, W. *Principles of psychology.* New York: Henry Holt, 1890.

Terrace, H. S. Stimulus control. In W. K. Honig, ed., *Operant behavior: Areas of research and application.* New York: Appleton-Century-Crofts, 1965.

9

Errorless Establishment of Visual Discrimination Using Fading Procedures

ROBERT MOORE / *Arizona State University*

ISRAEL GOLDIAMOND / *Institute for Behavioral Research, Silver Spring, Md.*

In laboratory discrimination experiments, the establishment of discrimination often requires numerous extinction trials. In programmed instruction (Holland, 1960), on the other hand, the experimental aim is to program the presentations to preclude such trials, which are considered to be "errors." In the present investigation, such errorless procedures were applied to a laboratory situation to minimize S^Δ responding, using preschool children as *S*s, in a task involving form discrimination.

The procedure is adapted from an experiment by Terrace (1963), who minimized the considerable S^Δ responding previously associated with the establishment of responding to vertical rather than horizontal stripes by pigeons. The easier discrimination between red and green was first established. Each stripe was then embedded in a color, and the colors were then gradually faded out.

The discrimination was transferred to the stripes alone almost without error.

Method and Procedures

Six children attending private day nursery schools served as *S*s, with ages (to the nearest year), and sexes as follows: S-1, 3F; S-2, 5M; S-3, 4F; S-4, 5F; S-5, 4M; S6, 4M. They were children of working mothers, engaged mainly in clerical tasks (with one nurse and one teacher); the fathers included clerical, maintenance, and skilled industrial workers. The experiment was conducted in a special room at the nursery schools set aside for that purpose.

Reprinted with the permission of the senior author and the publisher from *Journal of the Experimental Analysis of Behavior*, 1964, Vol. 7, 269–72. Copyright 1964 by the Society for the Experimental Analysis of Behavior, Inc.

The *S* faced a Masonite panel, about 24 in. square, containing four small windows, each of milk plastic, 2 in. wide by 3 in. high. The sample window was centered toward the top of the panel, with the other three windows symmetrically arranged in an arc below it, so that the center of each was 4 in. from the center of the sample window. Arranged in an arc beneath each of the matching windows were three small buttons, the manipulanda, with a pilot light above each. This light went on when the correct button was pressed.

Two types of series were run, *full* presentations and *fading* series, for the same or different *S*s. In the full presentations, the sample window at the top went on, projecting a triangle at full 110 v intensity. The sample window then went off, and simultaneously, the current was switched to the three matching windows below, each of which contained a triangle presented at full 110 v intensity. One of these was matched in degree of rotation with the sample triangle, and the other two differed. The *S* was required to select the one that matched the withdrawn sample, a delayed matching to sample task (Ferster and Appel, 1961). In the fading series, the sample window was presented and withdrawn, as in the full series, but of the three windows, only the correct match was presented at full 110 v intensity, the two incorrect matches being presented at a lower intensity, ranging from 0 up. This distinction between correct and incorrect was enhanced by a marked phi-phenomenon effect as the current was switched from the sample to the correct matching window. This series began with three presentations of the incorrect windows at 0, then one presentation each at settings .35, .40, .50, .60, .65, .70, .75, .80, .83 (or .82), .86, .88, .90, .92, .94, .96, .98 of full voltage. There were then at least seven presentations at

1.00 (110 v) in this series. It will be noted that at this final level, the settings are identical to those of the full series, and that the gradual increase in voltage, whereby this identity is produced, represents a gradual fading of the brightness difference between incorrect and correct, since the latter is always presented at full intensity. A correct response advanced the presentation to the next in this series; an incorrect response resulted in a repetition of the step (with a new slide). Two consecutive errors resulted in a regression to a previous step.[1]

Three triangles differing in angle of rotation were used as stimuli (Reynolds, 1961). They were inverted isosceles skeleton triangles, altitude 1.75 in., base 1.25 in. centered in each window. The apex was either straight down (*D*), rotated 25° to the left (*L*), or to the right (*R*). All three appeared in the matching windows, in varied positions; the sample was also varied. The order of sample presentations (with match presentations in parentheses) was: *L* (*LDR*), *D* (*RLD*), *R* (*LRD*), *L* (*RDL*), *D* (*DRL*), *R* (*DRL*), *R* (*RDL*), *L* (*DLR*), *D* (*LDR*), recycle. Nine sheets of acetate formed the slides, which incorporated these presentations. They were inserted into position before each presentation, with all lights off.

The *S* faced the panel, with *E* visible at the side, and with controls behind the panel. The sample was illuminated for approximately 4 sec as *S* was told: "Look at the picture in the top window. See which way it's pointing." It was

---

[1] In four *S*s, the fading series was extended between two and four presentations by unsystematic errors by *E*, which seemed to have no effect upon the data. These errors included repeating the voltage of the preceding presentation, and increasing by steps of .05 where .10 was scheduled.

then turned off, illuminating the matching windows, and E said: "Find another pointing the same way; touch it and push the button underneath it." If a correct response was made, the pilot light above the button illuminated immediately, and S was handed a small consumable or trinket, which he had previously been instructed to put into a small plastic bag. If an incorrect response was made, nothing was said by E. Recording was manual.

Results

Results are presented in Fig. 1. The ordinate is cumulative correct responses, and the abscissa is number of presentations. Establishment of discrimination by the fading schedule is most clearly demonstrated by the curve for S-1, who was begun on the full series, with incorrect windows at voltage setting 1.00. Accuracy was no better than chance. At A, fading was introduced, with the incorrect windows set at 0. These were then increased in voltage to .60, at B. All responses in this series were accurate. The brightness differences between correct and incorrect were then elimi-

nated, with the full series replacing the fading series, from B to C, during which the settings of the incorrect windows were 1.00. Accuracy immediately deteriorated to chance values. At C, fading procedures were reintroduced, with the voltage setting at .60, where it had been before the total elimination of differences between the windows. Accuracy immediately returned, with only two errors occurring during the ascending voltage (but decreasing brightness difference) series. At D, the voltages of all three matching windows were the same, and it will be noted that accuracy was maintained under conditions where previously (the full series) it had been no better than chance. Stimulus control had been transferred from brightness to rotation.

Contrasting effects upon the establishment of discrimination using full and fading series are also demonstrated by S-2, who was begun on the full series, with accuracy no better than chance. At E, fading was introduced, with the incorrect windows set at 0. Discrimination immediately became errorless. At F, there were two errors in a row, and the voltage was lowered one step. Accuracy

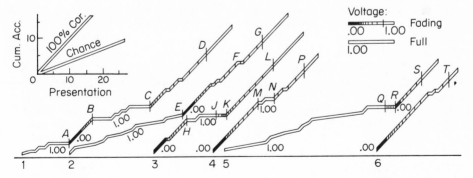

Fig. 1 Accuracy rates as functions of differential reinforcement of correct and incorrect matches of triangles when presented at full intensity during training (Full), as compared to initial presentation at differing intensities for correct and incorrect matches, with the difference gradually faded out (Fading), by increasing the intensity of the incorrect matches until they were as full as the correct matches.

returned, and the progression was reinstated, culminating in 1.00 at *G*, when the incorrect and correct windows were equal in brightness, the condition prior to *E*. In contrast to the latter period, which was under the full series, discrimination was now maintained without error.

The fading procedure initiated the sessions of *S*-3 and *S*-4, who accordingly began with errorless discrimination trials. For *S*-3, at *H*, the setting was .75, and the next settings were at 1.00, the full series, instead of .80 of the fading series. There was an immediate deterioration in accuracy. At *J*, the .75 setting was reintroduced, with no appreciable effect upon accuracy. The settings were then progressively reduced to .70, .65, and .60, at which point accuracy was reinstated (*K*), and the progression reestablished, with accuracy continuing thereafter through *L*, at the final setting of 1.00. For *S*-4, setting .82 was followed by full voltage at *M*, with breakdown to chance performance. Reinstatement of the fading procedure at *N*, when the setting was returned to .82, was followed by recovery of accuracy, which continued with one error into *P*, at the final setting of 1.00.

For *S*-5, the series was begun at full setting, with the chance performance characteristic of this procedure evident. At *Q*, the incorrect windows were lowered to .60 rather than 0, with no appreciable effect upon accuracy. At *R*, accordingly, fading was introduced by setting the incorrect windows at 0, with the complete instatement of accuracy which characterized this procedure. For this *S*, however, the fading series comprised three presentations at 0, four at .60, and six at 1.00. Errorless behavior was maintained during transitions whose abruptness disrupted discrimination in the other *S*s. Whether such behavior was a function of the individual

S, or of the long standard discrimination training period prior to *Q*, which characterized this record, and during which some discrimination may have been established, cannot be answered from these data. The record certainly contrasts, however, with that of *S*-6, who was begun using the fading procedure, and was continued on it without interruption. By *T*, the progression had reached 1.00 and was maintained without error. Discrimination was established with only two errors, and in the minimal time. His condensed performance contrasts sharply with that of the other *S*s, and the similarities of his record to those of other *S*s during fading series prompt the suggestion that it was the fading procedures themselves that were involved in the rapid establishment of discrimination.

Discussion

These results indicate that fading procedures may be extended to the errorless establishment of discrimination in matching to sample procedures.[2] Errors produce extinction trials which may make it more difficult to maintain the behavior being studied and serve to prolong the series. The economy of procedures which minimize error was depicted in the last *S* presented, whose learning was the most "perfect," with the least practice. Control of errorless behaviors by the procedures themselves was evident throughout the experiments by the reversibility and reinstatement obtained when the fading procedures were systematically dropped or instated. The results also reiterate that a major variable in the establishment of behav-

---

[2] Discrimination of selected letters of the alphabet, using parallel fading procedures, was also established without error with other children from the same nursery schools.

ior is the sequence (or program) of procedures utilized. On the response side, attention to sequence characterizes shaping, which can be considered a program of reinforcement of successive response ensembles, the succession being dictated by increasing presence of behavior along a criterion dimension. Thereby, novel response patterns are established, either for their own sake, or for use in other research. Analogously, in fading, E reinforces responses to stimulus differences successively approaching a criterion stimulus dimension. It is suggested that such procedures may be useful to establish novel discriminations and others required in psychophysical or other perceptual (*cf.* Goldiamond, 1962) or conceptual research (Goldiamond, 1964).

References

Ferster, C. B. and Appel, J. B. Punishment of S$^\Delta$ responding in matching to sample by time out from positive reinforcement. *J. Exp. Anal. Behav.*, 1961, 4, 45–56.

Goldiamond, I. Perception. In Bachrach, A. J., ed., *The experimental foundations of clinical psychology.* New York: Basic Books, 1962, pp. 280–340.

Goldiamond, I. A research and demonstration procedure in stimulus control, abstraction, and environmental programming. *J. Exp. Anal. Behav.*, 1964, 7, 216.

Holland, J. G. Teaching machines: an application of principles from the laboratory. *J. Exp. Anal. Behav.*, 1960, 3, 275–87.

Reynolds, G. S. Contrast, generalization, and the process of discrimination. *J. Exp. Anal. Behav.*, 1961, 4, 289–94.

Terrace, H. S. Discrimination learning with and without "errors." *J. Exp. Anal. Behav.*, 1963, 6, 1–27.

10

Application of Teaching Machine Concepts to Speech Pathology and Audiology

AUDREY L. HOLLAND / *University of Pittsburgh*

JACK MATTHEWS / *University of Pittsburgh*

Speech pathology and audiology is a borrowing field. We borrow from psychology, physics, anatomy, physiology, linguistics, anthropology—ad infinitum. A breakthrough in any of the areas from which we borrow may revolutionize concepts and procedures in speech pathology and audiology. Those of us responsible for the training of tomorrow's speech pathologists and audiologists must be alert to the applications of today's discoveries in the many disciplines related to communication processes and their disorders. On the basis of our research and clinical experience we feel that the recent work of B. F. Skinner and his associates (Holland, 1960; Skinner, 1957a; Skinner, 1954; Skinner, 1958; Skinner, 1953; Skinner, 1957b) may be a breakthrough in the science of behavior, which can significantly influence the field of speech pathology and audiology.

To many, the name B. F. Skinner immediately calls to mind teaching machines. Teaching machines did not originate with B. F. Skinner, nor are they a product of this decade in the history of psychology. The first teaching machine was patented in 1866 by Halcyon Skinner. In spite of many other patents in the area of automated teaching, there followed 60 years of relatively unsuccessful history interrupted briefly by the work of Sydney L. Pressey in the 1920's. Pressey (1926) envisioned a revolution in education as a result of the application of teaching machines. The revolution did not occur. Skinner attributes this failure to 'cultural inertia—a world which was not ready for it,' and to a lack of scientific interest in how the

Reprinted with the permission of the senior author and the publisher from *Asha*, 1963, Vol. 5, pp. 474–82.

organism learns, of what variables learning is a function, and of how to control those variables (Skinner, 1958).

Holland points out that the current interest and progress in teaching machines stems directly from the incorporation into them of principles developed in the science of behavior which permit precise control of behavior. 'The movement today is not simply the mechanization of teaching, but instead the development of a new technology—an attempt to obtain the kind of behavioral control shown possible in the laboratory' (Holland, 1960). In effect, present-day teaching machines are grounded in some of the better established facts of behavioral control.

This new technology was initiated by B. F. Skinner (1954, 1958), and the principles involved in teaching machines have emerged from the work of Skinner and his associates (Holland, 1960; Skinner, 1957a; Skinner, 1953; Skinner 1957b). Their discovery of the functional variables of learning has made possible a new applied technology—teaching machines. In an effort to explain why teaching machines of today provide both efficient and effective learning, their characteristics will be briefly discussed from the standpoint of the principles of learning incorporated in them:

IMMEDIACY OF REINFORCEMENT

Immediacy of reinforcement is a feature of the teaching machine. Correct responses are known to be reinforcers for human beings. When the student compares his answer to the correct answer on the machine, the reinforcement is immediate. Laboratory work shows that a delay between a response and its reinforcement greatly reduces the effectiveness of reinforcement (Holland, 1960).

EMITTING AND REINFORCING BEHAVIOR

In order that behavior be learned, it is necessary for it to be emitted and reinforced. Concerning this principle, Holland says:

. . . in the classroom, the student provides little verbal behavior. However, while working with a machine, the student necessarily emits appropriate behavior and this behavior is usually reinforced since the material is designed so that the student is usually correct. Not only is reinforcement needed for learning, a high density of correct items is necessary because material which generates errors is punishing. Laboratory experiments have shown that punishment lowers the rate of punished behavior (Holland, 1960).

SUCCESSIVE APPROXIMATION (GRADUAL PROGRESSION) IN THE DEVELOPMENT OF COMPLEX REPERTOIRES

Learning a subject-matter is not simply learning a response. It is a complex operant behavior. Teaching machines use exactly the same approach as that of the laboratory in attempting to develop complex operant behavior. First, a very, very simple behavior, a quite rough approximation to the behavior we wish to obtain in the end, is reinforced. On successive performances, we reinforce successively closer approximations to the criterion behavior. The teaching machine program runs through finely graded steps, working from simple to an ever higher level of complexity. Not only does gradual progression serve to make the student correct as often as possible (and thus be reinforced), but also it has been shown through laboratory research to be the fastest way to develop complex repertoires (Glaser, 1960; Holland, 1960).

GRADUAL WITHDRAWAL OF STIMULUS SUPPORT (FADING)

Gradual withdrawal is similar to the above principle of gradual progression. This principle insures that the student learning from a program is actually 'interacting' with the subject-matter. Skinner gives an example of teaching a student to recite a poem:

The first line is presented with several unimportant letters omitted. The student must read the line 'meaningfully' and supply the missing letters. The second, third and fourth frames present succeeding lines in the same way. In the fifth frame the first line reappears with other letters also missing. Since the student has recently read the line, he can complete it correctly. He does the same for the second, third and fourth lines. Subsequent frames are increasingly incomplete, and eventually, . . . the student reproduces all four lines without external help. . . . responses are first controlled by a text, but it is slowly reduced . . . until the responses can be emitted without a text, each member in a series of responses being now under the 'intraverbal' control of other members (Skinner, 1958).

CONTROL OF THE STUDENT'S OBSERVING AND ECHOIC BEHAVIOR

The experimental analysis of behavior has pointed out that observing behavior, or 'attention,' is subject to the same forms of control as other behavior. Classroom methods are effective only insofar as the student has some behavior with respect to the material being taught. Teaching machines control observing behavior in much the same manner as does the laboratory. For example, when the student becomes 'inattentive in the classroom, the teaching material flows on; with a machine, he moves ahead only as he finishes an item. Lapses in active participation result in nothing more than the machine sitting idle until the student continues. Further, it is simple to control the student's observing behavior by constructing items in which correct answers depend only upon his careful observation of the material in front of him' (Holland, 1960).

DISCRIMINATION TRAINING

Obviously, teaching machines can reinforce correct discriminations. However, little education consists of simple discrimination training. More often, it is abstraction or concept formation which is the subject of education. An abstraction is a response to a single isolated property of a stimulus which cannot exist alone. Through providing many examples employing the common property embedded in a wide range of other properties, the teaching machine program is a powerful device for accomplishing the teaching of concepts (Evans, Homme and Glaser, 1959; Holland, 1960).

The above are direct applications of laboratory principles. However, there are other advantages to the use of teaching machines, stemming from laboratory methodology. One of the most important of these is that of the ease of revision of teaching machine programs. The student's answers provide a detailed step-by-step record of his progress in learning the material, pointing up weaknesses and strengths in the program. The programmer is able to revise his material in view of the student's particular difficulties, as is not possible in other teaching techniques. In effect, the student writes the program; he cannot write the textbook. One further facet of teaching machines, inherent in most of the above discussion, should be emphasized. That is the ability of teaching-machine teaching to progress as the student is ready for it. Slow students can move through a program at a pace geared to their learning abilities without penalty. Brighter students may also move at their own best speed without having to wait for the slower students to 'catch up' before going on to a new topic.

Automated teaching today is effective because it is the result of the application of a scientific technology to the process of education, a process which Glaser calls 'the applied psychology of education' (Glaser, 1960). Similar technology is at work experimentally in the fields of psycho-pharmacology, neurology and nutrition—to name just a few (Skinner, 1957a).

We will describe an application of the technology to the field of speech pathology and audiology. Because much of the literature in the area of teaching machines devotes little attention to details of program construction and because we feel such information may be valuable to those interested in further research in this area, we have devoted considerable space to explaining how our program was constructed.

The Problem and Purposes

This study is a preliminary evaluation of the effectiveness of self-instruction techniques for teaching speech sound discrimination to children with defective articulation. The training of speech sound discrimination was chosen for programming, not only because it is recognizedly useful for the early phases of articulation therapy (Brong, 1948; Powers, 1957; Van Riper, 1954), but also because it appears especially suited to teaching machine programming.

The purposes of this study were to develop a series of experimental teaching machine programs for teaching discrimination of the [s] phoneme to children with defective [s] articulation, to develop an experimental teaching machine suitable for presenting the programs, and to evaluate the relative effectiveness of each of the programs. The study compared (a) a program which was patterned after the procedure suggested by Powers (1957); (b) a program which provided extensive training on discrimination of phonemes which were not embedded in phonetic context (isolated speech sounds); and (c) a program which trained exclusively in discriminating correct from misarticulated sound production within words. It was felt that the program which proved most effective should provide a close approximation to a useful automation of the early phases of articulation correction.

The Teaching Machine

The teaching machine developed for this study presented the auditory problem (single words, pairs of words or isolated sounds) by tape recorder. The subject's response to each problem (item) was to press one of three buttons. An incorrect response resulted in the tape recorder's immediately rewinding and replaying that problem. On correct responses the tape recorder simply continued to play uninterrupted. The clatter of the rewinding recorder was sufficient to delineate incorrect items without the assistance of auxiliary stimuli. Hence, the instrument meets qualifications for a teaching machine in presenting short problems, requiring the student to respond, and giving immediate information as to whether the response was correct or incorrect.

A Wollensak Model T-1600 tape recorder was modified for the purpose. This recorder was particularly adaptable because it contained internal wiring for rewinding as long as a switch was closed. An erroneous response resulted in the operation of a Hunter timer with its output switch wired in parallel with the rewind switch. The timer interval was adjusted to rewind the recorder past the missed item and into the silent period preceding it. At the end of the timed interval the recorder automatically resumed its forward motion, repeated the missed item, and if the response was then correct continued on to the next item.

The subject depressed one of the three large wooden buttons which operated electrical switches. The buttons, which were colored blue, red and green and had large white numerals (1, 2 and 3 respectively) painted upon them, were placed in a row on a metal panel. Each of the three types of response labeling (position, color and number) was of use in some particular phase of at least one of the programs.

Coding for the correct response was controlled manually by four keys on a small panel held in the experimenter's lap. This panel was always out of the subject's sight. Three of the experimenter's keys corresponded to the three keys on the subject's panel. The experimenter pressed the appropriate key at the beginning of each item. If the subject pressed either of the buttons which did not correspond to the key depressed by the experimenter, a simple switching network caused a pulse to be delivered to the Hunter timer and the rewinding operation ensued. The fourth key directly pulsed the timer. It was used only in the few cases when a subject failed to respond within the allotted time and resulted in repetition of the item.

The Programs

Each of the three programs developed for teaching auditory discrimination of

the [s] phoneme will be discussed separately.

PROGRAM I

Program I followed Powers' outline and had four distinct phases. Phase 1 involved discrimination of [s] in isolation from other isolated speech sounds. This was the grossest type of auditory discrimination within the program. For the 62 items in this phase, the subject pressed the blue button every time he heard [s] and pressed the red button when he heard any other sound. Isolated sounds were recorded so that there was a period of 5 seconds between the presentation of one sound and the sound following it. Good teaching machine programs are constructed so that in as many instances as possible the student is right. They attempt to shape complex forms of behavior by proceeding in small steps from quite simple material to more and more difficult material. The material in Phase 1 was thus constructed so that early presentations of [s] were longer and louder than non-[s] sounds. This was gradually faded until all the sounds were of roughly equal length and loudness. The earliest discriminations involved [s] and other speech sounds phonetically quite different from [s]. As this phase of the program continued, sounds which required finer discriminations were incorporated into the program.

In Phase 2, the subject was required to discriminate the sound in words. Again, an attempt was made to evolve from simplest to more complex discriminations. Since it is easier to discriminate sounds at the beginning of words, the first 83 items in this part of the program required the child to determine which one of a pair of words began with the [s] sound. If word number 1 began with the [s] sound, pressing button number one was correct. If word number 2 began with the [s] sound, pressing button number two was correct. Early items in the program stressed the word which began with the [s] sound. This emphasis was gradually eliminated (faded) as the program progressed. This part of the program began with items in which the whole phonetic structure of the non-[s] words was much different from the [s] words, gradually progressed through items in which the non-[s] words rhymed with the [s] words but began with much different sounds, went on through items where the initial sound of the non-[s] words was similar to [s] but which differed in the remaining phonetic context, and finally included items where the non-[s] words rhymed with the [s] words and in addition had initial consonants which were hard to discriminate from [s].

Following this, the child listened for words which ended in [s]. Pairs of words were again used, and a progression similar to the above was used, differing only in that final, rather than initial, [s] sounds were under consideration. After 81 items for discriminating final [s], the child was next exposed to problems of discriminating medial [s] sounds from other medial sounds. Pairs of words were again used. The same general principles of emphasis and fading out were followed here, and again the other word of each item gradually progressed toward greater and greater similarity to the paired [s] word.

Powers suggests that the next discrimination task should be that of identifying the position of the [s] sound within words. However, some transitional items were included to insure that the child listen to the whole word again, rather than concentrating on a part of a word, and to begin to establish his ability to recognize the position of sounds in words. The child was instructed that he

would hear some words one at a time. Some of the words had one [s] sound in them, some had two. He was to decide how many, and push the appropriately numbered button. There are only 30 items in this part of the program. However, gradual progression was an important factor. Early items had one or two quite obvious [s] sounds. Close to the end, the items required that the child discriminate between sounds which are similar to [s] in order to count the correct number of [s] sounds.

In Phase 3, the child was asked to identify the position of [s] within a word. The 95 items in this phase of the program forced the child to listen carefully enough to respond to the position of the [s] sound in each word. He had, by now, been trained in discriminating the [s] sound in every position in words; but now he had to respond differentially to the position taken by [s] in a given word. We pressed the first button for an initial [s], the middle button for a medial [s], and the end button for a final [s]. The earliest items had exaggerated [s] sounds, were easily recognizable as to [s] position, and furnished systematic practice with all three positions before the words were randomized as to position of [s] within them. Gradually, the changing of [s] position in a similar word was presented, and lastly final discriminations were forced with words which have within them, in addition to [s] sounds, sounds similar to that phoneme.

Phase 4 involved discrimination of correctly articulated from misarticulated [s] sounds within words. Omission of the [s] sound, nine substitutions of other phonemes, and four [s] distortions formed the basis for the program. All were discriminable on the tape recorder. These were arranged from most audibly different from [s] to least audibly different from [s]. Three initial [s] words, three medial [s] words, three final [s] words, and three [s] blend words were assigned to each 'error.' There were 168 items in all.

For each item, the child heard the same 'word' twice, once correctly and once misarticulated. Pressing button number one was the correct response if the first word was correctly articulated, while pressing button number two was correct if the second word was correctly articulated.

Two types of gradual progression were built into this phase. The first type was the gradual progression from most obvious to most subtle type of misarticulation. In addition, within each misarticulated segment the most discriminable items occurred first, and effort was made to exaggerate the misarticulation in early items. This was gradually faded out.

In accordance with good teaching machine technique, the program progressed through a finely graded series of more and more difficult auditory discriminations. Care was also taken throughout the program to insure that the items sampled [s] sounds adjacent to all possible vowels and all [s] blends. This follows programming technique, which suggests that we include as wide a variety of examples as possible in order to adequately establish a discrimination (Lumsdaine and Glaser, 1960). All of the words used in the program were checked with the Thorndike-Lorge lists (Thorndike and Lorge, 1944). Words which did not appear in the first 3,000 were not used unless it was clear that children would be familiar with them. Partial randomization within the items of the program determined which of a pair of words was correct. Initial, medial, and final words were also randomized for Phase 3. Restrictions were applied so that not more than six successive items were keyed to a particular

button. For all items following Phase 1, the time from the beginning of one item to the beginning of the next was eight seconds.

After Phase 1 of the program, every problem had at least one good [s] sound in it. This program format was chosen because such items forced the child to listen to at least one good [s] per item and furnished much more [s] stimulation than otherwise would have been available. Stimulation with good sound production is often mentioned in the clinical speech literature as important to articulation correction (Powers, 1957; Van Riper, 1954), and it was thus incorporated into Program I.

PROGRAM II

Program II was just an extension of Phase 1, Program I. It attempted to teach auditory discrimination by requiring the child to differentiate only between the [s] and other speech sounds when they were not embedded in phonetic context. The format was exactly like the isolation phase of Program I and differed only in that it was much longer, that it sampled all the consonants and vowels of English, and that there were a greater number of problems for each phoneme. There were 605 items in the program.

PROGRAM III

Program III, an extension of Phase 4 of Program I, was constructed in exactly the same manner, and had 588 items.

All three programs were tape recorded in a soundproof room, using the same recorder which served as the teaching machine. The tapes were recorded using the voice of a graduate student in speech pathology who was formerly a professional actor, chosen because of his excellent speech and imitative ability.

Subjects

Twenty-seven children (18 males and 9 females) between the ages of eight and eleven served as subjects. All of the children were of normal intelligence, as noted in their school records. All had been diagnosed by public school speech correctionists as having defective [s] articulation. None of the children was enrolled in speech therapy. The grade range was from the second through the fifth grades. In order to test the effectiveness of the training, a test for [s] discrimination was constructed which sampled the child's ability to discriminate sounds in isolation, to discriminate whether or not a word had [s] in it, to recognize [s] within words, and to distinguish correct from misarticulated [s] sounds within words. This test was administered before and following discrimination instruction.

Four other auxiliary tests were given before and after training. These tests were the Templin Short Test of Sound Discrimination, a test of general sound discrimination ability; a sibilant discrimination test constructed for the study in order to assess the child's ability to discriminate between sibilant sounds in similar fashion to the [s] discrimination test; a picture articulation test used to measure general articulation; and a picture articulation test designed to measure the child's ability to articulate [s] in the initial, medial, and final positions and [s] blends in the positions in which they occur in English. The three discrimination tests were recorded using the experimenter's voice. The subjects wrote their answers on special answer blanks for the discrimination tests, and their responses on the articulation tests were scored by the experimenter. For each of these tests, the child's score was the number of correct responses he gave.

The experimenter's reliability in judging correctness of articulation was checked by computing a percentage of agreement between original scorings and scorings of randomly selected recordings of the three children's articulation tests. This involved 288 sounds, and the percentage of agreement was 95%.

On the basis of the test scores, three matched groups were evolved. Children in Group I worked through Program I, children in Group II worked through Program II, and children in Group III worked through Program III.

The experimental procedure for each group was identical except for the contents of the programs.

Testing Procedure

Insofar as was possible, discrimination tests were administered to small groups. The children were informed that they had been selected to participate in a listening job and that before the job began a series of tests had to be given to determine if they listened well enough. Directions for each test were recorded on the test tape. If a child wished to hear a particular question over again, he was so permitted although the other children were not allowed to change their answers. Articulation tests were administered individually.

The programmed instruction was administered individually, in most cases during school time. At the beginning of the first session, the child was taught to operate the teaching machine. Throughout the entire program, each child was responsible for all of the operations involved in playing the recorder. Each child worked as long as he wanted to at each session. He was also allowed to hear items over again if he wished. The average time per session was 40 minutes; average time for completing the programs was 2 hours, 15 minutes for

Group I; slightly less then 2 hours for Group II; and for Group III, it was 2 hours, 25 minutes.

Each child was retested within three days following his completion of the program. The procedure for the post-test was exactly like the pre-program test procedure.

Results

In order to evaluate the effectiveness of the programs, scores from the tests given before and after the programs were compared. These comparisons were evaluated for statistical significance by a t-test for matched groups. . . . Only Group I showed significant improvement in [s] discrimination. Scores on the auxiliary tests improved significantly for Groups I and II on the sibilant discrimination test; for none of the groups on the Templin test; for all of the groups on [s] articulation; and for none of the groups on the general articulation test. The improvement in [s] discrimination for Group I represented improvement in eight of the nine subjects; the improved sibilant discrimination represented individual gains by six of the subjects in Group I and four subjects in Group II; and improvement in [s] articulation was noted in six children in Groups I and III and seven in Group II.

The relative effectiveness of the various programs was evaluated by comparing the degree of change in a child's scores on the two tests with that of his matched subject in each of the other two groups. These comparisons were also evaluated for statistical significance by a t-test for matched groups. . . . Only on the [s] discrimination test was there a statistically reliable mean change for Group I as compared to both Groups II and III.

· · ·

Discussion

DISCRIMINATION OF THE [s] PHONEME

It's not surprising to find Program I to be adequate in improving scores on the [s] discrimination test. A major reason for its success is that it makes more use of good programming principles than do the other programs. To be sure, all three were comprised of short problems to which the child had to provide a response which was reinforced if correct; all were constructed so that the density of reinforcement was high; all moved in gradual progression from easiest to successively more difficult items; and all attempted to control the student's observing behavior. However, an important basic difference between Program I and the other two programs is the way it proceeds in establishing a discrimination.

Adequate speech sound discrimination requires that the person be able to distinguish the sound in its full range of contexts. Such needs are characteristic of other situations which have been met in teaching machine work. It cannot be assumed that training in only a few representative cases in any training problem will lead to perfect transfer to the full range of cases. For this reason, an outstanding rule of teaching machine programming is to vary the examples, context, syntactic arrangement, etc. over as nearly the complete range as possible. One of the most striking features of Program I was its wide range of examples, stemming basically from this principle of program construction.

Appropriate variations were also used within each of the other programs, but the changing tasks of Program I allowed for a far greater breadth of possible examples and variations. In both Programs II and III, there was only one task in which these variations could take place.

An error analysis for the 160 items common to Programs I and III reflects this difference. These items comprise the final phase of Program I and thus were preceded by the varying tasks of the earlier phases. These items were spliced in Program III in sets of 12 for each of the 14 types of misarticulations. They followed immediately 28 items drilling on the same distortion. Despite this practice, students using Program III made many more errors on these items than did students using Program I. This provides confirmation of the worth of varied discrimination tasks like those in Program I.

The reactions of the children to each of the three programs shed some light on the question of their relative efficiency. Children in Group I enjoyed what they were doing; children in the other groups tired more easily, became bored and restless. Since it is unlikely that the groups were mismatched in enthusiasm, this too seems to be an added advantage of Program I.

Of particular interest was a spontaneous recitation, either aloud or whispered, of the items by most of the children in those phases of Program I where the items were composed of words. In the parts of Program I in which the children had to count the [s] sounds and in which they responded to the position of the [s] sound in words, all of the children recited the items. In a few instances in Phase 4, they not only repeated the correct word, but also imitated the misarticulated one as well. This behavior was noted for only a few children in Program III and was completely absent for the children working with Program II.

This spontaneous vocalization was unexpected, is at present unexplained, and might well be of considerable im-

portance. Program I provided most of the vocalization and also gave clear-cut improvement in [s] discrimination. Therefore, we cannot overlook the possibility that vocalization as such may play an important role in facilitating development of speech sound discrimination. These vocalizations might force careful observation of auditory cues, or they might provide supplemental kinesthetic stimuli which could be useful in close discriminations. On the other hand, the vocalizations may have no direct influence in discrimination establishment, but might, rather, reflect some other factor which is itself the important variable. The close difficult discriminations might also result in vocalization, whether actually useful or not. Similarly, both vocalization and adequate training may depend upon the interest of the student. Although there is no ready explanation for the vocalization and no information as to its importance in discriminating training, the possibilities raised are of considerable theoretical and practical importance.

Program I is clearly the superior of these programs for teaching [s] discrimination. This superiority is probably a direct reflection of the varying tasks within Program I. In addition, the wide range of tasks and the careful noticing of the [s] phoneme required from students using Program I point up two of the advantages of auditory discrimination training to articulation correction. When correct production of a sound is finally achieved, regardless of whether the etiology of defective articulation involves defective speech sound discrimination, the consistent conversational use of the correct sound depends upon reinforcement for using it. This reinforcement is automatic; that is, it results from 'hearing yourself say it correctly.' Careful noticing of a sound, within a wide range of phonetic contexts, sets up many more occasions upon which correct sound production can be reinforced. Careful auditory discrimination training would appear to be important in establishing stable correct articulation.

AUXILIARY TESTS

The Sibilant Test, the Templin Test, the [s] articulation, and the general articulation tests formed a secondary type of evaluation for the programs. They were included in an effort to test a number of hypotheses concerning the benefits of auditory training, but are, in the long run, side effects to the teaching of [s] discrimination.

The Sibilant Test. Since the sibilant sounds are among the most difficult to discriminate from [s], many items in Program I involved such tasks. Thus, training in discrimination of [s] gave training in discrimination of the other sibilants as well. It has been the clinical experience of the investigators that when correction of one sound has been achieved, the correction of similar sounds follows easily. The increased ability for Group I to discriminate sibilant sounds reflects this observation experimentally as far as discrimination training is concerned.

The reliable change in sibilant discrimination for Group II is less clearcut. Only four subjects contributed to this improvement, and the other five subjects showed no change. However, from the nature of the items in this program, children in Group II shared an advantage with children in Group I in that their program, too, was heavily loaded with sibilant sounds. The heightened ability to discriminate sibilants may reflect this.

Group III, whose program did not afford the increased sibilant discrimination practice noted for the other groups, showed no significant improvement. Lack of improvement on this task in addition to lack of improvement in [s] discrimination suggests that Program III was altogether inadequate in teaching speech sound discrimination.

The Templin Test. None of the three groups showed reliable changes in general speech sound discrimination as measured by the Templin Test. It is felt that this reflects the remote relationship between auditory training for a specific sound and auditory discrimination ability for a large number of speech sounds.

[s] Articulation Test. Viewed alone, the improved [s] articulation scores for all three groups is perhaps the most surprising finding of the study. For this reason, it must be cautiously interpreted. It is emphasized that the test for articulation involved three [s] sounds and fifteen [s] blends in a variety of positions in English words. The child's score was the number of sounds and blends he correctly articulated. Thus, an 'improved' score on this test does not indicate that the child who could not previously articulate [s] now could do so. It means, merely, that in the 24 phonetic contexts in which [s] was tested, the child was able to articulate [s] correctly more often. In order to satisfactorily modify his [s] sound for testing purposes, a child would have had to score 24 on the post-test. No child modified his [s] to this degree; all still had [s] problems, even in the testing situation, at the end of the study.

It is well known that few persons who misarticulate sounds do so in all possible phonetic contexts (Spriestersbach and Curtis, 1951). Twenty of the children in this study initially showed such inconsistency. The significant increase in correct [s] production noted for all three groups reflects simply an ability to articulate [s] within a few more phonetic contexts, not correct and stable [s] production. This gain is a beginning sign in articulation improvement and must be regarded as nothing more.

It will be remembered that no differences were shown to exist between the three groups as to their articulation gains. It is believed, however, that Group I, with its increased ability to discriminate [s], could capitalize upon the ability from these early gains.

General Articulation. The measure of general articulation ability was an attempt to gain an overall speech picture of each subject. This lack of improvement in general articulation following specific auditory discrimination training for a single sound was not surprising.

Conclusions

It seems clear from this study that techniques for improvement of [s] discrimination in children who misarticulate [s] are amenable to teaching machine programming. It is highly feasible that other sound discrimination programs can be developed following similar principles. At its most practical level, this study suggests that a clinical method is adaptable for automation. The same advantages which pertain to automated teaching in general—increased efficiency and effectiveness—also pertain here. The children in Group I, after spending approximately ten minutes learning to operate the tape recorder, worked through their program in an average of two hours and fifteen minutes and improved their [s] discrimination. With proper automation, this would involve only the student's time. Careful sound discrimination training by traditional methods usually takes considerably longer. The values of this time advantage lie, not only in accelerating the training, but also in freeing the clinician's time to work on sound production —a phase of articulation correction requiring the individual skill and knowledge of the clinician.

Challenging opportunities lie in the extension of teaching machine concepts to other areas of speech pathology and audiology. Aphasia rehabilitation, for example, may well be a promising area for automation of teaching. A library of programs for reshaping impaired language skills in adult aphasics would be an invaluable benefit to the aphasia clinician. Programs similar to this one —as well as programs for teaching arithmetic, reading, spelling, grammar, and foreign languages—should be examined and evaluated for use with aphasic adults. It is quite possible that such programs, and extensions and modifications of them, can form the beginnings of some excellent new concepts for rehabilitation of individuals with communication disorders.

Teaching machines can contribute to the field of speech pathology and audiology. The future should hold wide applications which go far beyond this simple start.

References

Brong, C. An evaluation of ear training as a pedagogical technique in improving sound discrimination. Unpublished doctoral dissertation, Northwestern University, 1948.

Evans, J., Homme, L. E. and Glaser, R. The RULEG system for the construction of learning programs. Unpublished paper, University of Pittsburgh, 1959.

Glaser, R. Christmas past, present, and future. *Contemporary Psychologist*, 1960, **5**, 24–28.

Holland, J. G. Teaching machines: An application of principles from the laboratory. In A. A. Lumsdaine and R. Glaser, eds., *Teaching machines and programmed learning*. Washington, D.C.: National Education Association, 1960.

Lumsdaine, A. A. and Glaser, R. *Teaching machines and programmed learning*. Washington, D.C.: National Education Association, 1960.

Powers, M. H. Clinical and educational procedure in functional disorders of articulation. In L. Travis, ed., *Handbook of speech pathology*. New York: Appleton-Century, 1957.

Pressey, S. L. *School and Society*, 1926, **23,** 586.

Skinner, B. F. *Science and human behavior*. New York: Macmillan, 1953.

Skinner, B. F. The science of learning and the art of teaching. *Harvard Educational Review*, 1954, pp. 86–97.

Skinner, B. F. The experimental analysis of behavior. *American Scientist*, 1957a, **45,** 343–71.

Skinner, B. F. *Verbal behavior*. New York: Appleton-Century, 1957b.

Skinner, B. F. Teaching machines. *Science*, 1958, **128,** 969–77.

Spriestersbach, D. C. and Curtis, F. F. Misarticulation and discrimination of speech sounds. *Quarterly Journal of Speech*, 1951, **37,** 483–91.

Thorndike, E. L. and Lorge, I. *The teacher's wordbook of 30,000 words*. New York: Columbia University Press, 1944.

Van Riper, C. *Speech correction: Principles and methods* (3rd ed.). Englewood Cliffs, N.J.: Prentice-Hall, Inc., 1954.

11

The Effect of Animation Cues and Repetition of Examples on Learning From an Instructional Film

A. A. LUMSDAINE / *University of Washington*

RICHARD L. SULZER / *National Aviation Facilities Experimental Center, Atlantic City, N.J.*

FELIX F. KOPSTEIN / *George Washington University*

The study reported herein deals with one specific aspect of the general question of what can be added to the training value of film material through the use of motion picture animation techniques. "Animation" techniques are, of course, many and varied. This report does not deal with the more complex sorts of animation, such as the figure-animation found in the animated cartoon. Rather, it is restricted to the study of simple "pop-in" labels superimposed over the pictures, moving arrows to direct attention of the student to successive salient parts of the pictorial material, and the like. The study also deals with the effects of increasing the number of instructional examples.

Method

INSTRUCTIONAL MATERIALS

The kind of animation effects studied can be characterized in terms of an illustrative excerpt taken from one of the experimental films used in the study. This portion of the film used an example to explain how to read a micrometer setting. It employed moving arrows, pop-in labels, etc. to match the narration. The basic illustration at the beginning of this excerpt is an extreme close-up of the micrometer scale, over which the accompanying narration begins as follows:

Reprinted in abridged form with the permission of the authors and publisher from A. A. Lumsdaine, Editor, *Student Response in Programed Instruction,* Publication 943, National Academy of Sciences—National Research Council, Washington, D.C., 1961. The original paper should be consulted for acknowledgements concerning support and assistance in the project, and for a more detailed statement of film and test content, procedures, and results, particularly with respect to the effects of repetition and how these were related to intelligence level.

"[The reading] is determined by first referring to the scale on the barrel. The figure seven" . . . (arrow pops in to point to the "7" on the barrel) . . . "indicates seven hundred thousandths." (Arrow moves over to one side of the micrometer and ".700" pops into the place where it now points.) "Two more graduations are seen." (Two arrows move in, to point to these.) "That's another .050, which is fifty thousandths . . ." (The two arrows move over, fuse and point to ".050" as it pops in under the ".700.")

The experimental film used in the study was adapted from a standard training film on the micrometer, produced during World War II by the U.S. Office of Education, and supplemented by additional footage shot specifically for purposes of the study. The experimental film also contained considerable material on the construction and care of the micrometer, but the present study focused mainly on the comparative effectiveness of different versions of the film in teaching men how to read micrometer settings. This instruction was conveyed primarily via the presentation of several examples of the kind illustrated above.

All films contained a short introduction explaining the purpose of the micrometer, its nomenclature, and the basic principles of its construction and use. This introduction was followed in each film by three or more examples of micrometer reading, showing how to read various settings of the instrument. These examples were inserted between interstitial or "enrichment" sections telling about the technique of using the "mike," how to care for it, malpractices to avoid in its use, how to check its accuracy, and so forth. The variation in "animation" versus "non-animation" was employed primarily in the examples that showed how to read the micrometer. In certain other portions of the presentation—for example, in explaining the principles of the micrometer's operation—identical animation techniques were used in both the animated-example films and the non-animated-example films.

The animated examples used in one set of experimental films were exactly paralleled in non-animated films. The instruction of micrometer reading in the non-animated films was identical with that in the animated films except for the absence of all animation (pointing, labeling, etc.) in the instructional examples. The corresponding animated and non-animated films used the same sound track and, except for the variation in presence or absence of animation effects, were substantially identical, frame for frame. Given these two sets of films, alike except for specific animation effects, the net contribution of the animation could be isolated and assessed.

Two additional experimental versions of both the animated and non-animated films were developed, one containing only three demonstrations of micrometer-scale readings, and the other containing those three plus three additional examples. Except for the addition of three examples, the two film versions were identical. Half of the trainees who saw the shorter film version, and half of those who saw the longer version, were also given a four-minute supplementary slide-film with a recorded commentary. This supplementary instruction concentrated on how to read difficult settings which fall just short of a division on the main scale, thereby requiring fine discriminations.

EXPERIMENTAL DESIGN AND PROCEDURE

The comparison between the films using animated examples and those using non-animated examples was actually made under eight different experimental conditions, with two class groups of students (Air Force basic trainees) using animated films and two using non-animated films for each of eight conditions. The eight conditions represented all eight possible combinations of these three factors: (a) whether or not a pre-film test on micrometer reading was given before the film; (b) whether the film presented six examples of micrometer reading, or only three examples; and (c) whether the film was or was not followed by a supplementary sound slide-film giving additional examples and pointers on how to avoid the commonest types of error in reading the micrometer. The combination of these three factors, plus the factor of animation versus non-animation, resulted in a 2 × 2 × 2 × 2 factorial design, requiring 16 class groups for a single replication. (Administrative considerations dictated the use of preformed class groups, rather than individuals or groups composed by random sampling, as the units for experimental instruction, testing, and hence analysis.) Two complete replications were tested, with all cells of the first replication being completed before the second replication was started. In the first replication each class group was a half-flight (about 25 to 30 men); in the second replication, full-sized flights (about 50 to 60 men) were used. Within each replication the assignment of animated versus non-animated films to successive class groups tested was determined by chance through the use of random-number tables.

Tests used to assess the students' ability to read micrometer settings consisted of a series of slides, each showing a micrometer setting. Each slide was projected on a screen for a fixed interval of time, and the men were instructed to write down the value of the setting on a test blank. (Previous experimentation had indicated that if men could read pictured settings correctly they could also read the settings when given an actual micrometer to read.) Five different settings were used to test the students' prior (pre-film) ability in reading the micrometer; fifteen different settings were used to test micrometer-reading ability after exposure to any one of the experimental films. In addition, other test questions were used to test effects of the film on knowledge of the nomenclature, construction, and principles of the micrometer.

Each group of men was shown one of the films and was tested immediately afterward. Film showing and testing were done in typical classroom buildings at an Air Force basic-training (indoctrination) center. Procedures and conditions of showing for both animated and non-animated films embraced considerable range and variety. In part this variability was deliberately introduced, for the purpose of increasing the generality of application of the results— that is, to avoid the possibility that the findings might apply only to particular, limited circumstances. But all controlled variations in conditions and procedures for the animated films were strictly paralleled by corresponding variations for the non-animated films. This practice, as well as other more technical aspects of the experimental design and procedure, was designed to assure an unbiased comparison of the effects of the two sets of films.

In all cases participants were told prior to the film showing that they would be tested after seeing the film. Carefully standardized instructions were used in all phases of instruction and testing; these instructions were read by specially trained proctors. Testing followed immediately after the conclusion of the instruction. In the post-film tests, as well as in the short pre-film tests given to half of the classes, each test-slide (micrometer setting) was shown for 30 seconds. On the tests, men were required only to write the correct total reading for each setting; they did not have to write down the component parts of the reading. Knowledge of nomenclature was tested by presenting a single slide on which five key parts of the micrometer were indicated by numbered arrows, and directing men to write in the names of these parts on a test blank, on lines numbered to correspond to the five parts indicated in the slide.

Results

INITIAL ABILITY

Prior to seeing the film, very few of the men could read the micrometer at all. On the pre-film test, 93 per cent of the men failed to answer any of the five test-items correctly. Training thus started virtually from scratch. The average pre-film test performance was only 3 per cent correct answers. Pre-film performance was comparable for the animation and non-animation groups. (Average scores were 2.6 per cent correct and 3.6 per cent correct, respectively.)

GAINS PRODUCED BY THE FILMS

Because of the very low level of pre-film knowledge or skill, test performance following the film is almost entirely attributable to gains produced by the film. On the average, half of the men got scores of 60 per cent or better on the micrometer-reading test after seeing one of the films. The average percentages (for all films) of fully correct answers given before and after the film showing were 3 per cent and 50 per cent, respectively, so that the average gain from the film is represented by a mean score increase of 47 per cent correct answers. A significant difference was found between the pre-film-test groups and the groups which did not receive the pre-film test. The mean for the former was 8.08 and for the latter, 6.86.

ADVANTAGE ACHIEVED BY ANIMATION DEVICES

The comparative levels of micrometer-reading skill achieved with the animated and non-animated film versions were as follows, as expressed in terms of the average percentage of correct answers on the micrometer-reading test:

> Animated films: 54.6 per cent correct
> Non-animated films: 45.0 per cent correct

The added gain produced by animation was shown by the highly significant difference of 9.6 per cent, which represents about 17 per cent of the possible room for improvement above the level attained by the non-animation film. Fifty-nine per cent of the "animated group" got more than half of the text questions correct, while only 46 per cent of the "non-animated" group did this well. In addition, animated films produced more learning for both high and low A.Q.E. (Airmen Qualifying Exam) score groups and for every educational level tested (eight years or less of school completed to twelve years or more).

Two things are evident from the results. First, the numerical measure that may be cited to indicate the margin of superiority for the animated films varies somewhat, depending on how the results are expressed. Thus the absolute values of the percentages themselves should not be taken too seriously. Second, any way the pie is sliced, a clear and substantial margin of superiority is shown to result from the use of the animated films.

STATISTICAL SIGNIFICANCE AND CONSISTENCY OF RESULTS

Analysis of variance and other statistical tests show that the superiority of the animated films is highly reliable—at better than the 99 per cent level of confidence ($P < .01$). The reliability of the results can also be gauged from the fact that a number of different showing conditions were used in the study, and that the films using animated examples were superior in every one of eight experimental conditions employed. Specifically, the animated films produced better learning than the non-animated films: (1) regardless of whether or not the film was preceded by a preliminary quiz orienting participants to the nature of the task to be learned; (2) regardless of whether longer films (with six instructional examples) or shorter films (three instructional examples) were used; (3) regardless of whether or not a follow-up supplementary slide-film was used following the film showing; and (4) under all eight possible combinations of the above three factors. The animated films were also superior to the non-animated films regardless of: (5) whether the films were shown under relatively favorable temperature conditions (morning showings) or under extremely hot, humid conditions; (6) variations in the size of the audience and distances men sat from the screen; and (7) whether proficiency in micrometer-reading after the film was strictly scored (fully correct answers) or more leniently scored (credit given for partially correct answers).

EFFECTS OF ADDITIONAL EXAMPLES

The group receiving the shorter film achieved a mean of 6.48 on the post-film test whereas the group receiving the longer version (six examples) achieved a mean of 8.46 (15-item test), representing about one-fourth of the maximum possible improvement. This difference between means is a highly reliable one (P < .001), as is the difference in means between the group receiving supplementary instruction (8.68) and the group not receiving it (6.30). Although the supplementary film was helpful after

both the three- and six-example film, the effect was much greater with the shorter film.

EFFECTS OF DIFFERENT ANIMATION TECHNIQUES ON LEARNING OF NOMENCLATURE

In addition to comparing the effects of animated versus non-animated examples on proficiency at reading micrometer settings, effects of two different presentations (used in an introductory section of the films) were compared as to their relative effectiveness in teaching the nomenclature of the micrometer. One of the two kinds of presentation compared (Technique A) employed simply pop-in arrows, with no labels, to identify the parts of the micrometer as they were orally named. Technique B employed more complex animation, with camera effects such as "dissolves," and the labels were faded on and off the screen as the narrator described each part. (The narration was identical for Techniques A and B.)

Test results on the comparative effectiveness of these two techniques showed that Technique B (using labels, etc.) was on the average significantly superior to Technique A (simple, no labels). The average percentage of parts correctly named by the groups of men taught by Technique A was only 16 per cent; the corresponding score for Technique B was 29 per cent. The margin of superiority for Technique B was thus a score gain of 13 percentage points.

Further analysis showed that the more elaborate Technique B—employing labels and camera "dissolves"—was advantageous primarily for terms not recurring frequently in later portions of the film. Other terms, used repeatedly in other connections, were evidently conveyed well enough by oral repetition so that for these terms the more elaborate labeling and animation technique showed less advantage. Thus the average percentages of fully correct answers for terms occurring frequently in other parts of the film (mentioned 16 to 19 times in all) were 22.7 per cent for Technique A and 27.2 per cent for Technique B, giving a difference (advantage of B over A) of only 4.5 per cent; but, by comparison, the results for terms occurring infrequently (only two or three times in the film)—and hence dependent on the introductory nomenclature section for getting them across—were 7.0 per cent for A and 32.8 per cent for B, with a much larger advantage (25.8 per cent) for B over A.

This pattern of results was, like the findings for effects of the films on micrometer-reading ability, consistent for groups of trainees differing in intelligence and educational level. It was also consistent regardless of whether knowledge of nomenclature was strictly scored (correct spelling of terms) or loosely scored (credit given for a reasonably close approximation to the correct name). This suggests that the technique of using labels helped fix the names of the parts in the men's memories, in addition to giving them the correct spelling of the terms.

As anticipated, a material improvement in learning was effected by the use of the simple animation techniques employed. Several points concerning practical implications of this finding deserve discussion.

"MOVIE" TECHNIQUES FOR TEACHING "STATIC" MATERIAL

The training objective of the experimental films was the teaching of what may be termed a non-moving or "static" subject matter. The essential skill to be taught did not depend primarily on perception of motion. The task was to read correctly a fixed instrument display (micrometer setting). Nevertheless, the use of animation techniques, characteristic of the instructional motion picture, was effective in increasing the training value of the instruction. This outcome raises a question concerning the frequently expressed opinion that, for so-called "static" subject matter, the choice of moving-picture film as the training medium is not warranted—that a static presentation (e.g., the typical film strip) is necessarily as good for presenting "static" material. The findings of the present study obviously do not tell the whole story, but they do furnish an example of improvement in teaching a static subject (reading fixed micrometer settings) resulting from the utilization of a characteristic motion-picture technique (overlay animation).

ALTERNATIVE METHODS

However, it is important to consider the probable reasons for the superiority of the animated films. Here we should distinguish clearly between underlying psychological or pedagogical factors and the production techniques employed for implementation. A good assumption is that much of the superior effectiveness of the kind of animation techniques studied here lies in the way they stress and clarify specific informational content, and in the way they direct attention to key aspects of a complex visual scene by precise timing of visual indicators keyed to the narration. It is worth noting that these stressing and attention-directing functions can also be achieved in other ways. Specifically:

1. In designing a motion picture presentation, other cinematic techniques such as live-action pointing, indicating, and writing—using suitable models, mockups, or other props—might serve the same attention-getting and stressing functions more cheaply, and as well or even better than in the present instance by overlay animation.

2. A logically important alternative technique not included in the present experimental work is the free use of arrows, labels, etc. in a static (non-moving) visual presentation such as a film-strip or series of slides. However, within the limitations imposed by usual production practices and commonly used still-projection equipment (a limited number of frames and relatively slow rate of changing frames), this alternative would generally be restricted to simultaneous rather than rapidly changing pointing to (and labeling of) the successively identified display elements.

3. By employing static visual materials —films, strips, slides, etc.—a first-rate classroom instructor who uses a pointer, suitable "chalk talk," etc., might achieve the same instructional effects as the animated films here used, thus serving the stressing and attention-direction functions by classroom utilization rather than by film production. A good instructor *might* do this. Whether the average instructor generally *will* in fact do it, and do it as effectively as the film can, seems doubtful. There is one important advantage in programming the pointing-and-stressing devices into the film, by animation or equivalent technique: Namely, effective implementation of these instructional functions can be effected once and for all, in advance—in standardized, well-timed fashion—by incorporating them into the film program itself.

AMOUNT OF IMPROVEMENT ACHIEVED

The problem to which this study was addressed, as stated at the outset, was: "Do trainees actually learn more through the use of motion picture animation techniques?" Granted an affirmative answer, within the limits of the specific techniques compared in this study, the further question—how much more they learn, and how the amount of improvement can be assessed—can be

dealt with. Is it, in particular, worth the added cost of providing the animation?

Present research techniques obviously do not provide an absolute, hard-and-fast answer to these latter questions. [Compare, however, Edwards (1956), Lumsdaine (1962), and other approaches to the estimation problems involved here.] An absolute standard of comparison is lacking. For one thing, as noted earlier, the results can be expressed in various ways, yielding somewhat different comparative figures. Thus, the averages and percentages themselves have only a relative significance, not an absolute one. We can, however, provide a very rough yardstick in terms of comparative instructional potency of other elements in the film-training situation. The advantage gained by animating the three initial examples of micrometer reading (used in the "baseline" film) was appreciably less than that achieved by the presumably less expensive device of adding three more examples (which required, however, two extra minutes of class time.) These comparative results give some basis for evaluating the improvement made by animation. It might further be inferred from the data that animation of the instructional material would be unnecessary, provided time is allowed for additional examples. This conclusion does not necessarily follow. In the present instance, use of animation in the examples produced an added gain, above and beyond that attained by the maximum amount of repetition.

IMPROVEMENT IN TEACHING NOMENCLATURE PRODUCED BY ANIMATION EMPLOYING VISUAL LABELS

In teaching nomenclature, Technique B was found to be superior to Technique A. These techniques differed in two respects: (1) Technique B used printed labels giving the name of each part visually as it was named by the narrator, whereas Technique A did not use these labels; and (2) Technique B "dissolved in" each part as it was named, whereas in Technique A all parts of the micrometer were present throughout the presentation of nomenclature, with each part identified, as it was named, by a pop-in arrow. Since the two techniques differed simultaneously with respect to two factors—labels and camera dissolves—the present data do not establish which factor was responsible for the superiority of Technique B. However, it seems reasonable to suppose that the use of labels to strengthen the verbal identification of the parts was probably a critical factor. Until more data are at hand it seems plausible to assume that free use of visual labels in pictorial film material will markedly improve the learning of nomenclature, particularly when insufficient opportunity is given for learning the names of the parts in other sections of the film.

Summary

The training value of simple animation techniques as cues in teaching an instrument-reading skill was studied by a controlled field experiment. The study was performed by testing 32 classes of Air Force basic trainees to find out how well they could learn to read micrometer settings from seeing one of several specially prepared experimental training films on the micrometer. The films seen by half of the men employed simple animation devices—pop-in labels, moving arrows, etc.—superimposed over the pictorial material. These animation devices were designed to stress and direct attention to key aspects of the pictures. The films seen by the other half of the men were identical except for the omission of these animation devices in key sequences of the films. Test data for approximately 1,300 trainees showed that use of the animation cue devices consistently produced a marked increase in the amount men learned from the film, thus lending factual support to the practice of using such devices in technical films.

The use of multiple demonstration examples is one obvious way to obtain the advantages of repetition in an instructional program. The results of this study show that where this form of repetition is appropriate it can produce very substantial gains in the training value of a film. In fact, adding only three additional examples produced roughly twice as much gain as did the use of overlay animation techniques. How much repetition is optimal depends upon both the difficulty of the material and the intelligence level of the audience.

References

Edwards, W. D. The use of statistical decision functions in making practical decisions. In G. Finch and F. Cameron, eds., *Symposium on Air Force human engineering, personnel, and training research.* Washington, D.C.: National Academy of Sciences—National Research Council, 1956. Pp. 115–24.

Lumsdaine, A. A. Instruments and media of instruction. In N. L. Gage, ed., *Handbook of research on teaching.* Washington, D.C.: American Educational Research Association—National Education Association, 1962.

12

"Superstition" in the Skinnerian[1]

JOHN OLIVER COOK / *North Carolina State College*

Let me begin with a thumping platitude. Though all true Skinnerians would scoff at the idea, in a loose sense of the word "theory," everyone's behavior reflects some theory or other. This is as true of those of us who are engaged in programed instruction as it is of anyone else. In instances where the person cannot give a reasonable account of why he is doing what he is doing, the theory in question is not so much a theory as it is an empirical generalization about the person's behavior. I shall neglect this instance and turn my attention to the case in which the theory that is reflected in the person's behavior is in fact a deliberately used guiding principle.

Teaching machines were the outgrowth of the Skinner box, and they

bear—particularly the early models—unmistakable marks of their origin. Thus, the design of teaching machines not only reflects certain theoretical principles about behavior, it also exhibits a number of irrelevant features of the Skinner box—features that had to be incorporated into it because of the very limited symbol-manipulating capacity of rats and pigeons. In short, I am saying that the teaching machine, even today, is just too faithful a copy of the Skinner box.

The analogy that comes to mind is the early attempts to build airplanes that flapped their wings, because that is the way birds fly. The principles of physics that underlie the flight of birds and the flight of rigid-wing airplanes are the same, but the manner in which these two things operate in the air is quite differ-

---

[1] Note from the Editor. Skinnerian: a hypothetical construct sometimes invoked to explain the behavior of psychologists employing a distinctive methodology and/or embracing a particular view of natural phenomena.

Reprinted with the permission of the author and the publisher from *American Psychologist*, 1963, Vol. 18, 516–18.

ent. Flapping wings are not a feature that is necessitated by the underlying physical principles. It would be a mistake to think that they are—a mistake that seriously limits the scope of our experimental efforts. To be sure, programmers and teaching machine designers enjoy a good deal more success in their efforts than the early flapping-wing plane designers did, but I still think that they are making the same mistake—the mistake of confusing features that are dictated by theoretical principles with features that are dictated by the specific characteristics of the learning task, by the nature of the learning organism, or by some other nontheoretical consideration.

There is, in the behavior of devout Skinnerians, as in the behavior of pigeons (Skinner, 1948), a strong element of superstition. In making the transition from training a pigeon in a Skinner box to training a human being with a teaching machine, religious Skinnerians seem to have a certain reluctance to change any detail of the ritual

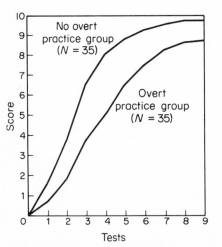

Fig. 1 Mean scores on a paired-associate task (from Cook and Spitzer, 1960).

for fear that the beneficial results that they enjoyed with the Skinner box might not be forthcoming with the teaching machine.

Pigeons being trained in a Skinner box make overt responses. What is more natural, then, than to require human beings who are being trained by teaching machines to make overt responses? Yet it has been repeatedly demonstrated for a variety of tasks that it makes no difference whether the subjects make overt responses or implicit ones. Indeed, in the case of some tasks, implicit responses produce better results than overt ones.

Here (Figure 1) is a case in point. These two groups learned the same paired-associate task under exactly the same conditions, the only difference being that one group was required to make overt responses and the other was not. The difference in performance, as you see, is large and (I might add for the benefit of non-Skinnerians) for the first six tests the difference is significant far beyond the .01 level. This finding at least illustrates my contention that overt responding is not an essential feature of programed instruction and that, in fact, it may even be a deleterious one in some cases. I think this point, though, is a dead horse and not worth the beating, because it is pretty clear now that we would secure general agreement among Skinnerians, as well as those outside the faith, that implicit responding may be quite effective.

Now let me turn to an issue that is alive and kicking: the matter of reinforcement. In working with a Skinner box we always reinforce the pigeon *after* it has made the correct response and not before it. Analogously, it is the common practice in programed instruction to evoke a response from the learner and then confirm (reinforce) it by showing him the correct response. What would

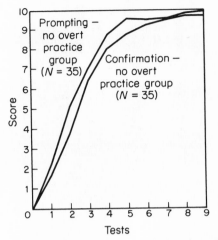

(Three training trials preceded each test)

Fig. 2 Mean scores on a paired-associate task (from Cook & Spitzer, 1960).

happen in, say, a paired-associate task if we showed the learner the correct answer *before* he made his response instead of after? The answer to this question is shown in Figure 2.

These data and those in Figure 1 are part of the same experiment. The top curve in Figure 1 is the bottom curve in Figure 2. These data show that giving the learner the correct answer before he responds, rather than afterwards, has no harmful effect upon his performance. In fact, it results in a slight, but insignificant, improvement.

Let me show you the same thing in serial learning. Here (Figure 3) the task consisted of learning a path through a punchboard maze. The apparatus consisted of a 12 × 12 array of buttons with a light above each button. In the confirmation condition the learner was informed of the correctness of each correct response after he had made that response. (The light went on over the correct button.) In the prompting condition, pressing the correct button in one

row lit the light above the correct button in the next row. Thus the subject in this condition was informed of the correctness of the response *before* he made it. Subjects in both treatments were given alternate training and test trials. They were not given any knowledge of results on the test trials. In terms of trials to criterion the prompting condition is clearly superior. The difference (again for the non-Skinnerians) is significant at the .01 level. This finding is in direct opposition to what I take to be the current belief of Skinnerians—that a student will not learn merely by being guided through a performance. He will learn; in fact, he will learn faster.

This story has three morals, but they are all very simple. The first is that not all the features of a gadget are dictated by theoretical principles. The second is that what works beautifully in one context may not work so beautifully in another. The third moral is that superstitious behavior is not restricted to pigeons.

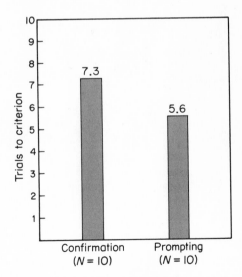

Fig. 3 Mean scores on a serial learning task (from Cook, Miller, Grier, & Staman, 1962).

References

Cook, J. O., Miller, H. G., Grier, J. B. and Staman, J. W. A generalized "plan" for serial learning. In J. O. Cook and H. G. Miller, eds., *Studies in guided learning.* Cooperative Research Project No. 1242, Washington, D.C.: U.S. Office of Education, Department of Health, Education, and Welfare, 1963.

Cook, J. O. and Spitzer, M. E. Supplementary report: Prompting versus confirmation in paired-associate learning. *J. Exp. Psychol.,* 1960, **59,** 275–76.

Skinner, B. F. "Superstition" in the pigeon. *J. Exp. Psychol.,* 1948, **38,** 168–72.

13

The Effects of Strong Formal Prompts
in Programed Instruction

RICHARD C. ANDERSON / *University of Illinois*

GERALD W. FAUST / *Office of Educational Services, U.S. Army Medical Field Service School*

Authors of self-instructional programs are often cautioned to avoid "over-prompting." It has never been demonstrated experimentally that "over-prompting" inhibits learning. In fact, there is surprisingly little research on prompting, considering the lengthy discussions and strongly stated opinions which appear in treatises on programed instruction (Anderson, 1967). Current conceptions of prompting seem to be based largely on Skinner's (1957) speculative analysis of verbal behavior and the practical experience of programers (Markle, 1964).

Most of the actual research on prompting has involved paired associate lists. It has been repeatedly demonstrated that people learn faster under a prompting procedure, in which both the stimulus term and response term appear before the response is required, than under the anticipation method, or confirmation method, as it has been called

in these studies (Cook and Spitzer, 1960; Sidowski, 1961; Levine, 1965). On the basis of these experiments, Cook (1963) has argued that the student should be shown the correct answer *before* he makes the response. Cook seems to be suggesting that the "copying frame" is an especially effective sort of teaching device. The further implication is that there is no such condition as "overprompting."

Our contention is that copying frames and, presumably, under some conditions, other kinds of strongly prompted frames as well, do have a serious shortcoming. The following is an obvious copying frame from a program on the menstrual cycle (Biological Sciences Curriculum Study, 1965, p. 11):

Reprinted with the permission of the authors and the publisher from *American Educational Research Journal*, 1967, Vol. 4, 345–52.

When an egg cell is released from the ovary, the wall of the uterus is thin.

When an egg cell is _____ from an ovary, the wall of the uterus is _____.

Students who repeatedly encounter such obvious copying frames may begin to fill in the blanks without carefully reading all of the frame. As a consequence, the student may sometimes fail to notice the stimulus that it is hoped will elicit the response in the future.

Even somewhat more subtle copying frames may not force attention to the discriminative stimulus. This should be especially true when the frames include additional prompts that make the desired responses more salient. It is hypothesized that when prompts such as underlining are used in conjunction with elaborated copying frames, it is once again possible for the student to answer correctly without attending to the bulk of the material contained in the frame. Figure 1 traces the *minimal* eye movements (a potentially observable aspect of attention) needed to complete a blank correctly in a stylized frame, depending

upon whether or not the frame contains a formal prompt.

One need not look far to find examples in actual instructional programs of augmented copying frames that include additional prompts, such as underlining or italicizing. For instance, the following is one of a number of such frames which appear in Holland and Skinner's (1961, p. 143) program *The Analysis of Behavior:*

An S^D is the *occasion* upon which a given operant may be reinforced. The dinner bell, as an S^D, is the _____ upon which going to the table will be reinforced.

On a frame of this kind it is possible for the student who is looking for shortcuts to pick out and write in the desired response without reading the whole frame carefully.

The purpose of the experiment described in this paper was to investigate the effects of strong, formal prompts, more particularly the effects of underlining the response terms in copying frames. The predication was that routine

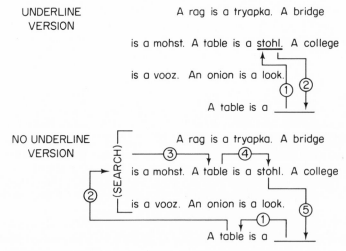

Fig. 1 Two versions of a stylized copying frame. The lines trace the minimal eye movements required to locate the response term.

use of such prompts would impair performance by permitting attenuated inspection behavior, because when the subject can respond correctly without noticing the discriminative stimulus, high levels of associative learning are unlikely.

Method

SAMPLE

Sixty-one graduate student volunteers enrolled in an educational psychology course acted as subjects. Students who reported any experience with Russian were excluded from the sample.

PROCEDURE

Each of two groups of Ss received a training sequence entailing 10 presentations of 16 English-Russian word pairs, a recall test, a stimulated recall test, a writing speed test, a second stimulated recall test, and a recognition test. After the testing all Ss completed a questionnaire that inquired into attitudes toward the experiment and effort expended in learning the words.

The Russian words used in the program were selected from a list of 212 four- to seven-letter Russian words. Pronounceability ratings were obtained for each of these words from 34 summer institute participants, using the procedure described by Underwood and Schulz (1960). All of the words employed in the program had mean ratings of less than 3.00 (relatively easy to pronounce). The list was further constrained to contain: (1) only words with common English meanings, (2) no two Russian or English words with the same initial letter, (3) no two words with very similar phonetic or orthographic construction, (4) no Russian word with an obviously strong association to its English equivalent.

Each frame in the "program" consisted of a prompt sentence containing an English word as the subject and its Russian equivalent as the predicate nominative, a context of four other English-to-Russian sentences and a repetition of the prompt sentence with the Russian word replaced by a blank. Over the ten training trials the prompt sentence for a given word pair appeared twice in each of the five ordinal positions within the paragraph. The filler sentences which made up the remainder of the paragraph were not systematically chosen. The order of frames was randomly determined for each trial independently of other trials. Two versions of the program were prepared, one in which the Russian word to be written into the blank was always underlined (Underlined version), and a second in which no words were underlined (No-Underline version). Sample frames from the two versions appear in Figure 1. Though Markle (1964) has classified underlining as an "emphasis prompt," in the Russian vocabulary program it seemed to operate as a "formal prompt" because it indicated the physical form of the response.

The program appeared as a mimeographed booklet stapled along the left edge. The pages, each of which contained a single frame, were 8½ in. wide and 3½ in. long. The S wrote his responses directly into the program booklet. After every sequence of 16 pages constituting a trial, a colored sheet appeared upon which S was instructed to record the time. The tests were presented in booklets and on pages separate from the program.

The recall test instructions asked students to "write all of the Russian words you can remember." The two stimulated recall tests consisted of frames containing a sentence with an English subject and a blank in place of the Russian predicate nominative. Each of these two tests required recall of all 16 overtly-practiced Russian words.

On the writing speed test, four new Russian words, each followed by a blank, were presented on each of eight pages. The Ss recorded the time it took to copy the Russian words while being "sure to spell each word correctly." The final recognition test was a simple matching test in which the S selected the English equivalents of the 16 Russian words from a list of 20 English words. A strict scoring procedure, in which a Russian word was counted correct only if it was spelled correctly, was employed on all tests.

The questionnaire which Ss completed after finishing the tests inquired into attitudes toward the experiment and effort expended to learn the words. Six open-ended essay questions, presented first in the hope that Ss would volunteer information, asked for comment on the amount of rehearsal or self-testing, interest, persistence in attempting to learn the words, shortcuts used in filling in the blanks, etc. Ss were then asked to complete nine multiple-choice questions intended to elicit the same information as the open-ended questions, but which were more pointed in wording. The answers to each of the open-ended questions were rated on a five point scale by raters who worked independently using a cue-sort method. The interrater reliability coefficients were all above .80.

Groups of between four to eight Ss completed the experiment at one time. Prior to the first session the training booklets for the two groups were placed in a single stack in random order. After the Ss were seated, the materials were taken from the top of this stack and passed out clockwise around the table. This procedure was continued for each session until all the stacked booklets had

been issued. The Ss read the instructions that came with their programs and then were instructed by the E on how to record the time after each trial. All Ss sat facing an assistant who displayed numbered cards representing the time. A card was turned every five seconds. As S completed a booklet or test page, it was collected and the next item was handed out. An E and the timekeeper were always present during sessions. An S completed the training and all tests in a single session. The average time to complete the experiment was 34.5 minutes.

Results

On the two stimulated recall tests, the No-Underline group recalled a mean of 25.3 words, while the Underline group recalled a mean of 22.1 words ($t = 1.91$, $df = 59$, $p < .05$), a superiority of 14.8 percent for the former group. Thus, this experiment did demonstrate the reality of overprompting, under limiting conditions at least. When a program consists entirely of copying frames, then performance is impaired when a prompt that makes the response term more noticeable appears in every frame.

The data further suggest that the reason performance was impaired was that underlining the response term opened the door to attenuated inspection behavior. The student who wanted to take short cuts could copy the response term without paying attention to the stimulus. It must be emphasized that underlining was expected to have a detrimental effect only when it resulted in inadequate inspection of the stimulus. Underlining should not have had an adverse effect on Ss who read carefully. The Ss within each group were divided into quartiles on the basis of time taken to complete the program. The stimulated recall means for each training time quartile appear in Figure 2, which reveals that the superiority of the No-Underline pro-

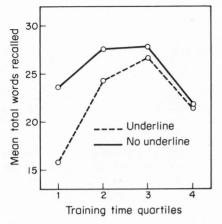

Fig. 2 Stimulated recall for Ss in each training time quartile.

gram was almost entirely due to the superior performance of No-Underline Ss in the first two time quartiles. Among Ss with faster-than-median training times, the mean recall for the No-Underline program was significantly higher than that for the Underline version ($t = 2.80$, $df = 29, p < .05$). The difference for Ss who were slower than the median was not significant. Since Ss who attempt to shortcut the blank filling procedure by simply copying response terms would be expected to take less time than their counterparts who are using a more meticulous and methodical approach to the program, the superior performance of the first and second quartile Ss who used the No-Underline program and the nearly identical performance of the two groups in the third and fourth time quartiles are understandable. The same sort of relationship between training time and recall has appeared in two previous experiments (Faust and Anderson, 1967), so it is a phenomenon in which we have reasonable confidence. Evidently frame design that insures that the discriminative stimulus will be noticed puts a floor under the performance of Ss who hurry through a program.

The questionnaire data supported the analysis of inspection behavior that has been advanced, particularly the interpretation of training time. Subjects with faster-than-median times in both of the groups reported a significantly greater tendency ($t = 3.79, df = 59, p < .05$) to "just try to fill in the blanks as quickly as possible [without spending] extra time studying the words." Many of those with fast training times actually reported using the "inadequate inspection behaviors" mentioned previously. The two groups were divided at the median on the basis of answers to the six open-ended questions. Among Ss above the median, who more frequently and more emphatically reported using short cuts and trying to get through the program as quickly as possible, those who received the No-Underline program recalled significantly more words ($t = 2.29, df = 29, p < .05$) than those who got the Underline version. For relatively conscientious Ss (those below the median), there was no significant difference between the programs.

The No-Underline group showed slightly, but not significantly, higher scores on the matching test and the free recall test than did the Underline group. The presence of a ceiling in the matching test, as evidenced by the fact that over 50 percent of the Ss in both groups correctly matched all 16 word pairs, constricted the possible difference between groups on this test. Since the inspection behavior hypothesis does not allow a differential prediction of amount of response learning and therefore of the program means on a free recall test, which should represent primarily response learning rather than associative learning, it is no surprise that the difference between the groups on this test was not significant.

As can be seen in Figure 2, there was a curvilinear relationship between training time and recall. The poor performance of Ss in the fourth time quartile was not expected, since decrement had not appeared in the two previous experiments that also employed Russian vocabulary programs (Faust and Anderson, 1967). The most plausible explanation seems to be that Ss in the fourth time quartile were studying the English-Russian word pairs that formed the context surrounding the prompt sentence in each frame and, as a result, learned or partially learned associations that interfered with the overtly-practiced word pairs. When asked "How often did you read all of the sentences on the pages in the booklet?" 50 percent of all Ss in the experiment checked "Almost never." Only one S in the fourth time quartile checked this alternative. A record was kept on occurrences on the free recall test of Russian words that had appeared in the context. Six of the ten Ss who recalled any words appearing in the context were in the fourth training time quartile.

Discussion

This experiment provides new evidence that learning is facilitated when steps are taken to control "attention," "inspection behavior," or, as Rothkopf (1965) prefers to call it, "mathemagenic behavior." Previous research has emphasized the role of the response requirement in the control of attention (Holland, 1965; Rothkopf, 1966). In this experiment and an earlier one (Faust and Anderson, 1967), the authors have demonstrated that, holding the response requirement constant, manipulations of the stimulus have an effect on attentional processes, which in turn facilitate or inhibit learning.

We feel that the findings of this experiment can be cautiously generalized to any kind of prompt, most especially to the entire class of "formal prompts." Markle (1964) defines formal prompts as those which provide information about the form of the desired response, such as number of letters, the initial letter or the sound pattern. Repetitious use of strong prompts of this nature may have a detrimental effect on the performance of some students. Furthermore, this effect need not be confined to programs using only copying frames.

Of course, prompts are not ordinarily used in such a heavy-handed and routinized fashion as they were in the Underline program. Usually a formal prompt acts to constrain the number of possible responses rather than to completely determine the response. The degree of constraint that a prompt imposes, that is, the strength of the prompt, is not always apparent from examination of the frame in which the prompt appears. There is a regrettable tendency in many programs to require one or another of a very small number of responses within any short sequence of frames. When this condition prevails, it seems likely that the student can often select the correct response from currently active responses by attending to the formal prompts alone and ignoring the rest of the frame.

References

Anderson, Richard C. Educational psychology. *Annual Review of Psychology,* **18,** 129–64, 1967.

Biological Sciences Curriculum Study. *Hormone control of the menstrual cycle in the human female.* Boulder, Col.: BSCS, 1965. 47 pp.

Cook, John O. "Superstition" in the Skinnerian. *American Psychologist*, **18**, 516–18, August 1963.

Cook, John O. and Spitzer, Morton E. Supplementary report: Prompting versus confirmation in paired-associate learning. *Journal of Experimental Psychology*, **59**, 275–76, April 1960.

Faust, Gerald W. and Anderson, Richard C. The effects of incidental material in a programed Russian vocabulary lesson. *Journal of Educational Psychology*, **58**, 3–10, January 1967.

Holland, James G. Response contingencies in teaching-machine programs. *Journal of Programmed Instruction*, **3**, 1–8, Spring 1965.

Holland, James G. and Skinner, B. F. *The analysis of behavior*. New York: McGraw-Hill, 1961. 337 pp.

Levine, Jerrold M. Prompting and confirmation as a function of the familiarity of stimulus materials. *Journal of Verbal Learning and Verbal Behavior*, **4**, 421–24, October 1965.

Markle, Susan M. *Good frames and bad*. New York: Wiley, 1964. 278 pp.

Rothkopf, Ernst Z. Some theoretical and experimental approaches to problems in written instruction. In John Krumboltz, ed., *Learning and the educational process*. Chicago: Rand McNally, 1965. Pp. 193–221.

Rothkopf, Ernst Z. Learning from written instructive materials: I. An exploration of the control of inspection behavior by test-like events. *American Educational Research Journal*, **4**, 241–50, November 1966.

Sidowski, Joseph B., Kopstein, Felix F., and Shillestad, Isabel J. Prompting and confirmation variables in verbal learning. *Psychological Reports*, **8**, 401–6; June 1961.

Skinner, Burrhus F. *Verbal behavior*. New York: Appleton-Century-Crofts, 1957. 478 pp.

Underwood, Benton J. and Schulz, Rudolph W. *Meaningfulness and verbal learning*. Chicago: Lippincott, 1960. 430 pp.

IV

The
Student
Response

To be effective all instruction must be accompanied by some form of active responding on the part of the student. Active responses may be divided into two broad classifications: covert and overt. *Covert responses* are those which are not publicly observable. Thus, when a student is required to think an answer or to work a problem "in his head," he is being asked to make an explicit, yet, covert response. *Overt responses*, on the other hand, are observable. They include such activities as writing, speaking, pushing a button, and pointing.

During the early 1900's there were many investigations of the value of requiring an overt response or, as it was then called, "recitation." These investigations generally led to the conclusion that requiring active recitation increases learning. The programed instruction movement, with its emphasis on the importance of overt constructed responses, led many investigators to reevaluate the importance of student responding in all forms of instruction. Oddly enough, early studies of programed instruction typically found that students who are required to make overt constructed responses don't learn more than students who merely "think" the answers or read programed frames with the response blanks filled in. This finding seemingly contradicts both prevailing theory and the findings of the earlier research. Fortunately more recent research has helped to explain this paradox and has at the same time clarified the role of response mode in programed instruction.

In the first article in this section, Rothkopf presents a model for learning from prose material; at the same time he makes some conjectures concerning the conditions under which overt responses can be expected to promote learning. He proposes that the response requirement has considerable effect upon the way a student inspects the training materials. Rothkopf's model generates many testable hypotheses concerning the conditions under which the requirement of an overt response will have positive training effects. Although much of Rothkopf's discussion is concerned with programed instruction, his conjectures are generalizable to other forms of instruction as well.

In Chapter 15 Rothkopf attempts to test some of the hypotheses proposed in Chapter 14. He demonstrates that testlike events have an effect on the student's attentional response to written materials. Whether or not these testlike events have effects consistent with training objectives is to a large degree determined by their placement in the instructional sequence. Testlike events which are interspersed throughout training passages yet follow the material they are testing increase the likelihood that an appropriate attentional response will be made to the passages. That is, they make it more likely that the student will read the passages carefully. Teachers who use study questions in conjunction with reading assignments would do well to reevaluate their procedure in the light of Rothkopf's data.

The attentional effect of requiring an overt response during class discussion is demonstrated in Chapter 16 by Travers, Van Wagenen, Haygood, and McCormick. They show that it does make a difference whom the teacher calls on during a class discussion. Students who are very seldom or never called on have a tendency to be "attentional dropouts"; that is, even their covert active responses are extinguished, and they cease attending to the instruction. The possibility that covert responding will not occur is also pointed out in Chapter 17 by Kaess and Zeaman. They, like Rothkopf, feel that the value of an overt response is that it increases the likelihood that the students will actively respond to the instruction. Furthermore, they found that allowing students to make errors during instruction is a dangerous procedure. Students learn what they do, and if we allow them to make errors during instruction, they are very simply learning the wrong responses—responses they are likely to make again in the future. This point is central to the programing approach to instruction, and it is the main reason why prompting and fading techniques (see Section III) have been so well received by the developers of programed instruction.

In her chapter Williams deals with the specific nature of overt responses. She asks the question, "Does it make any difference whether the student is required to construct a response during instruction or whether he is only required to select the correct response from a list of alternatives?" The answer is "Yes, it does make a difference." When there is considerable response learning to be done (such as is the case when new, complex, or technical terms are to be learned), then a constructed response is to be preferred. When response learning is at a minimum (for example, when the student merely needs to learn new stimulus situations in which to use previously learned responses), then other forms of responding should be considered.

Williams also demonstrates that constructed response tests are better able to differentiate between training methods in which response learning has been important. This finding is supported by the Roderick and Anderson study. In addition to assessing the relative effectiveness of short-answer and multiple-choice tests, Roderick and Anderson consider the value of small-step instruction. That is, they consider the question, "How often should we require an overt response?" Their results indicate that the level of a student's entering behavior determines how often an overt response should be required. The more naïve the student, the greater the value of small steps and abundant overt responding. Roderick and Anderson suggest that programed materials are often overly redundant. One way to check for such redundancy is to compare the program with a textbook-style summary of the material covered in the program.

In the last chapter of this section, Kemp and Holland describe the blackout ratio, an ingenious technique for determining the degree to which correct responding is contingent upon mastery of the instructional material. This chapter presents strong evidence to suggest that overt responding will lead to performance increments if, and only if, the response is contingent upon the instructional material. This point is similar to that made by Anderson and Faust in Chapter 13.

14

Some Conjectures about Inspection Behavior in Learning from Written Sentences and the Response Mode Problem in Programed Self-Instruction

ERNST Z. ROTHKOPF / *Bell Telephone Laboratories, Incorporated*

The requirement for frequent written responses by the student has been the most visible general characteristic of self-instructional programs. Most commonly, one or more words are deleted from each frame, and S is instructed to supply the missing term(s). The role of these written responses in learning has been the subject of considerable debate. Skinner, in a remarkably influential paper (1958), has suggested that Ss be required to "compose" responses frequently throughout the instructional program. This recommendation was made with circumspect caution, and other writers (e.g., Holland, 1960; Homme, 1960) have carefully distinguished between the emission of appropriate behaviors during study and the written responses which the program formally requires of S. But the relationship between behaviors that are appropriate in terms of the training objectives and the formal response requirements have not been successfully stated, nor have the conditions under which the response requirement plays either a necessary or advantageous role in the instructive process been clearly specified. As a consequence many investigators have interpreted Skinner's recommendations in the strong sense and have treated the response requirement as if it were a simple programing variable and a necessary condition for effective learning. This has led to a number of experiments in which the *over-all* effectiveness of instructional programs which made frequent response requirements was compared with that of programs which made no response requirement at all (e.g., Evans, Glaser, & Homme, 1960; Della-Piana, 1961; Shettel & Lindley, 1961; Goldbeck & Campbell, 1962). No de-

Reprinted with the permission of the author and the publisher from *Journal of Programmed Instruction*, 1963, Vol. 2, No. 4, 31–45.

tailed review of these studies will be attempted here since most of them have been well summarized by Alter and Silverman (1962). With few exceptions (e.g., Holland, 1961; Williams, 1963) these investigators have not found any substantial differences between the effectiveness of programs that require written responses and comparable programs in which S simply reads each frame and which employ no deletions (response blanks) whatsoever. It should also be noted that none of these studies has examined the effect of a written response in a particular frame on the acquisition of behaviors which that frame was supposed to establish.

The purpose of this paper is to define some conditions in which response requirements can be expected to promote appropriate learning and to distinguish these from other situations for which it is predicted that the response requirement will hinder learning or will have no effect on learning at all. In order to rationalize these predictions, it will be necessary to describe a somewhat speculative conceptual model of learning from written sentences and of learning from self-instructional programs composed chiefly of written sentences. Some critically important conjectures about a class of activities called inspection behaviors will also be described. Although the conceptual model and the conjectures about inspection behavior have a very incomplete empirical basis, the brashness in proposing such notions at this time was felt justified because they lead to a number of apparently testable predictions.

The present conceptualization, unlike most previous formulations in programed instruction, does not rely exclusively on the vocabulary of operant conditioning but also makes use of some of the theoretical concepts and the empirical findings of the verbal learning laboratory.

Effective Stimuli and Some Concepts of Stimulus Objects

In the discussion of learning from written verbal material, two categories of stimuli will be distinguished—stimulus objects and effective stimuli. A stimulus object is any part of the written material to which S is exposed. It can be determined by physical measurement. An effective stimulus is the psychological consequence of the exposure to the stimulus object. An effective stimulus cannot be directly observed. It appears intuitively obvious, however, that the distinction between stimulus object and effective stimulus is useful. This kind of distinction is commonly made in psychophysics, e.g., frequency and pitch, or frequency difference and j.n.d.s. (just noticeable differences). It has also been made in connection with learning problems (Hovland, 1937; Hull, 1943; Rothkopf, 1957). In learning from written material, it is clear that the effectiveness of a stimulus object—for example, a phrase or a sentence—is different for an illiterate person than for someone who can read; a similar distinction can be made for Ss who read the material carefully and for Ss who "skim." The character of the effective stimulus in learning from written verbal material depends on certain responses made by S, including potentially observable responses such as eye movements or hypothetical responses such as subvocal articulation responses. Response, then, like stimulus, is used in two senses—an inferred hypothetical event (a covert response) and an observable event. The latter category includes, of course, what S does when he writes his answer in the deleted portions of a frame sentence.

When referring to an effective stimulus or a covert response, neither particular stimulus consequences nor the topography of covert responses can be specified. This poses a number of problems,

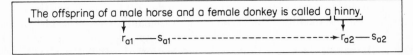

Fig. 1 Paradigm of learning from a written sentence. Articulatory responses are indicated by r_{a2}. Stimulus consequences of articulatory responses are marked s_a. Solid lines with arrows indicate a previously conditioned connection. Dotted lines with arrows indicate a connection being formed.

which are, for the present purposes, however, unimportant.

The need for specifying particular stimuli and responses is important when we speak about the connection between a stimulus and response; i.e., when it is necessary to describe what has been learned. This specification can be made in terms of a test item. Whatever is presented to S in the test item is called *stimulus object*. Whatever written answer S gives is the *response*. A conditional relationship is said to exist between a stimulus object and a response when we can conclude that S will *reliably* make the response when confronted by the test stimulus. This definition allows for the possibility that exposure to a written sentence results in several learned contingencies, since it is imaginable that any exposure will produce new and reliable responses to a number of different test questions.[1]

Learning

The conceptualizations proposed here are restricted to learning from programs that consist of written sentences. The model is an extension of the formulations proposed by Cook and Kendler (1956) for paired-associate learning. Content learning is assumed, in the main, to depend on temporal contiguity. For literate Ss, written letters, or words, or groups of words are previously conditioned stimuli which elicit appropriate articulatory responses; i.e., they are read. When S is exposed to a sentence and makes the appropriate articulation responses, the stimulus consequences of any articulatory response may gain control of other articulatory responses. This process is illustrated in Fig. 1. The sentence segment "The offspring of a male horse and a female donkey is called" plays the role of conditioned stimulus in this illustration. It results in the articulatory response r_{a1} which in turn produces stimulus consequences s_{a1}. The stimulus s occurs in close temporal contiguity with the previously conditioned stimulus "a hinny" and therefore r_{a2}. In this way the association s_{a1}–r_{a2} may be established, and the stimulus object "The offspring of a male horse and a female donkey is called" can become conditional for the response "hinny." The segmentation of the sentence into stimulus and response components in Fig. 1 was quite arbitrary. Conditioning may be backward or circular in that words occurring near the end of a sentence may become effective cues in a test situation for words which occurred near the beginning of the sentence. Nor is it assumed that backward associations are necessarily weaker constraints than forward associations. The structure of the

---

[1] Rules about the classes of test questions which become answerable through exposure to the same training sequence offer an interesting objective for experimental inquiry. The learning outcomes described as *schemes* or *plans* (Miller, Galanter, & Pribram, 1960) bear some resemblance to rules of this kind.

sentence probably does impose some constraints on the likelihood of various associative pairing. There is some evidence (Rothkopf, 1962; Rothkopf, 1963) that words occurring early in the sentence in training are better stimuli for words toward the end of the sentence rather than vice versa. But this effect appears weak, and the conditions under which the phenomenon occurs are poorly understood (see Anderson, 1963).

Temporal contiguity among articulation responses may be a necessary but is certainly not a sufficient condition for the formation of appropriate associations among sentence components. Consider, for example, the demonstration training series described by Woodworth and Schlosberg (1954, p. 711) "John Smith is a psychologist. Henry Jones is an astronomer. Walter Hodge is a biologist." Following exposure to this series, the majority response to the question "Who is the psychologist?" is "John Smith." This is found despite the fact that "John Smith" is more remote from the word "psychologist" with respect to other interposed words than "Henry Jones." Thorndike (1932, p. 64–73), who obtained results consistent with this demonstration, thought that these observations illustrated the principle of "belongingness." This principle, in effect, implies that the period and other grammatical features act as a kind of psychological barrier which reduces the likelihood that temporarily contiguous terms, on opposite sides of this barrier, become associated with each other. Any adequate theory of learning from strings of sentences must account for these "belongingness" effects. It is hypothesized here that "belongingness" depends on the prosodic or rhythmic patterns in which S emits articulatory responses when reading a passage. The intonation or timing which underlies these patterns

is under control of syntactic and probably semantic cues. The fact that stress and temporal patterning influence the formation of associations has been demonstrated experimentally. It has been shown, for example, that when lists of nonsense syllables are read in trochaic rhythm (i.e., feet consisting of one long or accented and one short or unaccented syllable), associations between adjacent syllables within the same foot are more strongly formed than between syllables which were also adjacent but not within the same trochee (Muller & Pilzecker, 1900; Muller & Schumann, 1894). Of course, we cannot observe these intonation patterns directly when S is reading silently. However, we can conjecture that these hypothetical intonation patterns occur somewhat as they would if the sentences were read aloud. For simple sentences an adequate intonation pattern may be achieved after a single inspection of the sentence. Difficult sentences probably involve repeated scanning of the stimulus sentences and repeated changes in intonation patterns. Such changes have been observed by Miller (1962) when extremely difficult sentence structures are repeatedly read aloud. The behaviors which lead to stable intonation patterns are probably acquired by Ss during their early attempts at learning from written materials. If the process is successfully completed for a given passage, S arrives at patterns of intonation and timing which functionally separate sentence from sentence and which differentiate and group the terms within a sentence. By observing how Ss intone when reading a given passage aloud, we can infer what the characteristics of the covert intonation pattern would be for that passage. If this assumption is correct, experimental investigations of the relationships between sentence structure and intonation pattern on the one hand, and intonation pattern and learning on the other, are feasible.

The Deletion Technique and the Learning Model

The most common technique for requiring Ss to make written responses in self-instructional programs is to delete one or more words from a frame sentence. S attempts to supply the missing term(s) and is then provided with the correct answer. In the early stages of learning, some prompting stimulus is generally supplied which is capable of inducing S to respond with the word that has been deleted from the sentence. The prompt can be supplied here to act as a previously conditioned stimulus. The prompting stimulus may be part of the sentence in which the deletion has been made. Alternatively it may have been in some other part of the instructional frame, or it may have been presented to S in a frame that has just preceded the individual item in question. The prompting stimulus plays a similar role

in learning as the deleted word would, were it still part of the sentence; i.e., it evokes the appropriate articulatory response. This is illustrated in Fig. 2. The stimulus word *smaller* acquires stimulus control over the articulatory response *hinny* in the first sentence of the frame. In the second sentence, the word *smaller* brings about temporal contiguity between s_{a1} and r_{a2} (i.e., *hinny*) by evoking r_{a2}. If the prompt is inadequate or absent and the appropriate articulation response, r_{a2}, does not occur, then the correct answer supplied to S will evoke r_{a2}. However, this eventuality may, in some circumstances, result in increased temporal delay between s_{a1} and r_{a2}.

Inspection Behavior

It is clear from the conceptual model described that the formation of associations appropriate to the training objectives depends on the character of the effective stimulation which results from exposure to the written training materials. For written stimulus material,

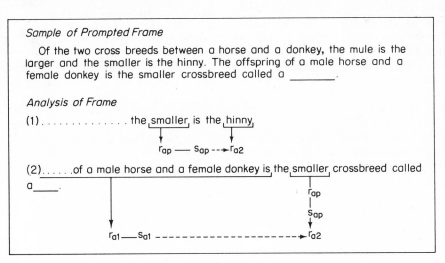

Fig. 2 Analysis of a prompted frame. The notational system is the same as in Fig. 1.

the character of this effective stimulation depends in turn on the activities that *S* engages in when confronted with the stimulus object. These activities will be referred to as inspection behaviors. *Inspection behavior* is used here in a very broad sense to include everything *S* does when exposed to the stimulus material, whether these activities are conducive to learning or not. Inspection behavior may involve yawning (a not uncommon activity among *S*s exposed to printed training materials) or close reading of the training sentences.

Learning from written sentences is hypothesized to depend on three classes of inspection behaviors: (1) those resulting in articulation responses for each component of the sentence; (2) those leading to intonation patterns; and (3) *mathemagenic* processing. The character of the first two types has been discussed earlier. The last, mathemagenic processing (from Greek *mathemema*, that which is learned; and *genic*, to form, to give birth), includes both rehearsal-like activities and the emission of mediating response chains or problem solving. Rehearsal involves silent repetition of the stimulus materials or silent self-testing. The evocation of mediating response chains or problem solving is thought to take place when *S* successfully responds to such frames as those shown here.

It can be conjectured that mathemagenic processing varies among *S*s and that its topography probably emerged from earlier experience in "trying to learn" from written verbal materials.

No attempt will be made to distinguish rigorously among the three classes of inspection behaviors, nor can inspection behavior be defined by direct measuring operations at present. For this reason inspection behavior is proposed as a hypothetical activity that can be either adequate relative to the training objectives or incomplete. Certain conditions to be described later are hypothesized to result in incomplete inspection behavior.

The adequacy of inspection behaviors can also be inferred from observations made on *S* while studying, for example, eye movements or inspection time, and also from poststudy measurements of training results. The conjectures made above about the character of various inspection behaviors were offered in order to enrich intuitive appreciation of the construct.

Inspection Behavior as an Operant

Inspection behavior, whether consistent with efficient learning or not, bears some resemblance to operants (see Skinner, 1957, p. 68, 69) that are under general

---

Sample Frame 1:

City X is due west of city Y. City Y is due north of city Z. City X is ___ ____ of city Z.

Sample Frame 2:

12 x 1036 = _____ ? _____

Sample Frame 3:

Frame X1 The ghosts who protect the Gruanda men in battle are called Komores.

X5 Sacrifices of black pigs are made to the Komores.

X8 The Gruanda sacrifice

_____   _____

to the ghosts who protect the men in war.

stimulus control and the rate and topography of which can be brought under the control of general reinforcing events. These reinforcing events probably arise from the character of the passage which is read and also from some of the consequences of written and other responses which S makes to frames. Prominent among these consequences is knowledge of results in testing. Very little direct evidence is available on the conditioning and maintenance of the inspection operant. Some of the work on eye movements in reading appears relevant to some degree. Tinker (1936), for example, has shown that inspection behaviors depend on the character of the reading material by demonstrating that the number of fixations per line, the duration of the fixations, and the frequency of regressive movements vary as a function of reading content. Some indirect evidence from eye movement studies also suggests that testing provides a state of affairs in which eye movements in reading are maintained at a high level. Carmichael and Dearborn (1947, p. 358–371), by interposing short quizzes throughout the experimental period, maintained reading behavior with little loss in efficiency throughout a six-hour reading period. By contrast, Hoffman (1946), who had Ss read equivalent material for four hours but did not use quizzes, observed decrements in number of fixations after only thirty minutes. The quizzes administered by Carmichael and Dearborn did not afford knowledge of results for S; yet they appeared to have been instrumental in maintaining inspection behavior. Knowledge of results, under some circumstances, probably does enhance the effectiveness of tests in this respect. The observations of Angell and Lumsdaine (1960) have some bearing on this hypothesis. They found that the use of periodic anticipation trials (i.e., testing with knowledge of results) in a

paired-associate training sequence consisting otherwise of all prompted trials resulted in generally higher recall performance than a training series composed entirely of prompted presentations. Both treatments included, in addition, testing trials *without* knowledge of results; so it is unlikely that the "test" character of the interposed anticipation trials is sufficient to account for the obtained differences. It is also interesting to note that while the prompting-with-interspersed-anticipation-trials treatment produced better results than the pure prompting condition, the prompting treatment was found to be in turn better than training consisting *only* of anticipation trials (Cook, 1958; Cook & Kendler, 1956).

Other interpretations of the Angell and Lumsdaine findings are possible (see Angell & Lumsdaine, 1960). However, their results do provide some support for the hypothesis that, for appropriately motivated Ss, success in providing correct responses to frames that contain deletions may be a reinforcer for inspection behaviors. The situation is perhaps like the behavior which leads to hand-raising responses in the classroom when a question is asked. Persistent failure in producing the correct answer when called is likely to extinguish the hand-raising responses and eventually the processing behaviors which precede hand raising. On the other hand, conspicuous success in providing the correct answer is likely to produce more frequent and more persistent attempts to solve the problems and to answer the questions. By analogous reasoning, in self-instructional programs, success at providing the correct response should strengthen the inspection behaviors consistently associated with correct responses.

This argument does not imply, however, that all inspection behaviors which produce correct responses are necessarily consistent with efficient achievement of training objectives. For efficient learning, inspection behavior must transform each term of the training sentences into appropriate effective stimuli. Thus the minimum requirement for inspection behavior is that it result for every sentence in a string of covert articulatory responses which have close correspondence to the sentence that serves as stimulus object. If inspection behaviors that yield these consequences also frequently result in correct responses, then the desirable inspection behaviors will be strengthened. This is consistent with the achievement of training objectives. Under certain conditions, however, inspection behaviors will yield only partially complete strings of articulatory responses but will nevertheless produce correct written responses. This will result in inappropriate learning and in the strengthening of inspection patterns which are not consistent with efficient achievement of the training goals.

Several factors determine the initial occurrence of inspection behaviors necessary to generate the appropriate stimulus consequences from a training sentence. These include the inspection tendencies S brings into the training situation, the structure of the individual sentences, and the manner in which the response requirement is used. One of these, the manner in which the response requirement is met, also can determine to a large degree whether incomplete inspection patterns can result in correct written responses.

The Response Requirement and Control of Inspection Behavior

One of the main theses of this paper is that inspection behavior can be to some degree controlled by use of the response requirement; i.e., by the character and location of the deleted term in a frame. It will be argued that certain uses of the response requirement will dispose S toward adequate inspection behaviors. Other uses will tend to result in incomplete inspection behavior and hence in diminished training effectiveness.

In general, making a written response in the vicinity of the stimulus object makes it more likely that all or part of the stimulus sentence has been read (i.e., that at least some articulation responses have been made) than do simple instructions to read the content of frames from which no deletions have been made. The written-response requirement, therefore, offers a general training advantage *provided* that making the correct written response is always contingent on complete inspection of the training frames. Whether this training advantage is measurable, however, depends in part on the inspection behaviors S brings to the instructional situation. If Ss are disposed to make proper articulation responses when reading, then reliable differences between a written response and a reading treatment will be difficult to obtain. Positive training effects of written-response requirements tend therefore to be restricted to populations which are unlikely to engage in initial careful reading of the program content or which are not likely to persist in careful reading. In certain sentences, however, even careful readers may benefit from the use of the written-response requirement. This occurs when it is suspected that the unaltered stimulus object is not adequate to produce the desired articulation responses. Grounds for such suspicion exist when novel or "different" terms are introduced in a sentence and when perfect orthography is required as terminal behavior. It is a commonplace observation that people will frequently learn, from written material, to assign appropriate names to objects or words but will not be able to spell these names or words properly even though they have read them many times. It appears as if *S* simply learns to generate the appropriate sounds. In the case of certain words and proper names, it is difficult to reconstruct the spelling from the sound, e.g., *occasion*. The skillful use of written-response requirements may aid here in producing the desired spelling articulations. Here is an example of a frame with this character:

> Sample Frame:
>
> In international law, a nation which exercises control over another nation is said to exercise suzerainty over it. A country having paramount control over another exercises suzer__nty over it.

Previous language habits may also result in discrepancies between the stimulus object and articulation. This may happen by substitution or by omission. In the first case an inappropriate articulation response is made because the articulation response is only partially under the control of the misread word due to strong context effects from the remainder of the sentence. Certain sentence components act as associative determinants for words which do not occur in the sentence. Under these circumstances the occurrence of inappropriate articulation responses is particularly probable when the term which actually appears in the critical position has some formal similarity with the likely but incorrect word. An example of this type of undesirable construction is "Our breakfast consisted of ham and eels." *Our breakfast consisted of ham and* is a previously conditioned stimulus

for the response *eggs,* which is inappropriate here; i.e., the phrase acts as an erroneous prompt. It would probably have been safer to write "We ate eels for breakfast and also ham," but the inclusion of a test sentence with response requirement in the frame e.g., a "copy frame," (Meyer, 1960) may also guard against the formation of inappropriate associations.

Incomplete articulation sequences may also occur when key small words such as *no* and *only* are part of the sentence. The reader can rarely detect the omission of this kind of word if the faulty sequence can still be judged a grammatical English sentence. The conjecture is made that ungrammaticalness or unusualness is an error signal by which *S* may be able to judge that he has misread the sentence. Constructions such as "The neutron has *no* electrical charge" or "The neutron does *not* have an electrical charge" should therefore be avoided. The sentence "The neutron is *without* electrical charge" appears preferable. But here again the use of an appropriate written response requirement within a copy frame may guard against inappropriate articulation sequences even for *S*s who bring relatively effective inspection behaviors into the training situation.

Response Requirements and Undesirable Inspection Behaviors

Response requirements increase the general likelihood that some articulation responses will be made to the training sentence and diminish the chances that a sentence or some critical portion thereof will be passed without being read at least in part. If the response requirement is improperly used, however, the procedure may dispose toward inspection behaviors which result in articulation responses to only narrow segments of the sentences as, for example, when the correct response can be supplied by reading only part of the sentence in which the deletion has been made or when the response requirements of a given sentence can be satisfied from only partial inspection of the sentences (or frames) which precede it. One of the criteria proposed here for deciding whether the response requirements of a program are likely to result in incomplete inspection behavior is the *predictability of the response requirement* (henceforth referred to as PRR). By way of illustration, PRR may occur if the last word of the first sentence of a frame is very frequently identical with the response term which has to be supplied for the second sentence.

When the response requirement of a sentence can be predicted from some part of an immediately preceding sentence, partial inspection behavior of both the preceding sentence and the sentence containing the deletion can be expected. This is because S can, under these circumstances, supply the response term from short-term memory; i.e., from echoic responses or continuing rehearsal of the response term. The silent assumption made here is an extension of the law of least effort to learning. When S can supply some response either from short-term memory or by learning a new association through inspection, he is more likely to attempt to provide the response term from short-term memory. Hence PRR, which disposes toward use of short-term memory, interferes with the formation of new associations by restricting inspection.

Two alternative operations are proposed by which PRR can be detected in a self-instructional program. In the first of these, Ss are presented with a training series consisting of n frames. The nth frame is presented without any deletion whatsoever and Ss are asked to

guess what term would have been deleted if such a deletion had been made. PRR must be suspected if Ss are able to make such a guess with substantially greater accuracy than a group of Ss who have not seen the preceding frames of the instructional sequence. An alternative procedure is to list for each frame: (a) the required response term; (b) the first few major conceptual classes to which the response term belongs (e.g., food, metal, technical term); (c) whether the term has been in the immediately preceding sentence; and (d) if so, where it occurred in the preceding sentence. If the same entry occurs with excessive frequency in rubrics a, b, or d and positive entries occur commonly in c, then PRR can be suspected. Whether these frequencies are excessive can probably be decided by comparing the obtained frequencies with the frequency of similar entries for an arbitrarily selected, equally large sample of substantive, nonresponse words from the program.

The second procedure for determining PRR is predicated on the assumption that excessive consistency with respect to (a) conceptual category of the response term and (b) location of the response word in the sentences just preceding the critical frame disposes toward partial inspection behavior. This assumption is supported by a recent experiment by Rothkopf and Coke (1963) in which a training sequence about the religious beliefs of a fictional primitive tribe was constructed. Ss proceeded through the sequence, which included eight experimental sentences, at self-determined rates. Each of the experimental sentences included a name and a food word within the context of an assertion about food sacrifices made to some supernatural beings (e.g., the Kirbys are offered melons). Initial presentation of each sentence was immediately followed in all relevant cases by a second presentation in which one of the words was deleted. Ss were instructed to write in the missing term and received immediate knowledge of results. In two treatments, NO (name only) and FO (food only), the same term (i.e., name term for NO or food word for FO) was deleted for all eight sentences. In another treatment, FAN (food and name), four of the sentences had the food term deleted while the name term was deleted in the remaining four sentences. In the fourth treatment, AM (all modes), the food and the name terms were deleted for two sentences each, while the remaining four sentences involved either simply rereading the repeated sentence or no repetition at all. In terms of the second procedure for determining PRR, it was highest for the NO and FO conditions and became progressively less for the FAN and AM treatments. Further, the response term to be supplied during repetition could easily be cued by instructionally irrelevant processes since repetition was immediate and the response requirement could be satisfied from short-term memory. Performance on a recall test, administered five minutes after the completion of training, supported the prediction that PRR interferes with learning. Percentage correct recall for relevant items was 13.7% for the FO and NO treatments, 16.3% for FAN, and 22.5% for AM. The difference between NO-FO and AM was significant beyond the .01 level (as estimated from an analysis of variance, d.f. = 300). For the FAN:AM comparison, P was just at .05. The NO-FO:FAN difference was not reliable.

If the assumption about the relationship between PRR and inspection behavior were correct, the FAN treatment should have disposed toward more complete inspection of each sentence than the NO or FO conditions. Therefore, if inspection takes time, Ss under the FO or NO conditions should complete study sooner than those under the FAN treatment. This prediction was confirmed by the data ($\bar{X}NO\text{-}FO = 6.6$ min., $\bar{X}FAN = 7.0$ min.) although the difference does not reach the conventional significance level ($.1 < P < .2$). Still longer study time should have been expected for the AM treatment, but the comparison could not be made because some of the sentences of this treatment were not repeated and there were consequently fewer times in the training sequence.

In the study described above, category of response term and location of the response word in the preceding sentence are confounded because the structure of the experimental sentences was held constant. The name word was always the subject of the sentence. Further experimental work is needed to separate the two factors which have been assumed to underlie PRR.

Inspection Behavior and the Location of Prompts

The partial inspection behaviors described above resulted jointly from the use of the response requirement and from some attribute of a preceding sentence in which the required response word was used. The response requirement can be expected to produce incomplete inspection under certain conditions which depend solely on the location of formal prompts in the sentence for which the response requirement is made. Consider an introductory frame as having three components, namely, the discriminative stimulus (S), a prompt (P), and the response requirement (R). Any such frame can be written in six orders—SPR, SRP, PSR, PRS, RSP, and RPS. The minimum requirement for appropriate learning which the present conceptual model makes for such a sentence is that adequate articulatory responses must be made to S and that P be sufficient to elicit the required response. If it is assumed that inspection of a sentence tends to stop as soon as the required response is made, then if both P and R occur before S in the sentence (*PRS, RPS*), appropriate articulation responses to S may not occur. For this reason the appropriate contingencies between S and R would not be established. Further, since incomplete inspection would be followed by correct responding, incomplete inspection would become more likely for subsequent sentences. Whether the remaining alternatives *SPR, SRP, RSP*, and *PSR* differ in training effectiveness is an open question. It is possible that with more rigorous and specific assumptions the conceptual model may produce some differential predictions for the four alternatives. However, it seems unlikely that differences among sequences *SPR, SRP, RSP, PSR* in training effectiveness are of sufficient magnitude to emerge over the noise level ordinarily found in verbal learning experiments.

Of course, other reasons for the use of response requirements have little direct bearing on inspection behavior. Response requirements, for example, may be used to diagnose learning difficulties in self-instructional programs that are being developed. But even here the program writer must be mindful that some uses of the response requirement may have induced some of the learning difficulties he has detected.

Summary

This paper has described a conceptual model for learning from written sentences and for learning from self-instructional programs consisting chiefly of written sentences. The model postulates temporal contiguity as an important association-forming principle for subject-matter content. The Thorndike "belongingness" effect is explained in terms of temporal characteristics of internal speech. Basic to the formation of appropriate subject-matter associations is the transformation of written stimuli (stimulus objects) into effective stimulation. This is accomplished through activities called inspection behaviors, which are thought to include three classes of activity: (1) those resulting in articulation responses; (2) those leading to intonation patterns in internal speech; and (3) mathemagenic processing. Inspection behaviors resemble free operants. It is hypothesized that inspection behaviors are shaped, altered, and maintained through reinforcing events arising from content, testing operations, and knowledge of results.

The conceptual model was built on very incomplete empirical foundation, but it generates several testable hypotheses about the use of written-response requirements in programed instruction. It also raises a serious question as to whether gross comparison of programing strategies that employ written responses with those that do not can ever yield useful experimental results.

References

Alter, Millicent and Silverman, R. E. The response in programed instruction. *J. Program. Instr.*, 1962, **1**, 55–77.

Anderson, B. The short-term retention of active and passive sentences. Unpublished doctoral dissertation, the Johns Hopkins Univ., 1963.

Angell, D. and Lumsdaine, A. A. *Prompted plus unprompted trials versus prompted trials alone in paired-associate learning.* Report AIR-314-60-IR-219. Pittsburgh: American Institute for Research, 1960.

Carmichael, L. and Dearborn, W. F. *Reading and visual fatigue.* Boston: Houghton Mifflin, 1947.

Cook, J. O. Supplementary report: Processes underlying learning a single paired-associate item. *J. Exp. Psychol.*, 1958, **56**, 455.

Cook, J. O. and Kendler, T. S. A theoretical model to explain some paired-associate learning data. In C. Finch and F. Cameron, eds., *Symposium on Air Force human engineering, personnel, and training research.* Publ. No. 455. Washington D.C.: Science-National Research Council, 1956, pp. 90–98.

Cook, J. O. and Spitzer, M. E. Supplementary report: Prompting versus confirmation in paired-associate learning. *J. Exp. Psychol.*, 1960, **59**, 275–76.

Della-Piana, G. M. An experimental evaluation of programed learning: Motivational characteristics of the learner, his responses, and certain learning outcomes. Salt Lake City: University of Utah, 1961.

Evans, J. L., Glaser, R. and Homme, L. E. An investigation of "teaching machine" variables using learning programs in symbolic logic. *J. of Ed. Research*, **55**, 433–52, June–July 1962.

Goldbeck, R. A. and Campbell, V. N. The effect of response mode and response difficulty on programed learning. *J. Educ. Psychol.*, 1962, **53**, 110–18.

Hoffman, A. C. Eye movements during prolonged reading. *J. Exp. Psychol.*, 1946, **36**, 95–118.

Holland, J. G. Teaching machines: An application of principles from the laboratory. In A. A. Lumsdaine and R. Glaser, eds., *Teaching machines and programmed learning.* Washington, D.C.: National Education Association, 1960, pp. 215–28.

Holland, J. G. Evaluating teaching machines and programs. *Teachers College Record*, 1961, **63**, 56–65.

Homme, L. E. The rationale of teaching by Skinner's machines. In A. A. Lumsdaine and R. Glaser, eds., *Teaching machines and programmed learning.* Washington, D.C.: National Education Association, 1960, pp. 133–36.

Hovland, C. I. The generalization of conditioned responses. I. The sensory generalization of conditional responses with varying frequency of tone. *J. Gen. Psychol.*, 1937, **17**, 125–48.

Hull, C. L. *Principles of behavior.* New York: Appleton-Century, 1943.

Meyer, S. R. Report on the initial test of a junior high-school vocabulary program. In A. A. Lumsdaine and R. Glaser, eds., *Teaching machines and programmed learning.* Washington, D.C.: National Education Association, 1960, pp. 229–46.

Miller, G. A. Some psychological studies of grammar. *Amer. Psychol.*, 1962, **17**, 748–62.

Miller, G. A., Galanter, E. and Pribram, K. H. *Plans and the structure of behavior.* New York: Holt, Rinehart & Winston, 1960.

Muller, G. E. and Pilzecker, A. Experimentelle Bietrage zur Lehre vom Gedachtniss. *Z. Ps.*, 1900, Supplementary Vol. 1.

Muller, G. E. and Schumann, F. Experimentelle Bietrage zur Untersuchung des Gedachtnisses *Z. Ps.*, 1894, **6**, 1–190.

Rothkopf, E. Z. A measure of stimulus similarity and errors in some paired-associate learning tasks. *J. Exp. Psychol.*, 1957, **53**, 94–101.

Rothkopf, E. Z. Learning from written sentences: Effect of order of presentation on retention. *Psychol. Rep.*, 1962, 667–74.

Rothkopf, E. Z. Learning from written sentences: Within-sentence order in the acquisition of name-class equivalences. *J. Verb. L. & Verb. Behav.*, 1963, **2,** 470, 475.

Rothkopf, E. Z. and Coke, E. U. Repetition interval and rehearsal method in learning equivalences from written sentences. *J. Verb. L. & Verb. Behav.*, 1963, **2,** 406–16.

Shettel, H. H. and Lindley, R. H. An experimental comparison of two types of self-instructional programs for a SAGE system paired-associate task. Contract AF19 (604)-5951. Pittsburgh: American Institute for Research, 1961.

Skinner, B. F. Teaching machines. *Science*, 1958, **128,** 969–77.

Skinner, B. F. *Verbal behavior.* New York: Appleton-Century-Crofts, 1957.

Thorndike, E. L. *The fundamentals of learning.* New York: Teachers College, Columbia University, 1932.

Tinker, M. A. Eye movement in reading. *J. Educ. Res.*, 1936, **30,** 241–77.

Williams, J. P. Comparison of several response modes in a review program. *J. Educ. Psychol.*, 1963, **54,** 253–60.

Woodworth, R. S. and Schlosberg, H. *Experimental psychology.* New York: Henry Holt, 1954.

15

Learning from Written Instructive Materials: An Exploration of the Control of Inspection Behavior by Test-Like Events

ERNST Z. ROTHKOPF / Bell Telephone Laboratories, Incorporated

The main purpose of the present experiment was to find out: (a) whether adjunct, test-like questions have generally facilitating effects on learning from written instructional materials and (b) whether it matters where the experimental questions are asked in the course of reading. Rothkopf (1963, 1965) has hypothesized that test-like events, such as questions, have a generally facilitating effect in learning from written material. These effects have been identified with a class of activities called inspection behavior.[1]

Hershberger and associates (Hersh-

berger, 1963; Hershberger and Terry, 1965a, 1965b) have provided recent evidence that adjunct questions increase the amount learned from a written passage. However the experimental procedures used in these and in other related studies (see McKeachie, 1963, pp. 1154–1156), allow the possibility that the observed facilitated performance was due to specific instructive effects of the experimental questions rather than a generally facilitating learning set.

Test-like events with knowledge of results, e.g., the anticipation method in paired-associate learning, are well known to have direct instructive effects, and to produce improvement in recall performance on the material tested. Even without knowledge of results, test-

---

[1] I actually prefer the term *mathemagenic* behavior or *mathemagenic responses* to *inspection behavior* because the last tends to be understood in an overly narrow sense. The roots of the new word are *mathema:* learning, that which is learned and *gignesthai:* to be born. This seems an appropriate reference to a class of responses which give birth to learning.

Reprinted with the permission of the author and the publisher from *American Educational Research Journal*, 1966, Vol. 3, 241–49.

like events have been observed to improve subsequent recall performance (Estes, 1960; Estes, Hopkins, and Crothers, 1960; Levine, Leitenberg, and Richter, 1964). As a consequence, it cannot be decided whether Hershberger's results were due to generally facilitating effects of test questions because in his and in other related studies (see McKeachie, 1963, pp. 1154–1156) the subject matter on which Ss tested while reading was identical or closely related to the material on which the final criterion examination was based.

The present study attempts to evaluate the facilitative effects of adjunct questions under conditions in which the direct instructive consequences of questions were eliminated. The logic of experimentation was to use adjunct test-like questions based on materials which had little or no transfer of training to the criterion examination. In this way any facilitative effects of testing could not be attributed to the specific training effects of the experimental test-like questions. Several conditions for using test questions were explored and compared with a control group which did not use adjunct tests.

Method

MATERIALS

Subjects were asked to read a 5200 word selection from Rachel Carson's book *The Sea Around Us*.[2] It described marine life at the greater ocean depths. Although the content of the selection was topically related, adjacent paragraphs frequently dealt with relatively independent factual domains.

The text was multilithed on 20 pages

---

[2] Permission for the experimental use of these copyrighted materials was kindly granted by the publishers, Oxford University Press, 417 Fifth Avenue, New York 16, New York.

of approximately 260 words each. These materials were divided into seven sections. The first of these consisted of pages 1 and 2; the remainder of three successive pages each. Six questions were constructed from the material in each of four sections and five questions from each of three sections, for a total of 39 questions. Questions were of the completion type, requiring a one or two term answer. From the pool of 39 questions, two were chosen from every section. The resulting set of 14 questions (to be referred to as *EQs*—experimental questions) were used in the main experimental manipulations of this study. The *EQs* were selected so as to minimize transfer of training from the portions of text underlying these 14 questions to the material underlying the remaining 25 items.

The main experimental comparisons were based on two criterion tests which were administered after the completion of training. The first of these was the General Test (*GT*), intended to measure general facilitative effects of *EQs*. This test was composed of the 25 questions that were not used as *EQs*. Two forms of this test (*A* and *B*), differing only in question sequence, were used. The second criterion test was intended to measure specific learning which resulted from the *EQs*. This test, which will be referred to as *EQRT* (*EQ* relevant test), consisted simply of all 14 *EQs* bound in a booklet.

TREATMENTS

Five experimental treatments and one control group were used. These differed mainly in the location of *EQs* in the textual sequence and in whether knowledge of results (correct answers) was provided for *EQs*. The experimental treatments were as follows:

SBA. (*EQs* shortly before, with answers); just *before* starting on any section, *S* read the two *EQ*s for that section and was instructed to guess the correct answer for each. After writing his guess, *S* obtained the correct answer by removing a mask from it. The general directions which accompanied this experimental condition and all other treatments in which *EQ*s were given prior to the readings stressed that the *EQ*s were samples of the kinds of questions which could be asked about the experimental materials.[3]

SB. (*EQ*s shortly before, no answers); same treatment as *SBA* except that the correct answers were not provided after *S* made his guess.

LBA. (All *EQ*s given before starting the chapter, with answers); just *before* starting to read the chapter, *S*s were given all 14 *EQ*s *en bloc*. They were instructed to guess the answer to each *EQ* and write it in the appropriate space. The correct answer was then provided as in *SBA*.

SAA. (*EQ*s shortly *after* each section, with answers); immediately after reading each section, *S* was asked to respond to each of the two *EQ*s appropriate to the section he had just read. The correct answer was provided as soon as *S* responded to each question. The general directions which preceded this treatment and subsequently described *SA* stressed that the *EQ*s were samples of the kind of questions which could be asked about the experimental materials and also that they provide *S* with information about how much he was remembering about the material he was reading.

SA. (*EQ*s shortly after each section, no answers); same as *SAA* except that

the correct answers were not provided after *S* responded to questions.

CONTROL GROUP

No *EQ*s were given in this treatment and *S*s were simply exposed to general directions which were composed of portions of those used in the other treatments. These stressed that *S*s should try to remember as much of the experimental chapter as they could and that they would be tested later.

Two additional groups of *S*s were used for the purposes described below.

DIRECTION REFERENCE GROUP (DRG)

The purpose of this group was to provide a reference level which could be used to determine the relative magnitude of *EQ*-effects compared to hortatory care-inducing directions. This group was treated exactly as the *control* condition except that the general directions included statements that the reading material contained much detailed factual information and that the text should be read carefully and slowly.

TRANSFER EVALUATION GROUP (TE)

This group was used to assure that there was no transfer of specific training between *EQ* and *GT*. Group *TE* did not read the experimental text at all. Instead it completed one form of the *GT* and then studied the *EQ*s and the correct answers to them by a modification of the anticipation method. When they could answer each *EQ* perfectly regardless of order of presentation, the *S*s were again given the *GT*, but in an alternate form.

PROCEDURE AND DESIGN

General directions, *EQ*s when and where appropriate, and the experimental text were bound in looseleaf notebooks and given to each *S* without substantial ad-

---

[3] Copies of the test questions and of the experimental directions used for each treatment have been deposited with the American Documentation Institute. Order Document No. 9018, remitting $1.75 for 35-mm microfilm or $2.50 for 6 by 8 in. photocopies.

ditional directions. The *S*s were brought into the experimental room individually and worked in one of seven booths which visually screened them from other *S*s who were working in the room at the time. Each *S* worked through the book at his own rate. While reading through the textual material, *S* recorded the time he started and finished reading each page directly on the page. A large digital clock, projected on a screen in the experimental room, served as time standard.

Each *EQ* was printed on the right half of a 5–7/16 × 8–3/8 in. sheet of paper which had notebook ring perforations along its left edge. Most of the left half of each of these sheets was obscured by a cardboard mask. This mask was also equipped with binding perforation and was bound into the notebook in a way that covered the left-hand portions of any *EQ* sheet until *S* tore the question sheet out of the notebook. For the *LBA*, *SBA*, and *SAA* treatments, the correct answer was printed close to the left edge of the *EQ* sheet. For the other treatments it was not given. After giving a response all *S*s tore the question sheet out of the notebook. In this way the *LBA*, *SBA*, and *SAA* treatments obtained correct answers after responding, while the other treatments did not. After use, the *EQ* sheets were placed into a slotted ballot-type box.

The two final criterion tests were administered immediately after *S* had completed reading the chapter and the notebook had been collected. The 25-item *GT* was administered first. Half of the *S*s in each treatment were given Form *A*, and the remainder Form *B*. After the *GT*, *S*s were given the 14-item *EQRT*.

SUBJECTS

Paid student volunteers ($N = 159$) from Fairleigh Dickenson University in Madison, N.J., served as *S*s. All had stated that they had not read *The Sea Around Us* before. Only 12 *S*s were used for *TE*. For each of the other treatments, $N = 21$.

One *S* was dropped from condition *SAA* because he did not follow directions. The first 12 *S*s who participated in the experiment were not given the *EQRT*.

Results

NO SPECIFIC TRANSFER FROM EQ TO GT

Data from the Transfer Evaluation Group (*TE*) verify that *EQ*s were properly constructed and that no substantial, specific transfer of training exists between *EQ*s and *GT*. Pre-training *GT* score for *TE* was 1.8 correct responses (7.2%). After mastery of *EQ*s, this figure was 2.6 (10.4%). This gain of 3.2% in *GT*-performance as a function of learning *EQ*s without reading the text is not reliable statistically. However, as an added safeguard against specific transfer which may have resulted from exposure to *EQ*s, the four *GT* questions which were responsible for the slight gain in group *TE* were eliminated from all comparisons involving the *GT*.[4] After removal of these four questions, mean correct responses on the pre-tests and post-tests of the *Control T* group were 1.58 and 1.50, respectively.

GENERAL FACILITATIVE EFFECTS OF EQs

Because of the evidence and measures described above, it is safe to assume that facilitated *GT* performance which is

---

[4] It should be noted that the elimination of these four items did not change the findings in any manner.

Table 1

PERCENTAGE CURRENT RESPONSES ON THE TWO FINAL TESTS
AND MEAN AND S.D. OF MEDIAN READING TIMES PER PAGE
FOR THE SEVERAL EXPERIMENTAL TREATMENTS

Treatment	GT	EQRT	Reading time (sec.)	S.D. of Reading Time*
Control	33.14	28.57	69.9	4.22
LBA	35.62	77.82	68.2	6.84
SB	30.10	65.36	69.0	8.16
SBA	34.67	77.82	71.6	6.62
SA	43.24	62.58	79.9	9.38
SAA	40.40	82.35	70.5	6.73
DRG	42.67	41.07	82.1	9.04

* Reading times for the first page were not included in the computations since they are considerably higher than any of the other pages.

produced by *EQ*s in the major experimental treatments is the result of a general set-like factor rather than the direct instructive consequences of *EQ*s. Performance on *GT* for the various treatments is shown in Table 1. The treatments in which *EQ*s were administered immediately after each section (i.e., *SAA, SA*) resulted in better general test (*GT*) performance than the *Control A* group. The Direction Reference Group (*DRG*) also exceeded the performance of the Control. The general facilitative effects due to *EQ*s which were administered *after* each section, and that due to *DRG* direction, amounted to an approximately 10% rise in correct responses. An analysis of variance showed between-treatments effects to be significant ($F = 2.44, d.f. = 6,139, P < .05$). The *SA* treatment ($t = 2.21, d.f. = 139, P < .01$) and *DRG* ($t = 2.09, d.f. = 139, P < .05$) produced significantly higher *GT* scores than the Control Group. The difference between *SAA* and the control did not reach the conventional significance level ($t = 1.59, P < .20$). All of the treatments which involved *EQ*s administered prior to reading the relevant segment of text (i.e., *LBA, SBA, SB*) performed at about the same level as the control condition.

SPECIFIC INSTRUCTIVE EFFECTS OF EQs

Specific instructive effects of *EQ*s can be estimated from performance on the *EQRT*, which is shown in Table 1. Analysis of variance indicated that differences due to treatment were significant beyond the .01 level ($F = 28.62, d.f. = 6,127$). All treatments involving previous exposure to *EQ*s resulted in substantially higher performance than either group without this exposure, i.e., *Control A* ($t = 10.54, P < .01$) or *DRG*. Subjects which obtained the correct answer after responding (*LBA, SBA, SAA*) responded correctly more often than those taking *EQ*s without feedback of any kind (i.e., *SB, SA; t = 4.54, P < .01*). No substantial changes in *EQRT* performance were found to be associated with location of the *EQ*s in the text.

It should be noted that the performance on *EQRT* of *DRG* and the Control Group, neither of which had been exposed to *EQ*s before, was at nearly the same respective level as on *GT*. The facilitating effect associated with the experimental directions in the *DRG* condition was of the same magnitude as before. It elevated the *EQRT* performance of *DRG* about 10 percent over *Control A* ($t = 2.37, P < .02$).

READING TIME

Median reading time per page was determined for each condition. The means and standard deviations of these over all 20 pages are also shown in Table 1. Two treatments, *DRG* and *SA* resulted in markedly slower reading than the other conditions. These two treatments also result in the highest *GT* performance. It is not clear why the *SAA* treatment, which is like *DRG* and *SA* with respect to *GT* performance, differs so markedly from these two treatments with respect to reading time.

The change in reading speed over successive sections of the experimental passage is shown in Fig. 1. The first

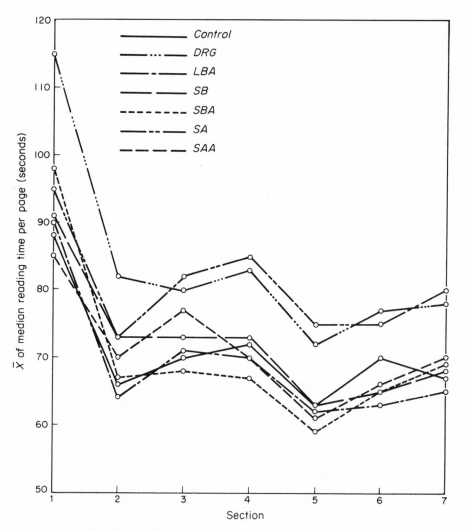

Fig. 1 Means of the median reading time per page for the seven sections of the experimental test. The first section contains two pages and the remaining sections three pages each.

section was read very slowly. The amount of time spent per page dropped sharply in the second section but the curves decelerate. The slower reading time found in the *DRG* and *SA* treatment maintains itself throughout the experimental text. An analysis of individual page reading times gives some indication that pages which followed *EQs* tended to have longer reading time and that increasingly less time was spent on the subsequent pages of the section. It is difficult to reach a definite conclusion in this matter, however, because the analysis is complicated by differences in reading speed between pages. It is notable, however, that the control group was observed to have less variability in reading time from page to page than the other treatments (see S.D.s in Table 1).

Discussion

Test-like questions which are presented *after* reading the relevant text passage have apparently both specific and general facilitative effects on post-reading performance. The general facilitative effects were found to be of the same magnitude as those of specially prepared hortatory directions.

Test-like questions which were presented *before* the relevant text passage was read produced only question-specific facilitative effects. These question-specific effects were greater when the correct answer was given to the student after he had made his response than when no knowledge of results was available. However, even without knowledge of results, the specific training effects which resulted from exposure to *EQs* were very marked.

The fact that *LBA, SBA,* and *SB* treatments did not result in general facilitation effects could have been due to the distracting influence of *EQs* in the *LBA, SBA,* and *SB* treatments, but the data do not support this view. According to this hypothesis, *EQs* which are administered prior to reading the material on which they are based resulted in greater attention to the *EQ*-specific materials in the experimental passage. As a consequence, less inspection activity was devoted to the material on which the general test questions were based. This however implies that the *LBA, SBA,* and *SB* treatments would perform better on the *EQ* relevant test (*EQRT*), and this was not found to be the case.

The results of this experiment are consistent with the view that, when a written passage is studied, Ss learn not only the specific content but also may acquire some general facilitative skills, namely inspection behaviors consistent with the training objectives (Rothkopf, 1963, 1965). The present experiment provides evidence that test-like questions on material which has just been read—questions which are self-administered after approximately every 1000 words of text—are one of the environmental controls of these inspection behaviors. These short tests induced effective inspection behaviors even when correct answers were *not* supplied after the student made a response.

The directions used in *DRG* treatment resulted in *GT* performance improvements of the same order of magnitude as the 14 experimental questions (*EQs*) of the *SA* treatment. It must *not* be concluded, however, that this result argues for the practical advantage of admonitions over adjunct tests in promoting learning from written material. The data from the *EQ* relevant test (*EQRT*) clearly prove that *EQs* and other adjunct tests are in themselves instructive and that they are more so when correct answers are provided after responding. Hence, adjunct tests unlike hortatory directions not only may shape effective inspection behavior but are also useful in teaching specific skills.

References

Estes, William K. Learning theory and the new "mental chemistry." *Psychological Review*, **67**, 207–23, 1960.

Estes, William K., Hopkins, Billy L., and Crothers, Edward J. All-or-none and conservation effects in the learning and retention of paired associates. *Journal of Experimental Psychology*, **60**, 329–39, 1960.

Hershberger, Wayne A. *Learning via programmed reading and cue versus response in programmed reading*. American Institute for Research, Technical Report AIR-C28-7/63-TR, July 1963.

Hershberger, Wayne A. and Terry, Donald F. Typographical cueing in conventional and programmed tests. *Journal of Applied Psychology*, **49**, 55–60, 1965. (a)

Hershberger, Wayne A. and Terry, Donald F. Delay of self-testing in three types of programmed test. *Journal of Educational Psychology*, **56**, 22–30, 1965. (b)

Levine, Marvin, Leitenberg, Harold, and Richter, Martin. The blank trials law. The equivalence of positive reinforcement and non-reinforcement. *Psychological Review*, **71**, 94–103, 1964.

McKeachie, Wilbert J. Research on teaching at the college and university level. In Nathaniel L. Gage, ed., *Handbook of Research on Teaching*. Chicago: Rand McNally, 1963. Pp. 1118–72.

Rothkopf, Ernst Z. Some conjectures about inspection behavior in learning from written sentences and the response mode problem in programmed self-instruction. *Journal of Programmed Instruction*, **2**, 31–46, 1963.

Rothkopf, Ernst Z. Some theoretical and experimental approaches to problems in written instruction. In J. D. Krumboltz, ed., *Learning and the educational process*. Chicago: Rand McNally, 1965. Pp. 193–221.

Rothkopf, Ernst Z. and Coke, Esther U. Repetition interval and rehearsal method in learning equivalences from written sentences. *Journal of Verbal Learning and Verbal Behavior*, **2**, 406–16, 1963.

16

Learning as a Consequence of the Learner's Task Involvement Under Different Conditions of Feedback

R. M. W. TRAVERS / *Western Michigan University*

R. K. VAN WAGENEN / *Arizona State University*

D. H. HAYGOOD and MARY McCORMICK / *University of Utah*

In a previous study by Van Wagenen and Travers (1963) subjects learning in groups of eight were exposed to two main learning conditions. Four of the subjects learned by a recitation procedure, interacting with the experimenter who functioned as a teacher. These subjects were referred to as the direct subjects. The remaining four were able to learn the task only by observing the performance of the direct subjects and their interaction with the experimenter. The latter four subjects were referred to as observer subjects and, according to current custom, their learning is designated as vicarious learning. The task involved in the study was the acquisition of German vocabulary. The experimenter-teacher presented the German words, one at a time, on large cards accompanied by two English words, one of which was the equivalent of the German word. The words were printed in large letters clearly visible to the entire group. After a direct subject, designated by the experimenter, selected one of the English words as the equivalent of the German word, he was either told by the experimenter, "That is right," or was told nothing when the response was incorrect. Although the observer subjects were provided with an equal amount of information when the direct subject responded correctly as when he responded incorrectly, evidence was found that they learned better when they observed a correct response than when they observed an incorrect one. This led to the hypothesis that the specific nature of feedback provided by the experimenter in such a situation would be an important factor in determining the learning

Reprinted with the permission of the senior author and the publisher from *Journal of Educational Psychology*, 1964, Vol. 55, 167–73. The table summarizing the analysis of variance has been deleted.

141

of the observer subjects. This is the central problem on which the present study focuses.

While little research has been undertaken on learning in situations which simulate those of the classroom, a considerable amount of information has been obtained on the relationship of feedback to learning under conditions where only one learner is involved at a time.

Most of the studies have been concerned with the effect of the experimenter saying "right," "wrong," or nothing, or combinations of these. The results of such research are difficult to fit together into a consistent pattern because of the varied nature of the subjects used.

Buss, who has conducted a series of researches with various associates (Buss, Braden, Orgel, & Buss, 1956; Buss & Buss, 1956; Buss, Wiener, & Buss, 1954), and Ferguson and Buss (1959) have generally found that the combination of *no comment* (N) for correct responses and "wrong" (W) for incorrect, or "right" (R) for correct responses and "wrong" for incorrect, produces more rapid learning than the combination of R-N. Buchwald (1959a, 1959b) has taken the position that N acquires positive reinforcing properties when given in the combination N-W and negative reinforcing properties in the combination N-R. Meyer and Seidman (1960) found that N appeared to have reinforcing properties with an 8–9 year old group but not with a 4–5 year old group. The younger, prekindergarten group seemed unable to utilize the information provided by silence on the part of the experimenter when the response was correct. Clearly, providing the best form of feedback is a relatively complex problem even in situations involving only one learner. The present study explores the relative effectiveness of different forms of feedback in a simulated classroom situation in which there are pupils who interact with the teacher and pupils who learn by observing the interaction.

Method

EXPERIMENTAL DESIGN

In the present study, as in the previous one by Van Wagenen and Travers (1963) a simulated classroom situation formed the context of the study. Eight "pupil" subjects sat in a row facing the experimenter who functioned in the teacher role. The experimenter interacted with the odd numbered subjects, but not with the even numbered ones, except on a single demonstration trial when he interacted with all the subjects. The experimenter presented a German word together with two English words which were printed in large letters on an 11×14 inch card. When presenting a card the experimenter turned to a designated subject and said, "Your word is [German word]." The designated subject then read both English words and selected one as the correct translation. After the subject had made his selection, he received knowledge of results according to the treatment to which his group had been assigned. The four feedback treatment modes were as follows: Treatment 1—(a) subject correct, "That's right," (b) subject incorrect, "No, that's wrong." Treatment 2—(a) subject correct, the experimenter said nothing when the subject made a correct response, (b) subject incorrect, "No, that's wrong." Treatment 3—(a) subject correct, "That's right," (b) subject incorrect, "No, that's wrong; [German word] means [English word]." Treatment 4—(a) subject correct, the experimenter said nothing when the subject made a correct response, (b) subject incorrect, "No, that's wrong; [German word] means [English word]."

Nine groups of eight subjects each were assigned to each one of the treatments; and in each group four of the subjects, the direct learners, interacted with the experimenter, while four, the observer subjects, learned the task by observing the interaction. The work was undertaken in an empty room of a school.

SUBJECTS

The subjects ($N = 288$) were fourth, fifth, and sixth graders drawn from three public elementary schools in Salt Lake City, Utah. Two of the schools were located in an older residential section of the city, and the third school was situated in a newly developed suburb.

TASK

The task in the present study consisted of learning to match 60 German words with their English equivalents. This learning occurred over 3 consecutive days beginning on Monday. The design of the task has been fully described in the previous study already referred to.

PROCEDURE

Three learning sessions for each group took place on Monday, Tuesday, and Wednesday mornings. Sessions lasted between 25 and 30 minutes. Usually three experimental groups were seen per week. On Friday a recognition test was given to the week's subjects to measure the amount of word learning which had taken place.

On the basis of either reading scores (obtained from the Metropolitan Achievement Test or the Science Research Associates Battery) or an intelligence quotient (from the Pintner General Abilities Test), 8, 16, or 24 subjects were selected from each of the fourth, fifth, and sixth grade classes available in a school. Reading scores or IQs were ranked for each class, and subjects were chosen by counting up and down from the mean score. Thus experimental groups chosen from a class were kept as homogeneous as possible with respect to reading grade placement or IQ of the group's members. If a chosen subject was absent on Monday, another class member was substituted, keeping the reading score or IQ as equivalent as possible to those of the rest of the group. If a subject was absent on a Tuesday or Wednesday, a substitute from his class was chosen for the learning days, but only the data of the original subject were used in the analysis. Children with any previous knowledge of German were eliminated from the sample. In one or two cases it was discovered after the experiment had been run that a child with a German background had been used as a subject. In those cases the subject's data were not used in the analysis.

After assigning subjects to seats in the row of chairs, which was 6 feet in front of the experimenter, the experimenter gave the group the following instructions:

> Although this is part of school, it is more like a game than anything else. What we do here won't have any effect on the rest of your grades. Only Miss H [the second experimenter, who acted as recorder and observer] and I will know what you do here. You will be learning some words from a foreign language, but to make it more fun, I'm not going to tell you what language you're learning until we're all through working in your school. It is important that you pay very careful attention, even though I may not be talking directly to you. Don't worry about your turn to answer. Instead, try to learn the meaning of the foreign word. Some people won't be asked for many answers, but we'd like everyone to learn all the words he can. You'll be learning words Monday, Tuesday, and Wednesday. On Thursday we won't come at all. But, on Friday we'll come again and see how well you remember the words you learned. So try to remember as many words as you can. [At this point the experimenter put a task card on a stand which was placed on a table in front of her.]
>
> Now let's practice. I'll call somebody's name, and then I'll read the foreign word aloud. The person whose name I call will then read aloud the two English words which are underneath the foreign word. Then that per-

son will guess which one of those two English words means the same thing as the foreign word. The person I call on will know if he's right or wrong because I will tell him so [in the case of Treatments 1 and 3]. [When using Treatments 2 and 4, the experimenter said, "If (subject) makes a wrong guess, I'll tell him so, but if he's correct, I won't say anything at all."] I'll call on only one person at a time, and only he should answer. Let's have a few practice tries. O.K. [one of the observer subject's names], your word is STIRN. Read the two English words aloud and then tell me which one you think means the same thing as the foreign word. At first it will be like a guessing game, but after a while you'll be more sure of your answer. Miss H is the scorekeeper for this game. [The subject read the words, the experimenter gave appropriate feedback, and the experimenter gave a practice word to each of the three other observer subjects.]

All right, are there any questions? Now let's start with the first word that's really part of the game.

During each learning session 20 new words were introduced. The words were presented on 40 cards. Cards Number 21 through 40 provided the same words presented on cards Number 1 through 20, but the order of presentation and position of the English choice words were altered in order to avoid a serial or position effect. On card Number 1 the English words were arranged thus:

Home
Part

whereas on the next presentation of that item, the order of the words was reversed.

The 40 cards were presented once, then the subjects had a few minutes' rest. Following this, the cards were presented once more, making a total of 80 presentations in one learning session. Each word was thus presented 4 times. Direct subjects responded directly to only 5 of the 20 words. While one direct subject was responding orally, the remaining three were learning by observation. Such circumstances provided that, three fourths of the time, direct subjects (the odd-numbered ones) learned by observation in the same fashion as the subgroup of four subjects whose total learning was by observation only (even-numbered subjects). After the learning session, the children were sent back to their regular classrooms.

On Friday all the children who had been subjects for the week took the recognition test at the same time. The items offered four response choices: the R and W choice words which had appeared on the task cards, and two distractor choices selected from the total pool of response words.

In administering the test the experimenter read the German word aloud and then paused for 10 seconds to allow the subjects to indicate their choices on the test paper.

Results

EFFECTS OF FEEDBACK MODE, SUBJECT INVOLVEMENT, AND DAYS OF LEARNING

An analysis of variance based on the recognition test data of 288 subjects was conducted. These test data, obtained on Fridays, examined separately the learning which had occurred the previous Monday, Tuesday, and Wednesday. The data also provided separate measures for those subjects involved directly in learning German vocabulary and for those who learned by observation only. In addition, equal numbers of subjects learned under each of four feedback (knowledge-of-results) conditions. All main effects were highly significant.

A Scheffe Test of Multiple Comparisons was used to assess differences between individual feedback conditions. These comparisons are given in Table 1. A relationship seems to exist between information content of the feedback condition and extent of learning. For

Table 1

SCHEFFE TEST OF MULTIPLE COMPARISONS FOR LEARNING
PERFORMANCE ACCORDING TO FEEDBACK CONDITIONS

Source	F^a
A. Treatment 4, "No, that's wrong; _____ means _____," versus Treatment 2, "No, that's wrong."	46.31***
B. Treatment 3, "That's right" and "No, that's wrong; _____ means _____," versus Treatment 2, "No, that's wrong."	29.85***
C. Treatment 1, "That's right" and "No, that's wrong," versus Treatment 2, "No, that's wrong."	15.99**
D. Treatment 1, "That's right," and "No, that's wrong," versus Treatment 4, "No, that's wrong; _____ means _____."	7.88*

Note: All other comparisons were not significant.

^{a} F standard with 3 and 284 df: 7.8 at .05 level, 11.34 .01 level, 16.26 .001 level.

* $p < .05$.
** $p < .01$.
*** $p < .001$.

example, under Conditions 3 and 4, which were the most information laden of the four feedback conditions, highest performance on the criterion test occurred. Learning under Feedback Condition 4 was slightly, but not significantly, better than under Condition 3.

Under the latter two conditions not only was a wrong response indicated, but the stimulus word and appropriate response were repeated by the experimenter in close temporal contiguity. This circumstance provided redundant information, since, in a binary choice situation saying "No, that's wrong" gives complete information concerning the correct response choice. It should be noted that the correct response was the last phrase heard by the subjects under Feedback Conditions 3 and 4.

Condition 3 provided, in addition to the feedback given in Condition 4, the utterance "That's right" given by the experimenter when the subject responded correctly. This additional phrase, however, did not seem to add to the effectiveness of the feedback.

Condition 1 differed from Condition 3 only in that it failed to add the phrase

"_____ means _____." According to the Scheffe Test learning under Condition 3 was not significantly more effective than under Condition 1.

It is obvious that Feedback Condition 2, "No, that's wrong," was significantly inferior to all other conditions studied. No redundant information was provided by the experimenter and perhaps of consequence is the fact that "No, that's wrong" emphasizes a wrong response, thus increasing its availability for some subjects.

Primacy in learning was superior to recency under all conditions studied ($p < .001$). That is, the words learned on Monday were, under all feedback conditions, better retained on the Friday test than those learned on Tuesday or Wednesday. That which was learned on Tuesday was also better retained than the learning accomplished Wednesday.

Subjects directly involved in learning the task (odd-numbered subjects) were thus involved for only one fourth of the task items while they learned as observers during the presentation of three fourths of the items. This is to say that each of the directly involved subjects received only 5 of the 20 items presented on Monday, on Tuesday, and on Wednesday directly. The remaining 15 items could be learned each day by observing the interaction of other subjects with the experimenter. These two different conditions for learning were combined ($\frac{1}{4} + \frac{3}{4}$) in the analysis of variance.

Since the learning for direct subjects was measured separately on those items learned directly and those learned by observation, these performances together with those for subjects whose total learning experience was by observation have been represented as percentages of the task learned and are provided in Table 2. In a previous study (Van Wagenen & Travers, 1963) a knowledge-of-results condition, "That's right," was employed in an experimental paradigm similar to the one used here. The percentage values from the earlier study are included in Table 2 as Feedback Condition 5. While the subjects in the two investigations were from different elementary schools, with a different person who was of the same sex serving as the experimenter, other conditions such as grade in school, sex of the subject, and reading test scores appeared to be comparable. The "That's right" feedback mode resulted in less learning than any of those from the present study.

Retention of the task was measured again after the passing of about 5 months and is given in Table 3 as per-

Table 2

PERCENTAGE OF THE TASK RETAINED AT THE TIME OF THE FRIDAY TEST

		Direct subjects		
Task	Feedback condition[a]	$\frac{1}{4}$ items direct	$\frac{3}{4}$ items by observation	Observer subjects (all items by observation)
Monday				
(20 items)	1	68	71	66
	2	62	63	63
	3	69	65	67
	4	76	69	71
	5[b]	72	62	60
Tuesday				
(20 items)	1	54	51	48
	2	61	49	46
	3	66	59	50
	4	61	54	51
	5[b]	50	42	39
Wednesday				
(20 items)	1	65	51	46
	2	58	45	43
	3	63	52	45
	4	68	52	46
	5[b]	52	35	33
Total				
(60 items)	1	62	58	53
	2	60	52	51
	3	66	59	54
	4	68	58	56

[a] $N = 72$ under each feedback condition.

[b] Feedback condition, "That's right," from earlier study.

Table 3

PERCENTAGE OF THE TASK RETAINED AFTER APPROXIMATELY 5 MONTHS

Task	Feedback condition	Direct subjects		Observer subjects (all items by observation)
		¼ items direct	¾ items by observation	
Monday (20 items)	1[a]	65	45	55
	2[a]	43	49	47
	3[b]	57	55	50
	4[b]	56	56	50
Tuesday (20 items)	1	40	38	41
	2	35	33	33
	3	48	41	40
	4	45	38	41
Wednesday (20 items)	1	25	31	37
	2	38	38	30
	3	44	32	33
	4	41	33	34

[a] $N = 16$.
[b] $N = 72$.

centage retained. This measure was acquired at only one of the schools where the sample was originally drawn. The retest was administered to 176 subjects, but these were not equally distributed across feedback conditions as may be observed in Table 3. It is worth noting that the proactive inhibition effect (advantage for primacy over recency) was still apparent; that is, Monday's task was better retained than Tuesday's, etc. In general, it appears that the knowledge-of-results conditions retained approximately the same relative order of effectiveness, with Conditions 3 and 4 being high, and Condition 2 showing poorest retention.

INTERACTIONS

An interaction between extent of subject involvement in learning and days of learning was significant at the .05 level. This interaction does not take into account the fact that the direct subjects learned under two conditions and, when

these two conditions are separated, an additional component is added to the interaction. This is illustrated in Figure 1. Variance due to other interactions

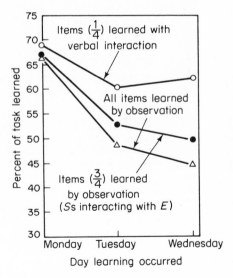

Fig. 1 Interaction between extent of subject involvement and days when learning occurred.

was in each case not significant. These included Feedback-Mode Conditions × Days, Feedback-Mode × Extent of Involvement, and the triple interaction of all main effects.

Discussion

Each one of the four learning conditions described provided all of the information necessary for the acquisition of correct responses, but the feedback differed in the amount of redundancy provided. The situations thus differed from those studied by Buss, Buchwald, and others, for they provided different forms of feedback giving equal information. The amount of redundancy is related to the degree to which the task is learned— with greater redundancy favoring learning. Of interest is the fact that those forms of feedback in which the last item of information transmitted was the correct response was significantly more effective than those in which other information was the last transmitted. This finding is in contrast with studies of R, N, and W as reinforcers in which the combination R-N has generally proven to be less effective than the other two combinations.

Another point of interest raised by the study is that the subjects who interacted with the experimenter performed better not only on the items on which they interacted but also on the items which they learned by observation. The data suggest the interpretation that the direct interaction procedure raises the level of arousal of the direct subjects which, in turn, influences acquisition on the items which they learn by observation.

References

Buchwald, A. M. Experimental alteration in the effectiveness of verbal reinforcement combinations. *J. Exp. Psychol.*, 1959, **57**, 351–61. (a)

Buchwald, A. M. Extinction after acquisition under different verbal reinforcement combinations. *J. Exp. Psychol.*, 1959, **57**, 43–48. (b)

Buss, A. H., Braden, W., Orgel, A. and Buss, E. Acquisition and extinction with different verbal reinforcement combinations. *J. Exp. Psychol.*, 1956, **52**, 288–95.

Buss, A. H. and Buss, E. The effect of verbal reinforcement combinations on conceptual learning. *J. Exp. Psychol.*, 1956, **52**, 283–87.

Buss, A. H., Wiener, M. and Buss, E. Stimulus generalization as a function of verbal reinforcement combinations. *J. Exp. Psychol.*, 1954, **48**, 433–36.

Ferguson, Elsie L. and Buss, A. H. Supplementary report: Acquisition, extinction, and counterconditioning with different verbal reinforcement combinations. *J. Exp. Psychol.*, 1959, **58**, 94–95.

Meyer, W. J. and Seidman, S. B. Age differences in the different reinforcement combinations on the acquisition and extinction of a simple learning problem. *Child Develpm.*, 1960, **31**, 419–29.

Van Wagenen, R. K. and Travers, R. M. W. Learning under conditions of direct and vicarious reinforcement. *J. Educ. Psychol.*, 1963, **54**, 356–62.

17

Positive and Negative Knowledge of Results on a Pressey-Type Punchboard

WALTER KAESS / *University of Connecticut*

DAVID ZEAMAN / *University of Connecticut*

A list of dependable principles of human learning is likely to include some form of Judd's conclusion of 1905 that performance improves most rapidly when *S* is given knowledge of results. The validity of the principle has been demonstrated on tasks as diverse as perception, judgment, sensory discrimination, motor skills, and concept formation. Ammons (1956) found the literature sufficiently coherent to propose 11 tentative generalizations or subprinciples. Wolfle, when summarizing the applications of learning principles states, "laboratory studies are unequivocal in emphasizing the importance of giving a subject as specific and as immediate information as possible concerning the outcome of his efforts" (1951, p. 1267). Both Ammons and Wolfle wisely postpone a discussion of what classes of information constitute effective knowledge until more data is available.

The work of Pressey, who for some 30 years has used several devices which provide human *S*s with immediate knowledge of results, has recently attracted the attention of psychologists interested in "teaching machines." The work with multiple-choice questions keyed to a punchboard which provides knowledge of results is most extensively described in Pressey (1950); and the related work of Angell and Troyer (1948), Jensen (1949), and Little (1934) has been evaluated by Porter (1957) and Skinner (1958).

Porter and Skinner acknowledge the pioneering nature of Pressey's device, but they find fundamental weaknesses in it as a "teaching machine." The assumed weaknesses are based not upon research on the punchboard but rather

Reprinted with the permission of the senior author and the publisher from *Journal of Experimental Psychology*, 1960, Vol. 60, 12–17. Two tables have been deleted.

upon assumptions which the authors have made concerning the most effective method of giving S knowledge of results. Both writers emphasize the importance of S making a physical response, one which will provide behavioral feedback. Porter, who accepts the punchboard as a "teaching machine" is the more emphatic. Any device which presents S with a stimulus but which does not require observable motor action is merely a teaching aid since, "it must be supplemented by some means, usually a teacher in order to be effective" (Porter, 1957, p. 127). Both writers also assume that knowledge of results is most effective when S's behavior is always or nearly always correct. This assumption applies to the punchboard in two ways: the value of alternatives and programming. Porter mentions the "conditioning of incorrect answers" and Skinner (1958, p. 970) states, "effective multiple-choice material must contain plausible wrong responses, which are out of place in the delicate process of 'shaping' behavior because they strengthen unwanted forms." Skinner has another reason for classifying the punchboard as primarily a self-testing device rather than a "teaching machine"—it violates his programming dictum which is, "each step must be so small that it always can be taken, yet in taking it the student moves somewhat closer to fully competent behavior" (Skinner 1958, p. 970). The punchboard had been used with difficult material which S learned by the elimination of incorrect choices.

This paper is primarily concerned with two aspects of the punchboard: the types of information available to S, and the importance of behavioral feedback. A multiple-choice item keyed to a punchboard can provide two types of knowledge: positive, when S's punch perforates the paper signifying "this is

the correct answer," and negative, when the punch does not break the paper and signals "this is not the correct answer." The experimental strategy is to hold constant the amount of positive information Ss receive and to systematically vary the amount of negative information. The importance of behavioral feedback is studied by making its presence or absence an independent variable. The data can be used to test some of the assumptions made by Porter and Skinner as to the nature of effective knowledge of results.

Method

Experiment 1.—Each S received a test booklet containing 150 multiple-choice items and an IBM answer sheet stapled to a cardboard template which provided immediate knowledge of results. The test items concerned the definition of psychological terms. One set of 30 items was used throughout the test. Trial 1 consisted of Items 1–30; Trial 2, Items 31–60, the original items in a new sequence; Trial 3, Items 61–90, a different sequence of the same items, etc. The sequence of items for each trial was determined by a table of random numbers, as was the order of choices within each item. Thus serial-position effects for the items and position effects for the placement of the correct answer within an item were controlled.

The independent variable, amount of negative information, was manipulated by varying the number of item-choices available to Ss on Trial 1. Condition 5 offered 30 5-choice items; Cond. 4, 30 4-choice items; Cond. 3, 3-choice items; and so on for Cond. 2 and 1. The elimination of a distractor for a given condition was made at random from the next highest condition number. This procedure reduced the possibility of systematically eliminating attractive or unattractive distractors. Trials 2–5 used only 5-choice items which were the same for all conditions.

The IBM answer sheet (ITS 1000B

108) was converted into a punchboard by means of a cardboard template containing 150 $\frac{1}{4}$-in. holes which were positioned so as to be directly beneath the correct item-choice. A blank sheet of paper was inserted between the answer sheet and the template to reduce tactile and visual cues. This assembly was then stapled to a solid sheet of cardboard.

The experimental conditions were determined by the test booklet S received. The Ss, students enrolled in the introductory psychology course, were tested in groups of about 30. All conditions were used in each student group, the test booklets being distributed in a predetermined random fashion. The random assignment of conditions within groups equated Ss in the different conditions for initial knowledge of psychology. The Ns for each condition were: 5NC, 88; 5, 75; 4, 64; 3, 62; 2, 73; 1, 73.

The control condition 5NC, no correction, on Trial 1 used a modified version of the punchboard. The template was solid beneath the items of Trial 1. The Ss marked their choices in the conventional manner by a vertical line between the choice markers and received no knowledge of results. Trials 2–5 used the holes in the template as a punchboard, and thus gave knowledge of results.

Experiment II.—An effort was made to evaluate the importance of behavioral feedback, the reinforcement value of punching on a punchboard. Test booklets for the first trial of Cond. 1 and 5 were modified by underlining with a red pencil the correct answer. The Ss were instructed to read carefully all available choices and to note the choice underlined since it was the correct answer. The Ss made no use of the punchboard until they began Trial 2. These modifications constitute Cond. 1A and 5A. Condition 5B was established by using the form of test booklet used for Cond. 5A, but Ss were instructed to punch the correct choice on the answer sheet. All Ss worked on the same material on Trials 2–5. The Ns for each condition were: 1A, 49; 5A, 30; 5B, 40.

Results

PRESENCE OR ABSENCE OF KNOWLEDGE OF RESULTS

The Ss in Cond. 5 and 5NC took the same tests on Trials 1 and 2. On Trial 1 the punchboard provided Ss in Cond. 5 with knowledge of results, while Ss in Cond. 5NC took a multiple-choice test in the usual manner. As can be seen from Fig. 1, there is little overlap in the dis-

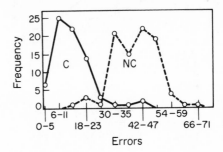

Fig. 1 Distribution of errors on Trial 2. On Trial 1, Ss in Cond. 5NC, no correction, took multiple-choice test without knowledge of results while Ss in Cond. 5 received knowledge of results from 5-choice punchboard.

tribution of errors made by the two groups on Trial 2. The t of 27.86 indicates the magnitude of the effect of the modified punchboard with vocabulary items.

NEGATIVE KNOWLEDGE

On the punchboard S receives negative knowledge when he punches an item-choice and is informed "this is not a correct answer." The mean number of errors on Trial 1 for each condition in Fig. 2 can be interpreted as the number of times the "average" S in the group received negative knowledge. All groups received the same amount of positive knowledge, since they punched each

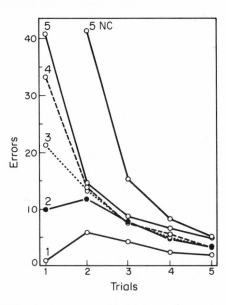

Fig. 2   Mean errors made on punchboard by groups having 1 to 5 item choices available on Trial 1. Items for Trials 2–5 had 5 choices.

item until there was a perforation signaling the correct answer. Errors on Trial 2 can be taken as the dependent variable. It appears from Fig. 2 that the more negative knowledge a group receives, the more errors it makes. A simple analysis of variance of Trial 2 errors, control group excluded, gave an F of 13.36 ($df = 4, \infty; P < .001$).

Negative knowledge could produce a relative increase in errors on subsequent trials in at least two ways: (a) negative information makes it less likely that S will mark the correct answer again and S distributes his picks randomly among the remaining available choices; (b) negative information makes it more likely that S will repeat the original error. Condition 2, where S is presented with but two choices, one being correct, is the easiest place to evaluate the two explanations. For each item of Trial 1, Ss can be classified into a "rights" group which chooses the correct answer

and receives positive information, and a "wrongs" group which selects the choice we will term the *prime distractor* and receives negative information (and on the second try receives positive information). The "rights" and "wrongs" groups can be further classified by their performance on the same item on Trial 2. The behavior of the "wrongs" group is pertinent. The essentials of 30 separate item analyses can be summarized by using the mean percentages of the Trial 2 response categories: correct 53%; prime distractor alone 27%; prime distractor and other errors 15%; errors but not prime distractor 5%. Since the prime distractor for each item was selected by using a table of random numbers, there is no reason to believe that these 30 distractors are more attractive choices than the population of distractors from which they were selected. If we assume that 53% of the "wrongs" group learned the correct answer on Trial 1, we would expect about 12% of the errors to be assigned to each of the *four* distractors on Trial 2. The conclusion is that negative information increases the probability that S will repeat his error.

The item analysis suggested that item difficulty may be related to the effect of negative information. Negative information seemed to have little effect on easy items which were missed but a strong effect on difficult items. This can be expressed by using the number of Ss in the "rights" group as an index of the difficulty of an item. A second index, one of the effectiveness of negative information, is based upon the percentage of the "wrongs" group which answers an item without error on Trial 2. The product-moment correlation between the two indexes is +.62. This tentative conclusion cannot be adequately tested with our data. The test items were purposely made difficult, but fortunately in some cases we underestimated the student's psychological vocabulary.

REPEATED TRIALS

Previous studies of learning on the punchboard seem to have used only a single time through the test material. Repeated trials could result in the rapid reduction of errors or a slow reduction of errors to an asymptote considerably above perfect performance. The shape of the curve would likely depend upon the relative strengths of positive and negative knowledge. The error curves of Fig. 2 bear on this matter. The curve for Cond. 5 shows a rapid reduction in errors for the early trials but seems to be flattening out in the later trials. After completing four trials with 5-choice items the Ss in Cond. 5 are making about the same number of errors as Ss in Cond. 1 make after one trial. The strong resistance of the effects of negative knowledge to correction with a 5-choice punchboard is shown not only in Fig. 2 but also in Fig. 3, where the errors on Trials 2–5 are the result of varying the amount of negative information on Trial 1. It seems reasonable to

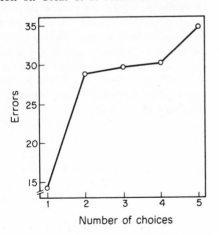

Fig. 3 Mean total errors on Trials 2–5 as a function of the number of item choices available on Trial 1.

conclude that the 5-choice punchboard rapidly reduces errors on beginning trials but soon reaches a point of diminishing returns. Part of this effect is due to the negative information received.

BEHAVIORAL FEEDBACK

The relative importance of overt vs. covert behavior remains one of the fundamental questions of learning. Experiment II was designed to evaluate the importance of the punchboard. The results of Exp. II and Cond. 1 of Exp. I were analyzed by a double classification analysis of variance, using adjustment for unequal numbers. The main effects between Punch-Observe and between 1–5 Choices and their interaction did not remotely approach conventional levels of statistical significance.

The similarity of the mean scores of the experimental conditions suggests that Ss received only positive knowledge. The Ss seem to neither profit from nor be hindered by the number of choices. The presence or absence of overt behavior does not seem to influence the learning. If this information is combined with the demonstrated effect of punching an incorrect choice found in Exp. I, we reach an interesting hypothesis: If an incorrect answer, as well as a correct answer, is read under instructions to note especially the underlined answer, the incorrect answer does not "stick." But if an incorrect answer is punched, in the absence of underlining of the correct answer, the incorrect answer tends to "stick" as a correct answer but, even so, may be overcome on later trials. Alternative explanations may be found, but there are data which further support the conclusions used in the chain of reasoning; namely, the essential equality of performance of the four groups used and the fact that the curves for each of the three conditions of this experiment are for Trials 2–5 almost identical with that of Cond. 1 of Fig. 2.

Discussion

The two kinds of knowledge of results, positive and negative, when presented through tactile and kinesthetic cues on the punchboard, differentially effect performance. Knowledge that an item choice is correct reduces errors; information that an item-choice is not a correct answer leads to a relative increase in errors beyond that observed without such negative information. The assumption of Porter and Skinner that incorrect items interfere with the acquisition of correct responses is supported by the results of Exp. I. However, their analysis is not supported by either of the two findings of Exp. II. Negative information does not impair performance when it is presented for S merely to read, nor is the reinforcement of overt correct responses more effective than the reinforcement of covert behavior.

An interpretation of the interfering effects of negative information requires identification of the source of reinforcement for the observed tendency to repeat erroneous choices. Two possible hypotheses that may serve as a guide for future research are as follows: (a) The temporal contiguity of question stimuli and erroneous responses provides a sufficient condition for their connection. One difficulty with this interpretation is the fact that the punchboard requires the last or postreme response to every question to be correct. (b) A reinforcement interpretation may appeal to the reward-value of the punch feedback following a correct response. This may provide a delayed reinforcement for incorrect responses preceding the correct one. Since the effects of delayed reinforcement vary with the length of delay, a testable consequence of this latter view, at least, is the prediction that temporal spacing of questions and answers will be a parameter of the main effects of the present experiment.

Further experimental analysis of the efficiency of the punchboard as a training device may yield additional results of both theoretical and applied interest.

Summary

A modified Pressey-type punchboard was used to study the influence of positive and negative knowledge of results and the importance of punch feedback. The rate of multiple-choice learning of definitions of psychological terms was found to vary inversely with the number of available wrong answers when overt error responses (punches) were made, but not when wrong answers were merely read. No corresponding differential effect of punch feedback on correct answers was observed. Reading these was as effective in producing learning as reading and punching.

References

Ammons, R. B. Effects of knowledge of performance: A survey and tentative theoretical formulation. *J. Gen. Psychol.*, 1956, **54**, 279–99.

Angell, G. W. and Troyer, M. E. A new self-scoring device for improving instruction. *Sch. Soc.*, 1948, **67**, 84–85.

Jensen, B. T. An independent-study laboratory using self-scoring tests. *J. Educ. Res.*, 1949, **43**, 134–37.

Little, J. K. Results of use of machines for testing and for drill, upon learning in educational psychology. *J. Exp. Educ.*, 1934, **3**, 45–49.

Porter D. A critical review of a portion of the literature on teaching devices. *Harv. Educ. Rev.*, 1957, **27,** 126–47.

Pressey, S. L. Development and appraisal of devices providing immediate automatic scoring of objective tests and concomitant self-instruction. *J. Psychol.*, 1950, **29,** 417–47.

Skinner, B. F. Teaching machines. *Science,* 1958, **128,** 969–77.

Wolfle, D. Training. In S. S. Stevens, ed., *Handbook of experimental psychology.* New York: Wiley, 1951. Pp. 1267–70.

18

Effectiveness of Constructed-Response and Multiple-Choice Programing Modes as a Function of Test Mode

JOANNA P. WILLIAMS / *University of Pennsylvania*

Recent studies have suggested that there is no simple answer to the question of what is the most appropriate mode of response in programed instruction. For example, Williams (1963) found that the relative effectiveness of two training modes may depend on the type of item used in the criterion test. In that experiment, college students worked through a program which reviewed previously learned material, and a constructed-response criterion test was administered. It was found that constructed-response training was superior to multiple-choice training on test items requiring the use of novel or technical terminology which had been introduced by the program, but not on items requiring general, familiar vocabulary. The present experiment was designed to extend this finding to a situation (*a*) where the content of the program was novel, and not review; and (*b*) where the subjects were elementary school pupils. In addition, the present experiment utilized not only a con-

structed-response criterion test but also a multiple-choice test, in order to determine whether the latter would also be sensitive enough to show the predicted interaction between response mode in training and type of test item.

In the previous study, only posttest scores were available; here, the criterion test was also administered as a pretest, so that the relationship between the variables could also be investigated in terms of the actual gains made as a result of having gone through the program.

A second purpose of the experiment was to examine the relationship between performance on programed materials and aptitude. It is reasonably well established at the present time that aptitude

Reprinted with the permission of the author and the publisher from *Journal of Educational Psychology*, 1965, Vol. 56, 111–17. Two tables summarizing analyses of variance have been deleted.

and achievement, as measured by post-test performance, are positively related when programed materials are used (Gleason, 1964; Lambert, Miller, & Wiley, 1962; Williams, 1963). However, in most cases, these correlations may have been due to differences which were present before the program was administered; for it is to be expected (and indeed Gleason, 1964, has found) that pretest performance is also a function of aptitude. It may be, as has been suggested, for example, by Ferster and Sapon (1958) and by Stolurow (1961), that when actual gains are assessed, there is little or no correlation between aptitude and performance. In the present experiment, the relationship of achievement and aptitude was examined both in terms of posttest performance and in terms of amount of gain from pretest to posttest.

Method

SUBJECTS

The subjects were 108 sixth-grade pupils who had not previously been exposed in school to the material taught in the program. Half the subjects were taken from high-aptitude classrooms (mean IQ about 125) and half, from average-aptitude classrooms (mean IQ about 100). Aptitude scores (Philadelphia Verbal Ability Test) were normally distributed, and the variances of the scores at the two aptitude levels did not differ. The subjects were run in two replications, 60 in the first and 48 in the second. Twenty-five additional subjects were dropped, 19 for failure to complete all training and testing sessions, and 6 (randomly) in order to equate N in each group.

MATERIALS

The first 120 frames of the Coronet Program, "Grouping Animals: What is a Mammal?" (1962), were reproduced in booklet form. Each frame appeared on a separate page, with the correct response presented alone on the following page. The program was reproduced in two forms: (a) constructed response (CR): standard format, in which the subject was required to write out answers for every frame; and (b) multiple choice (MC): under each item, presented in the standard way, two response alternatives were printed, and the subject was instructed to underline his choice. All subjects recorded their responses on separate answer sheets.

An objective test was made up of 16 items which required constructed responses. Half the items required the subject to utilize technical terms introduced in the program (such as vertebrae and phylum), and the other half were items to which the subject could respond with familiar words in his standard vocabulary. An additional 16 items, which required a choice between two alternative answers, were also given; half demanded technical terms as responses, and half were of the familiar vocabulary type. These were analyzed as two separate tests, but they were presented to the subject as one test, in which items of both kinds—constructed response and multiple choice—were mixed together.

Items were balanced so that every technical term which was used as a response appeared both on the CR and on the MC tests. In addition, the test was divided into two parts, each of which had to be completed independently. In each half, each response term appeared either as a MC *or* as a CR item, so that there could be no cueing from one type to the other. Half the subjects were given Part 1 first and then Part 2, and for the other subjects, the order was reversed.

PROCEDURE

Subjects were randomly assigned to one of the two training conditions (CR or MC). All subjects were given the objective test as a pretest, and 16 minutes were allowed (8 minutes for each half). On each of 3 successive days of training, starting 4 days after the pretest, subjects worked through 40 frames of the program. The time taken by each subject to work through each day's assignment was recorded. On the day following completion of the program, the subjects were again given the objective test with the same time limits as in the pretest. All subjects finished within the time allowed.

Before the experimental training, subjects were told that this was an experiment in programed instruction and that their class had been specially chosen for participation. It was pointed out that their test scores would not count as part of their school grades, but that they should try to work as well as possible. This type of introduction was chosen on the basis of advice from classroom teachers, and it was felt that it provided good motivation.

Results

Because there were no differences between the two replications in the mean number of correct responses on the pretest as a function of response mode (High Aptitude—HA—: $F < 1$, $df = 1/50$; Low Aptitude—LA—: $F = 1.23$, $df = 1/50$) or on the posttest (HA: $F = 1.67$, $df = 1/50$; LA: $F = 1.73$, $df = 1/50$), or in aptitude (HA: $F = 1.62$, $df = 1/50$; LA: $F = 1.02$, $df = 1/50$), the two replications were combined for analysis.

Means and standard deviations of the performance measures are presented in Table 1. Both pretest and posttest scores were normally distributed, and, contrary to previous findings (Williams, 1963), the variances of the two training modes did not differ on the posttest. There was a significant increase from pretest to posttest on both the constructed-response (CR) test and the multiple-choice (MC) test. A group of subjects who were given no experimental training showed no increase from pretest to posttest.

Table 2 presents the mean number correct on the constructed-response criterion test as a function of training mode, aptitude, and type of test item. As indicated by analysis of variance, there were no differences on the pretest as a function of response mode in training. HA subjects scored signficantly higher than LA subjects, and scores on general vocabulary items were higher than those for technical items. There were no interactions. On the posttest, as on the pretest, aptitude (HA > LA) and type of test item (general > technical) showed significant effects. In addition, subjects who had CR training scored significantly higher than those who had MC training. As predicted, there was a significant interaction between training

Table 1

MEAN NUMBER CORRECT ON THE CRITERION TEST

Test mode	Training mode	Pretest		Posttest		
		M	SD	M	SD	t
CR	CR	4.00	2.22	9.68	3.29	8.67*
	MC	3.48	2.16	7.70	3.35	7.81*
	None	4.20	2.37	5.15	2.78	1.10[a]
MC	CR	10.76	2.05	13.67	1.45	8.56*
	MC	10.31	2.33	13.68	1.54	8.87*
	None	10.35	2.32	11.05	1.70	1.14[a]

* $df = 106$, $p < .001$.
[a] $df = 38$, not significant.

mode and type of test item, and analysis of the simple effects indicated that the difference between the two training modes appeared on technical terms, but not on general terms. There was also an interaction between aptitude and type of test item: The difference between scores on technical items and general items was larger for the LA group than for the HA group.

Table 2

MEAN NUMBER CORRECT ON THE
CONSTRUCTED-RESPONSE CRITERION TEST

		Pretest		Posttest	
Train- ing mode	Apti- tude	Gen- eral items	Tech- nical items	Gen- eral items	Tech- nical items
CR	High	3.59	1.15	6.22	5.41
	Low	2.56	0.70	4.52	3.22
MC	High	2.89	1.22	5.30	4.18
	Low	2.26	0.59	4.07	1.85

Table 3 presents the data from the multiple-choice test. On the pretest, HA subjects scored significantly higher than did LA subjects, and there was a tendency for scores to be higher for technical terms than for general terms ($p <$ .10). Training mode was not a significant effect, and there were no interactions. On the posttest, aptitude (HA > LA) and type of test item (technical > general) were significant effects. There was no significant difference between the training modes, and there were no interactions. It should be noted that two of the three within-subjects error terms exceeded the corresponding between-subjects error terms. Although the data are not available to make a satisfactory assessment, the possibility that the MC test was not highly reliable should be considered.

The difference between pretest and

Table 3

MEAN NUMBER CORRECT ON THE
MULTIPLE-CHOICE CRITERION TEST

		Pretest		Posttest	
Train- ing mode	Apti- tude	Gen- eral items	Tech- nical items	Gen- eral items	Tech- nical items
CR	High	5.52	6.26	6.89	7.40
	Low	4.78	4.96	6.15	6.89
MC	High	5.44	5.78	6.89	7.48
	Low	4.59	4.81	6.04	6.96

posttest scores was taken as a measure of the amount gained from the experimental training, and the results are presented in Table 4. Analysis of the gains on the CR test show results very similar to those of the analysis of CR posttest performance: subjects who had CR training gained more than those who had MC training, and HA subjects gained more than did LA subjects. There was no interaction between these two variables. There was more gain on items requiring technical terminology than on general items. The predicted interaction between training mode and type of test item was significant. Analysis of the simple effects showed that the difference between gains made by the two training modes appeared only on the technical items; on general terms, the two training modes gained equally. The interaction between aptitude and type of test item was also significant, as in the posttest analysis: for HA subjects, there was more gain on technical terms than on general terms, while for LA subjects, the gains on the two types of items were equal.

Table 4 also shows the mean gains on the multiple-choice test. LA subjects gained significantly more than did HA subjects. No other main effect was significant. There was one significant interaction, between training mode and aptitude, such that for HA subjects the two training modes were equal, but for LA subjects the CR training group gained more than did the MC training group.

Table 4

MEAN GAIN (POSTTEST MINUS PRETEST) ON EACH CRITERION TEST

Training mode	Aptitude	CR test		MC test	
		General items	Technical items	General items	Technical items
CR	High	2.63	4.22	1.37	1.18
	Low	1.92	2.44	1.37	1.92
MC	High	2.41	2.96	1.44	1.70
	Low	1.81	1.26	1.52	2.15

CR training took significantly longer ($M = 47.5$ minutes) than MC training ($M = 35.8$ minutes) ($F = 45.60$, $df = 1/104$, $p < .001$). There was no significant difference between the two aptitude groups ($F = 1.50$, $df = 1/104$), and the two variables did not interact ($F = 2.35$, $df = 1/104$). An efficiency score was calculated for each subject by dividing his posttest score by his training time, giving a measure of amount learned per unit of learning time (Goldbeck & Campbell, 1962). MC training was significantly more efficient than CR training ($F = 9.82$, $df = 1/104$, $p < .01$); HA subjects were more efficient than LA subjects ($F = 26.34$, $df = 1/104$, $p < .001$); and the two variables did not interact ($F < 1$). An efficiency measure based on actual gains (difference score divided by training time) showed a slightly different pattern, however. As before, HA subjects were more efficient than LA subjects ($F = 8.00$, $df = 1/104$, $p < .01$), but there was no effect of training mode ($F < 1$). There was an interaction ($F = 4.00$, $df =

$1/104$, $p < .05$), such that for HA subjects there was no difference between the training modes, but for LA subjects, MC training was significantly more efficient.

Discussion

The predicted interaction between training mode and type of test item was significant both on the CR posttest and also when the CR difference scores were analyzed. This finding supports the initial hypothesis of the experiment, namely, that CR training is more effective than MC training when complex technical terminology introduced by the program is required, as compared to when general and familiar vocabulary is required.

The fact that the main effect of training mode was significant on the posttest was unexpected, for to the writer's knowledge, no previous study utilizing a typical continuous-discourse program has shown CR and MC modes to differ significantly. The only previous study showing a significant overall difference between these two modes was that of Fry (1960). In that experiment, the test items required the use of newly acquired Spanish vocabulary; these clearly would fall into the category of technical terminology. In Williams' (1963) experiment, where the overall comparison of CR and MC training did not reach significance but a comparison involving only technical terms did, the criterion test was taken from material designed as part of an actual instructional program. Less than one third of the items required technical terms as responses, and it is likely that tests used with continuous-discourse programs generally include a relatively low ratio of items which require difficult, complex "technical" responses. The present data suggest that CR training is superior to MC training to the extent to which the test demands use of such terms.

There was no effect of training mode in terms of the multiple-choice test, however, nor was there any interaction between training mode and type of test item, indicating that the more difficult constructed-response test reflected differences in the training procedures to which the relatively less-demanding multiple-choice test was not sensitive.

The results show clearly that there is a relationship between aptitude and posttest score. Indeed, if we consider posttest score as the index of achievement—and this is how achievement is usually assessed in the classroom—the conclusion is inescapable that achievement on programed materials is a function of aptitude. Moreover, there is a relationship between aptitude and pretest score, as Gleason (1964) found, indicating that there were differences even before the experimental training. In contrast, however, to studies which showed little or no relationship between aptitude and the amount actually gained from programed materials (e.g., Ferster & Sapon, 1958; Porter, 1959; Williams & Levy, 1964), the present results clearly indicate such a relationship when the more sensitive CR test is analyzed. The posttest differences as a function of aptitude are thus partly attributable to differences present prior to the experiment and partly to the effects of the experimental training.

On the multiple-choice test, however, LA subjects showed higher gains than did HA subjects. This anomalous result is probably due to the ceiling imposed by the test: Some of the HA subjects scored the maximum 16 points on the MC posttest, and it is most likely that they would have shown more improvement if the test had allowed it. Indeed, of those subjects who achieved a maximum score, 86% were in the HA group. In any event, HA subjects were still significantly superior to LA subjects on both posttests, and it is evident that differences in proficiency already present at the start of the experiment were not removed by administering the program, as expected by those who claim that with effective methods of teaching, such as programed instruction, aptitude differences tend to lose their value in predicting achievement.

It should be noted that the fact that there was no effect of training mode on the MC test is not due to a ceiling effect. If such were the case, it would be expected that more CR training subjects (*or* MC training subjects) should score at the maximum, suggesting that that group might have made further gains which the test could not show. However, the subjects who scored at the maximum were almost equally divided between CR and MC training subjects (43% and 57%, respectively), so that the likelihood of achieving the maximum score was not different for the two groups.

While the CR training group scored significantly higher than the MC training group, the size of the difference was relatively small. It might be felt that for practical purposes such small increments are not worth the greater amount of time taken in training. However, the experimental program was a relatively short one, and the small effects seen here would be expected to cumulate. Thus, in any actual instructional sequence, or over the course of several instructional sequences, the differences between these two training modes would be large enough to be of some consequence.

It has often been suggested that several different response modes should be incorporated into a sequence of frames for the purpose of introducing variety into the program. The present data sug-

gest that the effectiveness of such variation would be increased if the constructed-response mode were used on
frames requiring novel, complex, or
technical terminology, and other modes
were introduced elsewhere.

References

Ferster, C. B. and Sapon, S. M. An application of recent developments in psychology to the teaching of German. *Harvard Educational Review*, 1958, **28,** 58–69.

Fry, E. B. A study of teaching machine response modes. In A. A. Lumsdaine and R. Glaser, eds., *Teaching machines and programmed learning*. Washington, D.C.: National Education Association, 1960. Pp. 469–74.

Gleason, G. Programmed learning in sixth grade arithmetic. Paper presented at American Educational Research Association, Chicago, February 1964.

Goldbeck, R. A. and Campbell, V. N. The effects of response mode and response difficulty on programed learning. *Journal of Educational Psychology*, 1962, **53,** 110–18.

Lambert, P., Miller, D. M. and Wiley, D. E. Experimental folklore and experimentation: The study of programmed learning in the Wauwatosa public schools. *Journal of Educational Research*, 1962, **55,** 485–94.

Porter, D. Some effects of year long teaching machine instruction. In E. H. Galanter, ed., *Automatic teaching: The state of the art*. New York: Wiley, 1959. Pp. 85–90.

Stolurow, L. M. Teaching by machine. *Cooperative research monograph no. 6*. Washington: United States Government Printing Office, 1961.

Williams, J. P. A comparison of several response modes in a review program. *Journal of Educational Psychology*, 1963, **54,** 253–60.

Williams, J. P. and Levy, E. I. Retention of introductory and review programs as a function of response mode. *American Educational Research Journal*, 1964, **1,** 211–18.

19

A Programed Introduction to Psychology Versus a Textbook-Style Summary of the Same Lesson

MARIANNE RODERICK / *University of Illinois*

RICHARD C. ANDERSON / *University of Illinois*

Critics of programed instruction often voice the complaint that programs present material in steps that are unnecessarily small, that they involve too much repetition, and that such features are not required to produce learning with "sophisticated" students. Pressey and Kinzer (1964) have completed a study that gives empirical support to doubts about the efficiency of "small-step" programs. They prepared a succinct, textbook-style summary of the first two sets of *The Analysis of Behavior* (Holland and Skinner, 1961). The summary consisted of 643 words, while the section of program upon which it was based contained 1,710 words and also entailed 84 written responses. Students took eight times as long to complete the program as they did to read the summary, yet those who received the summary scored higher on the posttest. Students who completed nine "auto elucidative" questions in addition to reading the summary obtained the highest posttest scores of all. The Pressey and Kinzer experiment suffered from methodological shortcomings. Instead of random assignment of subjects to treatments, whole classes received one treatment or another. The posttest consisted of an essay examination, which was described as "carefully graded" but about which no further information was provided.

The results of the Pressey and Kinzer study would appear to be inconsistent with the findings of other research that has employed *The Analysis of Behavior*. One time-consuming feature of this program is the frequent requirement to make written responses. Yet Williams (1963) has found that overt responding produces better achievement than reading the program

---

Reprinted with the permission of the authors and publisher from *Journal of Educational Psychology*, 1968, Vol. 59, 381–87.

with filled blanks. Casual inspection of *The Analysis of Behavior* suggests that it is a redundant program. It contains many groups of frames in which equivalent responses are required in the presence of identical or nearly identical stimuli. Herein lies another possible contributor to the inefficiency which Pressey and Kinzer seem to have found. However, Coulson and Silberman (1960) reduced a 104-frame section of *The Analysis of Behavior* to 56 frames by removing frames judged to be redundant. Subjects who received the standard program scored higher on the posttest than those who received the shortened version.

Still, it does seem possible that redundancy and overt responding are necessary to produce satisfactory achievement given, and only given, the constraints of a small-step program and that these time-consuming features are not necessary to attain satisfactory achievement from a text. In other words, the value of such features may depend upon the form of the material in which they are included.

There is a plausible argument for considerable redundancy. The presumption is that many apparently similar encounters with the material are necessary in order to arrange discriminations among the terms and concepts being taught. A single statement of a principle may be sufficient if one's goal is merely to have the student name the principle when it appears in the verbatim form employed during instruction. If, on the other hand, one wants the student to be able to recognize various expressions of the principle, to discuss the principle fluently in his own words, to identify new instances of the principle, and to apply the principle to novel cases not treated during the course of instruction, then it may well be necessary to require the student to deal with a variety of forms of the principle and a variety of examples.

There is also a plausible argument for requiring the student to make overt, constructed responses. People learn what they are led to do. A person may spontaneously make appropriate covert responses when reading a text. But then again he may skim, skip difficult sections, or render the material in a way different from that intended by the author. The argument is that the requirement to make overt responses helps to ensure that the student will actually make the responses necessary for learning.

It remains to be seen whether the theoretical advantages of redundancy and overt responding are obtained in practice. To a greater or lesser degree, depending upon the task, the student will already be capable of the responses and discriminations entailed in a lesson. Because of what he has previously learned, the student sometimes may almost spontaneously generalize to appropriate stimulus and response classes. These entering behaviors may be systematically undervalued by programers who have been exhorted to use small steps, keep error rate low, and leave nothing to chance. Students may often be compelled to endure a lengthy "program," when several pages of clear English could evoke the desired performance. Commonly employed techniques for the development and validation of programs do not protect against inefficiency. Presumably during the course of tryout and revision the programer will discover the instances in which he has *underestimated* the difficulty of teaching a concept. But what of the instances in which difficulty has been *overestimated?* As Markle (1967) has indicated in her excellent analysis of the problem, frames upon which students make few errors are very unlikely to be eliminated from a program. Nor will sections of a program be compressed when students do very well on criterion test items measuring what these sections teach. Programs inevitably grow longer rather than shorter when revised. There is no empirical technique in use to detect superfluous redundancy.

If programers tend to underestimate entering behavior in the intended target population, an empirical demonstration of the value of considerable redundancy and overt responding would be difficult. However, a lesson characterized by a gradual progression of small steps, repetition and review, and the requirement to make overt, constructed responses might show to advantage in a population less skilled than the intended target population. One purpose of the present experiment was to compare a small-step program and a textbook-style summary of the material taught by the program with students who were grossly deficient in the entering skills manifested within the population for which the program was designed. These students were assumed to have available few of the responses to be acquired and were assumed unlikely to discriminate and generalize spontaneously in an appropriate manner among stimuli and responses. Consequently, the program was expected to work much better (though not necessarily well in absolute terms) than the summary for the students relatively deficient in entering behavior but, perhaps, only slightly better than the summary for students from the target population. The program used in this study, *The Analysis of Behavior*, was designed for use with college students. The program and summary were compared with both college and high school students.

The redundancy in many small-step programs may not be necessary to produce adequate performance on an immediate test. However, it is well established that repetition and spaced review facilitate retention. Another purpose of the study reported herein was to compare a program and a succinct summary on both an immediate and a delayed achievement test. The program was expected to show to greater advantage on the delayed test than on the immediate test.

The final purpose of the present experiment was to compare a program and a summary on both short-answer test items and equivalent multiple-choice test items. The student may be adequately prepared to recognize a new technical term if he has simply read a passage within which the term was defined and illustrated. However, if he is expected to be able to produce the new term, there is good reason to believe that the requirement to produce the term during the course of instruction will be helpful.

Method

SUBJECTS AND EXPERIMENTAL DESIGN

Eighty-five college sophomores, juniors, and seniors enrolled in an introductory course in educational psychology and a heterogeneous group of 116 high school seniors served as subjects. One college S was dropped due to failure to complete the program, while five high school and seven college Ss were lost because they were absent for the delayed achievement test.

A $2 \times 2 \times 2 \times 2$ design was employed with a repeated measure defining one of the factors. The first factor was training method. Ss completed either the program or the summary. The second factor was subject status. Ss were either high school seniors or college undergraduates. Retention interval was the third factor. The final factor was test mode. Both a short-answer and a multiple-choice achievement test were given to all *S*s.

INSTRUCTIONAL MATERIALS

About half of the *S*s received the standard version of the first four sets of *The Analysis of Behavior*. Each frame occupied a $3\frac{2}{3} \times 8\frac{1}{2}$ in. page; the answer to that frame appeared at the top of the following page. The program was mimeographed on blue paper, through which the following page could not be read. Each set was stapled along the left margin to form a separate booklet.

The remaining half of the subjects studied a textbook-style summary of the first four sets of *The Analysis of Behavior*. The summary was initially written by "lifting" material from the program in the order in which it appeared there. The material was later condensed and arranged in paragraph form to make it readable. Technical terms were underlined upon their introduction into the text, but not again. One example was used to illustrate each principle; no other redundancy was included. Several psychologists read the summary and made suggestions for its improvement. All agreed that material coverage was adequate. Prior to the experiment about 50 high school seniors, attending a different school from the one in which the experiment was conducted, and about 25 college undergraduates, enrolled in an introductory educational psychology course, completed the achievement test on an "open summary" basis. They were asked to read the summary and then take the test, searching through the summary to find or verify answers. From 31% to 100% of the students answered each question correctly. The lowest percentages were obtained from the high school seniors on several

short-answer items. However, none of the latter items were answered correctly by any of the high school seniors in another group of 50 which was not exposed to the summary. These data indicate that all of the test items *could* be answered on the basis of material contained in the summary.

The final version of the summary contained 1,799 words.[1] The program contained 3,398 words and involved 142 written responses.

PROCEDURE

*S*s were assigned to treatments by issuing them "tickets" from a deck stacked in a predetermined random order. The ticket directed *S* either to a room in which the summary was employed or to a different room in which the program was used. The program and summary were not employed within a single room because the program takes more time. There could have been a reactive effect had those completing the program seen many others finishing early.

Subjects in the program group received directions similar to the standard program directions published in *The Analysis of Behavior*. Those who received the summary were told to read at their own rate and were expressly permitted to reread all or part of the material if they so desired.

All *S*s were told that they would receive a test when they finished the program or summary. Assistants completed a control sheet upon which were recorded the order in which *S*s com-

---

[1] For copies of the summary and the achievement test, order NAPS Document No. 00066 from ASIS National Auxiliary Publications Service, % CCM Information Sciences, Inc., 22 West 34th Street, New York, New York 10001, remitting $1.00 for microfiche or $3.00 for photocopies.

pleted the treatment and the time required for each to do so. As each pair of Ss finished the program or summary, one of the two was randomly assigned to receive the immediate achievement test, while the other received an irrelevant (verbal reasoning) test as a time filler and placebo. This procedure equated the immediate and delayed achievement test groups in terms of training time.

High school Ss received the delayed achievement test seven days after the immediate test. The interval between the two tests ranged from six to nine days for the college Ss. The delayed test was not announced, and the teachers and others cooperating in the experiment were asked not to reveal that a test would be given again. The delayed test was given at a regularly scheduled meeting of an educational psychology course in the case of college Ss. In the case of the high school Ss, assistants made what was presumably an unexpected visit to the cooperating school to administer the delayed test. We have no evidence that Ss expected a second test. On the contrary, many Ss seemed genuinely surprised when the delayed test was administered.

The same measure, consisting of 19 short-answer items and 19 equivalent multiple-choice items,[2] was used as both an immediate and delayed test. For pairs of short-answer and multiple-choice items, the item stems were identical. On each occasion the short-answer section was administered first and collected before the multiple-choice test was distributed. The short-answer section was scored on the basis of a criterion list of acceptable answers. The multiple-choice section was machine scored and corrected for guessing.

Results

Table 1 contains the achievement test means for the various experimental conditions. Since there were disproportionate numbers of cases per cell, an unweighted means analysis of variance was performed. This analysis did not include the delayed achievement test scores of Ss who had also completed the immediate test, but only the delayed test scores of Ss who had received an irrele-

---

[2] There were six additional multiple-choice items for which there were no matching short-answer items. The results with these six items are not reported herein, though these results did parallel those obtained with the rest of the test.

Table 1

MEAN PERCENT CORRECT ON THE ACHIEVEMENT TEST

| | | High school | | College | |
		Immediate	Delayed	Immediate	Delayed
	N	30	28	19	19
Program	SA	48.1%	40.0%	83.9%	73.1%
	MC	45.3%	41.5%	83.9%	77.8%
	N	28	25	22	17
Summary	SA	33.3%	29.3%	84.4%	57.6%
	MC	38.3%	36.8%	84.0%	71.5%

Note: Included are delayed test scores only of Ss who were taking the achievement test for the first time.

vant test immediately after the treatment and who were therefore taking the achievement test for the first time.

All four main effects were significant. The unweighted mean percent correct on the achievement test was 61.7 for those who completed the program and 54.4 for those who read the summary, 39.1 for high school students and 77.1 for college students, 62.6 when the test was given immediately and 53.5 when it was delayed, and 56.2 on the short-answer items and 59.9 on the multiple-choice items.

There were two significant interactions. The Training Method × Test Mode interaction is graphed in Figure 1. The figure shows that the advantage of the program over the summary was greater on short-answer items than it was on multiple-choice items. Figure 2 pictures the Retention Interval × Test Mode interaction. There was a smaller decrement over the retention interval on multiple-choice items than on short-answer items.

Completed also was a second analysis involving only delayed achievement test scores. The new variable of interest,

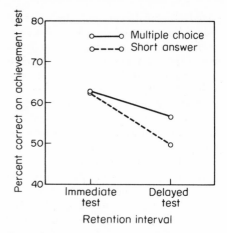

Fig. 2 Percent correct on short-answer and multiple-choice items as a function of Retention Interval.

which turned out to make a significant difference ($F = 8.68$, $df = 1/166$, $p < .01$), was whether S had received the immediate achievement test or an irrelevant test in its place. Those who received the immediate achievement test showed an unweighted mean percent correct of 63.5 on the delayed achievement test, while the percent correct for those who received the irrelevant immediate test was 53.5. Whether or not S took the immediate achievement test interacted significantly with test mode ($F = 9.75$, $df = 1/166$, $p < .01$). Taking the immediate achievement test (see Figure 3) had a greater effect on performance on short-answer items than on multiple-choice items contained in the delayed test.

Training time data indicated that Ss spent about five times as long to complete the program as they did to read the summary.

Discussion

Like Pressey and Kinzer (1964), we found that college undergraduates who

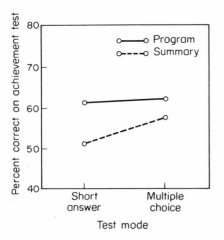

Fig. 1 Percent correct on the achievement test for groups that received the program or the summary as a function of test mode.

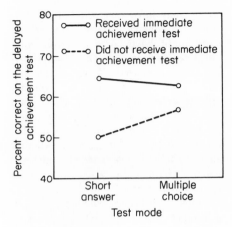

Fig. 3 Percent correct on the delayed achievement test for groups that did or did not receive the immediate achievement test as a function of test mode.

complete the initial sections of *The Analysis of Behavior* score no higher on an achievement test given immediately (83.9%) than do undergraduates who study a summary of the material contained in the program (84.2%). Furthermore, in the present experiment undergraduates spent about four times as long working on the program as they did reading the summary, once again approximately replicating Pressey and Kinzer. However, unlike the Pressey and Kinzer study, which was limited to the performance of college undergraduates on an immediate achievement test, the present study showed a significant overall achievement advantage for the program.

It was expected, for reasons outlined earlier, that the program would be most markedly superior to the summary (1) with high school rather than college students; (2) on the delayed rather than the immediate achievement test; and (3) on short-answer rather than multiple-choice test items. Each of the expected trends appeared in the data; however, only the latter one, the Train-ing Method × Test Mode interaction, was statistically significant in the overall analysis of variance. However, one-tailed t tests indicated that the program led to significantly greater achievement than the summary among high school students ($t = 2.14$, $df \simeq 90$, $p < .05$) but not among college students ($t = 1.23$, $df \simeq 90$, $p > .05$); and on the delayed test ($t = 2.15$, $df \simeq 90$, $p < .05$) but not on the immediate test ($t = 1.22$, $df \simeq 90$, $p > .05$).

The fact that receiving the immediate achievement test produced a significant increment on the delayed test is not surprising, since it has been well documented that responding to questions or test items during or shortly after training facilitates later performance, even when, as in the present case, no knowledge of results is provided (Spitzer, 1939; Michael and Maccoby, 1961; Rothkopf, 1966). There is the question of whether it is more effective to intersperse questions within the instructional materials, such as is done in a program, or more effective to ask a series of questions after a relatively lengthy presentation. The latter alternative proved more potent in the present study. Considering only performance on the delayed achievement test, it made a small (and nonsignificant) difference whether S completed the program (61.3%) or the summary (55.7%), but it made a somewhat larger (and significant) difference whether he received the immediate achievement test (63.5%) or not (53.4%). Among high school Ss, the program and the immediate test produced increments of the same size and these increments were additive. However, with respect to college undergraduates, for whom the program was designed, the optimum treatment was the summary followed by the immediate test (85.9%). This is an instance in which the "teach and test" policy often denigrated by advocates of programed instruction worked best.

Test mode interacted significantly with both training method and presence or absence of the immediate achievement test. In each case the short-answer items were more sensitive to the treatment variable than the multiple-choice items. It is possible that short-answer items are more sensitive than comparable multiple-choice items to *any* treatment difference. However, we prefer a different interpretation. Discounting the fact that it is often possible to eliminate one or more obviously wrong alternatives when considering a multiple-choice item, the presumption is that the two kinds of items require associative learning in about the same measure. The big difference between the item types is in the requisite level of response learning. An *S* will not be able to emit a poorly integrated response of low strength on a short-answer item, but he may be able to pick the response term from among a set of alternatives. The explanation for the greater sensitivity of the short-answer items in this experiment is that both the program, because of the overt response requirement, and the opportunity to practice the achievement test enhanced response learning. If this line of reasoning is correct, multiple-choice items might be as sensitive as short-answer items to treatments which do not differentially affect response learning.

The results of the experiment reported herein do provide some support for the rationale behind such program features as redundancy and overt responding. Nonetheless, as a practical matter, the most noteworthy finding was that for college students the program produced no better achievement than the summary, but took a lot more time. We want expressly to disavow any broad generalizations based on this single instance. Programs that are superficially similar may have very different instructional consequences. Indeed, this experiment might have come out differently had later sections of *The Analysis of Behavior* been used. If our analysis is correct, whether a particular program will outperform a summary will depend upon: the distance between actual entering behavior and desired terminal behavior, that is, "difficulty"; whether entering behavior is over- or underestimated; whether the programer has a bias toward "overkill" in the amount of redundancy included; whether empirical techniques are employed in program construction, testing, and development that guard against superfluous redundancy as well as detect gaps in the task analysis. Not mentioned previously, but obviously important, are such additional factors as the completeness of the task analysis and the adequacy of the design of individual frames.

A program with one or more defects may fail to outperform a summary. Most defects cannot be found in a simple examination of a program. Nor is the demonstration that students who complete a program do well on a posttest a guarantee of freedom from defects; students who get some other form of instruction might do better in less time. We should like to propose that, as a general quality control procedure, those who develop programs accept responsibility for demonstrating that their programs outperform summaries. The textbook-style summary of the material in a program makes a feasible trial horse because it can be prepared inexpensively, almost by formula. Because it contains minimal redundancy, a summary would be especially useful in detecting superfluous redundancy, but it could also provide a yardstick to gauge other shortcomings. Finally, if it were the common practice to compare programs with summaries as a step in validation, generalizations about the limits of programing techniques, as we know them today with various popula- tions and subject matters, might thereby arise.

References

Coulson, J. E. and Silberman, H. F. Effects of three variables in a teaching machine. *Journal of Educational Psychology,* 1960, **51,** 135–43.

Holland, J. G. and Skinner, B. F. *The analysis of behavior.* New York: McGraw-Hill, 1961.

Markle, S. M. Empirical testing of programs. In P. H. Lange, ed., *Programed instruction.* Part II, The 66th yearbook of the National Society for the Study of Education. Chicago, Ill.: University of Chicago Press, 1967.

Michael, D. N. and Maccoby, N. Factors influencing the effects of student participation on verbal learning from films: Motivating versus practice effects, "feedbacks," and overt versus covert responding. In A. A. Lumsdaine, ed., *Student response in programed instruction.* Washington, D.C.: National Academy of Sciences—National Research Council, 1961.

Pressey, S. L. and Kinzer, J. R. Auto-elucidation without programing. *Psychology in the schools,* 1964, **1,** 359–65.

Rothkopf, E. Z. Learning from written instructive material: An exploration of the control of inspection behavior by test-like events. *American Educational Research Journal,* 1966, **3,** 241–49.

Spitzer, H. F. Studies in retention. *Journal of Educational Psychology,* 1939, **30,** 641–56.

Williams, J. P. Comparison of several response modes in a review program. *Journal of Educational Psychology,* 1963, **54,** 253–60.

20

Blackout Ratio and Overt Responses in Programed Instruction: Resolution of Disparate Results

FREDERICK D. KEMP / *Harvard University*

JAMES G. HOLLAND / *University of Pittsburgh*

The rationale underlying programed instruction demands that there be a response to each item in a program. It has also been suggested that the response should be overt to assure that responses occur without fail. However, the now voluminous research literature contains inconsistent results for comparisons of posttest performance after overt response and after either the reading of completed statements or "thinking" the answer. Many studies have failed to find a statistically significant difference, but others have confirmed the advantage of an overt answer. (For a review of relevant studies see Holland, 1965.) One reason suggested for the frequent failure to obtain a significant difference has been that "poorly" programed or unprogramed material may have been used in many of the studies. This point received some support in the results of an experiment (Holland, 1964) in which a program was deliberately altered by leaving blank for the subjects' (*Ss*') completion (*a*) words that could be supplied quite easily, but for reasons relatively unrelated to the principal content of the items, and (*b*) words, which, although relevant to the critical content of the item, could not readily be given by *Ss*. Neither of the experimental programs showed significant differences from reading completed statements. However, the normal program, in which the answer term was both relevant to the critical content and was to be provided by *S*, showed a significant advantage for overt responding.

To determine experimentally whether response mode or other characteristics of programed materials are important, it is necessary to have an unequivocal,

Reprinted with the permission of the senior author and the publisher from *Journal of Educational Psychology*, 1966, Vol. 57, 109–14.

preferably quantitative, experimental definition of the degree to which the material used is programed. Such a measure has recently been developed (Holland & Kemp, 1965). This measure, the blackout ratio, consists of obliterating all material in a program which can be removed without affecting error rate. Such material is unprogramed in the sense that answers are not contingent upon (nor dependent upon) mastery of that material. The quantitative index is expressed as the ratio of the number of words that can be so obliterated to the total number of words in the material. By applying the blackout technique to programs used in previous response-mode studies, this experiment evaluates the claim that the frequent use of relative unprogramed materials has caused the existing ambiguity in the literature regarding the value of an overt response. Excluding high-error-rate programs from consideration, programs which revealed an advantage for overt responding would be expected to have a lower blackout ratio, on an average, than programs which failed to show a difference between overt and covert responding.

Method

BLACKOUT TECHNIQUE

The blacking-out procedure consists of physically obliterating those portions of an item judged to be unnecessary to the correct response. Generally, only whole phrases are blacked out; articles, prepositions, and auxiliary words are blacked out only with the full phrase. In calculating the blackout percentage, the unit used is, simply, words. Blanks are not counted as words and are never blacked out. Where diagrams, mathematical expressions, etc. appear in an item, they are treated somewhat arbitrarily, but consistently, as to what constitutes a "unit." Diagrams are

not blacked out (only the Cardiology Program contained many diagrams); thus, the blackout percentage refers strictly to verbal content. The supplementary materials ("panels") are not blacked out.

Figure 1 presents several samples of the same items from different programs, in normal and blacked-out forms. The range of the blackout ratio is apparent.

After blacking out the material (covering it with black crayon), the blacked-out and un-blacked-out versions are tested with two groups of *S*s to validate the assumptions that answers are independent of the material obliterated. When error rate has been significantly influenced, the blackout must be revised, and the new blackout tested until error rate is unaffected. In practice, the first blackout is often adequate, and there is seldom more than one revision required.

MATERIALS AND APPARATUS

Table 1 lists the programs used and the abbreviations by which they will be referred below. The Cardiology Program is listed on two rows because the Cummings and Goldstein (1962) study classified the items into those with verbal answers and those with pictorial. They had expected that overt responding would be important for pictorial but not for verbal items. However, they found an advantage for overt responding in both types of items.

To keep the size of the experiment within manageable and economical limits, the blackout ratio was determined usually for the first 50 items, but special considerations led to special exceptions. Only the 17 items in the appendix of a report (Roe, Massey, Weltman, & Leeds, 1960) were available for the Statistics Program. The full Cardiology Program was only slightly longer than the 100 items needed to obtain 50 pictorial items; 375 items were used for each of the two forms of the Analysis of Behavior because of the need for this information in relation to another experiment (Holland, 1964). Five programs— AB-A, AB-B, IBM, MG, and Elect (Z)— used supplementary material in the form

Table 1

EXPERIMENTAL PROGRAMS

Program and abbreviation	Author of program	Previous experiment(s) on overt vs. covert responding	No. items	Difference (D) or no difference (ND)
The Diagnosis of Myocardial Infarction —Pictorial Card P	Basic Systems (unpubl.)	Cummings & Goldstein (1962)	57	D
The Diagnosis of Myocardial Infarction —Verbal Card V	Basic Systems (unpubl.)	Cummings & Goldstein (1962)	124	D
Principles of Missile Guidance MG	TMI (Air Force— unpubl.)	Cartier (1963)	100	D
Analysis of Behavior— Version A AB-A	Holland & Skinner (1959)	Holland (1960, 1964) Williams (1963)	375	D
Genetics Genet	Kormondy (unpubl.) [a]	Kormondy & Van Atta (1962)	50	ND
Electricity Elect (Z)	U.S. Navy basic electricity course, Zuckerman, Marshall, & Groesberg (1961)	Zuckerman et al. (1961)	50	ND
Binary Numbers BN	Silverman & Alter (1961)	Silverman & Alter (1961)	50	ND
Experimental Programmed Course: IBM Sorters IBM	IBM (unpubl.)	Hartman, Morrison, & Carlson (1963)	41	ND
Basic Electricity Elect (S)	Silverman & Alter (1961)	Silverman & Alter (1961)	50	ND
Sets, Relations, & Functions Sets	Eigen (1961)	Lambert, Miller, & Wiley (1962)	50	ND
Analysis of Behavior— Version B AB-B	Holland & Skinner (1959)	Holland (1960, 1964)	375	ND
Statistics Stat	Roe et al. (1960)	Roe et al. (1960)	17	ND

[a] This program is considerably different from a published program which was based on it.

of panels, which were given to S at the appropriate times.

All programs, in either normal or blacked-out forms, were used in teaching machines in the Harvard Self-Instruction Room under supervision of a trained attendant. The AB-A and the AB-B programs were used in the Harvard disc machine; all others were used in the Rheem Didak #501 Machine. Some of the cardiology frames were too large for this machine and required a large answer space. For these items, a special booklet was arranged.

All blackouts in the present study were performed by the senior author. An addi-

Normal   Blocked out

Stat

This illustration shows Cells 1 and 2
filled in all the possible ways they can
be filled. Cell 1 = 3 ways, Cell 2 = 2
ways.

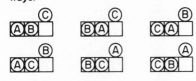

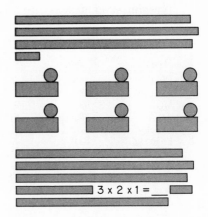

We can see in this illustration that
there is only <u>one</u> way (ball) left to fill
cell 3 when cells 1 and 2 are filled.
Thus, there are 3 x 2 x 1 =___ways
in which 3 balls can fill 3 cells.

Card-V

In the word "electrocardiogram"
indicate which parts mean "electrical",
"heart", and "record".

In the word "electrocardiogram"
indicate which parts mean "electrical",
"heart", and "record".

AB-A

If a response which has been
accidentally reinforced does not
happen to occur just before a
second operation of the magazine,
it will be____.

If a response which has been
accidentally reinforced does not
happen to occur just before a
second operation of the magazine,
it will be____.

AB-B

If a _____ which has been
accidentally reinforced does not
happen to occur just before a
second operation of the magazine,
it will be extinguished.

If a _____ which has been
accidentally reinforced

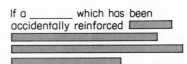

Fig. 1 Sample items from four programs as they appeared in the normal and blacked-out versions.

tional experiment served as a check on
his objectivity and on the objectivity of
the method itself. Ten naïve Ss were
trained using a teaching-machine program
on the blackout technique and compared
with one another and with the present
"blackout specialist" on the blackout ratios
for segments of seven programs. The blackout
ratios assigned by 9 of the 10 Ss correlated
highly with one another. The highest
correlation between naïve Ss' blackouts
was .988. Of the 45 coefficients 26 exceeded
.80, and 9 of the remaining involved the
deviant S. The 9 Ss whose blackouts
correlated with one another also yielded
high correlations with the blackouts of the
blackout specialist in the present study
(coefficients ranging from .614–.923).

SUBJECTS

A total of 195 undergraduates at Harvard
University and Radcliffe College served as

Table 2

PERCENT CORRECT ON EXPERIMENTAL PROGRAMS: MEDIANS AND
INTERQUARTILE RANGES FOR NORMAL AND BLACKED-OUT VERSIONS

	Normal		Blacked-Out	
Program	Median	Interquartile range	Median	Interquartile range
Card P	75.4	54.4–86.4	77.2	73.2–86.0
Card V	68.6	60.3–83.3	71.8	68.4–79.8
MG	93.0	92.0–96.5	93.0	87.2–94.2
AB-A	78.0	61.7–88.4	78.4	70.8–82.9
Genet	82.0	77.5–94.0	82.0	68.0–90.5
Elect (Z)	84.0	73.0–94.0	84.0	72.0–91.0
BN	90.0	81.5–96.0	88.0	77.5–92.0
IBM	85.4	81.7–90.2	80.5	67.7–91.5
Elect (S)	82.0	69.5–92.0	76.0	66.0–84.5
Sets	98.0	96.0–100.0	94.0	91.5–98.0
AB-B	93.6	85.3–97.2	91.7	89.5–93.3
Stat	94.1	82.4–95.6	88.2	80.9–95.6

Note: No p's reached significance.

Ss. They were paid a flat fee for participating in the experiment, based on a rate of $1.50 an hour for a number of hours estimated to be sufficient for relatively slow workers.

PROCEDURE

The basic procedure involved a comparison between 15 Ss taking the normal version of the program and 15 Ss taking the blacked-out version. Most of the data were collected in the summer of 1964. At that time, 30 Ss took AB-A; 30 took AB-B; 30 took Card, Elect (Z), and Sets; and 30 took IBM, Genet, Elect (S), and BN. Earlier, 30 Ss took Stat (Spring 1964), and 30 took MG in the fall of 1965.

Preliminary data indicated the necessity of revising the blacked-out versions of four programs—Stat, IBM, Elect (Z), and Sets. This was done in the fall of 1965, when 15 Ss took the revised version of all four programs. The data were then compared with the data from the normal program which had been gathered earlier.

Results and Discussion

BLACKOUT VALIDATION

Table 2 presents the medians and quartiles of the percentages of correct responses on the various programs for the normal and blacked-out versions of each. Differences in percentage points between normal and blacked-out versions range from 7.4 (Stat) to -3.2 (Card V), but *no* program showed a significant difference in error rate, as measured by the Kolmogorov-Smirnov two-sample test, one tailed (Siegel, 1956).

BLACKOUT RATIOS

Figure 2 shows the percentage of material blacked out of each of the programs. Those programs which have previously shown a difference favoring overt responding are darkened, while those which have shown no difference

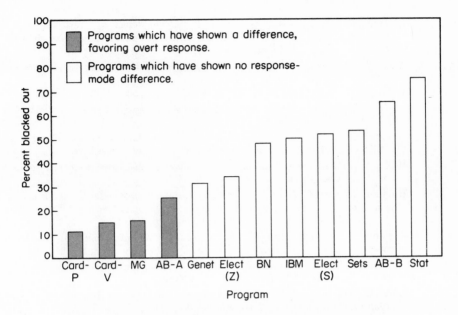

Fig. 2 Percentage of the total number of words which were blacked out of each of the 12 sets of material. (The programs are arranged in rank order from the lowest to highest blackout ratios.)

are plain. The 12 programs yielded a wide range of blackout ratios (11.1%–74.6%). Aside from the primary purpose of this study, it indicates that the blackout ratio as a measure of program adequacy can vary considerably. In theory the measure can vary from 0%–100%, but in practice the extremes are most unlikely. However, a range of 64 percentage points among 12 programs which were not specifically chosen to explore the range is promising for the blackout measure of programing.

It is readily apparent from Figure 2 that the four sets of material from which the least material could be removed are those which in previous research yielded results favoring an overt response. These had blackout ratios ranging from 11.1–25.4, while the other eight sets of material, for programs previously yielding no difference between overt and covert responding, had blackout ratios ranging from 31.0–74.6. In short, the degree to which material is programed is related to whether or not overt responding is important. If the response is unrelated to the critical content on which *S* is later to be posttested, it makes no difference whether, much less how, he responds, but if *S* is tested on things which have served as a contingency for correct responses, overt responding is important.

References

Cartier, F. A. Comparison of overt and covert responding on a programed lesson assigned as homework. *Journal of Programed Instruction*, 1963, **2**, 13–19.

Cummings, Allana Q. and Goldstein, F. S. The effect of overt and covert responding on two kinds of learning tasks. Technical Report No. 620919, Center for Programed Instruction, 1962.

Eigen, L. D. *Sets, relations, and functions.* New York: Center for Programed Instruction, 1961.

Hartman, T. F., Morrison, B. A., and Carlson, M. E. Active responding in programed learning materials. *Journal of Applied Psychology,* 1963, **47,** 343–47.

Holland, J. G. Design and use of a teaching machine program. Paper read at American Psychological Association, Chicago, September 1960.

Holland, J. G. Response contingencies in teaching-machine programs. *Journal of Programed Instruction,* 1964, **3,** 1–8.

Holland, J. G. Research on programming variables. In R. Glaser, ed., *Teaching machines and programmed learning: II. Data and direction.* Washington, D.C.: National Education Association, 1965. Pp. 66–117.

Holland, J. G. and Kemp, F. D. A measure of programing in teaching-machine material. *Journal of Educational Psychology,* 1965, **56,** 264–69.

Holland, J. G. and Skinner, B. F. A self-tutoring introduction to a science of behavior. Harvard University, 1959. (Mimeo)

Kormondy, E. J. and Van Atta, E. L. Experiment in self-instruction in general biology. *Ohio Journal of Science,* 1962, **4,** 4–10.

Lambert, P., Miller, D. M., and Wiley, D. E. Experimental folklore and experimentation: The study of programmed learning in the Wauwatosa public schools. *Journal of Educational Research,* 1962, **4,** 4–10.

Roe, Anne, Massey, Mildred, Weltman, G., and Leeds, D. Automated teaching methods using linear programs. Automated Learning Research Project No. 60–105, University of California, 1960.

Siegel, S. *Nonparametric statistics.* New York: McGraw-Hill, 1956.

Silverman, R. E. and Alter, Millicent. Response mode, pacing, and motivational effects in teaching machines. United States Naval Training Device Center, Port Washington, N.Y., Technical Report No. 507-3, 1961.

Williams, Joanna P. A comparison of several response modes in a review program. *Journal of Educational Psychology,* 1963, **54,** 253–60.

Zuckerman, C. B., Marshall, C. R., and Groesberg, S. Research in the automation of teaching. United States Naval Training Device Center, Port Washington, N.Y., Technical Report No. 661-1, 1961.

V
Reinforcement and Feedback

A *reinforcer* is any stimulus that increases the probability of responses that precede it. That is, when reinforcement follows a particular response, that response is more likely to occur in the future. A large body of research on reinforcement has been accumulated, and the importance of reinforcement for human behavior is beyond question.

Two broad classes of reinforcers may be distinguished: primary and secondary, or conditioned, reinforcers. *Primary reinforcers* are those which serve an obvious biological function. They derive their strength from a state of need or deprivation. Thus, food is a powerful reinforcer for a hungry animal; water is a powerful reinforcer for a thirsty animal, and so on. We can use these reinforcers to produce some desired behavior. Thus, if we want a dog to come when we whistle, we reinforce the hungry animal with food each time he does so. By being reinforced for his behavior, the dog will soon respond to the whistle almost every time he hears it. We may then say that the dog has learned to come when we whistle. Reinforcement has made this response more likely or probable.

Primary reinforcers can also be powerful reinforcers of human behavior. Hungry people will go to great lengths to obtain food. Yet they have limited applicability in the classroom. Primary reinforcers derive their strength from a state of deprivation. And one cannot withhold food, water, or any basic necessity from a child in order to improve his classroom performance.

The second class of reinforcers, however, does have wide applicability in the classroom. This is the class of secondary, or conditioned, reinforcers. *Conditioned* means learned or acquired. The reinforcing value of conditioned reinforcers comes through a process of association with primary reinforcers. Perhaps the best example of a conditioned reinforcer is money. Money has no reinforcing value to a very young child. But through a process of associating money with such things as candy, popsicles, and toys it comes to have reinforcing properties to the child, even though it serves no biological function. Another example of a conditioned reinforcer is social approval. Through a process of learning, the child comes to value social reinforcements administered by his parents, his peers, and his teacher. If this process of social learning proceeds normally in the child, social reinforcement can be a powerful reinforcer throughout his life.

That social reinforcement can serve as a useful and powerful reinforcer in modifying classroom behavior is demonstrated nicely by Allen and her associates in Chapter 21. They describe the use of reinforcement principles to control hyperactivity in a four-year-old boy. This child—very active and having only a limited attention span—would race from activity to activity, never really completing anything. Allen and her associates wanted to get him to stick to one task until it was completed; that is, they wanted to increase his attention span. They used a procedure called differential reinforcement. In *differential reinforcement,* one withholds reinforcement from an undesired activity (such as not maintaining attention) and reinforces the desired activity (such as maintaining attention). This procedure entails another principle of reinforcement: Responses that are not reinforced are *extinguished,* meaning that they become less and less likely to occur. Thus, in this case the experimenters hoped to strengthen the boy's attending behavior and extinguish his hyperactivity. At the beginning of the differential reinforcement training, it was rather difficult to observe any instance of attending behavior that could be reinforced. The child would spend only short amounts of time at any one activity. Hence, the experimenters began with a very low criterion of attending behavior. Gradually the standard for this was raised. (This process of gradually increasing the standards of acceptable behavior is known as *successive approximation.* When an experimenter or teacher applies differential reinforcement to successive approximations of the desired performance, the process is called *shaping.*) Allen and her associates shaped attending responses, using social approval as the reinforcer. Applications of this type of procedure to the classroom should be obvious. A student cannot learn if he does not pay attention to the task. Allen *et al.* have illustrated an effective method of getting the student to pay attention.

O'Leary and Becker (Chapter 22) demonstrate another application of reinforcement—dealing with unwanted behavior in the classroom. They instituted a token reinforcement system to reduce the level of "deviant" behavior (talking, gum chewing, getting out of seats, etc.) in a classroom. The tokens consisted of marks in booklets which could later be exchanged for inexpensive toys and trinkets. Few teachers enjoy the role of disciplinarian, and they often find that negative control is not very effective. An alternative is a reinforcement system such as that employed successfully by O'Leary and Becker. The time-honored methods of yelling at children who misbehave in the classroom, threatening them, punishing them, or sending them to the principal may actually reinforce troublemakers by gaining attention for them from teacher and classmates. If the teacher reinforces or pays attention only to nondeviant behavior, children regarded as troublemakers will often come to engage in nondeviant behavior to receive attention they formerly received for deviant behavior. That such procedures can effect remarkable changes in the classroom is amply demonstrated by O'Leary and Becker.

A note of caution is in order, however. In a subsequent paper provocatively entitled "How to Make a Token System Fail," Kupyers and Becker (1967) illustrate the shortcomings of mishandled applications of reinforcement. Similarly research described by Irwin Lublin in Chapter 23 shows that the effectiveness of social reinforcement depends upon the experimenter's skill in identifying instances of desired behavior and quickly and consistently reinforcing them. Thus, training for administrators of a reinforcement program seems to be recommended.

A prominent feature of programed instruction is the provision for immediate knowledge of results (showing the student the correct answer) after each response. One rationale for this practice is that a knowledge of results serves as a reinforcer. It may not seem intuitively plausible, but it is well established that intermittent reinforcement—providing reinforcement for some, but not all, acceptable responses—brings about greater student persistence than continuous reinforcement. Shirley Lublin (Chapter 24) reasoned, from such research, that intermittent knowledge of results should improve performance in a self-instructional program. Actually the earlier research did not allow a clear prediction, since when new responses must be learned, intermittent reinforcement or knowledge of results usually has a negative effect (Jenkins and Stanley, 1950; Schultz, 1965). For one thing, knowledge of results provides corrective feedback and supplementary information to the student when he makes a mistake. However, no one could have predicted the results Lublin actually obtained. Her surprising finding was that the less frequently knowledge of results was provided, the better the performance, with the group receiving none whatsoever performing best of all. This is inconsistent with either a reinforcing or corrective feedback function for knowledge of results. Lublin interpreted her findings to mean that when knowledge of results was withheld "each frame demanded more attention from the subjects and required the subjects to study each frame more carefully." More research will be required to check this interpretation, as well as several other possible interpretations.

Within programed instruction it is not at all clear at this time whether, or under what conditions, knowledge of results is helpful. However, such knowledge does help students learn more when it is used in conjunction with most forms of instruction, including lecture-discussion techniques in the classroom. This is illustrated in the study by Sassenrath and Garverick described in Chapter 25. They compared three procedures for providing feedback on midsemester tests in a course in educational psychology. On final examination questions which had been included in one or another of the midsemester tests, all three conditions that provided feedback were found superior to those which provided none.

References

Jenkins, W. O. and Stanley, J. C. Partial reinforcement: A review and a critique. *Psychological Bulletin*, 1950, **47**, 193–234.

Kupyers, O. S. and Becker, W. C. How to make a token system fail. Office of Instructional Resources, University of Illinois, Urbana, Illinois, 1967.

Schultz, R. W. Learning of paired associates as a function of pronounceability and percentage occurrence of stimulus or response members. *Journal of Verbal Learning and Verbal Behavior*, 1965, **4**, 494–97.

21

Control of Hyperactivity by Social
Reinforcement of Attending Behavior

K. EILEEN ALLEN / *University of Washington*

LYDIA B. HENKE / *Eugene, Oregon*

FLORENCE R. HARRIS / *University of Washington*

DONALD M. BAER and NANCY J. REYNOLDS / *University of Kansas*

There exists now a series of experimental field studies applying reinforcement principles to problem behaviors of preschool children. These studies have dealt with crying (Hart, Allen, Buell, Harris, & Wolf, 1964), regressive crawling (Harris, Johnston, Kelley, & Wolf, 1964), isolate play (Allen, Hart, Buell, Harris, & Wolf, 1964), passivity (Johnston, Kelley, Harris, & Wolf, 1966), noncooperative behaviors (Hart, Reynolds, Brawley, Harris, & Baer, 1966), self-mutilative scratching (Allen & Harris, 1966), autistic behavior (Brawley, Harris, Peterson, Allen, & Fleming, 1966; Wolf, Risley, & Mees, 1964) and classroom disruptiveness (Allen, Reynolds, Harris, & Baer, 1966). In each instance, the behavior under examination was highly responsive to adult social reinforcement. The present study was conducted to ascertain whether similar social reinforcement procedures could alter the hyperactivity of a 4-year-old boy who tended to flit from activity to activity.

Attending behavior, commonly referred to as "attention span," has long been recognized as a crucial and desirable alternative to hyperactivity. What has not always been clear is the extent to which attending is a behavior which teachers can help a child to develop, althought Patterson (Patterson, Jones, Whittier, & Wright, 1965) has done work in this area with older children. Thus it is of interest to determine if systematic social reinforcement can increase the duration of a young child's attending to an activity, and also to analyze the successive steps a teacher might take in helping a child to main-

Reprinted with the permission of the senior author and the publisher from *Journal of Educational Psychology*, 1967, Vol. 58, 231–37.

tain his attention to an activity for increasingly long periods.

One of the ultimate objectives of preschool education is, of course, to develop a child's skills in using materials constructively and creatively. An essential first step toward this objective sometimes must be to increase the time the child spends engaging in each activity. Fortunately, duration of attention can be defined, observed, and reliably recorded in the field situation.

Method

SUBJECT

James was one of 16 normal children of middle-socioeconomic status who comprised the 4-year-old group in the Laboratory Preschool. At the inception of the study, he was 4 years, 6 months old and had been attending school for 3 months.

James was a vigorous, healthy child with a well-developed repertoire of motor, social, and intellectual skills. Although he made a comfortable adjustment to school during the first few weeks, a tendency to move constantly from one play activity to another, thereby spending little time in any one pursuit, was noted early. Since such behavior is common to some young children in a new situation, his teachers merely continued their friendly efforts to engage him in more prolonged and concentrated use of materials.

After 12 weeks James showed no diminution in number of activity changes during play periods. An observer then was assigned to record his behavior, noting his activities and the time spent in each. Records kept over 5 school mornings showed that although occasionally James stayed with an activity for 1, 2, or 3 minutes, the average duration of an activity was less than 1 minute. The parent reported that the same kind of "flightiness" had long caused concern at home. It was agreed that a study be made of ways of helping James to increase his attending behavior.

PROCEDURE

The procedure for increasing the duration of time spent in any activity was to make adult social reinforcement contingent solely on the subject's (*S*'s) emitting attending behavior for a specified minimum period of time. Attending behavior was defined as engaging in one activity. This included play activity (*a*) with a single type of material, such as blocks or paint; (*b*) in a single location, such as in the sandbox or at a table; or (*c*) in a single dramatic role, such as sailor or fireman. Adult social reinforcement (Bijou & Baer, 1965) was defined as one or more of the following teacher behaviors: talking to *S* while facing him within a distance of 3 feet, or from a greater distance using his name; touching *S*; and giving him additional materials suitable to the ongoing activity. Withholding or withdrawing social reinforcement consisted of turning away from *S*; not looking or smiling at him; not speaking to him; and directing attention to some other child or activity.

One teacher was assigned major responsibility for maintaining reinforcement contingencies. However, since the two other teachers might at times also deliver or withhold reinforcement, each had to remain constantly aware of the conditions in force.

The design of the study required four successive experimental stages, as delineated by Harris, Johnston, Kelley, and Wolfe (1964).

Base line. The existing rate, or operant level, of activity changes prior to systematic application of adult social reinforcement was recorded for several play sessions.

Reinforcement. Social reinforcement was presented immediately when attending behavior had been emitted for 1 unbroken minute. Reinforcement was maintained continuously until *S* left the material or the area or verbalized a change in his play role. Immediately consequent upon such a shift in play activity, social reinforcement ceased until 1 minute of attending behavior had again been emitted.

The procedure was continued until attending behaviors had materially increased.

Reversal. Then, to ascertain whether social reinforcement was, in fact, the determining factor in modifying the behavior under study, reinforcement was again delivered on a noncontingent basis such as had been in effect during the base-line period. This reversal of contingencies was carried out long enough to yield a clear assessment of the effects of the changed conditions.

Reinstatement. During this period, the procedures in effect during the second stage, Reinforcement, were reinstituted. After attending behaviors had again increased in duration, the criterion for presenting social reinforcement was raised to 2 minutes.

RECORDING

The *S*'s attending behavior and adult social reinforcement, as previously defined, were coded and recorded in successive 10-second intervals by an observer using a stopwatch and a red flashlight with a magnet attached. The recording system was similar to that described by Allen *et al.*, (1964). Each period of attending to one activity was enclosed in brackets. Since an increase in attending behavior brought a corresponding decrease in the number of activity changes, data on attending behavior were counted and graphed in terms of the number of activity changes occurring within successive 50-minute time units. In general, but not necessarily, two 50-minute periods indicated 1 day of recording of play time exclusive of teacher-structured or teacher-directed activities.

During the two reinforcement stages, the observer used a flashlight to inform teachers when *S* reached criterion for social reinforcement. The cue consisted of placing the flashlight on top of the metal clip of the clipboard as soon as *S* had emitted 1 minute, and later 2 minutes, of attending behavior. When the behavior stopped, the observer removed the flashlight and placed it under the clipboard, where it remained out of sight until criterion attending behavior had again been emitted. Teachers were instructed to maintain awareness of the flashlight position and to check it before giving *S* any social reinforcement.

Periodically throughout the study, observer reliability on attending behaviors, activity changes, and adult social reinforcement was checked by an independent observer. Agreement of records ranged between 97% and 100%. No post checks of attending behavior could be made because the study was terminated by the close of the school year, at which time the family moved to another city.

In addition to the behavior under study, some assessment of whether social aspects of *S*'s behavior were affected by changes in his attending behavior seemed desirable. Therefore, *S*'s verbalizations, proximity to, and cooperation with other children were defined, coded, and recorded. The quality of the child's social behavior was estimated by considering cooperative behavior as high-level social behavior and mere proximity as low-level social behavior, in contrast to isolate behavior, which was considered non-social. Interrater reliability on these parameters ranged between 84% and 92%.

Results

Base line—Stage 1. The number of activity changes that James made in each of 21 successive 50-minute periods of free-choice play, both indoors and out, is shown in Figure 1. The fewest number of activity changes was 33 during Period 12, with an average duration of 1 minute 29 seconds per activity. The greatest number of activity changes occurred in Period 14, with 82 changes and an average duration of 37 seconds per activity. The overall average for the base-line stage (the operant level of the behavior under study) was 56 activity changes per 50-minute period, with an average duration of 53 seconds per activity.

The amount of teacher reinforcement presented to James on a random, noncontingent basis averaged 16% of each session. This rate was within the normal range in this preschool of amount of teacher attention per child.

Reinforcement—Stage 2. This stage comprised seven 50-minute periods, as shown in Figure 1. Activity changes ranged from a high of 41 in Period 22 (the first period of experimental procedures) to a low of 19 in Period 28 (the last period of experimental procedures). The overall average of activity changes for the seven periods was 27, with an average duration of 1

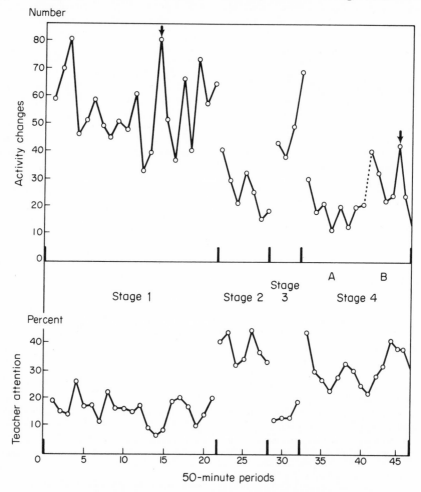

Number

Fig. 1 Number of activity changes of *S* during 50-minute periods throughout study, compared with concurrent percentage of time *S* received teacher attention. (Stage 1, base line of activity change under noncontingent attention. Stage 2, attention contingent on 1 minute of attending. Stage 3, base-line condition. Stage 4, contingent attending as in Stage 2, at dotted line, criterion for attending raised to 2 minutes. Arrows indicate days *S*'s mother visited.)

minute 51 seconds per activity, or twice that of the base-line stage. Teacher reinforcement during Stage 2 averaged 38% of each period.

Reversal—Stage 3. During the four-period reversal stage (Figure 1, Stage 3), activity changes rose markedly. An average of 51 activity changes per period occurred, with an average duration of 59 seconds per activity. Both measures (number of changes and average duration) were comparable to the base-line stage. During the reversal teacher attention averaged 14% of each period.

Reinstatement—Stage 4-A and B. Reinforcement contingencies during Stage 4-A, Figure 1, were the same as those in effect during Stage 2. Under these conditions, the rate of activity changes again dropped markedly, with a high of 31 and a low of 12 (Periods 33 and 36, respectively). The overall average of activity changes for the eight period of Stage 4-A was 20, with an average duration of 2½ minutes per activity. Teacher reinforcement during Stage 4-A averaged 31% of each period.

In Period 41 (Figure 1, Stage 4-B) the criterion for delivery of social reinforcement was raised to 2 minutes of attending behavior. Some increase in number of activity changes occurred during Period 41, with a subsequent leveling off. During this part of Stage 4, the greatest number of activity changes was 45, occurring in Period 45; the fewest number, 16, occurred in Period 47. The average number of activity changes during Stage 4-B was 32 per period, with an average duration of 1 minute 34 seconds per activity. Teacher reinforcement averaged 33% of each period.

The overall average for Stage 4 (A and B combined) was 27 changes per session, with an average duration of 1 minute 51 seconds per activity.

Social behavior. The quality of social behavior was defined and measured as high, low, and isolate. Although not under experimental manipulation, it merits remark for its constancy throughout the experimental procedures. The averages per session were as follows:

	High	*Low*	*Isolate*
Stage 1	45%	37%	16%
Stage 2	50%	38%	12%
Stage 3	48%	40%	13%
Stage 4-A	49%	39%	13%
Stage 4-B	41%	44%	15%

These figures were well within the range of the preschool's normative social behavior.

Discussion

The data presented in Figure 1 give strong support to the hypothesis that attending behavior is "teachable" in the sense that it can be shaped and maintained by teachers. Moreover, adult social reinforcement again appears to be a powerful instrument for this purpose. When adult social reinforcement was given in a systematic fashion, solely as an immediate consequence of continuing attending behavior, the number of activity changes diminished to half the number that occurred under the more usual, nonsystematic adult procedures of the base-line and reversal stages.

The continuing fluctuation of the data which occurred during each of the experimental periods may merit comment. Behavior does, of course, vary somewhat from day to day. The factors responsible for this variability were not brought under experimental control. Many of them are inherent in the field setting of a preschool, and could hardly be controlled in that setting. It is apparent, though, that systematic control of adult social reinforcement, which is readily achieved, is sufficient to override these factors (Baer & Wolf, 1966).

Two of the high points in activity changes, Periods 14 and 45, suggest possible examples of such uncontrolled factors. During Periods 14 and 45 James's mother was present for the entire morning. She interacted with him freely each time he contacted her and went with him frequently when he requested her to come and look at a particular object or play situation. In addition, she made frequent suggestions that he "settle down" and paint her a picture, build with blocks, or "tend to his own business." The mother appeared to have more reinforcing value than the teachers on these novel occasions, a fact not surprising in itself. The fact that the mother was often reinforcing behaviors incompatible with the behavior that teachers were shaping strengthened the original hypothesis that the child's short attention span was in fact a function of adult social reinforcement.

No formal attempt was made to secure data on the quality of James's attending behaviors. In the judgment of the teachers, however, the quality improved steadily. During Stage 4, James frequently spent 15 to 20 minutes pursuing a single activity, such as digging, woodworking, or block building. Within these activities he made frequent excursions to get additional materials relevant to his project, such as a wheelbarrow or a dirt sifter. By definition, such departures were recorded as activity changes, even though he returned and continued with the same play. Such occasions, clearly delineated in the data, teachers considered evidence of improved quality of attending, for the side trips were relevant to a core activity, rather than a series of unrelated activity changes as were typical of Stages 1, 2, and 3. The data thus are probably a conservative estimate of the degree of change produced in James's attention span.

The data on social behavior are of particular interest, for they answer in part the often-asked question regarding peripheral effects on overall behavior patterns when one aspect of behavior is under intensive treatment. As was indicated, there was no change in the quality of James's social interaction, already deemed satisfactory by teachers at the start of the study, though the number of separate contacts did decrease, as was predicted. These data add to the evidence that only the behavior specifically being worked on increases or decreases as a function of the reinforcement contingencies.

Throughout the study, the child's mother was informed of procedures and progress in frequent parent conferences. However, no systematic attempts were made to program presentation of social reinforcement from the family. For one thing, the mother worked, and there were frequent changes of babysitters. Nevertheless, the mother reported that James had "settled down" considerably at home. She kept no data to substantiate these statements, but did relate several incidents which indicated that there was some generalization from preschool to home. Both the mother and the teachers judged that James was eminently more ready for kindergarten at the end of the study than he had been prior to it. The importance of intensive attending behavior to future learning is obvious. The ease of socially altering attending behavior in *either* direction, while perhaps less obvious, is no less important to an analysis of children's intellectual, perceptual, and social development.

References

Allen, K. E., Hart, B. M., Buell, J. S., Harris, F. R., and Wolf, M. M. Effects of social reinforcement on isolate behavior of a nursery school child. *Child Development*, 1964, **35**, 511–18.

Allen, K. E. and Harris, F. R. Elimination of a child's excessive scratching by training the mother in reinforcement procedures. *Behaviour Research and Therapy*, 1966, **4**, 79–84.

Allen, K. E., Reynolds, N. J., Harris, F. R., and Baer, D. M. Elimination of disruptive classroom behaviors of a pair of preschool boys through systematic control of adult social reinforcement. Unpublished manuscript, University of Washington, 1966.

Baer, D. M. and Wolf, M. M. The reinforcement contingency in preschool and remedial education. Paper presented at the meeting of the Carnegie Foundation Conference on Preschool Education, Chicago, January 1966.

Bijou, S. W. and Baer, D. M. *Child development.* **2.** New York: Appleton-Century-Crofts, 1965.

Brawley, E. R., Harris, F. R., Peterson, R. F., Allen, K. E., and Fleming, R. E. Behavior modification of an autistic child. Unpublished manuscript, University of Washington, 1966.

Harris, F. R., Wolf, M. M., and Baer, D. M. Effects of adult social reinforcement on child behavior. *Young Children*, 1964, **20**, 8–17.

Harris, F. R., Johnston, M. K., Kelley, C. S., and Wolf, M. M. Effects of positive social reinforcement on regressed crawling in a preschool child. *Journal of Educational Psychology*, 1964, **55**, 35–41.

Hart, B. M., Allen, K. E., Buell, J. S., Harris, F. R., and Wolf, M. M. Effects of social reinforcement on operant crying. *Journal of Experimental Child Psychology*, 1964, **1**, 145–53.

Hart, B. M., Reynolds, N. J., Brawley, E. R., Harris, F. R., and Baer, D. M. Effects of contingent and non-contingent social reinforcement of the isolate behavior of a nursery school girl. Unpublished manuscript, University of Washington, 1966.

Johnston, M. K., Kelley, C. S., Harris, F. R., and Wolf, M. M. An application of reinforcement principles to development of motor skills of a young child. *Child Development*, 1966, **37**, 379–87.

Patterson, G. R., Jones, R., Whittier, J., and Wright, M. A. A behavior modification technique for the hyperactive child. *Behaviour Research and Therapy*, 1965, **2**, 217–26.

Wolf, M. M., Risley, T., and Mees, H. Application of operant conditioning procedures to the behavior problems of an autistic child. *Behaviour Research and Therapy*, 1964, **1**, 305–12.

22

Behavior Modification of an Adjustment Class: A Token Reinforcement Program

K. DANIEL O'LEARY / *State University of New York at Stony Brook*

WESLEY C. BECKER / *University of Illinois*

Praise, teacher attention, stars, and grades provide adequate incentive for most pupils to behave in a socially approved way. However, for some students —notably school dropouts, aggressive children, and some retarded children— these methods are relatively ineffective. Where the usual methods of social approval have failed, token reinforcement systems have proven effective (Birnbrauer, Bijou, Wolf, and Kidder, 1965; Birnbrauer and Lawler, 1964; Birnbrauer, Wolf, Kidder, and Tague, 1965; Quay, Werry, McQueen, and Sprague, 1966). Token reinforcers are tangible objects or symbols which attain reinforcing power by being exchanged for a variety of other objects, such as candy and trinkets, which are back up reinforcers. Tokens acquire generalized reinforcing properties when they are paired with many different reinforcers. The generalized reinforcer is especially useful since it is effective regardless of the momentary condition of the organism.

For the children in this study, generalized reinforcers such as verbal responses ("That's right" or "Good!") and token reinforcers such as grades had not maintained appropriate behavior. In fact, their teacher noted that prior to the introduction of the token system, being called "bad" increased the children's inappropriate behavior. "They had the attitude that it was smart to be called bad. . . . When I tried to compliment them or tell them that they had done something well, they would look around the room and make faces at each other." It is a moot question whether the poor academic performance of these children was caused by their

---

Reprinted with the permission of the senior author and the publisher from *Exceptional Children*, 1967, 637–42. Two tables have been deleted.

disruptive social behavior or vice versa. It was obvious, however, that the disruptive behaviors had to be eliminated before an academic program could proceed.

Although classroom token reinforcement programs have proved effective in modifying behaviors, the pupil-teacher ratio has usually been small. In the study by Birnbrauer, Wolf, et al. (1965), a classroom of 17 retarded pupils had four teachers in the classroom at all times. Quay (1966) had one teacher in a behavior modification classroom of five children. One purpose of this project was to devise a token reinforcement program which could be used by one teacher in an average classroom; a second purpose was to see if a token system could be withdrawn gradually without an increase in disruptive behavior by transferring control to teacher attention, praise, and grades, with less frequent exchange of back up reinforcers.

Subjects

The subjects for this study were 17 nine-year-old children described as emotionally disturbed. They had IQ scores (Kuhlmann-Anderson) ranging from 80 to 107. They had been placed in the adjustment class primarily because they exhibited undesirable classroom behaviors, such as temper tantrums, crying, uncontrolled laughter, and fighting. The children were in the classroom throughout the day with the exception of some remedial speech and reading work. Although the token reinforcement system was in effect for the whole class, the study focused on the eight most disruptive children.

Method

The children's deviant behaviors were observed by two students in the classroom from 12:30 to 2:10 three days a week. A third student made reliability checks two days a week. Among the behaviors recorded as deviant were the following: pushing, answering without raising one's hand, chewing gum, eating, name calling, making disruptive noise, and talking. Each student observed four children in random order for 22 minutes each session. Observations were made on a 20 second observe/10 second record basis. Deviant behaviors were recorded on observation sheets. During the observations, the children had three structured activities: listening to records or stories, arithmetic, and group reading. During these activities, instruction was directed to the whole class, and the children were expected to be quiet and in their seats.

BASE PERIOD

The teacher was asked to handle the children as she normally did. To obtain data which reflected the frequency of deviant pupil behavior under usual classroom procedures, a base period was used. The observers were in the classroom for three weeks before any baseline data were recorded. At first the children walked up to the observers and tried to initiate conversation with them. As the observers consistently ignored the children, the children's approach behaviors diminished. Thus, it is likely that initial show-off behavior was reduced before baseline measures were obtained.

The average interobserver reliability for individual children during the four week base period, calculated on the basis of exact agreement for time interval and category of behavior, ranged from 75 to 100 percent agreement. A perfect agreement was scored if both observers recorded the same behavior within a 20 second interval. The reliabilities were calculated by dividing the number of perfect agreements by the number of different responses observed. The percentage of each child's deviant behavior for any one day was calculated by dividing the number of intervals in which one or more deviant behaviors occurred by the number of observed intervals for that day. As can be seen from Figure 1, there was a fairly stable base rate of deviant behavior with a slight increasing trend.

TOKEN REINFORCEMENT PERIOD

On the first day of the token period, the experimenter placed the following instructions on the blackboard: In Seat, Face Front, Raise Hand, Working, Pay Attention, and Desk Clear. The experimenter then explained the token procedure to the children. The tokens were ratings placed in small booklets on each child's desk. The children were told that they would receive ratings from 1 to 10 and that the ratings would reflect the extent to which they followed the instructions. The points or ratings could be exchanged for a variety of back up reinforcers. The reinforcers consisted of small prizes ranging in value from 1 to 29 cents, such as candy, pennants, comics, perfume, and kites. The total cost of the reinforcers used during the two months was $80.76. All the pupils received reinforcers in the same manner during class, but individual preferences were considered by providing a variety of items, thus maximizing the probability that at least one of the items would be a reinforcer for a given child at a given time.

The experimenter repeated the instructions at the beginning of the token period each day for one week and rated the children to provide a norm for the teacher. It was the teacher, however, who placed the ratings in the children's booklets during the short pause at the end of a lesson period. The ratings reflected the extent to which the child exhibited the appropriate behaviors listed on the blackboard. Where possible, these ratings also reflected the accuracy of the child's arithmetic work.

The number of ratings made each day was gradually decreased from five to three, and the number of points required to obtain a prize gradually increased. For the first three days, the tokens were exchanged for reinforcers at the end of the token period. For the next four days, points were accumulated for two days and exchanged at the end of the token period on the second day. Then, for the next 15 days, a three day delay between token and reinforcers was used. Four day delays were employed for the remaining 24 school days. During the three and four day delay periods, tokens were exchanged for reinforcers at the end of the school day. By requiring more appropriate behavior to receive a prize and increasing the delay of reinforcement it was hoped that transfer of control from the token reinforcers to the more traditional methods of teacher praise and attention would occur.

After the first week, the teacher made the ratings and executed the token system without aid. Procedures were never discussed when the children were present.

The children also received group points based on total class behavior, and these points could be exchanged for popsicles at the end of each week. The group points ranged from 1 to 10 and reflected the extent to which the children were quiet during the time the ratings were placed in the booklets. The number of group ratings made each day was gradually decreased from five to three as were the individual ratings. However, since the children were usually very quiet, the number of points required to obtain a popsicle was not increased. The points were accumulated on a thermometer chart on the blackboard, and the children received popsicles on seven of the eight possible occasions.

At first, the teacher was reluctant to accept the token procedure because of the time the ratings might take. However, the ratings took at most three minutes. As the teacher noted, "The class is very quiet and usually I give them a story to read from the board while I give the ratings. One model student acts as the teacher and he calls on the students who are well behaved to read. . . . This is one of the better parts of the day. It gave me a chance to go around and say something to each child as I gave him his rating. . . ."

The rating procedure was especially effective because the teacher reinforced each child for approximations to the desired final response. Instead of demanding perfection from the start, the teacher reinforced evidence of progress.

In addition to the token procedure, the teacher was instructed to make comments, when appropriate, such as: "Pat, I like the way you are working. That will help your rating." "I am glad to see everyone turned around in their seats. That will help all of you get the prize you want." "Good, Gerald. I like the way you raised your hand to ask a question."

A technique used by the teacher to extinguish the deviant behavior of one child was to ignore him, while at the same time reinforcing the appropriate behavior of another child. This enabled the teacher to refrain from using social censure and to rely almost solely on positive reinforcement techniques, as she had been instructed.

The investigators also were prepared to use time out from positive reinforcement (Wolf, Risley, and Mees, 1964) to deal with those behaviors which were especially disruptive. The time out procedure involves isolating the child for deviant behavior for a specified period of time. This procedure was not used, however, since the frequency of disruptive behavior was very low at the end of the year.

The average interobserver reliability for individual children during the token period ranged from 80 to 96 percent. The reliabilities were recorded separately for the base and token periods because reliabilities were higher during the token period when the frequency of deviant behavior was low.

Results

As can be seen from Figure 1, the average percentage of deviant behavior at the end of the year was very low. The daily mean of deviant behavior during the token procedure ranged from 3 to 32 percent, while the daily mean of deviant behavior during the base period ranged from 66 to 91 percent. The average of deviant behavior for all children during the base period was 76 percent, as contrasted with 10 percent during the token period. The change from the base period to the token period was highly significant ($p < .001$). Using an omega squared, it was estimated that the treatment accounted for 96 percent of the variance of the observed deviant behavior.

An examination of the individual records (Figure 2) shows the small degree of individual variation and differences in deviant behavior from the base to the token period. Although subjects 2 and 7 exhibited more deviant behavior than others during the token period, the percentage of deviant behavior was obviously less than during the base period. The percentage of deviant behavior declined for all pupils from the base to the token period.

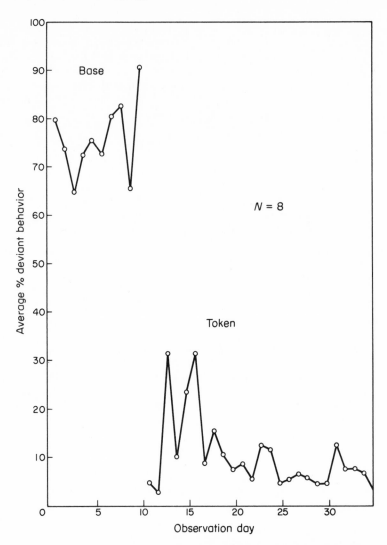

Fig. 1 Average percentages of deviant behavior during the base and token periods.

Discussion

At least two variables in addition to the token procedure and social reinforcement possibly contributed to the change in the children's behavior. First, during the baseline and token phases of this demonstration, the teacher was enrolled in a psychology class which emphasized operant and social learning principles. The influence of this class cannot be assessed, although the dramatic and abrupt change from the base to the token phase of the demonstration makes it seem highly implausible that the psychology class was the major variable accounting for the change. However, in a replication of this study now being

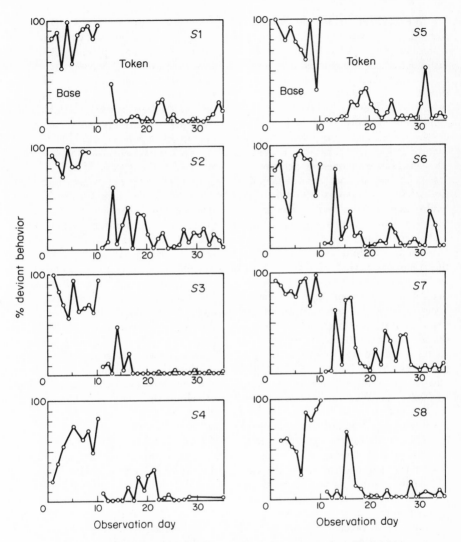

Fig. 2 Percentages of deviant behavior for individual children during base and token periods.

planned, the teacher will receive only a short introduction to the basic principles and subsequent instruction by the experimenter throughout the procedure.

Secondly, the reduction in deviant behavior enabled the teacher to spend more time giving children individual attention during the token phase of the experiment. She had time to correct and return the children's work promptly, thus giving them immediate feedback. She was also able to use teaching materials not previously used. Some children who had not completed a paper for two years repeatedly received perfect scores. The immediate feedback and new materials probably contributed to the maintenance of appropriate behavior.

An experiment within the Skinnerian paradigm involves the establishment of a stable base rate of behavior; next, environmental contingencies are applied and the maladaptive behavior is reduced. The contingencies are then withdrawn and there is a return to base conditions. Finally, the environmental contingencies are again instituted and the maladaptive behavior decreased. This procedure of operant decrease, increase, and finally decrease of maladaptive behavior in association with specific environmental conditions demonstrates the degree of stimulus control obtained by the technique.

A return to base conditions early in the treatment period of this study was not carried out because of a concern that the enthusiasm and cooperation generated by the program throughout the school system might be severely reduced. There is little doubt that a return to base conditions following three or four weeks of the token procedure would have resulted in an increase in disruptive behavior. When a reversal was used by Birnbrauer, Wolf, et al. (1965), a number of children showed a decline in the amount of studying and an increase in disruptive behavior. As an alternative, it was planned to return gradually to baseline conditions during the following fall, but radical changes in pupil population prevented this reversal.

Without a reversal or a return to baseline conditions, it cannot be stated that the token system and not other factors, such as the changes that ordinarily occur during the school year, accounted for the observed reduction of deviant behavior. To demonstrate clearly the crucial significance of the token procedure itself, a systematic replication with different children and a different teacher is planned. As Sidman (1960) noted, "An investigator may, on the basis of experience, have great confidence in the adequacy of his methodology, but other experimenters cannot be expected to share his confidence without convincing evidence" (p. 75).

Two interesting implications of this study are the effects of delay of reinforcement and generalization. The use of tokens provides a procedure which is intermediate between immediate and delayed tangible reinforcement. In Birnbrauer, Wolf, et al.'s (1965) class of severely retarded children, this delay was extended from a few seconds to over an hour. Some educable children studied for many days for check marks only and, presumably, the knowledge that they were approaching a goal. All the children in the present study worked for four days without receiving a back up reinforcer. In addition, more than one child made the comment toward the end of school that next year they would be old enough and behave and work well without the prizes.

Anecdotal records indicate that after the token procedure was put into effect, the children behaved better during the morning session, music, and library periods. These reports suggest that a transfer to normal classroom control using social reinforcement and grades would not be very difficult. Also, the gang behavior of frowning upon "doing well" disappeared. Some children even helped enforce the token system by going to the blackboard just before class began and reading the instructions to the class.

References

Birnbrauer, J. S., Bijou, S. W., Wolf, M. M., and Kidder, J. D. Programmed instruction in the classroom. In L. P. Ullman and L. Krasner, eds., *Case studies in behavior modification.* New York: Holt, Rinehart and Winston, 1965. Pp. 358–63.

Birnbrauer, J. S. and Lawler, Julia. Token reinforcement for learning. *Mental Retardation*, 1964, **2,** 275–79.

Birnbrauer, J. S., Wolf, M. M., Kidder, J. D., and Tague, Cecilia E. Classroom behavior of retarded pupils with token reinforcement. *Journal of Experimental Child Psychology*, 1965, **2,** 219–35.

Quay, H. C., Werry, J. S., McQueen, Marjorie, and Sprague, R. L. Remediation of the conduct problem child in the special class setting. *Exceptional Children*, 1966, **32,** 509–15.

Sidman, M. *Tactics of scientific research.* New York: Basic Books, 1960.

Wolf, M. M., Risley, T. R., and Mees, H. L. Application of operant conditioning procedures to the behavioral problems of an autistic child. *Behavior Research and Therapy*, 1964, **1,** 305–12.

23

Sources of Differences in Effectiveness Among Controllers of Verbal Reinforcement

IRWIN LUBLIN / *California State College at Los Angeles*

Since the publication (1955) of Joel Greenspoon's now-famous dissertation of 1950 reporting the operant conditioning of plural nouns through verbal reinforcement, a large number of investigators have reported success in conditioning a variety of response classes, utilizing several different verbal reinforcers (Krasner, 1958; Salzinger, 1959). On the other hand, a number of investigators have reported failure to obtain conditioning effects of this sort. At least four studies have reported failure to replicate Greenspoon's experiment itself (Mandler & Kaplan, 1956; Matarazzo et al., 1960; Spielberger & DeNike, 1962; Sullivan & Calvin, 1959). Furthermore, for every published unsuccessful attempt to demonstrate verbal conditioning, there are many unpublished failures known to workers in this area. These failures make it clear that verbal conditioning is a more elusive phenomenon than was at first supposed.

The present study examined certain variables which might underlie this elusiveness. Specifically, it examined those variables relating to the experimenter as a dispenser of verbal reinforcements and sought to relate them to variations in the degree to which experimenters obtain conditioning effects.

Although a few studies (Binder et al., 1957; Kanfer, 1958; Reece & Whitman, 1962; Solly & Long, 1958) have found differences in effectiveness between different experimenters within the same experimental situation, they have not related these differences to variations in the established parameters of the reinforcement situation. Indeed, they have neither measured nor standardized these parameters. Therefore, it is very difficult to say what may have been the

Reprinted with the permission of the author and the publisher from Proceedings of the 73rd Annual Convention of the American Psychological Association, 1965.

198

determinants of success in some instances or of failure in others.

In the experimental literature of operant conditioning, three variables play a well-established role as determinants of the effect of reinforcement: (a) delay of reinforcement, (b) probability of reinforcement, (c) magnitude of reinforcement. In the verbal reinforcement of verbal responses, one might then expect that the following characteristics of the experimenter would be important determinants of his effectiveness: (a) *speed*, i.e., *E*'s typical delay after a word in the chosen response class is uttered before he utters his reinforcement; (b) *consistency*, i.e., *E*'s overall success in emitting reinforcement when it is appropriate and withholding it when it is not; and (c) *potency*, i.e., one would expect that personality differences among *E*s would make the approval utterances of some *E*s more 'potent' secondary reinforcers than the utterances of others (more rewarding to the *S*s).

Method

The present investigation was designed to assess individual differences among *E*s in the skill (speed and consistency) with which they dispensed verbal reinforcements, to assess the *E*s on a number of personality variables, and then to relate these skill and personality differences to differences among the *E*s in their ability to condition *S*s.

SUBJECTS

There were actually two categories of subject: the subjects proper (*S*s), of whom there were 255, and the experimenter-subjects or experimenters (*E*s), of whom there were 11. Of the 11 *E*s, six (three male, three female) were volunteers from an introductory psychology class; four (all male) were graduate students in clinical psychology; and one

was a female social worker. The 220 experimental *S*s were comprised of 118 males and 102 females. The 35 control *S*s included 19 males and 16 females. All *S*s were recruited from introductory psychology classes. Neither the *E*s nor the *S*s were told anything about the nature or design of the study until its completion.

PROCEDURE

Two different tape-recorded stories with different narrators (one male, one female) were used to assess the *E*s on speed and consistency of reinforcement. In individual sessions, each *E* was asked to listen to the stories and to say "mm-hmm" following each mention of the father in the story, whether by name, pronoun, or descriptive title. These pretest sessions were themselves recorded to allow auditors to score each *E*, using exact typescripts of the standard stories.

An *E*'s speed score was defined as the mean number of words *E* allowed to intrude following the utterance of a word in the designated response class before he began to utter his reinforcement. In this manner, it proved possible to measure the individual delays with great precision. *E*'s consistency score was defined as the number of times on the test tapes that he followed an instance of the designated response class ("father") with a reinforcement, minus the number of times that he failed to reinforce or did so erroneously.

Following this pretest for skill, each *E* was assigned a random sample of 20 *S*s. In individual, tape-recorded sessions, he asked each *S* to tell a ten-minute story about a child and his father, and again, as in the pretest, was to say "mm-hmm" following each mention of the father in the story. A control group of 35 *S*s was run by the investigator with the same story instructions but no reinforcement. Each *E*'s effectiveness score was then computed as the mean ratio (per cent) of father references to child references for his 20 Ss.

Following this conditioning phase of the investigation, each E was asked to take the Edwards Personal Preference Schedule (PPS), which yields scores on 15 personality "needs" and is widely viewed as a psychometrically sophisticated instrument for the delineation of 'normal' personality variation (Edwards, 1954).

Results

The skill measures taken from the pretest tapes differentiated the 11 Es reliably. Their speed ranks on the two different stories were virtually identical, yielding a Spearman correlation of .96, while the rank correlation for consistency scores was .70 ($p < .01$). This stability justified combining the scores from the two pretest stories in the remainder of the data analysis.

Eight of the Es exceeded the control group in their effectiveness scores with a mean superiority of 9.12%. Three Es scored slightly below the control group (mean difference of 1.85%). The Wilcoxon test gives the probability of such differences between the control group and the experimental groups as .01 under the null hypothesis (that no conditioning took place).

The question of whether there were ordered differences among the 12 treatment groups in a direction predictable by the Es' ranks on speed or on consistency of reinforcement was tested by application of the Jonckheere analysis-of-variance technique (Jonckheere, 1954). The Jonckheere test for treatments ordered according to the Es' ranks on speed yielded a p value of .017. It was concluded that there were significant differences among the treatments in a direction predictable by the respective

Es' relative speed of reinforcement. The Jonckheere test for treatments ordered according to the Es' consistency ranks was not significant ($p = .20$).

Spearman correlations were computed between the Es' ranks on conditioning effectiveness and their ranks on each of the 15 PPS personality scales. Two-tailed tests were made in accordance with the exploratory nature of this part of the investigation. None of the correlations approached significance with the prominent exceptions of those involving need for Abasement and need for Endurance, which were high and significant ($-.75$ and .70, respectively). Neither of these was correlated with speed-of-reinforcement scores.

Discussion

The results of the present study permit the conclusions that: (a) experimenters differ from one another in their skill as dispensers of verbal reinforcement; (b) one aspect of this skill, i.e., speed of reinforcement, is related to effectiveness in verbal conditioning; (c) need for Abasement and need for Endurance (PPS) predict verbal-conditioning effectiveness fairly well. (Abasement is a negative influence.) Subject to cross-validation, it seems likely that these personality variables are related to that dimension of reinforcement described in the present context as "potency."

These results are consistent with the operant conditioning literature. Delay of reinforcement has long been known to be crucial within narrow limits. The negative findings with respect to consistency are to be viewed against the general picture obtained from 25 years' work with partial or intermittent reinforcement in animals. Many studies have indicated that lowering the percentage of trials on which reinforcement is given does not necessarily lead to a weaker response tendency. With respect to the effects of personality variables on verbal-reinforcement effectiveness, it will be recalled that differences in "potency" among reinforcements were considered roughly analogous to differences in the magnitude of reinforcement in animal operant conditioning, where quality and quantity of reinforcement have long been known to affect performance (Hall, 1961).

In general, it appears that the present results confirm the proposition that the parameters of verbal reinforcement operate in much the same fashion as the parameters of primary reinforcement. Hence, they suggest why some experimenters fail to obtain verbal conditioning effects. The answer may lie in their failure to optimize the parameters of the reinforcement situation.

References

Binder, A., McConnell, D., and Sjoholm, Nancy A. Verbal conditioning as a function of experimenter characteristics. *Journal of Abnormal and Social Psychology*, 1957, **55**, 309–14.

Edwards, A. L. *Edwards personal preference schedule.* New York: Psychological Corporation, 1954 (manual revised 1957).

Greenspoon, J. The reinforcing effect of two spoken sounds on the frequency of two responses. *American Journal of Psychology*, 1955, **68**, 409–16.

Hall, J. F. *Psychology of motivation.* Chicago: Lippincott, 1961.

Jonckheere, A. R. A distribution-free k-sample test against ordered alternatives. *Biometrika*, 1954, **41**, 133–45.

Kanfer, F. H. Verbal conditioning: Reinforcement schedules and experimenter influence. *Psychological Reports*, 1958, **4**, 443–52.

Krasner, L. Studies of the conditioning of verbal behavior. *Psychological Bulletin*, 1958, **55**, 148–70.

Mandler, G. and Kaplan, W. K. Subjective evaluation and reinforcing effect of a verbal stimulus. *Science*, 1956, **124**, 582–83.

Matarazzo, J. D., Saslow, G., and Pareis, E. N. Verbal conditioning of two response classes: Some methodological considerations. *Journal of Abnormal and Social Psychology*, 1960, **61**, 190–206.

Reece, M. M. and Whitman, R. N. Expressive movements, warmth, and verbal reinforcement. *Journal of Abnormal and Social Psychology*, 1962, **64**, 234–36.

Salzinger, K. Experimental manipulation of verbal behavior: A review. *Journal of General Psychology*, 1959, **61**, 65–94.

Solley, C. M. and Long, J. When is "uh-huh" reinforcing? *Perceptual and Motor Skills*, 1958, **8**, 277.

Spielberger, C. D. and DeNike, L. D. Operant conditioning of plural nouns: A failure to replicate the Greenspoon effect. *Psychological Reports*, 1962, **11**, 355–66.

Sullivan, M. W. and Calvin, A. D. Further investigation of verbal conditioning. *Psychological Reports*, 1959, **5**, 79–82.

24

Reinforcement Schedules, Scholastic Aptitude, Autonomy Need, and Achievement in a Programed Course

SHIRLEY CURRAN LUBLIN / *California State College at Los Angeles*

It is generally agreed that programed instruction might be one way of increasing teaching efficiency. Since about 1955, there has been a wealth of studies investigating important variables in programed instruction (e.g., Coulson, 1962; Lumsdaine & Glaser, 1960). The present study investigated three questions relating to programed instruction.

The first question investigated was whether or not different schedules of reinforcement are differentially related to achievement in a programed course. W. D. Edwards (1960), on the basis of an interview with Skinner, reports that a variable-ratio schedule should be the most advantageous. Porter (1957) and Fry (1963) both suggest that schedules of reinforcement might make knowledge of results in programed instruction a more effective reinforcer. On the other hand, Amsel (1960) and Lumsdaine (1962) are both critical of the application of reinforcement schedules to pro-

gramed instruction. Amsel states that programed instruction shapes a complex behavior pattern, each step of which should be reinforced. And Lumsdaine feels that program writers should stress prompting cues, rather than reinforcement schedules. Krumboltz and Weisman (1962), using four levels of fixed-ratio confirmation and two levels of variable-ratio confirmation in a 177-frame programed textbook, found no evidence that the various schedules of confirmation (reinforcement) produced different effects on a criterion test.

The second question investigated in the present study was derived from Skinner's (1958) suggestion that programed instruction should tend to reduce individual differences in performance due to aptitude. Several

Reprinted with the permission of the author and the publisher from *Journal of Educational Psychology*, 1965, Vol. 56, 295–302.

studies (Ferster & Sapon, 1958; Irion & Briggs, 1957; Porter, 1959) have shown no relationship between scholastic aptitude (intelligence) and achievement in programed instruction. Yet, other studies (Ashbaugh, 1962; Hartman, Morrison, & Carlson, 1962; Lambert, Miller, & Wiley, 1962; McNeil & Keislar, 1961) did find such a relationship.

The third question investigated in this study was whether autonomy need is related to achievement in a programed course. The nature of programed instruction is such that it requires the student to be somewhat self-governing, self-sufficient, or autonomous. That is to say, programed instruction requires the student to work alone, evaluate his own work, and be satisfied with little personal feedback from the teacher.

Method

SUBJECTS

The subjects consisted of 219 students enrolled in an introductory psychology course at Pennsylvania State University during the spring term, 1964. No student had taken a psychology course prior to this one. The students were enrolled in a wide variety of curricula, both science and nonscience.

MATERIALS

The Programed Course. The first 27 sets (1,144 frames) of Holland and Skinner's (1961) *The Analysis of Behavior* were used. The content of the course and examination items were unfamiliar to the students. The 27 sets of the programed course were mimeographed on $8\frac{1}{2} \times 14$ inch paper, with the frames appearing in sequence, the answer to any given frame immediately following the frame itself. At the beginning of each set the title, number of frames, and estimated time to complete the set were also reproduced for the stu-

dent. There were four versions of each set, corresponding to the four treatment groups, as follows: (a) continuous reinforcement, where each frame was followed by the correct response; (b) variable-ratio 50% reinforcement, where a random 50% of the frames of each set were followed by the correct response; (c) fixed-ratio 50% reinforcement, where every other frame (even numbered) was followed by the correct response; (d) no reinforcement, where all answers were omitted. Occasionally a set within the program included an exhibit, for example, some tables or a graph, to which the subject was to refer throughout the set. Each subject was allowed to pace himself on the program. The program was the constructed-response (fill-in-the-blank) type.

The Criterion Test. The test items (also constructed response) were selected from the review items supplied in *The Analysis of Behavior* and written by Holland and Skinner (1961). No test item was a duplication of an item or frame found within the programed course. The criterion test contained 55 frames, calling for 100 responses for which the subjects were required to provide answers. Thus, the total of possible points on the criterion test was 100; scores from this test constituted the dependent variable. The reliability of the criterion test (Kuder-Richardson Formula 21) was computed to be .88.

Scholastic Aptitude Measure. The Pennsylvania State University academic aptitude examination (referred to as the Moore-Castore), taken by all freshmen at the University, was used as a measure of scholastic aptitude. The reliability of the Moore-Castore (Kuder-Richardson Formula 20) is .94. According to Marks (1964), correlations between the Moore-Castore and the Educational Testing Service Scholastic Aptitude Test vary from .42 to .73, depending on the sample and revision of the test used.

Personality Measure. The Edwards Personal Preference Schedule (EPPS) was used to measure each student's level of autonomy need. (For the sample used in this study, the Pearson r between scholastic aptitude and autonomy need is .14, which is significant at the .05 level.)

Programing Device. All sheets required for any given unit of work were inserted into a manila envelope measuring $11\frac{1}{2} \times 14\frac{1}{2}$ inches. During the first class meeting before the programed portion of the course began, each student was given a mimeographed copy of the following instructions, which were elaborated upon in class:

> At the next class meeting, you will receive the first part of your textbook. You will receive an additional section during each class meeting. You will work on each section handed you during the class meeting. Each section of the textbook builds upon the previous section; therefore, you *must* work on the sections in order. . . . *How you will use the book:* When you come to class next time, you will receive a manila envelope with the first section of the book in it. You will take the stack of sheets out of the envelope, keeping them in correct order. Place the envelope over the stack, and use is as a cover sheet. Slide the envelope down until the first sentence, or frame or item, of the text is revealed. Read it. Write in the blank the correct response called for. Slide the cover sheet down slowly, and reveal what the correct response should have been. Then go on to the next item, or frame. Uncover only one item at a time—this is essential. It is also essential to *write* your response *before* looking to see if the correct answer is there. For some of you, the answer will not always appear. It is essential that you follow these instructions. When you glance ahead without first putting down an answer, you commit yourself to only a vague and poorly formulated guess. This is not effective and in the long run makes the total task more difficult. It is important to do each item in its proper turn. Do not skip. Avoid careless answers. When you have completed page one of the stack, place it on the bottom of the

deck, and proceed to page two, working until you have finished all the material.

Proctors circulated throughout the classroom during each class meeting. Their task was to help distribute and collect materials, and to see that the above instructions were followed. It was found to be financially unfeasible to supply teaching-machine devices for the large experimental sample.

Each student paced his own work and was allowed to leave when finished. There was always ample time in the class period for the student to complete the programed material assigned for that period. Each student had his own manila envelope. Pasted on the front of each envelope was a sheet upon which the student recorded the time required to complete each set.

Anonymous Attitude Questionnaire. The attitude questionnaire, filled out anonymously by all students after completion of the programed course, was designed to (a) obtain some indication of the students' attitudes towards the programed portion of the course, (b) determine how much and what type of outside reading in psychology had taken place during the course of the experiment, (c) determine how many students had seen the programed material prior to the experiment, and (d) determine whether the students knew the source of the programed material.

PROCEDURE

The 219 subjects were randomly assigned to the following four treatment groups: continuous-reinforcement, variable-ratio 50% reinforcement, fixed-ratio 50% reinforcement, and no-reinforcement. Within each of the four treatment groups, subjects were subsequently designated as in one of two aptitude groups (above average or below average, using norms for science and nonscience curricula). An analysis of variance was performed on this 2×4 factorial design. Again, within each of the four treatment groups, subjects were subsequently assigned into one of three autonomy-need groups (high-autonomy-need, average-autonomy-need, or low-autonomy-need). Subjects with autonomy scores falling above the eighty-fifth percentile (using norms for college men and women, reported by Edwards, 1959) were placed in the high-autonomy-need group. Subjects with autonomy scores falling between the seventeenth and eighty-fourth percentiles were placed in the average-autonomy-need group. Finally, subjects with autonomy scores falling at or below the sixteenth percentile were placed in the low-autonomy-need group. An analysis of covariance was performed on this 3×4 factorial design.

The experimenter conducted three regularly scheduled class meetings per week, during which time the subjects worked on the programed material. When the subjects arrived for each class meeting, they found in their assigned seats their own individual envelopes containing the programed material for that day. Each subject began on the materials when he arrived, worked independently, and left upon completion of the materials. The experimenter decided how much material was to be covered each day, using as a guide the estimated times provided by Holland and Skinner (1961) for each set. Care was taken to assign little enough material so that the self-pacing aspect of the situation was not violated. All subjects worked on the same material on any given day; that is, no subjects were ahead or behind other subjects in course content, unless a subject had missed a class, in which case that subject was behind until the weekly make-up class. All subjects began and finished the material on the same date. The subjects were not told the authors of the programed materials until the end of the course. The subjects understood that there would be an examination on the programed material, but they were not told exactly when this test would be given.

Upon completion of the programed material, which lasted 4 weeks, all subjects took (a) the criterion test, (b) the EPPS, and (c) the anonymous attitude questionnaire.

Table 1

ORIGINAL AND ADJUSTED MEANS FOR EACH GROUP OF THE AUTONOMY NEED $\times$ SCHEDULES OF REINFORCEMENT DESIGN

Group	SD	Mean criterion Test scores Original	Adjusted
Continuous-rein-forcement	11.99	55.88	55.63
Variable-ratio 50% reinforcement	11.72	61.60	61.55
Fixed-ratio 50% reinforcement	14.09	57.75	57.86
No-reinforcement	13.08	62.88	63.09
High-autonomy-need	14.70	57.97	56.99
Average-autonomy-need	12.58	59.34	59.58
Low-autonomy-need	12.76	62.80	64.01

Results

The performance of the several groups on the criterion test is shown in Table 1. An analysis of variance was computed for the hypothesis regarding schedules of reinforcement and aptitude, using scores on the criterion test (described above) as the dependent variable. The effect of schedules of reinforcement exceeds the critical value for a .05-level test ($F = 3.29$). Hence, the data permit the conclusion that the different reinforcement schedules produced different amounts of learning. The no-reinforcement group scored highest, followed by the variable-ratio 50% group, followed by the fixed-ratio 50% group. The continuous-reinforcement group scored lowest. Significance was also reached for the effect of aptitude, the observed F ratio (27.77) exceeding the critical value for a .01-level test. The above-average-aptitude group scored higher. No interaction effect was observed between schedules and aptitude.

An analysis of covariance was computed to test the hypothesis regarding schedules of reinforcement and autonomy need. (The assumptions underlying analysis of covariance were met.) The adjusting variable was Moore-Castore scores; the dependent variable was total items correct on the criterion test. The Pearson r between Moore-Castore scores and criterion-test scores was .46 ($p <$ .01). The F ratio provides a test of the hypothesis concerning schedules, after the criterion data have been adjusted for the linear trend on the covariate (aptitude). This test was significant beyond the .01 level ($F = 4.74$). Thus the experimental data again indicate statistically significant differences between the criterion-test scores for the four reinforcement groups. The test on the effect of autonomy need exceeds the critical value for a .05-level test ($F = 3.28$). Surprisingly, the low-autonomy group scored higher on the criterion. Thus, there are statistically significant differences between levels of autonomy need. The test for an interaction effect does not reach the required significance level.

Since a significant F ratio was found for both schedules of reinforcement and levels of autonomy need, it is appropriate to employ the Tukey b analysis (Winer, 1962) to determine whether each mean is significantly different from each of the others. From this analysis, it is concluded that on the criterion test: (a) the continuous-reinforcement group scored significantly lower than both the variable-ratio 50% group ($q = 3.84$, $p < .05$) and the no-reinforcement group ($q = 4.84$, $p < .05$); (b) the fixed-ratio 50% group scored significantly lower than the no-reinforcement

group ($q = 3.44$, $.05 < p < .10$),[1] but not significantly lower than the continuous-reinforcement or the variable-ratio 50% groups on the criterion test; and (c) the high-autonomy-need group scored significantly lower than the low-autonomy-need group on the criterion test ($q = 4.10$, $p < .05$).

In order to evaluate some factors that might be related to differences found among groups, the results of the anonymous questionnaire and the working times per set data were analyzed. The results from the anonymous questionnaire indicated that the continuous-reinforcement group did the most outside reading in psychology during the experiment; nevertheless, they scored lowest on the criterion test. Although the continuous-reinforcement group and the no-reinforcement group represent, respectively, lowest and highest groups on the criterion test, they seemed to express the most similar attitudes towards the experiment. These two groups expressed the most unfavorable attitudes towards the programed portion of the course. It is unlikely then that differences in attitude towards the program or experiment account for the differences obtained between the two groups. Only two subjects (one in the no-reinforcement group and one in the variable-ratio 50% group) had seen the program before the experiment, and so this factor could not have accounted for the observed differences between these large groups.

An evaluation of the average time spent on each set of the program revealed that the no-reinforcement group spent more time, on the average, than the other three groups on 25 of the 27 sets. Time spent on set, then, is related

---

[1] Previously, the Duncan multiple-range test (A. L. Edwards, 1960) had been computed on these data. This particular comparison reached significance at the .05 level.

to score on the criterion test. The cause of this relationship is not discernible from the present data, for many factors may have been operating during the extra time spent on the sets. One factor, for example, may be number of times the subjects read each frame.

Discussion

The finding of significantly higher criterion-test scores obtained by the no-reinforcement group adds to a recent finding reported by Holland (1964). Using a 140-item program, Holland obliterated 68% of the words in the program (all material obliterated was noncontingent response material). One group of subjects used the obliterated program; the control group worked on the normal, nonobliterated program. Results showed no differences between the two groups of subjects in terms of error rate on the program. Holland suggests that the obliterated portion of the program was "not truly programed" (i.e., did not require a response from the subject). An alternative interpretation is that in both the present study and in the Holland study, obliteration of part of each frame demanded more attention from the subjects and required the subjects to study each frame more carefully. In the present study, omission of the answers may have caused the subjects to look for confirmation of their responses in succeeding frames.

According to Moore,[2] the frames within a program can be so over prompted, or so over cued, that the subject can work through the entire program emitting a correct response for each frame without learning the mate-

rial within the frames at all. This suggests that making the program too easy for a subject may interfere with learning. Such an effect may have been operating within the continuous-reinforcement group in the present study. An analysis of the set-time records showed that this group always spent the least amount of time on a set. The task required of this group of college students may have been so unchallenging, or so uninteresting (due to the 100% predictability that the right answer would immediately be supplied), that they were not attending to the concepts being taught in the frames.

Exactly why the no-reinforcement version of the program should have produced higher criterion-test scores is impossible to determine within the framework of this particular study. It may be added, however, that the form of the criterion test was most like the form of the no-reinforcement version of the program, and the subjects in this group were accustomed to responding to that type of frame or question found on the criterion test. The adjustment required for going from the program directly to the criterion test may have been a handicap for the subjects in the remaining treatment groups.

The finding that the no-reinforcement version produces higher criterion-test scores may also be related to the question of optimal step size in programs. Skinner (1954), Holland (1960), and Lumsdaine and Glaser (1960) state that small steps (i.e., more steps in the program) are a more desirable feature in programs than are large steps (i.e., fewer steps to cover the same amount of material). Presumably this is because small steps give the subject more support and more prompts and allow the subject to proceed from one frame to another with a large percentage of reinforcement and a low

[2] J. W. Moore, personal communication, March 1964.

probability of making an error. One might consider that removal of reinforcement, as in the case of the no-reinforcement and ratio versions of the program in the present study, had the effect of making the steps larger and more difficult. Yet such a feature may have required the subject to formulate and test his own hypotheses as he went along. He may have been more careful about the response he chose to write down and thus may have made fewer errors on the program. This feature may in turn have improved retention of the material being taught. If so, the present study lends some support to the hypothesis that programs should be written with large steps rather than small steps. Perhaps subjects who have to "work" for their reinforcement profit most from the program. The no-reinforcement subjects in this study probably had to remain more active and more attentive to obtain their reinforcement.

Another factor that may have been operating in the no-reinforcement group is something similar to the Zeigarnik effect. That is to say, confirmation following a correct response may actually detract from retaining that response. A form of "closure" may have caused the subjects to dismiss the item from further consideration. The no-reinforcement subjects, on the other hand, may have retained responses for long periods of time, until they found confirmation for them in subsequent frames, if indeed they found reinforcement for them at all.

Finally, the unpredictability of confirmation found in the variable-ratio 50% program may have produced a novelty effect which did not obtain in the continuous-reinforcement and fixed-ratio 50% programs. Such a novelty effect may have increased the motivation of the subjects in the former group. Slot machines are on a variable-ratio schedule, a schedule which produces highly motivated responding. Skinner (1959, p. 139) points out that this particular schedule produces what seems to be "excited" behavior, where the subject responds not for the net amount of reinforcement, but rather for the excitement that such a schedule produces.

The "wash-out" effect of programed instruction on scholastic aptitude suggested by Skinner is not confirmed in this study. Those subjects having above-average academic ability performed significantly better on the criterion test than did those subjects possessing below-average academic ability. It seems that no matter how well written the program, high-ability subjects learn the concepts better than lower-ability subjects.

Level of autonomy need was found to be related to success on the criterion test. The direction of the relationship, however, was unexpected. That is, the low-autonomy-need subjects scored significantly higher on the criterion test than did the high-autonomy-need subjects. The average-autonomy-need subjects scored between these two extreme groups, but not significantly different from either one. It is possible that the high-autonomy-need subjects felt that, since they were required to come to class, make up all classes missed, work on just that material handed them by the experimenter, and return all material at the end of each class, their needs for autonomy were frustrated. These same aspects of the experimental sessions may have made the low-autonomy-need subjects feel more comfortable. This fact may have contributed to their higher criterion-test scores. Presumably then, if all the subjects had been given the entire program and left on their own, the difference would have favored the high-autonomy-need subjects.

References

Amsel, A. Error responses and reinforcement schedules in self-instructional devices. In A. A. Lumsdaine and R. Glaser eds., *Teaching machines and programmed learning: A source book.* Washington, D.C.: National Education Association, 1960. Pp. 506–16.

Ashbaugh, W. H. The effect upon achievement of written responses to programmed learning material for students of differing academic ability. Unpublished doctoral dissertation, Pennsylvania State University, 1962.

Coulson, J. E., ed. *Programmed learning and computer-based instruction.* New York: Wiley, 1962.

Edwards, A. L. *Edwards personal preference schedule (manual).* New York: Psychological Corporation, 1959.

Edwards, A. L. *Experimental design in psychological research.* New York: Holt, Rinehart, & Winston, 1960.

Edwards, W. D. Skinner's teaching machines. In A. A. Lumsdaine and R. Glaser, eds., *Teaching machines and programmed learning: A source book.* Washington, D.C.: National Education Association, 1960. Pp. 611–14.

Ferster, C. B. and Sapon, S. M. An application of recent developments in psychology to the teaching of German. *Harvard Educational Review,* 1958, **28,** 58–69.

Fry, E. B. *Teaching machines and programmed instruction.* New York: McGraw-Hill, 1963.

Hartman, T. F., Morrison, Barbara, and Carlson, Margaret. Active responding in programmed learning materials. Unpublished manuscript, IBM Thomas J. Watson Research Center, October 1962.

Holland, J. G. Teaching machines: An application of principles from the laboratory. *Journal of Experimental Analysis of Behavior,* 1960, **3,** 275–87.

Holland, J. G. Isolation of nonresponse contingent portions of teaching-machine programs. Paper read at Eastern Psychological Association, Philadelphia, April 1964.

Holland, J. G. and Skinner, B. F. *The analysis of behavior.* New York: McGraw-Hill, 1961.

Irion, A. L. and Briggs, L. J. Learning task and mode of operation variables in use of the subject matter trainer. Technical Report No. AF PTR C-TR 57–8, October 1957, Air Force Personnel and Training Research Center, Lowry Air Force Base, Colorado.

Krumboltz, J. D. and Weisman, R. G. The effects of intermittent confirmation in programed instruction. *Journal of Educational Psychology,* 1962, **53,** 250–53.

Lambert, P., Miller, D. M., and Wiley, D. E. Experimental folklore and experimentation: The study of programed learning in the Wauwatosa public schools. *Journal of Educational Research,* 1962, **55,** 485–91.

Lumsdaine, A. A. Some theoretical and practical problems in programmed instruction. In J. E. Coulson, ed., *Programmed learning and computer-based instruction.* New York: Wiley, 1962. Pp. 134–54.

Lumsdaine, A. A. and Glaser, R., eds. *Teaching machines and programmed learning: A source book.* Washington, D.C.: National Education Association, 1960.

Marks, E. Evaluation of the Pennsylvania State University academic aptitude examination. University Park: Pennsylvania State University, April 1964.

McNeil, J. D. and Keislar, E. R. Individual differences and effectiveness of auto-instruction at the primary grade level. *California Journal of Educational Research,* 1961, **12,** 160–64.

Porter, D. A. A critical review of a portion of the literature on teaching devices. *Harvard Educational Review,* 1957, **27,** 126–47.

Porter, D. A. Some effects of year long teaching machine instruction. In E. Galanter, ed., *Automatic teaching: The state of the art.* New York: Wiley, 1959. Pp. 85–90.

Skinner, B. F. The science of learning and the art of teaching. *Harvard Educational Review,* 1954, **24,** 86–97.

Skinner, B. F. Teaching machines. *Science,* 1958, **2,** 137–58.

Skinner, B. F. *Cumulative record.* New York: Appleton-Century-Crofts, 1959.

Winer, B. J. *Statistical principles in experimental design.* New York: McGraw-Hill, 1962.

25

Effects of Differential Feedback from Examinations on Retention and Transfer

JULIUS M. SASSENRATH / *University of California, Davis*

CHARLES M. GARVERICK / *State University of New York at Buffalo*

Educators and psychologists often urge teachers to discuss—or in some way feed back to students—detailed results regarding the students' performances on examinations and other school work in order that the work can be a learning as well as an evaluation situation. One of the earliest experiments on feedback from examinations by Plowman and Stroud (1942) showed that high school students who could look over an examination with their errors corrected eliminated about 50% of their errors on a retest a week later. More recently Page (1958) reported that most students who received comments on their examination papers did better on their next examination than students who received no comments. Page's experiment like the earlier one by Hurlock (1925) on verbal praise and blame emphasized encouragement or incentives and their effect on learning. The present experiment focuses more on cognitive rather than motiva-

tional aspects of feedback, inquires into both the retention and transfer effects of feedback, and deals with university rather than elementary and secondary school students.

Although most of the available research has focused on feedback versus no feedback, two exceptions that bear closely on the present experiment are those by Curtis and Wood (1929) and Stone (1955). Curtis and Wood compared four methods of scoring examinations and found that, although all four were worthwhile, methods providing for discussion were the best. Stone proposed that the value of feedback would be proportional to the amount of information contained in it. Stone obtained superior results on retests for students who were informed as to why alternative

Reprinted with the permission of the senior author and the publisher from *Journal of Educational Psychology*, 1965, Vol. 56, 259–63.

answers were wrong. Students who received less complete information did less well.

In the present experiment it is hypothesized that, with an increase in the amount of information from feedback on midsemester examinations, there will be an increase in scores on a retention section and a transfer section of a final examination. In terms of increasing amounts of information, (a) one group would receive no feedback, (b) a second group would check over their answers from correct ones placed on a blackboard, (c) a third group would have the questions discussed by the instructor, and (d) a fourth group would reread material for questions they answered incorrectly as well as correctly.

Method

SUBJECTS AND DESIGN

Four-hundred eighty-seven students from classes in introductory psychology participated in the experiment. Five instructors each handled two of the four feedback treatments in an effort to control for instructor effects. Due to differences in number of students enrolling in and completing the course in the various classes, there were 129 subjects in the control-no-feedback group, 97 subjects in the group which checked their answers on the board, 116 subjects in the group in which instructors discussed the questions, and 145 subjects in the group which looked up the answers in the book. The subjects were not randomly assigned to the classes but were registered depending upon their class schedules and attempts by the instructors to keep classes approximately equal in size. Subjects did not know which instructor would teach what class.

PROCEDURE

Cronbach's (1963) *Educational Psychology*, second edition, was the basic text for the course. Multiple-choice items covering textbook readings were selected jointly by the five instructors from Test Item File Series 1 by J. S. Orleans, which accompanies the text. Items were selected if they met the following criteria: (a) evaluated the more major objectives of the course, (b) evaluated the subject's knowledge of concepts and principles rather than facts, names, etc., and (c) were short and clear. Three 40-item multiple-choice midsemester examinations were given to each of the classes. In addition, each instructor had some multiple-choice, completion, or essay questions which were not common to all the classes. These examinations occurred approximately at the end of the first, second, and third months after the semester began.

Two days after taking each of the three midsemester examinations, classes were given one of the following experimental treatments:

1. The subjects in the control-no-feedback group were given their total scores on the examination and their letter grades but had no opportunity to see their examinations.
2. The subjects in the check-on-board group were given back their examinations, and the correct answers were placed on the blackboard. They were told to spend the class period checking over their examinations to see which items were right or wrong and why they were wrong.
3. The subjects in the discussion group were given back their examinations, and each question was briefly discussed by the instructor.
4. The subjects in the reread group received the corrected examinations, and the page numbers in the textbook from which each question was taken were placed on the blackboard. Subjects were instructed to find the place on the pages, particularly for those questions they missed, and to reread those passages.

Those subjects who had their examinations returned were also given their total score and letter grade. At the end of the 45-minute class period their examinations were collected.

The final examination at the end of the semester consisted of (a) 45 items, 15 from each of the three midsemester examinations, (b) 30 multiple-choice items from the test-item file that had not appeared on any of the previous midsemester examinations, and (c) a varying number of questions unique to each instructor. The dependent variables for the experiment consisted of the 45-item "retention" and the 30-item "transfer" parts of the examination that were common to the four groups.

Results

Table 1 presents the means and standard deviations for the four groups on the first, the retention, and the transfer examinations. A one-way classification analysis of variance on the scores for the first examination, with a correction for disproportionality, indicated that there was no significant difference among the groups ($F = 1.59$, $df = 3/483$, $p > .05$). Fortunately, these results indicated that there was no sampling bias in the average initial ability in educational psychology among the groups that subsequently received the four experimental treatments.

Nevertheless, following a suggestion by Feldt (1958), a 4 levels (ability in education psychology) × 4 feedback

treatments analysis of variance was applied to the data on both the retention and transfer tests, employing a correction for disproportionality. The analysis for the retention test showed that the effect of both the feedback treatments ($F = 16.27$, $df = 3/471$, $p < .001$) and the ability levels ($F = 45.82$, $df = 3/471$, $p < .001$) are significant. The interaction is not significant ($F = 1.22$, $df = 9/471$, $p > .05$).

In order to further analyze the retention data Duncan's new multiple range test with Kramer's correction for unequal sample size was used. These results showed that all three groups receiving feedback were significantly ($p = .05$) different from the control-no-feedback group and that the group receiving discussion of their examination questions was significantly ($p = .05$) different from the group that looked up the answers in the textbook. Thus, as far as retention is concerned, it would appear, as may be seen in Table 1, that the better feedback treatment for this population is discussing the items in class. However, the group which checked over items from the correct ones on the board just barely missed being significantly different from the group which looked up the answers in the textbook.

A 4 levels (ability in educational psychology) × 4 feedback treatments analysis of variance of the transfer data showed that the effects of both the treat-

Table 1

MEANS AND STANDARD DEVIATIONS ON THE FIRST, RETENTION, AND TRANSFER EXAMINATIONS FOR FOUR GROUPS

Examination	Control–no feedback		Check answers on board		Discuss answers in class		Reread in book	
	M	SD	M	SD	M	SD	M	SD
First	29.43	5.76	28.49	5.31	30.25	6.55	29.28	5.84
Retention	30.36	5.13	33.89	6.48	34.49	5.58	32.60	5.59
Transfer	20.74	3.69	21.72	4.05	22.18	3.51	21.46	3.32

ments ($F = 4.52$, $df = 3/471$, $p < .001$) and the ability levels ($F = 69.60$, $df = 3/471$, p < .001) are again significant. Also the interaction is again not significant (F < 1.00). Duncan's new multiple range test with Kramer's correction for unequal sample size showed that the group which had the questions discussed was significantly (*p* = .05) different from the control-no-feedback group in the transfer examination. The group which checked over the items from the correct ones on the blackboard just barely missed being significantly different from the control-no-feedback group on the transfer examination. However, discussing items in class apparently improves performance slightly more than providing no feedback, even on items that had not appeared on a previous examination.

Discussion

This experiment tested the general hypothesis that, with an increase in amount of information from feedback on examinations, there would be an increase in the retention and the transfer scores on a final examination. It was assumed that the group receiving no feedback would have the least amount of information, the group which checked its answers from the correct ones on the blackboard would have slightly more information, the group which had the questions discussed by the instructor would have even more information, and the group which reread the material covering questions they missed would get the most amount of information.

Analyses of the results in general showed that on both the retention and transfer tests the group which had the questions discussed in class and the group which checked their answers from the correct ones on the blackboard were better than the control-no-feedback

group and the group that reread material on items they got incorrect on the three mid-semester examinations. These results particularly support the old study by Curtis and Wood (1929), with high school subjects, showing that methods of feedback that provide for discussion are best. One can only speculate on the reasons why the group that reread material they missed did not do as well as expected. One reason is that subjects in this group focused only upon questions they missed and spent very little, if any, time upon questions they got right—some of which they may have gotten correct primarily by chance. Consequently, they may not have actually received as much feedback information as initially assumed. Also a few subjects in this group forgot to bring their textbook to class the day of the feedback treatment and had to borrow a book from another student: again cutting into the amount of relevant feedback information they may have received. Thus, had this group, as a whole, received the amount of information they should have, perhaps they would have performed as well or better than the groups which received discussion or checked over their answers from the correct ones on the board.

Another methodological weakness of this experiment is that subjects were not assigned to treatment conditions at random. This procedure was precluded by subjects having class schedules which would have posed a conflict in the majority of cases. However, an analysis of the scores on the first examination indicated that there was no sampling bias between the treatment groups in initial performance in educational psychology.

One could also raise the question that a Hawthorne effect may explain the results of this study. However, it was not emphasized in classes that an experiment was underway, and also the treatments were not unusual but similar to those used by many instructors.

A further argument can be raised that the results are due to instructor effects, since it was not possible to perfectly counterbalance nor analyze for this variable. However, the five different instructors each taught two of the four different feedback treatments in an effort, at least, to partially control for instructor effects. Therefore, it seems most plausible to conclude that advising teachers to discuss examination questions with students or letting students check over their examinations is no idle suggestion. However, the type of feedback appears to be less important than the fact that they get it. Students receiving any of the three feedback conditions employed in this experiment did better than those receiving no feedback, as the absolute difference among the three experimental groups is not large.

References

Cronbach, L. J. *Educational psychology* (2nd ed.). New York: Harcourt, Brace & World, 1963.

Curtis, F. D. and Wood, G. G. A study of the relative teaching value of four common practices in correcting examination papers. *School Review*, 1929, **37**, 615–23.

Hurlock, E. B. An evaluation of certain incentives used in school work. *Journal of Educational Psychology*, 1925, **16**, 145–49.

Feldt, L. S. A comparison of the precision of the three experimental designs employing a concomitant variable. *Psychometrika*, 1958, **23**, 335–53.

Page, E. B. Teacher comments and student performance: A seventy-four classroom experiment in school motivation. *Journal of Educational Psychology*, 1958, **49**, 173–81.

Plowman, L. and Stroud, J. B. Effects of informing pupils of the consequences of their responses to objective test questions. *Journal of Educational Research*, 1942, **36**, 16–20.

Stone, G. R. The training function of examinations: Retest performance as a function of the amount and kind of critique information. Research Report No. AFPT RC-TN-55-8, 1955, USAF Personnel Training Research Center, Lackland Air Force Base.

VI

The Facilitation of Concept Learning

As Carroll has indicated in Chapter 26, ". . . education is largely a process whereby the individual learns either to attach societally-standardized words and meanings to the concepts he has already formed, or to form new concepts that properly correspond to societally-standardized words and meanings." Carroll presents an excellent overview of the process of concept learning. His discussion includes his thinking on the teaching of concepts and the relevance of psychological theory and research in guiding such teaching. He points out also that, while there has been a large amount of laboratory research on concept learning and utilization, little work has been done on the actual process of teaching concepts. Carroll's paper represents an imporant first step in this direction.

The remainder of this section presents experimental investigations of ways to facilitate the acquisition and utilization of concepts. Johnson and Stratton (Chapter 27) evaluated the relative effectiveness of several techniques for the teaching of concepts. The relative merit of each was determined by comparing the groups of subjects taught by each technique with each other, with a group trained by employing all the techniques, and with a group that received no training. The results showed each of the techniques to be superior to giving no training; however the "mixed" program using all of the techniques proved best. The study suggests that teachers should be flexible in their teaching of concepts, employing a variety of techniques to facilitate concept acquisition.

Concepts may be described as having certain features which are relevant or important for defining the concept. For instance, the feature of roundness is an important one in defining the concept of *ball*. However, any particular example of the concept, such as a bowling ball, may also contain features that are not relevant to the concept of *ball*. A bowling ball usually has three finger holes but not all balls have these holes. We may say, then, that the presence of finger holes is a feature that is irrelevant to the concept of *ball*.

Several studies have investigated the effect of irrelevant features in the teaching of concepts. Traub (Chapter 28) reports a study in which sixth graders were taught to add positive and negative numbers. All of the children were given basic instruction in which the concepts involved were explained and illustrated. One group of children then practiced solving problems which were very similar (in terms of both relevant and irrelevant features) to the examples used during instruction. Another group practiced solving problems which differed from the training examples in certain features that were irrelevant to the concepts being taught. Thus for this group, while the critical or relevant features of the concepts remained the same, the children were exposed to problems which contained a greater variety of irrelevant features. Traub refers to this latter type of problem as *heterogeneous*. When the groups were tested on an achievement test consisting of problems new to both groups, the second group scored significantly better.

One possible interpretation of Traub's results is that introducing irrelevant features (so as to make examples more heterogeneous) will aid concept acquisition. This is not necessarily so, especially early in the teaching of a concept. Irrelevant features may distract the student from inferring or noticing the "critical features" of the concept—that is, those features which define the concept (see Carroll's paper). For instance, Dwyer (Chapter 29) showed that simple line drawings of the human heart were more effective in teaching the anatomy of the heart than realistic photographs of the heart in which many irrelevant features were necessarily included. (Note that Traub did not introduce problem heterogeneity until after some previous instruction.) Probably a safe generalization is that the teacher should minimize irrelevant features initially, then gradually introduce some (especially those irrelevant features the student is likely to encounter).

One hotly contested issue in education is whether the student should be told the concepts he is to learn or should be led to discover them. Proponents of the discovery method have claimed that such a procedure is more motivating to the student and increases his ability to think and solve problems. Opponents have pointed out that discovery training is very time consuming and inefficient. It is simply easier to tell the student what you want him to know. Research comparing discovery and expository methods of instruction is uniformly inadequate, and the issue (if it really can be regarded as an either/or proposition) remains unresolved. One of the best studies on the topic has been completed by Guthrie (Chapter 30), who used a simple cryptogram unscrambling task. His results showed that expository teaching resulted in faster acquisition, but discovery teaching was superior when students were required to discover and use rules very different from those learned in instruction. More research on this issue is needed.

Barrett and Otto (Chapter 31) have extended the notion of concept learning to learning from written materials. These authors consider the problem of students' inducing main ideas or concepts from paragraphs of prose. Students were required to infer the main idea from paragraphs in which it was implied and not actually stated. Barrett and Otto manipulated several factors, one being the number of irrelevant features (the addition of modifying phrases and dependent clauses). Their results, fully consistent with the concept-learning literature, indicated that the fewer the number of irrelevant features, the easier it was to induce main ideas.

26

Words, Meanings and Concepts

JOHN B. CARROLL / *Educational Testing Service, Princeton, New Jersey*

The teaching of words, and of the meanings and concepts they designate or convey, is one of the principal tasks of teachers at all levels of education. It is a concern of textbook writers and programmers of self-instructional materials as well. Students must be taught the meanings of unfamiliar words and idioms; they must be helped in recognizing unfamiliar ways in which familiar words may be used; and they must be made generally aware of the possibility of ambiguity in meaning and the role of context in resolving it. Often the task that presents itself to the teacher is not merely to explain a new word in familiar terms, but to shape an entirely new concept in the mind of the student.

Whether the teaching of words, meanings, and concepts is done by the teacher, the textbook writer, or the programmer, it is generally done in an intuitive, unanalytic way. The purpose of this article is to sketch, at least in a

first approximation, a more analytical approach to this task. One would have thought that volumes would have been written on the subject, but apart from such brief treatments as those of Brownell and Hendrickson (1950), Serra (1953), Levit (1953), and Vinacke (1954), for example, one searches the literature in vain for any comprehensive treatment of concept teaching. One is reassured that there are gaps to be filled.

There is, in the first place, an unfortunate hiatus between the word "meaning" and the very word "concept" itself. *Meaning* and *concept* have usually been treated as quite separate things by different disciplines. *Meaning*, for example, has been considered the province

Reprinted with the permission of the author and the publisher from *Harvard Educational Review*, 1964, Vol. 34, 178–202. Copyright © 1964 President and Fellows of Harvard College.

of a somewhat nebulous and insecure branch of linguistics called *semantics*.[1]

----

[1] Even if a technical science of "semantics" is a comparatively modern invention,—dating, say, from Bréal's article on the subject published in a classical journal in 1883,—the field might be said to have been thoroughly discussed. The classic work of Ogden and Richards (C. K. Ogden and I. A. Richards, *The Meaning of Meaning* [3rd ed.; New York: Harcourt, Brace, 1930]), the somewhat faddish writings stemming from Korzybski's doctrines of "general semantics" (A. Korzybski, *Science and Sanity; an Introduction to Non-Aristotelian Systems and General Semantics* [8th ed.; Lakeville, Conn.: 1948]), and the recent work in psychology of Osgood *et al.* (Charles E. Osgood, George J. Suci, and Percy Tannenbaum, *The Measurement of Meaning* [Urbana, Illinois: Univ. of Illinois Press, 1957]), Brown (Roger Brown, *Words and Things* [Glencoe, Illinois: The Free Press, 1958]), and Skinner (B. F. Skinner, *Verbal Behavior* [New York: Appleton-Century-Crofts, 1957]) might be said to have disposed of most of the general problems of a science of meaning. On the other hand, Stephen Ullmann's recent book (Stephen Ullmann, *Semantics, an Introduction to the Science of Meaning* [Oxford: Basil Blackwell, 1962]) claims only to be in the nature of a "progress report," pointing to the "revolution" that has taken place in modern linguistics and the "advances in philosophy, psychology, anthropology, communication engineering and other spheres" that have had "important repercussions in the study of meaning."

There has been a rash of papers on the implications of linguistics for the teaching of English, the teaching of reading, the teaching of foreign languages, and so on. In fact, the idea that linguistics has much to contribute to educational problems in the "language arts" has become almost embarrassingly fashionable. One's embarrassment comes from the fact that despite certain very definite and positive contributions that linguistics can make to these endeavors, these contributions are of relatively small extent. Once we accept such fundamental tenets of linguistics as the primacy of speech over writing, the structure of the language code as a patterning of distinctive communicative elements, and the arbitrariness of standards of usage, and work out their implications in detail, we find we are still faced with enormous problems of methodology in the teaching

Concept is almost anybody's oyster: it has continually been the concern of the philosopher, but has received generous attention from psychology. While the meanings of these two terms can be usefully distinguished in many contexts, it is also the case that a framework can be made for considering the intimate interconnections.

Second, there is a gap between the findings of psychologists on the conditions under which very simple "concepts" are learned in the psychological laboratory and the experiences of teachers in teaching the "for real" concepts that are contained in the curricula of the schools. It is not self-evident that there is any continuity at all between learning "DAX" as the name of a certain geometrical shape of a certain color and learning the meaning of the word "longitude." Even if such a continuity exists, it is not clear how the relative difficulty or complexity of concepts can be assessed.

Third, a problem related to the second arises when we ask whether there is any continuity, with respect to psycho-

----

of such subjects as English, reading, and foreign languages. The position is particularly difficult in connection with the study of meaning, because most branches of linguistics have paid little attention to this study; some linguists have seemed to go out of their way to exclude the study of meaning from their concerns as linguists. Although there are recent attempts (Paul Ziff, *Semantic Analysis* [Ithaca, N.Y.: Cornell Univ. Press, 1960] and Jerrold J. Katz and Jerry A. Fodor, "The Structure of a Semantic Theory," *Language*, XXXIX [1963], 170–210) to systematize semantic studies, these efforts may be less than completely successful if they fail to take account of the fundamentally psychological problem of how individuals attain concepts and how these individually-attained concepts are related to word meanings. The treatment of this problem offered in the present paper is exceedingly sketchy and must be regarded as only a first approximation.

logical "processes," between the inductive, non-verbal type of learning studied in the psychological laboratory under the guise of "concept learning" and the usually more deductive, verbal-explanatory type of teaching used in the classroom and in typical text materials. Take, for example, the kind of concept learning that has been explored so fruitfully by Bruner and his associates (1956). The experimental setting they employed is essentially a game between the experimenter and the subject: the experimenter says he is thinking of a concept—and perhaps he shows an example of his "concept," whereupon the subject's task is to make guesses about other possible instances of the concept in such a way that he will eventually be able to recognize the concept as defined by the experimenter. But in every case, one feels that the experimenter could have "taught" the subject the concept by a very simple verbal communication like "three circles" (for a "conjunctive" concept in which two attributes must occur together) or "any card that has either redness or two borders" (for a "disjunctive" concept) or "any card with more figures than borders" (for a "relational" concept). Teaching a concept in school is usually not all that simple.

In an effort to fill these gaps, we will sketch out a framework for conceptualizing problems of Meaning and Concept. For reasons that will eventually become clear, we must start with the notion of Concept.

The Nature of Concepts

In a totally inorganic world there could be no concepts, but with the existence of organisms capable of complex perceptual responses, concepts become possible. In brief, concepts are properties of organismic experience—more particularly, they are the abstracted and often cognitively structured classes of "mental" experience learned by organisms in the course of their life histories. There is evidence that animals other than human beings behave with regard to concepts in this sense, but we shall confine our attention to human organisms. Because of the continuity of the physical, biological, and social environment in which human beings live, their concepts will show a high degree of similarity; and through language learning, many concepts (classes of experience) will acquire names, that is, words or phrases in a particular language, partly because some classes of experience are so salient and obvious that nearly every person acquires them for himself, and partly because language makes possible the diffusion and sharing of concepts as classes of experience. We use the term "experience" in an extremely broad sense—defining it as any internal or perceptual response to stimulation. We can "have experience of" some aspect of the physical, biological, or social environment by either direct or indirect means; we can experience heat or light or odor directly, while our experiences of giraffes or atoms, say, may be characterized as being indirect, coming only through verbal descriptions or other patterns of stimuli (pointer readings, etc.) that evoke these concepts.

One necessary condition for the formation of a concept is that the individual must have a series of experiences that are in one or more respects similar; the constellation of "respects" in which they are similar constitutes the "concept" that underlies them. Experiences that embody this concept are "positive instances" of it; experiences that do not embody it may be called "negative instances." A further necessary condition for the formation of a concept is that the series of experiences embodying the concept must be preceded, interspersed, or followed by other experiences that constitute negative instances of the concept. As the complexity of the concepts increases (i.e., as there is an increase in the number of interrelations of the respects in which experiences must be similar in order to be positive instances), there is a greater necessity for an appropriate sequencing of positive and negative instances in order to insure adequate learning of the concept (Hunt, 1962). At least this is true when the concept has to be formed from *nonverbal* experiences only, i.e., from actual exemplars or referents of the concept as contrasted with non-examplars. But concept learning from verbal explanation, as will be noted below, must, as it were, put the learner through a series of vicarious experiences of positive and negative instances. For example, in telling a child what a lion is, one must indicate the range of positive and negative instances—the range of variations that could be found in real lions and the critical respects in which other animals, tigers, leopards, etc., differ from lions.

We have been describing what is often called the process of abstraction. We have given a number of *necessary* conditions for the formation of a concept; exactly what conditions are *sufficient* cannot yet be stated, but in all likelihood this will turn out to be a matter of (a) the number, sequencing, or timing of the instances presented to the individual, (b) the reinforcements given to the individual's responses, and (c) the individual's orientation to the task. The evidence suggests that the learner must be oriented to, and attending to, the relevant stimuli in order to form a concept. The public test of the formation of a concept is the ability to respond correctly and reliably to new positive and negative instances of it; we do not wish to imply, however, that a concept has not been formed until it is put to such a test.

The infant acquires "concepts" of many kinds even before he attains anything like language. One kind of concept that is acquired by an infant quite early is the concept embodied in the experience of a particular object—a favorite toy, for example. As the toy is introduced to the infant, it is experienced in different ways—it is seen at different angles, at different distances, and in different illuminations. It is felt in different positions and with different parts of the body, and experienced with still other sense-modalities—taste, smell. But underlying all these experiences are common elements sufficient for the infant to make an identifying response to the particular toy in question—perhaps to the point that he will accept only the particular specimen that he is familiar with and reject another specimen that is in the least bit different. The acceptance or rejection of a specimen is the outward sign of the attainment of a concept —as constituted by the class of experiences associated with that particular specimen. The experiences themselves are sufficiently similar to be their own evidence that they constitute a class—a perceptual invariant, therefore, together with whatever affective elements that may be present to help reinforce the attainment of the concept (pleasure in the sight, taste, smell, and feel of the toy, for example).

Even the concept contained in a particular object represents a certain degree of generality—generality over the separate presentations of the object. But preverbal infants also attain concepts which from the standpoint of adult logic have even higher degrees of generality. A further stage of generality is reached when the infant comes to recognize successive samples of something—e.g., a particular kind of food—as equivalent, even though varying slightly in taste, color, temperature, etc. Because the different samples of food are about equally reinforcing, the infant gradually learns to overcome the initial tendency to reject a sample that is experienced as not quite the same as one previously experienced. That is, what seems to be initially a negative instance turns out to be a positive instance because it provides the same reinforcement as the earlier instance—the reinforcement being in this case a "sign" that the new experience is to be taken in the same class as former ones. An even higher stage of generality is achieved when the child will accept and make a common response to any one of a number of rather different stimuli—for example, any one of a number of different foods. In adult terms, he has attained the concept of "food" in some elementary sense. The explanation of this phenomenon may indeed draw upon the usual primary reinforcement theory (the equivalence of different foods in satisfying a hunger drive) but it also depends upon various secondary reinforcements, as when the parent punishes the child for eating something not considered "food," like ants or mud. This is an elementary case in which culture, as represented by parents, provides signs as to what the positive and negative instances of a concept are.

Direct experience, i.e., the recognition of experiences as identical or similar, allows the infant to attain concepts that in adult language have names such as redness, warmth, softness, heaviness, swiftness, sweetness, loudness, pain, etc. In some cases, the infant's concepts of sensory qualities may be rather undifferentiated. For example, because big things are generally experienced as heavy and strong, and small things are generally experienced as lightweight and weak, the infant's concept of size may not be adequately differentiated from his concepts of weight and strength. Without any social reinforcement to guide him, his concept of "redness" may range over a rather wide range of the color spectrum, and if he happens to have been born into a culture which pays little attention to the difference, say, between what we would call "red" and "orange," his concept of "redness" may remain relatively undifferentiated even after he has learned a language— just as it has been demonstrated that different varieties of blue are not well coded in everyday English (Brown and Lenneberg, 1954).

Furthermore, we can infer from various investigations of Piaget (Flavell, 1963) that the child's concepts of size, weight, and other physical attributes of objects do not contain the notion of "conservation" that his later experiences will teach him. For all the infant or young child knows of the physical universe, objects can change in size, weight, etc. in quite arbitrary ways. It is only at a later stage, when the child has had an opportunity to form certain concepts about the nature of the physical universe, that his concepts of size, weight, and number can incorporate the notion of constancy or conservation that mature thinking requires. Experience with objects that can expand or contract through stretching or shrinking gives the child a concept of size that can properly explain the fact that a balloon can be blown up to various sizes. Indeed, this explanation may involve the concepts of "expansion" and "contraction." At a still later stage, the child may learn enough about the relation of heat to expansion to explain why it is necessary to have seams in concrete roads, or why one allows for expansion in the building of large bridges. And it will be relatively unlikely that even as an adult he will learn enough about the concept of size to understand the concept of relativity—that the size of a body is relative to the speed at which it is traveling and the system in which it is measured.

Thus, concepts can in the course of a person's life become more complex, more loaded with significant aspects. Concepts are, after all, essentially idiosyncratic in the sense that they reside in particular individuals with particular histories of experiences that lead them to classify those experiences in particular ways. My concept of "stone" may not be precisely your concept of "stone" because my experiences with stones may have included work with pieces of a peculiar kind of vitreous rock that you have seldom seen. To a large extent, how I sort out my experiences is my own business and may not lead to the same sortings as yours.

Nevertheless, I can specify the way I sort out my experiences by noting the *critical attributes* that differentiate them. I can specify what sensory qualities and attributes are necessary before I will classify an experience as being an experience of what I call a stone. But it is not even necessary for a person to be able to specify such attributes. A child who has learned a certain concept—who has learned to recognize certain experiences as being similar—may not necessarily be able to verbalize what attributes make them similar; he may not even be aware of the fact that he has attained a certain concept, since it may be the case that only his behavior—the fact that he consistently makes a certain response to a certain class of stimuli—indicates that he has formed a concept. Such would be the case, for example, for the classic instance where the child is afraid of the barber because he wields instruments (scissors) that look like those of the doctor whom he has already

learned to fear, and because he wears a similar white smock.

Indeed, this last instance exemplifies the fact that concepts may include affective components. Because concepts are embodied in classes of experiences they include all the elements of experiences that may occur in common—perceptual and cognitive elements as well as motivational and emotional elements. My concept of "stone" may reflect, let us say, my positive delight in collecting new varieties of minerals, whereas your concept may reflect the fact that you had unpleasant experiences with stones— having them thrown at you in a riot, or finding lots of them in your garden. Osgood's "semantic differential" (Osgood, Suci and Tannenbaum, 1957), in which one is asked to rate one's concepts on scales, such as good-bad, strong-weak, fast-slow, active-passive, light-heavy, pungent-bland, is a way of indexing certain relatively universal cognitive and affective components of individual experiences as classed in concepts; it would perhaps more properly be called an "experiential differential" than a "semantic differential." The fact that fairly consistent results are obtained when concept ratings from different people are compared or averaged implies that people tend to have generally similar kinds of experiences, at least within a given culture.

It has already been suggested earlier that since man lives in an essentially homogeneous physical and biological environment and a partially homogeneous social environment, it is inevitable that a large number of concepts arrived at by individual people should be the same or at least so nearly identical in their essential attributes as to be called the same; these concepts we may call *conceptual invariants*. We can be sure that throughout the world people have much the same concepts of *sun, man, day, animal, flower, walking, falling, softness,* etc. by whatever names they may be called. The fact that they have names is incidental; there are even certain concepts that for one reason or another (a taboo, for example) may remain nameless.

It is probably when we enter into the realms of science and technology and of social phenomena that the concepts attained by different people will differ most. In science and technology concepts vary chiefly because of differences, over the world, in the levels of scientific and technological knowledge reached; and in the social sphere they will differ chiefly because of the truly qualitative differences in the ways cultures are organized. Nevertheless, within a given community there will be a high degree of commonality in the concepts recognized and attained, in the sense that there will be relatively high agreement among people as to the attributes that are criterial for a given concept. For example, even though types of families vary widely over the world, the concept of *family* within a given culture is reasonably homogeneous. At the same time, differences in intellectual and educational levels will account for differences in the sheer number of concepts attained by individuals within a given culture.

Words and Their Meanings

In the learning of language, words (and other elements in a linguistic system, including phonemes, morphemes, and syntactical patterns) come to be perceived as distinct entities, and in this sense they form one class of perceptual invariants along with the perceptual invariants that represent common objects, feelings, and events. The child must learn to perceive the various instances of a given sound or word as similar, and eventually to differentiate the several

contexts in which a given sound or sound pattern is used. (We know of an instance of a very young child who somehow learned to react violently to the word "no," but she would react just as violently to the word "know," even when it was embedded in a sentence. The process of differentiation took a considerable time.)

Many words or higher units of the linguistic system come to stand for, or name, the concepts that have been learned pre-verbally. Certainly this is true for a long list of words that stand for particular things or classes of things, qualities, and events. For the English language, these categories correspond roughly to proper and common nouns; adjectives; and verbs of action, perception, and feeling. It is perhaps less clear that "function words" like prepositions and conjunctions, or grammatical markers like the past tense sign can represent concepts, but a case can be made for this. For example, prepositions like *in, to, above, below, beside, near* correspond to concepts of relative spatial position in a surprisingly complex and subtle way; and conjunctions like *and, but, however, or* correspond to concepts of logical inclusion and exclusion, similarity and difference of propositions, etc.

The processes by which words come to "stand for" or correspond to concepts can best be described in psychological terms. Without going into the details here, we can only say that in every case there is some sort of reinforcing condition that brands a word as being associated with a given concept. This is true whether the word is learned as what Skinner (1957) calls a *mand* (as when a child learns the meaning of *water* as a consequence of having water brought whenever he says "water") or as a *tact* (as where the child is praised or otherwise reinforced for saying "water" when he sees or experiences water), because in either case the word is paired contiguously with the concept *as an experience*. The connection between a word and the concept or experience with which it stands in relation must work in either direction: the word must evoke the concept and the concept must evoke the word.

As a physical symbol, a word is a cultural artifact that takes the same, or nearly the same, form throughout a speech community. It is a standardized product on which the speech community exercises a considerable degree of quality control. Not so with concepts, which as we have seen may vary to some extent with the individual, depending on his experiences of the referents of the words. Society does, however, maintain a degree of "quality control" on the referential meaning of words. The conditions under which the use of words is rewarded or not rewarded—either by successful or unsuccessful communication or by direct social approval or disapproval—can be looked upon as constituting the "rules of usage" of a word, and these rules of usage define the *denotative meaning* of a term. Thus, there is a rule of usage such that the noun *mother* can be used only for a certain kind of kinship relation. One thinks of denotative meaning as something that is socially prescribed. Connotative meaning, however, banks heavily on those aspects of concepts that are widely shared yet non-criterial and perhaps affective (emotional) in content. "Mother" as a noun might evoke various emotional feelings depending upon one's experience with mothers.

Perhaps it is useful to think of words, meanings, and concepts as forming *three* somewhat independent series. The words in a language can be thought of as a series of physical entities—either spoken or written. Next, there exists a set of "meanings" which stand in complex relationships to the set of words. These relationships may be described by the rules of usage that have developed by the processes of socialization and communication. A "meaning" can be thought of as a standard of communicative behavior that is shared by those who speak a language. Finally, there exist "concepts"; the classes of experience formed in individuals either independently of language processes or in close dependence on language processes.

The interrelations found among these three series are complex: almost anyone can give instances where a word may have many "meanings," or in which a given "meaning" corresponds to several different words. The relationships between societally-standardized "meanings" and individually-formed "concepts" are likewise complex, but of a somewhat different nature. It is a question of how well each individual has learned these relationships, and at least in the sphere of language and concepts, education is largely a process whereby the individual learns either to attach societally-standardized words and meanings to the concepts he has already formed, or to form new concepts that properly correspond to societally-standardized words and meanings. A "meaning" of a word is, therefore, a societally-standardized concept, and when we say that a word stands for or names a concept, it is understood that we are speaking of concepts that are shared among the members of a speech community.

To the extent that individual concepts differ even though they possess shared elements, misunderstandings can arise. My concept of "several" may correspond to the range "approximately three to five," where yours may correspond to "approximately five to fifteen." Speech communities may differ, too, in the exact ranges in which they standardize meanings. The word *infant* seems to include a higher age range in Great Britain (in the phrase "infants' schools") than it does in the United States, and in legal contexts the word may even refer to anyone who has not attained some legal age like twenty-one years.

The fact that words vary in meaning according to context has given rise to one form of a "context theory of meaning" which seems to allege that the meaning of a word is to be found in its context; this is only true, however, in the sense that the context may provide a *clue* as to the particular meaning (or standardized concept) with which a word is intended to be associated. In fact, the clue usually takes the form of an indication of one or more elements of a concept. For example, in the phrase *A light load* the context suggests (though it does not determine absolutely) that *light* is to be taken as the opposite of heavy because loads vary more importantly in weight than in their color, whereas the context in *A light complexion* suggests the element of color because complexions can vary in color but only very improbably in weight. It is not surprising that normal language texts have been found to have redundancy, for the elements of concepts suggested by the words in a sentence are often overlapping.

Frequently context is the key to the fact that a word is being used in an archaic or unusual sense. A student who cannot square the usual meaning of *smug* with its use in the following lines from Shakespeare's *Henry IV (Part I)*:

"And here the smug and silver Trent shall run
In a new channel, fair and evenly"

had better resort to a dictionary, where he will find that an earlier meaning of *smug* is *trim, neat.* We cannot dwell here on the interesting ways in which words change in meaning historically, often in response to changes in emphasis given to the various criterial attributes embodied in the concepts corresponding to words. Just as one example, though, consider the historical change of meaning of "meat" from (originally) "any kind of food" to "edible part of animal body, flesh," where the criterial attribute "part of animal body" gradually came to be reinforced alongside the attribute "edible thing."

Definitions

What, by the way, is the function of a dictionary definition in the light of the system of ideas being presented here? Aside from the few instances where dictionary definitions present pictures or drawings of the items being defined, two main techniques are used in dictionary entries: (1) the use of verbal equivalents, and (2) the use of formal definition by stating *genus et differentia.* The use of verbal equivalents, as where we are told that *smug* can mean "trim, smooth, sleek," has the function of evoking either a (hopefully) previously known concept to which both the defined word and the defining word stand in the same relation, or a series of (hopefully) previously known concepts from whose common elements the reader can derive the concept to which the defined word properly stands in relation. The use of a formal definition, on the other hand, literally "marks off the boundaries of" the concept by first indicating what it has in common with other experiences (*genus*) and then indicating in what respects or attributes (*differentia*) it differs from other experiences. For example, if we are told that *tarn* is a small mountain lake or pool, we know that in many respects it is similar to other lakes or pools—that it is an enclosed, contained body of water, but that it is a special kind of lake of a given size and location. One could, therefore, presumably acquire the concept named *tarn* by learning to make this response only in connection with the criterial attributes defining it. What could be simpler, particularly if one is verbally told what the criterial attributes are? The only kind of intellectual mishap would occur, one would think, when one of the attributes is misunderstood or overlooked. Calling Lake George (in the Adirondacks) a *tarn* would be grossly to neglect or misunderstand the element of small size.

Concept Formation Research

We are now in a position to inquire into the possible relevance of concept formation research to the learning of the meanings and concepts associated with words in a language.

Practically all concept formation research since the days of Hull (1920) has been concerned with essentially the following task: the subject is presented with a series of instances which are differentiated in some way; either the task is finding out in what way the several instances match up with one of a small number of names, or (in the simpler case) it is one of discovering why some instances are "positive" (i.e., instances of the "concept" the experimenter has in mind) or "negative" (not instances of the "concept"). Typically the stimulus material consists of simple visual material characterized by a number of clearly salient dimensions—e.g., the color of the figures, the geometrical shape of the figures, the number of figures, the number of borders, the color of the background, etc. Occasionally the critical characteristics of the concept are not clearly in view—as in Hull's experiment where the critical stroke elements of Chinese characters tended to be masked by the rest of the figures, or as

in Bouthilet's (1948) experiment where the critical feature was the inclusion of letters found in the stimulus word. Sometimes the critical elements are semantic elements of words, as in Freedman and Mednick's experiment (1958) in which the task was to find the common semantic element in a series of words such as *gnat, needle, stone,* and *canary.*

Thus, there are two elements to be studied in any concept-formation task: (1) the attributes which are criterial to the concept—their nature and number, the number of values each attribute has and the discriminability of these values, and the salience of the attributes themselves—that is, whether the attributes command attention and are readily perceivable, and (2) the information-handling task required of the subject in view of the order in which positive and negative instances are presented and the amount of information concerning the concept that is furnished by each presentation. Most of what we know about this kind of concept attainment task can be summarized in the following statements:

1. Concept attainment becomes more difficult as the number of relevant attributes increases, the number of values of attributes increases, and the salience of the attributes decreases.
2. Concept attainment becomes more difficult as the information load that must be handled by the subject in order to solve the concept increases, and as the information is increasingly carried by negative rather than positive instances.
3. Various strategies for handling the information load are possible, and some are in the long run more successful than others.

Concept Learning in School

I suspect that anyone who has examined the concept formation literature with the hope of finding something of value for the teaching of concepts in school has had cause for some puzzlement and disappointment, because however fascinating this literature may be, as it wends its way through the detailed problems posed by the methodology itself, its relevance to the learning of concepts in the various school subjects is a bit obscure.

Let us look at the major differences between concept learning in school and in the laboratory.

(1) One of the major differences is in the nature of the concepts themselves. A new concept learned in school is usually a genuinely "new" concept rather than an artificial combination of familiar attributes (like the concept "three blue squares" such as might be taught in a psychological experiment).

(2) New concepts learned in school depend on attributes which themselves represent difficult concepts. In more general terms, concepts learned in school often depend upon a network of related or prerequisite concepts. One cannot very well learn the concept of derivative, in the calculus, until one has mastered a rather elaborate structure of prerequisite concepts (e.g., slope, change of slope, algebraic function, etc.). Further, the attributes on which school-learned concepts depend are frequently verbal, depending on elements of meaning that cannot easily be represented in terms of simple sensory qualities as used in concept formation experiments.

(3) Many of the more difficult concepts of school learning are of a relational rather than a conjunctive character; they deal with the relations among attributes rather than their combined presence or absence. Concept-formation experiments have thus far revealed little about the acquisition of relational concepts.

(4) An important element in school learning is the memory problem involved in the proper matching of words and concepts. Thus, the problems of paired-associate memory are added to those of concept learning itself. For example, a student in biology or social studies has to learn not only a large number of new concepts, but also a large number of unfamiliar, strange-looking words to be attached to these concepts. The rate at which new concepts can be introduced is probably limited, just as the rate at which foreign language words can be acquired is limited.

(5) The most critical difference between school concept learning and concept learning in psychological experiments is that the former is for the most part deductive and the latter is generally inductive. It would be relatively rare to find a concept taught in school by the procedure of showing a student a series of positive and negative instances, labeled as such, and asking him to induce the nature of the concept with no further aid. Such instances could be found, of course; perhaps they would exemplify a pure "discovery method," and perhaps there should be more use of this method than is the case. The fact is that a pure discovery method is seldom used, because it is rather slow and inefficient. Even if a teaching procedure incorporates "discovery" elements, it is likely to be combined with deductive elements. The concept to be taught is described verbally—perhaps by a rule or definition—and the student is expected to attain the concept by learning to make correct identification of positive and negative instances. For example, he is told what an "indirect object" is and then is given practice in identifying the indirect objects (positive instances) among other words (negative instances). Many simple concepts can be taught by a wholly deductive procedure. For most students, the dictionary definition of *tarn* will be a sufficient stimulus for attainment of the concept. On the

other hand, it is well known that purely deductive, verbal procedures are frequently insufficient to help learners attain concepts. Concept-formation experimentation would be more relevant to school learning problems if it could give more attention to examining the role of verbalization and other deductive procedures in concept attainment.

Nevertheless, there are certain similarities between concept attainment in school and concept formation in psychological experiments. These arise chiefly from the fact that not every concept is learned *solely* in a formalized, prearranged school setting. The school environment is in many ways continuous with the out-of-school environment; concepts are learned partly in school, partly out of school. The process whereby the elementary concepts of a language are learned closely parallels that of the psychological concept-formation experiment. A child learns the concept "dog" not by having the concept described to him but by learning to restrict his usage of the word *dog* to instances regarded as positive by the speech community. In this process there are many false responses—either false positives (calling a non-dog a dog) or false negatives (believing a dog to be a non-instance), before an appropriate series of reinforcements produces correct concept attainment. Similar phenomena occur with concepts in the school curriculum. A child who has been told that his cousins visiting him from Peoria are "tourists" may not realize that tourists do not need to be relatives, and when he is told that the Germans who have settled in his town are "immigrants," he may believe that all foreigners visiting his town are immigrants. Concept-formation experiments yield information as to the range and variety of instances that have to be furnished for efficient and correct concept

formation in the absence of formal instruction.

But if the foregoing statement is true, concept-formation studies should also yield insights as to what information has to be furnished for *deductive* concept formation, e.g., from a formal definition. Obviously, a formal definition is successful only to the extent that it correctly identifies and describes all the criterial attributes that are likely to be relevant for a concept, and to the extent that it communicates the proper values and relationships of these to the learner. The burden is both on the definition itself and on the learner. A student may fail to learn the concept *tarn* from the definition previously cited either because it omits some essential criterial attribute (e.g., that a tarn must contain *water* rather than, say, *oil* or *lava*), or because the student fails to comprehend the meaning of its elements (for example, how small is "small"?).

What is actually going on in most school learning of concepts is a process that combines in some way deductive and inductive features.

Descriptions and definitions provide the deductive elements of the process. The several parts of a description or definition specify the attributes and relationships that are criterial for the concept. The order in which these specifications are arranged in the description and presented to the student may have something to do with the ease of concept attainment, particularly in the case of complex concepts with many attributes and complex interrelationships (like the case of *tort* discussed below). As yet we have no well-founded generalizations about the order in which the criterial attributes for a concept should be presented.

At the same time, inductive procedures entail the citing of positive and negative instances of the concept. We know from concept-attainment research that learning is facilitated more by positive than by negative instances, even though the "information" conveyed by these instances is the same in a given experimental context. But in real-life concept learning, the number of dimensions that may possibly be relevant is less limited; the function of positive instances is as much to show *which* dimensions are relevant as it is to show what values of them are critical. We may speculate that the real value of what we are calling inductive procedures in concept learning is to afford the learner an opportunity to test his understanding of and memory for the elements of verbal descriptions and definitions. This testing may even involve the construction and testing of alternative hypotheses.

For example, consider the following verbal statement of what a "paradigm" (for research on teaching) is:

"Paradigms are models, patterns, or schemata. Paradigms are not theories; they are rather ways of thinking or patterns for research that, when carried out, can lead to the development of theory" (Gage, 1963).

As a verbal statement, this is hardly adequate; fortunately, Gage proceeds to exhibit a number of positive instances of "paradigms" by which his readers can test out their notions of what this concept might be. Many readers will still have difficulty, however, because he fails to exhibit *negative* instances of paradigms.

What is needed, eventually, is a scientific "rhetoric" for the teaching of concepts—assembled not only from the traditional rhetoric of exposition but also from whatever scientific experiments on concept teaching can tell us. We will be better off, however, if concept-attainment studies begin to give at-

tention to the manner in which real-life, non-artificial concepts can be taught most efficiently—presumably by combination of both deductive and inductive procedures.

Illustrations of Concept Teaching Problems

To suggest the kinds of problems that arise in the teaching of concepts or that might be investigated through formal research, I propose to analyze a small number of concepts of various types, at several levels of difficulty.

TOURIST VS. IMMIGRANT

A fourth grade teacher reported difficulty in getting her pupils to understand and contrast the meanings of the words *tourist* and *immigrant*. Neither word appears in Dale and Eichholz's (1960) list of words known by at least sixty-seven percent of children in the fourth grade, although *tour* (as a sight-seeing trip) was known by seventy percent. In the sixth-grade list, *immigrant* was known by seventy percent and *tourist* by seventy-seven percent; the figures are ninety-seven percent (for *immigration*) and ninety-six percent (for *tourist*) in the 8th-grade list.

To an adult, the differentiation between the concepts designated by *tourist* and *immigrant* looks almost trivially simple. Aside from the sheer memory problem in learning and differentiating the words themselves, what are the sources of confusion for the child? In specific cases, a tourist and an immigrant might have many common characteristics: both might be from a foreign country, or at least from some distance away from the local community; both might be of obviously non-native culture because of dress, complexion, speech, and behavior; both might be doing what would appear to be "sight-seeing," though possibly for different purposes. The differences between a tourist and an immigrant might not be very apparent, being primarily differences of motivation. Indeed, a tourist might become an immigrant overnight, just by deciding to be one.

As we have seen, there is a sense in which the concept-attainment experimental literature is relevant to the child's problem in learning the meanings of the words *tourist* and *immigrant.* If the child is presented with various instances of people who are either tourists or immigrants, properly labeled as such, but with no further explanation, it will be the child's task to figure out what attributes or characteristics are relevant to the differentiation of these concepts. This might occur either in school or outside of school. Most likely the instances of tourists and immigrants will be relatively sporadic over time, and the instances may not vary in such a way as to show what attributes are truly relevant. For example, all the tourists may be obviously American, whereas all the immigrants may be obviously Mexican, let us say. The tourists may all be well-dressed, the immigrants poorly dressed, and so on. If the natural environment is like a grand concept-formation experiment, it may take the child a long time to attain the concepts *tourist* and *immigrant;* indeed, the environment may not be as informative as the usual experimenter, since the child may not always be informed, or reliably informed, as to the correctness of his guesses. No wonder a child might form the concept that a tourist is any well-dressed person who drives a station-wagon with an out-of-state license plate!

The purpose of teaching is to short-cut this capricious process of concept attainment within the natural environment. Through the use of language, there should be relatively little difficulty in explaining to a child that an immigrant is one who moves from one country or region to another in order to change his permanent residence, while a tourist is one who travels around for pleasure without changing his permanent residence. One can use simple explanations like: "He's going to stay here, have his home here . . ." or "He's just traveling around for the fun of it while he's on vacation, and someday he'll get back home." There should be no difficulty, at any rate, if the child has already mastered certain prerequisite concepts. Among these prerequisite concepts would be: the concept of home or permanent residence and all that it implies; the concept of the division of world territory into different countries and those in turn into regions; and the concept of traveling for pleasure or curiosity. It is very likely that the child who is having trouble understanding the concept of tourist vs. the concept of immigrant has not got clearly in mind these prerequisite notions that constitute, in fact, the criterial attributes upon which the distinction hangs.

Alternatively, a child might be having trouble because he has not dispensed with irrelevant aspects of these concepts: he might think that a tourist has to be always an American, whereas an immigrant must be a foreigner, because he has seen *American* tourists and *foreign* immigrants, no *American* immigrants nor *foreign* tourists. The ingenious teacher will think of the possible misunderstandings that could arise through the influence of irrelevant attributes of tourists and immigrants.

TIME

K. C. Friedman (1944) pointed out that elementary school children have much trouble with various time concepts. A child sees no incongruity, for example, in saying, "My older brother was born a long time ago." According to Friedman, it was not until Grade VI that all children in his school could state the date or list the months in perfect order. They had difficulty, he reports, in forming a concept of the "time line" and then in recognizing the placement of various historical events on such a time line. It is easy to see why the child would have these difficulties; even as adults it is difficult for us to appreciate the significance of the fantastically long periods implied by geological time. It should be noted that our concept of a time line is essentially a *spatial* concept whereby we translate temporal succession in terms of spatial order and distances. For a child, times does not flow in a straight line nor in any other particular direction, unless it is around the clock, in a circular or spiral dimension! How can the child form a concept of time and its units? Is time a class of experiences? Does it have criterial attributes? The paradigms of concept-formation experiments do not seem to apply here readily. But let us examine the situation more closely. How can the child have experiences of time and generate the concept of a time line? Certainly there can be experiences of intervals of time—watching a second hand of a clock move through the second-markings, or experiencing the succession of night and day, noticing the change of seasons or waiting for the end of the school year. Moving from one time period to another could be likened to moving from one square of a sidewalk to the next. It should be an easy transition to thinking of the time line as a sidewalk of infinite extent in both directions—toward the past and toward the future. Marking off the days on the calendar and naming the days and months should help to reinforce this cognitive structure. Extrapolation of the

time line is like generalizing these time experiences to all possible such experiences.

One of the difficulties comes, presumably, from the fact that the far reaches of the past and the future cannot be immediately experienced, and one immediately has trouble if one attempts to show a time line that includes historical events in the distant past along with a representation of the relationship between today, yesterday, and the day before yesterday. (Incidentally, it is hard to believe Pistor's [1939] claim that young children cannot tell the difference between the present and the past, in view of the fact that they can correctly use the present tenses of verbs in simple situations.) Time lines of different scales must be used, and the concept of scale will itself be hard for children to understand unless it is carefully explained—perhaps by showing maps of the immediate environment in different scales. Only after such ideas have been mastered will it be possible for the child to have any appreciation of such concepts as *year, century, 1492* (as a date), *B.C., generation. Generation* and *eon,* by the way, would have to be introduced as somewhat flexible, arbitrary units of time, as contrasted with fixed, measurable units such as *year* and *century.*

QUANTITATIVE EXPRESSIONS LIKE "MANY," "FEW," "AVERAGE"

Ernest Horn (1937) pointed out that certain quantitative concepts like *many, few,* and *average* are often so difficult that children do not give reasonable interpretations of them. It is very likely that the source of the difficulty is that children tend not to be able to think in relative terms. Children (and perhaps their teachers) would like to be able to assign definite ranges of numbers for such words as *many, few, average, a sizable amount,* etc., when actually they are all relative terms. There has even been a psychological experiment to demonstrate this: Helson, Dworkin, and Michels (1956) showed that adult subjects will consistently give different meanings to a word like "few" when it is put in different contexts. For example, "few" meant about twelve percent on the average, in relation to 100 people, whereas it meant four percent, on the average, in relation to 1,728,583 people.

In teaching a child these relational concepts, the problem would be to exhibit or describe numerous instances in which the absolute base varies but in which the actual numbers of quantities meant would at the same time vary sufficiently to give the impression that these words do not indicate anything like exact amounts. It should be pointed out that 100 things might be "many" in some situations and "few" in others. The use of "average" in such a context as "There was an average number of people in church today" can be taught by drawing attention to its relation to the probable extremes of the numbers of people that might be in church, generalizing the concept to other situations like "I caught an average number of fish today." This might lead to the introduction of the average as a statistic or number that gives information about the "central tendency" of some frequency distribution. It may help to use an unfamiliar or unusual context to bring out this concept in sharp relief. For example, I like to illustrate the utility of the statistical mean or arithmetic average by asking students to imagine that the first space men to reach Mars discover human-like creatures there whose average height is—and this is where the mean becomes really informative—3 inches!

The basic concept of the mean arises in the context of experiences in which there is a plurality of objects measured in some common way. As a first approximation, as far as a child is concerned, the average is a number that is roughly halfway between the highest and lowest measurements encountered, and in some way "typical" of these measurements. Only at some later stage does the child need to learn that the mean is a number that can be computed by a formula and that it has certain properties.

LONGITUDE

It is difficult to understand why E. B. Wesley (1952) says that concepts related to the sphericity of the earth, like latitude and longitude, are not easily taught to the average child before Grades VI and VII. Wesley was writing before the advent of the space age when every child knows about space capsules traveling around the globe. Though it may still be difficult to get a child to see how the flatness of his immediate environment is only apparent and that the immediate environment corresponds to just a small area on the globe, it can certainly be done, well before Grade VI, through suitable demonstrational techniques. Having established the sphericity of the earth, one should be able to teach latitude and longitude as concepts involved in specifying locations on the globe. Their introduction should properly be preceded by simpler cases in which one uses a system of coordinates to specify location—e.g., equally spaced and numbered horizontal and vertical lines drawn on a blackboard with a game to locate letters placed at intersection of lines, a map of one's town or city in which marginal coordinates are given to help locate given streets or places of interest, and finally a Mercator projection map of the world with coordinates of latitude and longitude. Children exposed to the "new math" with its number lines and coordinates should have no trouble with this. Then let us show children by easy stages how a Mercator projection corresponds to the surface of the earth (certainly an actual globe marked off with latitude and longitude should be used), then how it is necessary to select a particular line (that passes through the Greenwich Observatory) as the vertical coordinate from which to measure, and how the circumference of the earth is marked off in degrees—180° West and 180° East from the Greenwich meridian.

The object is to build for the child a vivid experience of the framework or cognitive structure within which the concept of longitude is defined. The further complications introduced by the use of other kinds of world projections or by the use of regional or even local maps could then be explored. Easily-obtained U.S. Geological Survey maps of one's locality would concretize the meanings of further concepts, e.g., the division of degrees into minutes and seconds, and the fact that a degree of longitude will gradually shrink in length as one moves northward from the equator.

TORT

The concept of *tort* is very likely to be unfamiliar or at least vague to the average reader. Even a dictionary definition[2] may not help much in deciding whether arson, breach of contract, malicious prosecution, or libel are positive instances of torts. The case method used

---

[2] The *American College Dictionary* defines *tort* as "a civil wrong (other than a breach of contract or trust) such as the law requires compensation for in damages; typically, a willful or negligent injury to a plaintiff's person, property, or reputation."

in many law schools, whereby students examine many positive and negative instances of torts in order to learn what they are, is somewhat analogous to a concept-formation experiment of the purely inductive variety.

A study[3] of the various laws and decisions relating to torts yields the following approximate and tentative characterization of the concept as having both conjunctive and disjunctive aspects:

$$\text{TORT} = (A+B+C+D+E+F+G+H)$$
$$(I+J)(K)(-L)(-M)(-N)(-O)$$

where A = battery
B = false imprisonment
C = malicious prosecution
D = trespass to land
E = interference to chattels
F = interference with advantageous relations
G = misrepresentation
H = defamation
I = malicious intent
J = negligence
K = causal nexus
L = consent
M = privilege
N = reasonable risk by plaintiff
O = breach of contract

Within a parenthesis, terms joined by the sign + are mutually disjunctive attributes; a minus sign (−) within a parenthesis signifies "absence of"; the full content of each parenthesis is conjunctive with the content of every other parenthesis. Thus, we can read the formula as follows: "A tort is a battery, a false imprisonment, a malicious prosecution, a trespass to land, . . . , or a defamatory act which is done either

---

[3] For helping me in my treatment of the concepts of *tort* and *mass* I am indebted to my student, Mr. Edward A. Dubois.

with malicious intent or negligently, which exhibits a causal nexus with the injury claimed by the plaintiff, *and* which is done without the plaintiff's consent, *or* without privilege on the part of the defendant, *or* without a reasonable risk by the plaintiff, *or* which is not a breach of contract."

Thus, *tort* turns out to be a concept very much on the same order as *tourist* —a collocation of criterial attributes with both conjunctive and disjunctive features. Deciding whether an act is a tort requires that one check each feature of a situation against what can be put in the form of a formula (as done above). Presumably, a person presented with a properly organized series of positive and negative instances of torts could induce the concept, provided he also understood such prerequisite concepts as *battery, misrepresentation,* etc.

MASS VS. WEIGHT

One of the more difficult concepts to teach in elementary physics is that of *mass*. What kind of concept is it and how can one learn it and experience it? How can it be distinguished from the concept of weight? Actually, if we ignore certain subtle questions about mass, such as that of whether inertial and gravitational mass are demonstrably identical, the concept of mass is not as difficult as it might seem; the real difficulty is to teach the sense in which it is different from weight. In fact, weight is perhaps the more difficult concept, because the weight of an object can vary to the point that it can become "weightless."

The concept of mass, one would think, ought to develop for the learner (be he a child or an adult) in much the same way that concepts of other properties of the physical world develop— analogously, that is, to concepts of color, number, and volume. For mass is a property of objects that differentiates them in our experience: there are objects with great mass (like the earth, or a large boulder) and there are objects with small mass (like a feather or a pin or the air in a small bottle), and our experiences of objects with respect to mass can differ enormously, particularly in our proprioceptive senses. Further, mass is a property of objects that is *conserved* regardless of whether the object is in motion or at rest; conservation of mass is learned through experience just as conservation of other properties is learned. Even the physical definition of mass as that property of things which accounts for the relative amount of force which has to be applied to produce a certain amount of acceleration is perceived in common-sense terms as the property of objects that determines the amount of force or effort that one would have to exert to move or lift it. The well-known "size-weight" illusion (in which, for example, we exert an undue amount of effort to lift or push some large but relatively light object) illustrates the fact that our perceptions of an object typically include some impression of its mass. The physical operation of measuring mass by determining the ratio of force to acceleration is an operational extension of the kind of behavior we exhibit when we see how much force it will take to move a heavy trunk.

The real trouble comes in the fact that we are too prone to equate mass with weight, mainly because equal masses also have equal weights when compared by means of a balance, or when measured with a spring balance at the same point on the earth's surface (at least, at the same distance from the earth's center). If we were more easily able to experience the fact that the weight of an object of given mass changes as acceleration due to gravity changes—for example by going to the moon and observing the "weight" of objects there, or by experiencing "weightlessness" in an orbital flight around the earth, weight and mass might be just as easy to distinguish as size and mass. Since such experiences would be rather hard to come by, to put it mildly, we have to be content with the imaginal representation of weight as a *variable* property of objects that really depends upon a relation between the gravitational force exerted on an object and its mass (actually, the product of these two). A child might be made to understand how objects of different masses could have equal "weight"—a relatively large object on the moon and a relatively small one on the earth, for example—as measured by a spring balance which is sensitive to the pull of gravity; or how an object of constant mass would have different weights at different distances from the earth (the pull of gravity thus varying). We would have to conclude that weight, properly speaking, is a relational concept that can only be understood when the total framework in which weight can be defined is described. Mass, on the other hand, is a concept that corresponds much more directly to immediate perceptions of reality.

It will be noted that the teaching of mass and weight concepts involves several prerequisite concepts—e.g., the pull of gravity, the relation between the mass of an object like the earth or the moon and the gravitational force it exerts, and the concept of acceleration. The pull exerted by a magnet could be used for illustrating certain aspects of the concept of gravitational force; a large magnet and a small magnet could represent the respective gravitational pulls of earth and moon; the concept of acceleration can be introduced verbally as "how fast something gets started" and later as an accelerating curve of velocity.

Without really meaning to do so, this discussion of mass and weight has turned out to be a consideration of how such concepts might be taught at relatively early stages—say, somewhere in the elementary school. Nevertheless, some of the same teaching techniques might not be amiss even at high school or college levels. At these levels the chief problem is to give meaning to mathematical formulas such as

$$\text{mass} = \frac{\text{force}}{\text{acceleration}}$$

The implication of this formula, that mass is constant for a given object, can be illustrated by showing with actual physical materials that as force is increased, acceleration is increased proportionately. The effect of increasing mass could be shown by demonstrating that acceleration (roughly indicated by distance traveled against friction) under a constant force diminishes. To a large extent, such experiments can be considered as yielding in precise mathematical terms the relationships that are perceived in everyday experience and that lead to our intuitive understanding of such a concept as mass.

Above all, it should be noted that *mass* is a relational concept, a constant property of objects that reveals itself through the relation between the forces applied to the object and the resultant acceleration. Negative instances can only be properties of objects like weight, size, etc., that are not revealed in this way.

Summary

The basic concern of this paper has been with the teaching of concepts and the relevance of psychological and psycholinguistic theory and experimentation in guiding such teaching.

It has been necessary, first, to point out that concepts are essentially nonlinguistic (or perhaps better, *a*linguistic) because they are classes of experience which the individual comes to recognize as such, whether or not he is prompted or directed by symbolic language phenomena. Because the experiences of individuals tend to be in many respects similar, their concepts are also similar, and through various processes of learning and socialization these concepts come to be associated with words. The "meanings" of words are the socially-standardized concepts with which they are associated. One of the problems in teaching concepts is that of teaching the associations between words and concepts, and this is analogous to a paired-associate learning task.

At the same time, new concepts can be taught. One procedure can be called inductive: it consists of presenting an individual with an appropriate series of positive and negative instances of a concept, labeled as such, and allowing him to infer the nature of the concept by noticing invariant features or attributes. This is the procedure followed in the usual concept-formation experiment: although our present knowledge allows us to specify several *necessary* conditions for the formation of a concept, we still do not know what conditions are *sufficient*.

Another procedure for concept teaching may be called deductive, and it tends to be the favored procedure in school learning (and, in fact, in all expository prose). It is the technique of presenting concepts by verbal definition or description. This technique has received relatively little attention in psychological experimentation, but it seems to parallel inductive concept attainment in the sense that verbal descriptions are specifications of criterial attributes that can enable the individual to shortcut the process of hypothesis, discovery, and testing that typically occurs in the inductive concept-attainment procedure. Nevertheless, it is not known how relevant our knowledge of critical factors in inductive concept formation is for the guidance of deductive teaching procedures.

It is pointed out, however, that the efficient learning of concepts in school probably involves both inductive and deductive procedures. An analysis of typical concepts of the sort taught in school shows that they do indeed follow the models studied in psychological experimentation, but that they are more likely to involve complex relationships among prerequisite concepts. The difficulties that learners have in attaining a concept are likely to be due to their inadequate mastery of prerequisite concepts and to errors made by the teacher in presenting in proper sequence the information intrinsic to the definition of the concept.

References

Bouthilet, L. The measurement of intuitive thinking. Unpublished doctoral dissertation, University of Chicago, 1948.

Brown, R. W. and Lenneberg, E. H. A study in language and cognition. *Journal of Abnormal and Social Psychology*, 1954, **49**, 454–62.

Brownell, W. A. and Hendrickson, G. How children learn information, concepts, and generalizations. In N. B. Henry, ed., *Forty-ninth yearbook*, National Society for the Study of Education, Part I. Chicago: University of Chicago Press, 1950. Pp. 92–128.

Bruner, J. S., Goodnow, J. J., and Austin, G. A. *A study of thinking*. New York: Wiley, 1956.

Dale, E. and Eichholz, G. *Children's knowledge of words.* Columbus: Bureau of Educational Research and Service, Ohio State University, 1960.

Flavell, J. H. *The developmental psychology of Jean Piaget.* Princeton: Van Nostrand, 1963.

Freedman, J. L. and Mednick, S. A. Ease of attainment of concepts as a function of response dominance variance. *Journal of Experimental Psychology,* 1958, **55,** 463–66.

Friedman, K. C. Time concepts of elementary-school children. *Elementary School Journal,* 1944, **44,** 337–42.

Gage, N. L. Paradigms for research on teaching. In N. L. Gage, ed., *Handbook of research on teaching.* Chicago: Rand McNally, 1963. Pp. 94–141.

Helson, H., Dworkin, R. S., and Michels, W. C. Quantitative denotations of common terms as a function of background. *American Journal of Psychology,* 1956, **69,** 194–208.

Horn, E. *Methods of instruction in social studies.* New York: Scribner, 1937.

Hull, C. L. Quantitative aspects of the evolution of concepts. *Psychological Monographs,* 1920, p. 123.

Hunt, E. B. *Concept learning: An information processing problem.* New York: Wiley, 1962.

Levit, M. On the psychology and philosophy of concept formation. *Educational Theory,* 1953, **3,** 193–207.

Osgood, C. E., Suci, G. J., and Tannenbaum, P. H. *The measurement of meaning.* Urbana, Ill.: University of Illinois Press, 1957.

Pistor, F. Measuring the time concepts of children. *Journal of Educational Research,* 1939, **30,** 293–300.

Serra, M. C. How to develop concepts and their verbal representations. *Elementary School Journal,* 1953, **53,** 275–85.

Skinner, B. F. *Verbal behavior.* New York: Appleton-Century-Crofts, 1957.

Vinacke, W. E. Concept formation in children of school ages. *Education,* 1954, **74,** 527–34.

Wesley, E. B. and Adams, M. A. *Teaching social studies in elementary schools* (rev. ed.). Boston: D. C. Heath, 1952. P. 307.

27

Evaluation of Five Methods
of Teaching Concepts

DONALD M. JOHNSON / *Michigan State University*

R. PAUL STRATTON / *Michigan State University*

Most concept experiments require the subject (S) to learn to classify objects by practice with positive and negative instances and to label the positive instances with a nonsense syllable. Theoretical discussions often take this procedure as typical of concept learning. Carroll (1964) has questioned the relevance of such experiments to concept learning in school because the label is usually a standard word with a network of associations, and because teachers use several methods, some of which are more deductive than inductive. Serra (1953) was able to list a variety of methods by which teachers introduce concepts in elementary school, and inspection of a college textbook will also disclose a diversity of methods. There are at least three, in addition to the classification method, that have been frequently used by teachers and textbooks, but have not been experimentally

evaluated: defining a concept, using it in a sentence, and giving synonyms.

Experimental evaluation of these methods requires different tests of concept achievement appropriate to each, and different types of test item have been devised for regular testing of concept achievement in school also. Cronbach (1942) described several types of test item for diagnostic vocabulary testing. Hastings (1941) constructed six tests, each of a different item type, for testing achievement of 35 standard mathematics concepts and attained good reliabilities for each test. These studies have been concerned with blocks of related concepts within an area of knowledge, rather than single concepts, but the results suggest that achievement of

Reprinted with the permission of the authors and the publisher from *Journal of Educational Psychology*, 1966, Vol. 57, 48–53.

single concepts may also be evaluated by different tests which correspond to different teaching methods.

Evaluation of different teaching methods raises the critical question of amount of transfer. Classification practice may build up specific associations that suffice for a classification test, but lack the generality needed for a definition test. However, a recent experiment with 12-year-old children (Johnson & O'Reilly, 1964) found more transfer from classification training to definitions, when the definitions were carefully scored, than previous research had indicated. Since a set to learn concepts facilitates concept achievement (Reed, 1946), college Ss, who are used to studying concepts, may show even more transfer. The question can be systematically investigated by giving all tests to all Ss. This study proposes, therefore, to construct four tests of a few concepts, to teach these concepts by four corresponding methods and by a combination of the four, and to compare achievements on all tests following all teaching methods.

Test Construction and Analysis

Only standard concepts, designated by words, are relevant. The results of a preliminary study with a definition test and a multiple-choice synonym test gave some indication of suitable levels of difficulty. Words with Thorndike-Lorge frequency counts between 11 and 14 could be expected to be easy for college students. Words with counts between 1 and 6 could be expected to be difficult.

Selection was based on frequency and suitability to the four tests to be described. Only nouns, verbs, and adjectives with four synonyms could be used. Words with more than one meaning in an abridged dictionary and technical words that some Ss might currently be

studying were rejected. From the two pools of items that survived editing, the experimenters arbitrarily chose four easy words: controversy, vile, rustic, and vicinity, and four difficult words: alacrity, altercation, chide, and opulent.

TEST

There were two tests of the open-end or free-response type and two of the objective or multiple-choice type.

Definitions. Each word was printed with space for a short response. The instructions were: "There are four words to be defined. Explain briefly what each word means. Try each one, even if you have a guess."

Sentences. The incomplete-sentence technique is a way of embedding a word in connected discourse. The instructions were: "Here are some incomplete sentences to be finished. Please add a few words to give each sentence a meaningful ending. Try each one, even if you have to guess."

There were two sentences for each concept, and the eight sentences were printed in irregular order. Two examples follow: "A controversy ceases when _____."

"Something rustic would probably be found_____."

Classifications. Four short phrases were written to describe objects or events classifiable under each of the four concepts, together with four unrelated phrases. These 20 items appeared in irregular order with the following instructions:

Most, but not all, of the following items can be classified under four concepts: rustic, vile, controversy, vicinity. Read each item and mark each on your answer sheet thus: rustic 1, vile 2, controversy 3, vicinity 4, none of these 5.

Three sample items follow: "Two men of differing opinions discuss the social value of a book." "A weathered old barn." "An ex-criminal becomes a respected member of the community."

Synonyms. This conventional vocabulary test requires S to choose a synonym, but 10 choices were presented rather than the usual 5 in order to increase the reliability of the single item. Four such items were constructed for each concept; the 16 items appeared in blocks of 4, one for each word, in alphabetical order.

The tests were administered in the order given above to reduce the opportunity for learning from the alternatives on the multiple-choice tests. The two free-response tests were printed on separate sheets; each sheet was collected when completed. Time required was about 40 minutes.

SUBJECTS

Group 1, which had the easy concepts, consisted of 63 students in two classes in general psychology at Michigan State University. Group 2, which had the difficult concepts, consisted of 75 students in abnormal psychology. One foreign student was eliminated from each group.

RESULTS

The definitions were rated on a scale of 0–4 by two judges, using ordinary dictionary entries as criteria. The two sentence completions for each concept were treated as a unit and rated on a scale of 0–4 by the two judges because evaluation of a response seemed to be more stable when it was read in conjunction with another response related to the same concept. The criteria of judgment were based on the instructions to write meaningful endings and the assumption that Ss would try to demonstrate their knowledge. For both easy and difficult concepts, and for both definitions and sentences, the correlations between scorers were satisfactory for present purposes, ranging from .60–.97 with a median of .78. The sums of the two ratings were used in the analysis; hence the scores for each test ranged from 0–8.

The data from Classifications and Synonyms were treated as four-item tests with reliabilities computed by Kuder-Richardson Formula 20. For the easy concepts errors were infrequent, and reliabilities ranged from .19–.72 with a median of .48. For the difficult concepts the range was .65–.89 with a median of .79. The scores were doubled so that the range of scores on each test extended from 0–8.

Evaluation of Teaching Methods

A comparison of methods requires that each be used separately. Therefore four sets of teaching materials or programs, corresponding to the four tests, were prepared for teaching the four more difficult concepts. A mixed program was also prepared. Mean scores on the four tests of the four difficult concepts ranged from 2.6–5.2 as compared to a maximum of 8; hence there is room for improvement on each.

MATERIALS

Definitions. Definitions were written, with the help of several dictionaries, to characterize each term in a specific way and to place each in a higher-order class. An example follows:

> When two or more people express different opinions, get excited, and contradict each other, the event is called an *altercation.* Thus an *altercation* is a social interaction characterized by heated exchange of opposing arguments. Now write a definition of *altercation* in your own words.

The four definitions, with spaces for the responses, were printed on one side of one sheet of paper; hence all the material remained in view.

Sentences. Russell and Fea (1963) point out that wide reading is universally recommended as a method of building vocabulary, but that direct research on the value of reading in increasing vocabulary has yielded disappointing results. And the reason, they suggest, is the practice of trying to learn unfamiliar words from unfamiliar context.

For present purposes a short story of 174 words was written in which each of the four words appeared twice. The instructions were to read the story and learn the four words. Following Russell and Fea, the context was made easy; to most college students only the four words were unfamiliar. Then Ss were given four incomplete sentences with the request to finish them, using each of the four words once. All the material remained in view.

Classifications. Short descriptions of objects and events, similar to the test materials, were arranged in blocks of five, one classifiable under each of the four concepts, and one irrelevant. The four words and "none" were printed at the top of each block with instructions to classify each item by writing the appropriate word on a blank line next to the item. One such block appeared on the first page of a booklet, and the next page gave the answers to the first block, followed by a second block of five items. There were six blocks of 30 events to be classified, and correct answers were given to all. The arrangement of the booklet made it easy to turn back and check answers.

Synonyms. The first page of the booklet for the synonym training told Ss that their task was to learn the meanings of four concepts. Four short statements appeared next: "*Alacrity* means eagerness." "*Altercation* means squabble." "*Chide* means to criticize." "*Opulent* means luxuriant." Then each of the four concepts appeared next to a blank space, and four other synonyms were given, namely, reproach, quarrel, lavish, and promptness, to be matched with the four concepts by writing one synonym in each blank. The next page gave the answers to these and another block of four synonyms to be matched to the same four concepts. Four blocks of four synonyms were given, followed by answers on succeeding pages.

The arrangement of the booklet facilitated checking of answers.

Mixed Program. The review by Serra (1953) reported that teachers commonly use several methods together. Johnson and O'Reilly (1964) found that children with practice in classifying birds and defining the class learned more than children with only classifying practice. It is reasonable to suppose that, even if the amount of training is equated, a combination of methods would be more efficient than any single method.

The Mixed Program was constructed of materials used in the other four programs with necessary modifications. The definitions were abridged. Each concept appeared only once in the context of a sentence. Two synonyms and one example were given. An illustration follows:

> To chide someone is to talk to him to get him to correct his mistakes. *Chide* means to criticize or reproach. Thus a mother might chide her children for fighting with each other. An example might be a group of fellows poking fun at a boy with dirty clothes. Now write in your own words what *chide* means.

This was followed by one block of synonyms for matching and one block of events for classification, with correct answers.

The plan of the experiment required the formulation of certain rules in the preparation of the materials. The four teaching methods should be distinct. The definitions should not include synonyms. The words in context should not include definitions or examples to be classified. In respect to sentences, classifications, and synonyms the items used for teaching and testing should be different. This rule does not apply to the scoring of definitions because memorizing a definition is an accepted part of this teaching method. Each program should be an equally good representative of the method it embodies. This last is a goal that cannot be attained, but the attempt was made to make each program maximally effective.

Each program should require the same

time for completion. Differences in reading speed and care make this criterion difficult to attain also, but after some preliminary trials and adjustments it was expected that each program would require about 12 minutes for most college students.

PROCEDURE

Teaching and testing were conducted in a class of about 200 students in general psychology. The five sets of teaching materials, together with an irrelevant set of materials for a control group, were passed out serially so that approximately one-sixth of the class received each set, and neighboring Ss had different sets. Work was stopped and papers were collected at the end of 12 minutes. Nearly all Ss had finished.

The tests were given 9 days later. Absence of Ss on either day reduced the number in the five method groups to 22–28. The control group was increased to 40 by the addition of Ss who were present on the test day but absent on the teaching day. Scoring of the Definitions and Sen-

tences was carried out by the two judges who had attained the interjudge agreement mentioned above. The sums of the two ratings were used.

RESULTS

Table 1 shows the scores obtained by all groups on the separate tests and also the totals. The maximum score on any test of the four concepts is 32, and the maximum total is 128. In respect to total score all method groups exceeded the control group. These differences are large and, as Table 2 shows, highly significant.

The group that received the Mixed Program achieved higher total scores, as expected, than any group that received a single kind of training. These differences are significant with the exception of the group that had training on sentences, and this difference would be significant by a one-tailed test. Within the four groups that received a single kind of training there are no significant differ-

Table 1

MEANS AND STANDARD DEVIATIONS OBTAINED ON FOUR TESTS OF CONCEPT
ACHIEVEMENT BY SIX GROUPS WITH DIFFERENT TRAINING METHODS

| Method groups | N | Achievement scores | | | | |
		Def.	Sen.	Class.	Syn.	Total
Definitions	28	20.2	23.0	28.0	27.9	99.1
		8.4	8.3	5.3	5.3	22.6
Sentences	26	23.6	25.2	28.4	28.7	105.8
		7.9	5.4	4.0	4.0	17.1
Classifications	24	21.4	24.2	28.4	28.8	102.8
		8.2	6.6	5.6	4.5	21.0
Synonyms	25	19.9	24.3	26.1	27.6	97.9
		9.2	6.8	4.4	4.6	22.1
4 groups pooled	103	21.3	24.1	27.7	28.3	101.4
		8.5	6.2	4.4	4.6	20.8
Mixed program	22	26.5	27.4	29.3	30.5	113.6
		6.5	5.3	3.2	2.0	11.4
Control	40	12.8	17.6	23.5	23.4	77.2
		9.9	8.3	8.0	9.0	31.3

Table 2

SIGNIFICANCE OF DIFFERENCES BETWEEN TOTALS SHOWN IN TABLE 1

Method groups	Sen.	Class.	Syn.	Mixed	Control
Definitions	1.23	.61	.20	2.95**	3.34**
Sentences		.55	1.42	1.88	4.75**
Classifications			.80	2.19*	3.89**
Synonyms				3.12**	3.10**
4 groups pooled				2.66**	6.00**
Mixed program					6.56**

$* p < .05.$
$** p < .01.$

ences. For this reason these groups were pooled to form a group of 103 with a mean total of 101.4. The difference between this mean and that of the mixed group is highly significant.

The results for separate tests are similar to those for total scores, but the differences are not so clear-cut. All groups did better than the control group on all tests, and the mixed group did better than any single-method group. On the Definitions test no single-method group is significantly superior to any other, but when the four groups are pooled, the mean of the pooled group is superior to the control group ($p <$ .01), and the mixed group is superior to the pooled group ($p < .01$). The same statements can be made for the Sentences test and the Synonyms test. On the Classifications test the difference between the pooled-group mean and the control-group mean is significant ($p <$ .01), and the difference between the mixed-group and the pooled-group mean yields a t of 1.56. In general it is safe to say that each kind of training was effective in raising scores on all tests above the control group and that the mixed training was best.

Another way to look at the data is to examine the mean scores on each test of each concept. Each of the 16 concept means for the pooled group exceeded the corresponding mean for the control group, and 15 of the 16 means for the mixed group exceeded the corresponding means for the pooled group.

Discussion

The results show that construction of short tests of single concepts is feasible. The tests of the more difficult concepts yielded 16 reliable scores in about 40 minutes; each score measures knowledge of a single concept by a different response, and each is sensitive to the improvement resulting from a small amount of practice. The small standard deviations for the mixed group on Classifications and Synonyms suggest a ceiling effect, but this effect was not serious enough to prevent this group from exceeding the others.

Concepts of this kind can be taught to college students equally well by different programs of instruction which require different responses. The superiority of the Mixed Program supports the common practice of teachers and textbook writers.

The question about transfer may be phrased in this form: How much of what was learned by one method transferred to the tests constructed of materials used in the other methods? Since transfer effects are usually small, one might assume that each of the four single-method groups would get its highest score on the test corresponding to that method. The results of Table 1 do not support this assumption. The group that had practice in writing definitions actually was below the pooled-group mean on the Definitions test, but above the pooled-group mean on Classifications. The synonyms group was the lowest of the four on Synonyms; it was above the pooled-group mean only on Sentences. Overall, there is no evidence of specific relations between training method and test achievement; the picture is one of 100% transfer.

One interpretation for the large transfer effect is that S sets concept acquisition as his goal, varying his methods on his own initiative and testing himself so that the intended differences between training methods vanish. Thus each method takes over some of the advantages of the mixed method. An-other possibility is that the transfer occurs on the testing day when S treats the four tests as problems and uses whatever he can recall to solve them. One with training on sentences may recall the story, for example, and use this information to formulate a definition or to choose a synonym. Probably transfer occurs during both learning and testing.

The matter of interference should be mentioned. One might suppose that if S is given a definition or a synonym, there would be no more for him to learn. But he is given four definitions, or four synonyms, as well as verbal instructions; hence some interference can be expected. This may explain why the Sentences method, which depends on learning from context, usually considered inefficient, was as good as any. The continuity of the story probably reduced the amount of interference.

References

Carroll, J. B. Words, meanings and concepts. *Harvard Educational Review*, 1964, **34,** 178–202.

Cronbach, L. J. Analysis of techniques for diagnostic vocabulary testing. *Journal of Educational Research*, 1942, **36,** 206–17.

Hastings, J. T. Testing junior high school mathematics concepts. *School Review*, 1941, **49,** 766–76.

Johnson, D. M. and O'Reilly, C. A. Concept attainment in children: Classifying and defining. *Journal of Educational Psychology*, 1964, **55,** 71–74.

Reed, H. B. Factors influencing the learning and retention of concepts: I. The influence of set. *Journal of Experimental Psychology*, 1946, **36,** 71–87.

Russell, D. H. and Fea, H. R. Research on teaching reading. In N. L. Gage, ed., *Handbook of research on teaching.* Chicago: Rand McNally, 1963. Pp. 865–928.

Serra, M. C. How to develop concepts and their verbal representation. *Elementary School Journal*, 1953, **53,** 275–85.

28

Importance of Problem Heterogeneity to Programed Instruction

ROSS E. TRAUB / *McGill University*

In developing self-instructional programs for relatively complex tasks, such as solving linear equations in one unknown or adding signed numbers, a programmer faces the problem of identifying the skills needed to perform the task. Guidance in dealing with this problem may be obtained from the conceptual framework suggested by Gagné (1962). This framework consists of the analysis of a task into a set of subtasks, all logically necessary for the performance of the task. From this point of view, the skills needed to perform the task are those required for working the subtasks. Programing then involves devising ways to provide experience with the subtasks, the object being to develop the separate subtask skills and promote transfer of those skills to the performance of the task as a whole.

Experience with subtasks may be provided in at least two ways. One is to use instructions that tell about the subtasks (Gagné, 1962). An additional device, commonly used in teaching, is to give practice solving problems of the subtasks.

Several studies have used problems to provide subtask experience (Gagné, Mayor, Garstens, and Paradise, 1962; Traub, 1963; Tuckman, 1962). In general, these studies show that experience obtained from instructions *and* solving problems results in better performance of the task as a whole than experience obtained from instructions alone. However, the *kind* of problems used to provide subtask experience has not been systematically studied. In particular it is not known whether problem heteroge-

Reprinted with the permission of the author and the publisher from *Journal of Educational Psychology*, 1966, Vol. 57, 54–60. The Method section has been condensed.

neity, that is, variation in the contexts and the answers of a set of problems, is a factor in learning.

The main purpose of this experiment was to study problem heterogeneity as a factor in learning a complex task from a self-instructional program. To do this, a task was analyzed into subtasks. On some of the subtasks, one group of subjects was given heterogeneous problems to solve. These problems were heterogeneous in that they differed widely in their contexts and in several aspects of their solutions. Another group solved homogeneous problems, ones that were very similar in their contexts and in their solutions. A control group worked problems that reviewed the learning done on previous subtasks. This group was to provide a base line with which to compare the other two groups. After learning the subtasks, all subjects were tested on problems of the task as a whole. Performance of these problems was used to evaluate the effects produced by the different kinds of subtask problems.

Another aspect of the present experiment was to investigate the relation between problem heterogeneity and subject aptitude. The question asked was whether heterogeneous problems are better at one ability level and homogeneous problems at another ability level. To answer this question, scores on several aptitude and achievement examinations were used to test for an interaction between level of subject aptitude and the effects produced by the different kinds of subtask problems.

Method

THE LEARNING TASK AND THE EXPERIMENTAL VARIABLE

The task used in this study was graphical addition of positive and negative integers.

$$(^+7) + (^-3) = \underline{\hspace{2cm}}$$

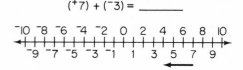

Fig. 1 A solved graphical integer-addition problem.

Graphical addition involves drawing an arrow on the number line to demonstrate the addition of two numbers. This is illustrated in Figure 1. Notice that the arrow starts at the location on the number line of the first integer to be added. The length and direction of the arrow represent the second integer so that the stopping point of the arrow locates the sum of the two numbers.

The graphical addition task was analyzed into subtasks, and a program of instructions was written by following the suggestions of Gagné (1962, p. 357). The program had four parts. The first part taught how to locate positive integers on the number line and how to draw arrows to represent positive integers. Part 2 of the program provided similar training for negative integers.

The third part of the program taught how to draw an arrow of specified length from the number-line location of a specified integer. This training involved two subtasks, one for arrows drawn in a positive direction, the other for arrows drawn in a negative direction. . . . In effect the instructions told the student to place his pencil at a certain point on the number line and draw the arrow representing a given integer. Then the student completed the task by identifying the integer found at the end of the arrow.

Three different kinds of problems were devised for the subtasks included in the third part of the program. These different problems constituted the experimental variable and may be described as follows.

Heterogeneous Problems. One set of 20 problems was made heterogeneous in two respects. First, the contexts of the problems were varied by providing a different 20-unit segment of the number line with each problem. Second, the heterogeneous problems were constructed so that their answers varied in certain ways from one problem to the next. . . . See Part A of Figure 2.

A
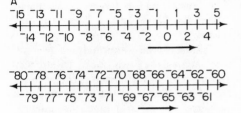

B
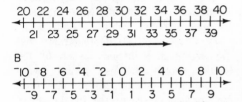

Fig. 2 Number-line segments and correct arrow responses for three heterogeneous subtask problems (Part A) and one homogeneous subtask problem (Part B).

Homogeneous Problems. A second set of 20 problems was homogeneous. The contexts of these problems were held constant by providing the same segment of the number line with each problem. Also the answers to the homogeneous problems were very similar. . . . See Part B of Figure 2.

Review Problems. A third set of 20 problems was not directly related to the skills taught in the third part of the program. These problems gave practice in drawing arrows to represent integers. That is, these were review problems giving additional practice of the skills learned in the first two parts of the program.

The fourth part of the learning program taught the graphical addition task and presented 26 graphical addition problems. These problems were designed to cover a wide range of difficulty. They con-

sisted of one- and two-digit integers presented for addition in the format illustrated in Figure 1. Each problem required two answers: the graphical one of an arrow drawn on the number line, and the integer answer.

SUBJECTS

The subjects were 294 sixth-grade children who were naïve about graphical integer addition. . . . The sample included 169 boys and 125 girls.

PROCEDURE

The learning program was presented in the form of a 150-page booklet. To work the program, each student read a page of the booklet, made a written response, and then checked his answer by looking on the back of the page. Wrong answers were corrected before the student continued. This was the procedure for the first 130 pages of the program. The last 20 pages were for the 26 graphical addition problems. Students could not check their answers to these problems.

As was previously indicated, the program had four parts. It was administered on four successive days, one part being given each day. On the first day, instructions for working the program were read. . . . Then the students worked Part 1 of the program. . . . On the second day of the experiment, Part 2 of the program was administered. Parts 1 and 2 were the same for all students.

For the third part of the program, worked on Day 3, the total sample of children was divided into four sections on the basis of their sex and school district. Each of these four sections was further divided at random so that the students in each of three subsections had the same range of arithmetic aptitude as measured by the Arithmetic Concepts Test of the Iowa Tests of Basic Skills. . . .

It will now be useful to talk in terms of three experimental groups constructed as follows: Each of the four sections formed by dividing the students on the basis of sex and school district contributed one of its three subsections to each of the three experimental groups. Thus an experimental group was made up of students of each sex from both school districts.

The experimental groups were given the same program of instructions on Day 3, but each got different subtask problems to work. One group got the 20 heterogeneous problems, another the 20 homogeneous problems, and the third the 20 review problems.

The fourth part of the program was worked on the fourth day. It was the same for all the students and contained the 26 graphical integer-addition problems. Responses to these problems were scored for the number of correct arrow answers and the number of correct integer answers. Also, the arrow errors were qualitatively analyzed and categorized.

Results

THE EFFECT OF PROBLEM HETEROGENEITY ON GRAPHICAL INTEGER ADDITION

The main results of this study are presented in Table 1, which gives the means and standard deviations for two measures of the performance of the experimental groups on the graphical integer-addition problems. It is clear that the best performance was achieved by the heterogeneous-problems group: Both the

arrow and integer means of this group were larger than the corresponding means of the homogeneous- and review-problems groups. Also evident from Table 1 is the fact that the homogeneous-problems group was not consistently superior to the review-problems group: The former had a larger arrow mean while the latter had a larger integer mean.

These results were analyzed by one-way analysis of variance. Differences among the experimental groups were significant for both the arrow-response measure ($p < .01$) and the integer-response measure ($p < .05$). Additional analyses using the Newman-Keuls procedure for group comparisons (Winer, 1962, p. 80) demonstrated that the arrow and integer means of the heterogeneous-problems group were significantly greater (p's $< .05$) than the corresponding means of the other two groups. However, the arrow and integer means of the homogeneous-problems group and the review-problems group were not reliably different.

THE INTERACTION BETWEEN PROBLEM HETEROGENEITY AND SUBJECT APTITUDE

No evidence was found of a reliable interaction between the effects of problem heterogeneity on graphical integer

Table 1

MEANS AND STANDARD DEVIATIONS OF ARROW AND INTEGER SCORES FOR EACH EXPERIMENTAL GROUP

Experimental group	N	Arrow mean	SD	Integer mean	SD
Heterogeneous problems	97	11.98	8.78	14.81	7.42
Homogeneous problems	93	8.85	7.80	11.90	7.04
Review problems	104	7.11	8.34	12.30	7.86

addition and subject aptitude. The test for an interaction was made in two ways. First, a two-way analysis of variance design was used in which the different experimental groups provided the categories for one main effect, and several levels of arithmetic aptitude as measured by the Arithmetic Concepts Test provided the categories for the second main effect (see the Treatments × Levels design of Lindquist, 1953, pp. 127–132). Eight such analyses were carried out, one for the arrow scores and one for the integer scores from each of four sections of the total sample. The four sections were obtained by dividing the subjects on the basis of sex and school district.[1] Only one of the eight analyses of variance had a significant interaction term ($p < .05$). It was interpreted as being caused by chance factors.

The second test for an interaction employed analysis of covariance (Gulliksen & Wilks, 1950). Two analyses were made, one with the arrow scores, the other with the integer scores as the dependent variable. For both these analyses, the independent variables were scores on several aptitude and achievement tests that were administered to the students as part of a more detailed study (Traub, 1964). The results confirmed the conclusion derived from the two-way analyses of variance: The heterogeneous subtask problems produced significantly better performance of the graphical integer-addition task independently of subject aptitude.

---

[1] Analysis of variance was performed separately on the data from each of the four sample sections because the sections contained unequal numbers of subjects and covered different levels of arithmetic ability. These conditions made it impossible to perform a higher-way analysis of variance including sex and school district as main effects.

OTHER RESULTS

Classes of Arrow-Response Errors. Three broad classes of errors were identified in the arrow responses to the graphical integer-addition problems. These were stereotyped, random, and omitted-response errors. Stereotyped errors had certain well-defined properties in relation to the problems they were to answer. For example, one stereotyped error had the arrow starting correctly at the location on the number line of the first of two integers being added. Instead of representing the second integer, these arrows were drawn *to the location* of the second integer. There were six other clearly identifiable kinds of stereotyped errors. The second class of errors was random; they could not be related in any way to the problem being answered. The third error type was the omitted response in which no arrow was drawn. . . .

The most interesting result involves the heterogeneous-problems group. This group made the lowest proportion of stereotyped and omitted-response errors, and the highest proportion of random errors.

The Effect of Heterogeneity on the Difficulty of Subtask Problems. Table 2 presents means and standard deviations for each experimental group on two measures of performance on Part 3 of the learning program. These measures were the number of errors made in working the 20 subtask problems and the time required for Part 3 of the program. It is clear from Table 2 that the heterogeneous-problems group committed more errors and required a longer working time than the other two experimental groups. The homogeneous-problems group had the second highest mean score on both measures, while the review-problems group had the lowest. All differences between the group means

Table 2

MEANS AND STANDARD DEVIATIONS FOR EACH
EXPERIMENTAL GROUP ON TWO MEASURES OF
PERFORMANCE ON PART 3 OF THE LEARNING PROGRAM

Experimental group	Errors on subtask problems		Working time (in min.)	
	M	SD	M	SD
Heterogeneous problems	3.43	3.94	34.53	8.78
Homogeneous problems	2.13	3.52	29.35	8.34
Review problems	.10	.32	24.22	6.39

reported in Table 2 were significant (p's < .01) when tested by the Newman-Keuls procedure. These significant group differences contrast with the non-significant differences found among the time and error means for Parts 1 and 2 of the program. Thus it follows that the differences obtained for Part 3 of the program were produced by differences in the difficulty of the three kinds of subtask problems. The heterogeneous problems were most difficult, the homogeneous problems second most difficult, and the review problems easiest.

Discussion

In this study, students who worked heterogeneous subtask problems performed the task significantly better than students who worked either the homogeneous problems or the irrelevant review problems. One reason for this finding is suggested by the results of the error analysis of responses to the graphical integer-addition problems. The experimental groups differed in the proportion of arrow responses that could be classified as stereotyped errors. In particular, the heterogeneous-problems group made the smallest proportion of stereotyped errors. Also, this group omitted the smallest proportion of responses. Thus, the heterogeneous-problems group made fewer stereotyped errors while answering more problems.

It is clear that one reason the heterogeneous-problems group did better on the final task was because they made fewer stereotyped errors and omitted fewer responses. The reason for this is probably that the heterogeneous problems contained more information about the task than the other kinds of subtask problems. Support for this suggestion is provided by the finding that the heterogeneous problems were the most difficult. It is likely that difficulty has a high correlation with the amount of information contained in a set of problems.

Additional and logically more direct support for the information interpretation comes from an inspection of the heterogeneous subtask problems and the graphical integer-addition problems. The fact is that both these sets of problems were heterogeneous in the sense of presenting problems in the context of several different number-line segments. Moreover, the different kinds of arrow answers required for the heterogeneous subtask problems were also required for the graphical integer-addition problems.

From the foregoing it is clear that, while all groups had the same instructions for solving the graphical integer-addition task, the heterogeneous-problems group had more information about certain aspects of the task. The homogeneous- and review-problems groups did not have the information, and hence for these groups the graphical integer-addition problems would have been relatively more complex. Apparently the effect of this greater complexity was to increase the probability of forgetting or confusing the correct procedure for solving the task. Consequently, the homogeneous- and review-problems groups adopted a problem-solving procedure that resulted in a stereotyped error, or else they gave no response at all.

In summary, the findings of the present investigation indicate that heterogeneous subtask problems can produce better learning of a complex task, such as graphical integer addition, when the teaching is done by a self-instructional program. The importance of heterogeneous problems is additionally emphasized by the negative finding of the study. This finding was that the different kinds of subtask problems affected learning independently of level of subject aptitude. Heterogeneous problems were best for students of high and low aptitude.

References

Gagné, R. M. The acquisition of knowledge. *Psychological Review*, 1962, **69**, 355–65.

Gagné, R. M., Mayor, J. R., Garstens, Helen L., and Paradise, N. E. Factors in acquiring knowledge of a mathematical task. *Psychological Monographs*, 1962, **76** (7, Whole No. 526).

Gulliksen, H. and Wilks, S. S. Regression tests for several samples. *Psychometrika*, 1950, **15**, 91–114.

Lindquist, E. F. *Design and analysis of experiments in psychology and education*. Boston: Houghton Mifflin, 1953.

Traub, R. E. Basic factor abilities: Their relation to rate of learning and to the effect of repetition on performance of a programmed learning task. Unpublished minor research paper, Princeton University, 1963.

Traub, R. E. The importance of problem heterogeneity to programmed learning. Princeton, N.J.: Educational Testing Service Research Bulletin No. RB-64-26, Office of Naval Research Technical Report, May 1964.

Tuckman, B. W. Ability and practice in the performance of non-reproductive tasks. Unpublished minor research paper, Princeton University, 1962.

Winer, B. J. *Statistical principles in experimental design*. New York: McGraw-Hill, 1962.

29

Adapting Visual Illustrations
for Effective Learning

FRANCIS M. DWYER, JR. / *The Pennsylvania State University*

It is relatively apparent that visual illustrations are rapidly becoming an almost universal means of instruction: slides, photographs, cartoons, transparencies, film strips, and sketches are now in use from kindergarten through college. Even though research has established that the use of carefully prepared and relevant visual aids can improve student achievement, there has been no attempt to determine the relative effectiveness of the various types of visual illustrations. Presumably not all types of visual illustrations will be equally efficient in promoting the learning of different types of educational tasks. Justification for the use of various types of visual illustrations should be based on their distinctive contributions to specific types of learning.

Related Research

A review of research in the field of visual education failed to locate any study investigating the relative effectiveness of visual illustrations possessing differing amounts of realistic detail and used in conjunction with oral instruction. In fact, the literature fails to reveal conclusive evidence that any one form of visual aid is more effective than another.

Some research evidence does exist, however, regarding the comparative effectiveness of two or three visual media, i.e., sound motion pictures, silent motion pictures, and still pictures. Many studies (e.g., McClusky and McClusky, 1924; Vernon, 1946; Heidgerken, 1948), have found no significant differences in the effectiveness of two or more visual media, such as films and filmstrips. Other studies (e.g., Carson, 1951; Hovland, Lumsdaine, and Sheffield, 1949;

Reprinted in abridged form with the permission of the author and the publisher from *Harvard Educational Review*, 1967, Vol. 37, 250–63. Copyright © 1967 President and Fellows of Harvard College.

Slattery, 1953; Ortgiesen, 1954) have shown the superiority of filmstrips over films, while some other studies (e.g., Goodman, 1942; Craig, 1956) have demonstrated the superiority of silent motion pictures over sound motion pictures. There have also been a number of studies (e.g., Vander Meer, 1949; Cogswell, 1953; Bathurst, 1954; Fullerton, 1956) which made comparisons along other dimensions. However, in these studies the illustrations displayed through the various media were seldom equivalent. Even when slides are made from frames of a film, they do not convey exactly the same content as the film. These studies seem to indicate that no valid comparisons can be made unless material equivalent in content appears in all of the media being compared. Caution is therefore needed in attempting to evaluate the research literature.

Each medium has unique characteristics which should be employed to achieve specific learning objectives. Films may be used when motion is required to convey manipulative tasks or processes. Still pictures may be effective in place of films where the film goes too fast, or shifts scenes too quickly, to stress important points. Slides and filmstrips enable the instructor to increase the time students may view the illustrations, to answer their questions, and to make comments.

Many studies attempt to compare the effectiveness of the various media in presenting the same information, but do not give adequate consideration to these inherent capabilities and limitations. In some instances, it would seem inappropriate to compare the effectiveness of a motion picture and a series of slides abstracted from the film in presenting the same information. Each medium should be evaluated in terms of the learning objectives for which it is best designed. Comparisons of different media in relation to one type of learning objective, or where specific objectives are not identified and reported, produce results which are uninterpretable.

Realism Theories

This study was motivated by the apparent inconsistencies between the results of some research on perception and certain established theories, specifically the iconicity theory identified by Morris (1946), the sign similarity orientation developed by Carpenter (1953), the theory of pictorial perception proposed by Gibson (1954), and Dale's (1946) cone of experience. For convenience, these will be referred to collectively as "realism theories."

The basic assumption of each of the realism theories is that learning will be more complete as the number of cues in the learning situation increases. Each posits a continuum of learning effectiveness extending from the object or situation itself to a simplified abstraction of it—from a motion picture with color and sound, for instance, through a photograph, to (least effective) a verbal description. Their contention is that the more qualities a visual shares with the object or situation to be depicted, the more realistic the visual, and, therefore, the easier the learning. Miller *et al.* (1957) support this assumption as they feel that the chances of an individual's learning in a particular situation are increased as the number of cues is increased. Following this assumption, many researchers, multiple-channel communicationists, have proceeded to fill all transmission channels, especially the pictorial, with as much information as possible (Hartman, 1960, 1961; Murry, 1960; Cropper *et al.*, 1961; Twyford *et al.*, 1964).

However, there is other theory and research suggesting that this assumption underlying the realism theories may be a tenuous one at best. Miller *et al.* (1957) have stated that it would be a mistake to assume that one cue added to another would increase learning by a linear increment. Their contention is that additional cues or excessively realistic cues may be distracting or possibly even evoke competitive responses in opposition to the desired learning. Such cues would be interference and would reduce rather than facilitate learning. Accordingly, Bruner *et al.* (1956) and Travers *et al.* (1964) have suggested that learners do not need a wealth of stimuli in order to recognize the attributes of an object or situation which place it in a particular category. Travers *et al.* (1964, p. 1.19) maintain that "merely confronting a person with stimuli identical to those emitted by the real environment is no guarantee that useful information will be retained."

Travers *et al.* (1964, p. 1.18) feel that the realistic presentation of much content provides unnecessary detail and that the real objective of visual education is "not so much to bring the pupil into close touch with reality, but to help students become more effective in dealing with reality." Travers and his associates feel that this can be done effectively by symbols. Broadbent (1958, 1965) has explained that the reduction of learning as cues increase is caused by the filtering process in the central nervous system which prevents many of the realistic stimuli from receiving active reception in the brain. Jacobson (1950, 1951) supports this point of view and states that the brain is capable of utilizing only minute proportions of the information perceived. Travers *et al.* (1964, p. 5.20) explain that in relation to auditory and visual channels "the amount of information which is utilized by the higher centers is vastly less than the informational capacity of the channels involved."

Attneave (1954) conducted research guided by the hypothesis that one function of the perceptual machinery was to reduce redundant stimulation and to encode incoming information so that only the essentials travel through the central nervous system to the brain. In support of his hypothesis, he states that (1954, pp. 185–86) "lines bordering objects provide the essence of the information to be conveyed." This he feels accounts for the effectiveness of cartoons and stick drawings as conveyors of information. Travers *et al.* (1964, p. 5.25) have stated that visual data are stored in the nervous system in some form isomorphic with line drawings, permitting the individual to remember and reproduce such information with greater facility than more realistic information. This would seem to indicate that those visuals closely representing line drawings and containing the essence of the information to be transmitted would be more effective and more efficient in facilitating learning than would more detailed illustrations, which would have to be coded initially by the central nervous system before being transmitted. Travers *et al.* (1964, p. 1.18) suggest that "inputs of information when received by the human organism are coded and most of the original stimuli initially presented to the senses not only never enters the perceptual system, but is not remembered by the system."

In summary, there is theory and research that seems to indicate, contrary to the assumption of the realism theories, that presenting a student with a wealth of stimuli that approximate "reality" is not necessarily the most effective way to facilitate learning. Because excesses of realism may actually interfere with the transmission of information and because certain kinds of stimuli may not be perceived, it seems necessary for educators concerned with the structure of visual illustrations to attempt to discover those characteristics that will facilitate particular kinds of learning.

This study compares the relative effectiveness of three types of visual illustration sequences used in the instruction of university freshmen about the human heart. It also attempts to determine which illustrated presentation most successfully facilitated four specific learning objectives: knowledge of the location of anatomical parts, transfer of learning (from the oral-visual presentation to a three-dimensional model of the heart), knowledge of terminology, and comprehension.

. . .

Methods and Procedures

The experimental population for this study consisted of 108 freshman students enrolled at The Pennsylvania State University. These students were assigned at random to one of four groups: Group I, N = 30; Group II, N = 27; Group III, N = 26; Group IV, N = 25. The three visual groups were considered to be the treatment groups and the non-visual group the control group.

All the students in each group took a pretest, received their respective presentation, and took four post-tests, all in one session. Students in all four groups listened to the same forty-minute recorded oral presentation; at the same time, each group was shown a sequence of thirty-nine black and white slides designed to complement the oral instruction. Basically the same information was presented to each group; the only difference in the treatments was in the degree of realism (detail) in the sequences of illustrations.

The oral presentation was by means of a Sony Photo-Sync tape recorder. The visual illustrations were presented via a Bausch and Lomb slide projector with an automatic time changer. The oral and visual materials were electrically synchronized, in such a way that students receiving the pictorial presentations viewed their respective visuals for equal amounts of time. Students in the control (oral) group were shown the name of the part of the heart being discussed during the time the students in the pictorial treatments viewed illustrations. The rate and number of words per minute were identical for each presentation.

. . .

Instruction

All students received the same recorded oral instruction. Group I saw no accompanying illustrations, but the names of the parts of the heart mentioned were projected on the screen.

Group II viewed abstract linear representations of the form and relative locations of the parts of the heart as they were mentioned in the oral presentation. These drawings, like the other illustrations used in the study, were similar to those in many science textbooks.

Group III was shown more detailed, shaded drawings representing the parts of the heart as they were mentioned.

Students in Group IV saw realistic photographs of the parts of the heart being described.

Criterion Tests

Each student received four individual criterion tests: Heart Model Test, Terminology Test, Drawing Test, and Comprehension Test. Scores received on these four tests were combined in a composite seventy-eight item test designed to measure total understanding of the concepts presented.

HEART MODEL TEST

Consisted of twenty identification items. This test required students to identify the numbered parts on a three-dimensional model of the human heart. Each part of the heart, which had been discussed in the oral presentation, was labeled on the heart model. The students were provided with an answer sheet with corresponding numbers on which they were to write in the name of the part of the heart which corresponded to the number. (Kuder-Richardson Formula 20 reliability, r = .923)

TERMINOLOGY TEST

Consisted of twenty fill-in type questions. This test attempted to evaluate the learner's knowledge of referents for specific symbols, whether presented orally or visually. For example, knowledge of the variety of symbols which may be used for a single referent, or knowledge of the referent most appropriate to a given use of a symbol were tested. (Kuder-Richardson Formula 20 reliability, r = .885)

DRAWING TEST

Consisted of eighteen identification items. This test emphasized symbols with concrete referents. Knowledge of positions and locations and recall of patterns, structures, or settings or parts within an entity could be included in a test of this nature. Students were required to draw a representative diagram of the heart and to place the identified parts in their respective positions. This test evaluated the student's ability to position correctly the various parts (i.e., valves, auricles, ventricles, etc.) on their diagram representing the heart.

(Kuder-Richardson Formula 20 reliability, r = .906)

COMPREHENSION TEST

Consisted of twenty multiple-choice questions. This test required the student to mentally reorganize material to achieve a particular purpose, perhaps to develop a new view of the material. Specifically, it consisted of multiple-choice items which referred to the position of specific parts of the heart during its functioning. The student was then asked to identify the position of other specified parts at that particular moment. This test required a thorough understanding of the heart, its parts, its internal functioning, and the simultaneous processes which occur during the systolic and diastolic phases.

TOTAL CRITERION TEST

Consisted of seventy-eight items. Scores received on the four criterion tests were combined in a composite seventy-eight item total criterion test designed to measure total understanding of the concepts presented. (Kuder-Richardson Formula 20 reliability, r = .873)

PHYSIOLOGY PRETEST

Consisted of thirty-six multiple-choice questions. This test was administered to all participants in an attempt to determine their prior factual knowledge of functional aspects of human physiology. Scores on this test were used as the adjusting variable in the analysis of covariance to evaluate the relative effectiveness of the various treatments. (Kuder-Richardson Formula 20 reliability, r = .728)

Analysis of Pretest

Analysis of covariance, using pretest achievement on the thirty-six-item physiology test to partial out previous knowledge in the subject area, was used to determine the significance of differences in immediate achievement for the four treatment groups. Comparisons among the individual means of the four groups, via Dunn's (1961) "c" procedure, were conducted to determine the effectiveness of the various treatment groups in enhancing student achievement on the four individual tests.

. . .

Results

Analyses of covariance were performed on the test scores in order to assess differences among the four groups. With respect to the Total Criterion Test, the abstract linear representation and the detailed shaded drawings were both more effective than either the oral presentation alone or the presentation of the realistic photographs ($p < .01$). There was no difference between groups having the abstract linear representation or the detailed drawing presentation, and the oral presentation was as effective as the realistic photographic presentation.

Analysis of scores on the Drawing Test yielded the same results as those of the Total Criterion Test. The Heart Model Test also produced the same results, except that the abstract linear presentation was more effective than the detailed shaded drawing presentation ($p < .01$). On the Terminology Test, groups receiving the abstract linear representations and the detailed shaded drawings performed better than the group receiving photographs ($p < .01$), although there was no difference between the two former groups. The oral presentation group was no worse than any of the others. Finally, there were no significant differences between any groups on the Comprehension Test.

Interpretation

In terms of instructional effectiveness, economy, and simplicity of production, the data suggest that abstract linear presentations should be used to teach overall concepts, specific locations and positions of patterns and parts of the heart, and to facilitate transfer of training. Oral presentations alone, however, are recommended for teaching term referents and reorganization of the material by the student. It appears that the simplest illustrations are the most effective.

Conclusion

This study represents an initial inquiry into the complex problems of comparisons between media, and of the use of different media to produce maximum learning. The results seem to indicate that the reduction of realistic detail in an illustration does not necessarily reduce its instructional effectiveness and in many cases improves it. Most importantly, there were significant differences in the effectiveness of different types of instruction for different educational objectives. In the final analysis, it is probably necessary to determine what details are crucial cues for particular lessons.

So far, there has been very little research to determine the specific effects of various types of visual illustrations for either general or particular educational objectives. What is needed is extensive research into and development of various types of visual illustrations, and how they may mediate learning.

It is readily acknowledged that the effects of visual illustrations on learning depend predominately on the characteristics of the students, the characteristics of the content, and the ways in which the content is organized. Even though this study was conducted in a specific content area with a specific type of student, it opens avenues for further research, some of which should involve different content areas, subjects of various ages and entering skills, various educational objectives, and student-paced as well as teacher-paced instruction. Such research would hopefully test the generalizability of the results reported herein.

References

Attneave, F. Some informational aspects of visual perception. *Psychol. Rev.*, 1954, **61**, 183–93.

Bathurst, L. H. The comparative effectiveness of using a wall model, motion picture films, filmstrips, and the standard slide rule in teaching the operation of a slide rule. Unpublished doctoral dissertation. Pennsylvania State Univer., 1954.

Broadbent, D. E. *Perception and communication.* New York: Pergamon Press, 1958.

Broadbent, D. E. Information processing in the nervous system. *Science.* Massachusetts: American Association for the Advancement of Science, 1965, **3695**, 457–62.

Bruner, J. S., Goodnow, J. J., and Austin, G. A. *A study of thinking.* New York: Wiley, 1956.

Carpenter, C. R. A theoretical orientation for instructional film research. *Audiovisual Commun. Rev.* 1953, **1**, 38–52.

Carson, D. The American way of life as portrayed in filmstrips: An experiment in visual education. Abstracted by Charles F. Hoban and Edward B. Van Ormer. *Instructional film research 1918–1950.* Technical Report, SDC-269-7-19, Special Devices Center, Office of Naval Research, Port Washington, New York, 1951.

Cogswell, J. F. A study of the effects of three dimensional sound motion pictures on the learning of a perceptual-motor task: The assembly of the breech block of the 40 mm anti-aircraft gun. Unpublished master's thesis. Pennsylvania State Univer., 1953.

Craig, G. Q. A comparison between sound and silent films in teaching. *Brit. J. of Educ. Psychol.*, 1956, **26**, 202–06.

Dale, E. *Audio-visual methods in teaching.* New York: The Dryden Press, 1946.

Dale, E. *Audio-visual methods in teaching.* New York: Henry Holt, 1959.

Dunn, O. J. Multiple comparisons among means. *Amer. Statist. Assn. J.*, 1961, **56**, 52–64.

Fullerton, B. J. The comparative effect of color and black and white guidance films employed with and without "anticipatory" remarks upon acquisition and retention of factual information. Unpublished doctoral dissertation, Univer. of Oklahoma, 1956.

Gibson, J. J. A theory of pictorial perception. *Audiovis. Commun. Rev.*, Winter, 1954, **2**, 3–23.

Goodman, D. J. Comparative effectiveness of pictorial teaching aids. Unpublished doctoral dissertation, New York Univer., 1942.

Gray, H. *Anatomy of the human body.* Philadelphia: Lea and Ferbiger, 1944.

Gropper, G. L., Lumsdaine, A. A., and Skipman, V. *Improvement of televised instruction based on student responses to achievement tests.* Pittsburgh:

Metropolitan Pittsburgh Educ. Television Station, and the American Inst. for Research, 1961.

Hartman, F. R. A review of research on learning from single and multiple channel communications and a proposed model with generalizations and implications for television communication. *Research on the communications process.* Division of Academic Research and Service: Pennsylvania State Univer., Oct., 1960, 6.1–6.40.

Hartman, F. R. Single and multiple channel communication: A review of research and a proposed model. *Audiovis. Commun. Rev.*, 1961, **9**, 235–62.

Heidgerken, L. E. An experimental study to measure the contributions of motion pictures and slide films to learning certain units in the course, introduction to nursing arts. Unpublished doctoral dissertation, Univer. of Indiana, 1948.

Hovland, C. I., Lumsdaine, A. A., and Sheffield, F. D. *Experiments on mass communication.* Princeton, N.J.: Princeton Univer. Press, 1949.

Jacobson, H. The informational capacity of the human ear. *Science*, 1950, **112**, 143–44.

Jacobson, H. The informational capacity of the human eye. *Science*, 1951, **113**, 292–93.

Kanner, J. H. and Rosenstein, A. J. Television in army training: Color vs. black and white. *Audiovis. Commun. Rev.*, 1960, **8**, 243–52.

Laner, S. The impact of visual aids display showing a manipulative task. *Quart. J. Exp. Psychol.*, 1954, **6**, 95–106.

McClusky, F. D. and McClusky, H. Y. Comparison of motion pictures, slides, stereograph, and demonstration as a means of teaching how to make a reed mat and a pasteboard box. In F. M. Freedman, ed., *Visual education.* Chicago: Univer. of Chicago Press, 1924, 310–34.

Miller, N. E., ed. Graphic communication and the crisis in education. *Audiovis. Commun. Rev.*, 1957, **5**, 1–120.

Morris, C. W. *Signs, language and behavior.* New York: Prentice-Hall, 1946.

Murry, J. R. The comparative effectiveness of condensed visualized methods versus taped-demonstration methods in teaching operation of the VM tape recorder and Victor 16mm projector. Unpublished doctoral dissertation, Pennsylvania State Univer., 1960.

Ortgiesen, L. The relative effectiveness of selected filmstrips and sound motion pictures in teaching soil conservation in ninth-grade social studies classes. Unpublished doctoral dissertation, Univer. of Nebraska, 1954.

Slattery, M. J. *An appraisal of the effectiveness of selected instructional sound motion pictures and silent filmstrips in elementary school instruction.* Washington, D.C.: Catholic Univer. Press, 1953.

Sparks, J. N. Expository notes on the problem of making multiple comparisons in a completely randomized design. *J. Exptl. Educ.*, 1963, **4**, 344–49.

Steel, R. G. D. and Torrie, J. H. *Principles and procedures of statistics.* New York: McGraw-Hill, 1960.

Travers, R. M. W., McCormick, M. C., Van Mondfrans, A. P., and Williams, F. E. *Research and theory related to audiovisual information transmission.* Utah: Bureau of Educational Research, Univer. of Utah, 1964.

Twyford, L. C., Church, J. G., McAshan, H. H., and Brown, R. M. *New media for improvement of science in instruction.* New York: Univer. of the State of New York, the State Education Department, Bureau of Classroom Communication, 1964.

VanderMeer, A. W. *Relative effectiveness of instruction by film exclusively, films plus study guides and standard lecture methods.* Technical Report, SDC-269-7-13, Special Devices Center, Office of Naval Research, Port Washington, New York, 1949.

VanderMeer, A. W. *Relative effectiveness of color and black and white in instructional films.* Technical Report, SDC-269-7-28, Special Devices Center, Office of Naval Research, Port Washington, New York, 1952.

Vernon, M. D. An experiment on the value of the film and filmstrip in the instruction of adults. *Brit. J. of Educ. Psychol.*, 1946, **16,** 149–62.

30

Expository Instruction Versus
a Discovery Method

JOHN T. GUTHRIE / *Johns Hopkins University*

It has been argued that the discovery method facilitates the retention of subject matter (Ausubel, 1963; Bruner, 1961). However, empirical research fails to sustain these opinions. When speed of learning and retention were used as criteria, instruction containing rules has proved superior to instruction without rules (Craig, 1956; Haslerud and Meyers, 1958; Kittell, 1957; Wittrock, 1963). In addition, the only two studies (Hendrix, 1961; Katona, 1940) which oppose this generalization are difficult to interpret because the control and experimental groups were incomparable.

A more popular stand is that the discovery method is primarily useful for producing transfer and general problem-solving ability (Bruner, 1961; Suchman, 1961). However, when transfer is used as the criterion for learning, the results have been equivocal. Craig (1956) found no difference between "independent" and "directed" groups on transfer to new rules. Haslerud and Meyers (1958) confirmed this finding, although this conclusion is suspect due to uncontrolled practice effects resulting from a within-subjects design. An advantage on transfer for instruction with "rule given" as compared with "rule not given" is reported by Wittrock (1963). However, the present author's examination of the rule group and the no-rule group with feedback present for both, indicates that there was an advantage ($t = 2.50$, $df = 145$, $p < .05$) for the no-rule group. Gagné and Brown (1961) also suggest that a "guided discovery" training procedure is superior to a "rule and example" procedure for producing transfer. Their treatment conditions, however, appear to have favored the

---

Reprinted with the permission of the author and the publisher from *Journal of Educational Psychology*, 1967, Vol. 58, 45–49.

"guided discovery" group. This group was trained on the specific type of behavior required by the criterion, whereas the "rule and example" group was taught a different type of behavior. Finally, Kittell (1957) concluded that giving a rule at the outset of instruction was superior to not giving a rule on all criteria: speed of learning, retention, and transfer. His conclusion, however, is unjustified since a substantial number of the subjects (*S*s) taught by the discovery method failed to meet the initial learning criteria. It is doubtful that *S*s would be able to transfer behavior which was never learned.

The above research clearly demonstrates that instruction with rules produces faster learning and better retention than instruction without rules. On the other hand, the empirical evidence concerning techniques for producing transfer is inconclusive. Consequently, the more central proposition that discovery learning facilitates transfer remains virtually untested. The purpose of the present experiment was to compare several methods of instruction, including both rules and examples and only examples, on the basis of several criteria of retention and transfer. It was hypothesized that instruction with rules and examples would facilitate retention, but not transfer. And training with only examples would facilitate transfer, but not retention.

Method

The *S*s were 72 students enrolled in an undergraduate educational psychology course. All *S*s were taught to decipher cryptograms. The cryptograms were taken from words 4–10 letters in length occurring 20–30 times per million in adult reading matter (Thorndike & Lorge, 1944). The letters were scrambled according to one of six rules. Rules 1, 2, and 3 were trans-

positional; 4, 5, and 6 were substitutional. Rule 1: Exchange the first and the last letters in each cryptogram. Rule 2: Reverse the order of the first half and the last half of the letters. Rule 3: Remove the first two letters and place them in the middle of the rest of the cryptogram. Rule 4: Replace the first letter with the letter succeeding it in the alphabet. Rule 5: Replace the numbers with the correct vowel (a, e, i, o, u equal 1, 2, 3, 4, 5). Rule 6: Replace the last letter with the letter preceding it in the alphabet.

There were four treatment conditions to which *S*s were assigned at random. In the Example-Rule group, examples of cryptograms were presented until a criterion of eight consecutive correct responses was attained. The rule was then taught with a programming technique until the *S*s could verbalize it upon request. Under the Rule-Example condition, the *S*s were first taught the rule through the program. Examples of cryptograms governed by the rule were then given until the criterion was met. The Example condition consisted of presenting only examples of cryptograms until the criterion was attained. The control group received no training on deciphering cryptograms, but spent a comparable amount of time learning Russian vocabulary. All groups were subdivided. Half the *S*s in each group were taught two transpositional rules (1 and 2); and half were taught two substitutional rules (4 and 5).

The test was composed of 30 cryptograms, and was subdivided into 3 parts. The first part contained 10 cryptograms formed from words not seen in training and governed by rules not used in training. The rules for this part were drawn from the opposite class of rules used in training. For instance, if *S* was trained to solve cryptograms composed from transpositional rules, this part required him to solve cryptograms composed from substitutional rules, and vice versa. This was considered the "remote" transfer task. The second part contained 10 cryptograms formed from words not seen in training, but governed by exactly the same rules as used in training. This was considered the retention task. In the third part, the 10 cryptograms were formed from new words and governed by rules not used in training. However, these rules were drawn from the same class of rules (transpositional vs. substitutional) as used in training. This was labeled the "near" transfer task.

The Ss were seated at a table facing an upright divider (2½ × 5 feet) with a small centered window (3 × 5 inches) in which the stimuli were presented. Written instructions were first given to each S on a sheet of paper. The instructions, which were minimal, directed the S to say the word suggested by each cryptogram and informed him that he would be tested. The instructions for the control group pertained only to the Russian vocabulary.

The Ss received successive presentation of cryptograms conforming to one of the rules. Each S was presented cryptograms until a criterion of 8 consecutive correct responses was attained or until 25 cryptograms had been presented. The order of presentation was randomized for each S. Each trial consisted of presenting a cryptogram and requiring S to verbalize the correct word. The length of the trials was 15 seconds. Feedback, which consisted of presenting the cryptogram with the correct word beside it, followed each trial. The duration of feedback was 5 seconds. The

time lapse between feedback and the following trial was about 5 seconds. Each S was taught to decipher cryptograms governed by two rules. After the two rules were learned, the test was given. Directions for the test informed the S of the test and stated that some of the correct answers were obtainable by substituting one letter for another letter in the alphabet, and other answers were obtainable by rearranging the letters within the cryptogram. The S was informed when he entered each of the test subdivisions. The approximate time required for the test was 10 minutes.

Results

The data were initially analyzed with a series of orthogonal planned comparisons, but the planned comparisons appeared too general to adequately represent the data. Consequently, simple one-way analyses of variance were computed for each of the test subdivisions including retention, near transfer, and remote transfer and for the trials to criterion. The means, standard deviations, and F ratios are presented in Table 1.

The overall significant differences permitted the use of the Tukey proce-

Table 1

MEANS AND STANDARD DEVIATIONS OF ERRORS AND TRIALS TO CRITERION

	Rule-example		Example-rule		Example		No training		
	M	SD	M	SD	M	SD	M	SD	F
Remote transfer	5.94	1.59	4.26	2.29	2.56	2.73	4.67	1.15	6.64**
Near transfer	5.23	2.26	2.84	2.00	2.27	1.05	4.50	1.21	8.94**
Retention	1.94	2.37	3.06	2.31	2.89	2.42	5.27	2.27	7.64**
Retention (Substitutional)	1.33	1.70	1.56	1.06	1.11	0.29	4.44	2.64	7.13**
Retention (Transformational)	2.55	1.37	4.56	2.26	4.67	2.25	6.11	1.41	4.80**
Trials to criterion	11.92	6.96	23.66	8.51	22.72	8.81	—	—	4.40*

Note: All test data are based on errors. Trials to criterion represent the total trials required to learn two rules.

   * $p < .025$.

   ** $p < .01$.

dure (Edwards, 1963) for comparing means (see Table 2). First, on the remote-transfer task, the Example group was significantly superior to all other groups. The Example-Rule group did not differ from No Training. And the Rule-Example group was significantly inferior to all other groups. On the near-transfer task, the Example group and the Example-Rule group were superior to No Training and Rule-Example, but did not differ from each other. The Rule-Example group was not different from the controls.

On the retention task, there do not appear to be any differences among the treatment groups, though all are superior to No Training. However, for reasons outlined in the discussion, it is believed that the retention test for those trained on substitutional rules was incapable of discriminating among treatments. Consequently, analyses of variance were conducted separately for *S*s trained on substitutional rules and *S*s trained on transformational rules. Significant differences were found on both groups (see Table 1). The Tukey procedure was then employed to compare the means (see Table 2). As expected, there were no differences among groups trained on the substitutional rule, though the control group was inferior to all treatment groups. However, for groups trained with transformational rules the Rule-Example was superior to all other groups. In addition, the Example and Example-Rule groups did not differ from the No Training group.

To analyze the time required for learning under various conditions, a one-way analysis of variance was conducted on all treatment groups using trials to criterion as the dependent variable. First, the general differences were significant. In addition, the Tukey comparison showed that the Rule-Example group learned faster than the other two groups; and that the Example and Example-Rule groups did not differ from each other.

Discussion

At the outset of the experiment, it was hypothesized that the rules would function as eliciting stimuli. In other words, it is suggested that rules in verbal learning are analogous to the unconditioned stimuli in classical conditioning. They serve to evoke a response which is then reinforced. For example, when the rule was presented in the Rule-Example group and a cryptogram was presented in close succession, specific deciphering behavior was evoked from *S*s. When these *S*s were presented a cryptogram, they manipulated the letters specifically according to the rule to form the word.

Table 2

TUKEY COMPARISON OF MEANS

Remote transfer	Near transfer	Retention	Retention substitution	Retention transformation	Trials to criterion
1. Example	Example	Rule-Example	Example	Rule-Example	Rule-Exampl
2. Example-Rule	Example-Rule	Example	Rule-Example	No Training	Example
3. No Training	No Training	Example-Rule	Example-Rule	Example-Rule	Example-Rul
4. Rule-Example	Rule-Example	No Training	No Training	Example	

Note: Treatments are in rank order. The treatments connected by a common line do not differ. All oth treatments differ significantly at the .05 level.

It was speculated that this behavior would then be reinforced through feedback, and acquired. That such behavior was, in fact, acquired is evident from the results indicating that *Ss* in the Rule-Example group performed well on retention tasks.

It was also reasoned at the outset that when no rules were given to *Ss*, their behavior would more closely approximate the operant conditioning paradigm. That is, presenting *Ss* a cryptogram would evoke searching, exploratory behavior which would be reinforced when a word was made from the cryptogram. That such explorative skill was acquired is evidenced from the result that the Example and Example-Rule groups surpassed the Rule-Example and the Control groups on the transfer, but not on the retention tasks.

It should be noted that the conclusions regarding retention have been drawn from the data of *Ss* taught transformational rules; and the data from *Ss* taught substitutional rules have been ignored. The reason for this is that one of the substitutional rules contained a number, whereas all other rules contained only letters. It is likely that this number acted as a distinctive cue which facilitated retention in all groups. Thus a ceiling effect for retention of *Ss* taught substitutional rules prevented differences on this measure from manifesting themselves.

References

Ausubel, D. P. *The psychology of meaningful verbal learning.* New York: Grune & Stratton, 1963.

Bruner, J. S. The act of discovery. *Harvard Educational Review*, 1961, **31**, 21–32.

Craig, R. C. Directed versus independent discovery of established relations. *Journal of Educational Psychology*, 1956, **47**, 223–34.

Edwards, A. L. *Statistical methods for the behavioral sciences.* New York: Holt, Rinehart & Winston, 1963.

Gagné, R. M. and Brown, L. T. Some factors in the programming of conceptual material. *Journal of Experimental Psychology*, 1961, **62**, 313–21.

Haslerud, G. N. and Meyers, S. The transfer value of given and individually derived principles. *Journal of Educational Psychology*, 1958, **49**, 293–98.

Hendrix, G. Learning by discovery. *Math Teacher*, 1961, **54**, 290–99.

Katona, G. *Organizing and memorizing.* New York: Columbia University Press, 1940.

Kittell, J. E. An experimental study of the effect of external direction during learning on transfer and retention of principles. *Journal of Educational Psychology*, 1957, **48**, 391–405.

Suchman, J. R. Inquiry training: Building skills for autonomous discovery. *Merrill Palmer Quarterly of Behavioral Development*, 1961, **7**, 148–49.

Thorndike, E. L. and Lorge, I. *The teacher's word book of 30,000 words.* New York: Bureau of Publications, Teachers College, Columbia University, 1944.

Wittrock, M. C. Verbal stimuli in concept formation: Learning by discovery. *Journal of Educational Psychology*, 1963, **54**, 183–90.

31

Elementary Pupils' Ability to Conceptualize the Main Idea in Reading

THOMAS BARRETT / *The University of Wisconsin*

WAYNE OTTO / *The University of Wisconsin*

The general purpose of this investigation was to examine the ability of pupils in the latter part of grades one through six to synthesize and state the main idea of brief, carefully controlled paragraphs which were written with one specific but implied main idea.

The first step was to develop an operational definition of "main idea" that would provide (1) a consensual framework for the implementation of the study, (2) guidelines with respect to structure of the experimental materials to be located or developed, and (3) guidelines for the development of a scale to be used in scoring responses. In view of these requirements, it was finally agreed that an adequate main idea statement would include two elements: (1) reference to a general topic, as illustrated in the statement "Birds build nests," and (2) a restriction placed on the general topic by reference to the specific content of the passage, e.g., "Birds build nests/in different places."

Consequently, a combination of general topic and specific referent was considered a correct response when children's main idea statements were subsequently evaluated. This operational definition is the referent when the term "main idea" is used in the discussion that follows.

Method

MATERIALS

When an extensive search failed to yield published children's materials that had well-structured paragraphs containing one implicit main idea, the decision was made to construct paragraphs. The basic

---

Paper read at the annual convention of the American Educational Research Association, Chicago, Illinois, February 1968. Reprinted in abridged form with the permission of the senior author.

problem then was to provide an appropriate reading task for first through sixth grade subjects. To accomplish this and to permit subsequent comparisons of responses across grade levels, the procedure was to establish general content and a specific main idea for base level, i.e., first grade, paragraphs and then to manipulate readability level across grades by application of existing readability formulas.

The initial work on the development of the paragraphs focused on the formulation of main ideas from the general area of "nature"—a sufficiently universal curriculum-interest area to insure at least a base level of meaningful vocabulary among first graders. Eventually three main idea statements were selected: (A) Animals help the farmer in different ways; (B) Birds build nests in different places; (C) Animals use claws for different things. Second, the operational decision was made to work with a structural formula that prescribed that four subjects of the same general classification—one for each sentence—be combined with predicates involving different tasks or functions.

At this point, three paragraphs were developed at the first grade readability level, in accord with the following guidelines: (1) In keeping with the accepted operational definition of the main idea, each sentence provided information about a subject performing an act (the general topic) and about the specific nature of the action (the restrictive element). For example, the main idea "Birds build nests in different places" was developed in four sentences, each of which included a reference to birds as the subject and to a specific place where birds build nests. (2) Each sentence was independent except for pronoun antecedents. (3) Each sentence contained a single idea that contributed to the main idea.

Once the initial three paragraphs were developed, it was decided to consider the effect of two constructions of the subjective element of the sentences used, since the degree to which children are required to synthesize is apt to vary in classroom materials. Accordingly, alternate forms of each sentence—designated Style A and Style B in the study—were written. In Style A, the subject of each sentence in a paragraph was the name of the general class being discussed, so synthesis was required only by the predicate element. In Style B, the subject of each sentence was the name of a specific member of the class being discussed, so both the subject and predicate elements required synthesis. Development of the main idea "Birds build nests in different places" with Style A and Style B sentences is illustrated in the following schema.

STYLE A

Subject elements	Predicate elements
Some birds	(Example 1) build nests under a roof.
Many birds	(Example 2) like nests in trees.
Concept given Some birds	(Example 3) even make nests in tall grass.
A few birds	(Example 4) make nests inside wood fence posts.

STYLE B

Subject elements	Predicate elements
(Example 1) Robins	(Example 1) may build nests under a roof.
(Example 2) Bluejays	(Example 2) like nests in trees.
(Example 3) Ducks	(Example 3) make nests in tall grass.
(Example 4) Woodpeckers	(Example 4) make nests inside wood fence posts.

When the base, or first grade, paragraphs were written, the sentences in each paragraph were expanded in terms of vocabulary difficulty and/or sentence length to bring the readability level up to subsequent grade levels, while keeping the kernel thought of each sentence intact. The Spache Readability Formula (1953) for grades 1–3 and the Dale-Chall Readability Formula (1948) for grades 4–6 provided guidelines for controlling readability. Due to limitations of the formulas, however, it was necessary to impose additional controls. Wherever possible, for example, words from the Stone List (1957) were used for the primary grades. When adherence to the list was not practicable, phonetically regular words were used. Care was taken to keep sentence length within reasonable limits. Finally, linguistic structure was arbitrarily regulated across grades by expanding the sentences with additional phrases and clauses. The procedure was arbitrary because the existing formulas make no provision for the control of this stylistic variable.

The first grade paragraph comprised four simple sentences with no more than a single phrase as a modifier, while at subsequent grade levels additional modifying phrases and dependent clauses were added.

Because there was no basis for predicting how much the readability controls would affect the subjects' ability to recognize and formulate the main idea of each paragraph, the decision was to have subjects at each grade level read either base level, first grade paragraphs (Type II) or paragraphs written for their grade level (Type I). The strategy, then, was to compare the responses to base level and to grade level responses in order to determine whether the readability level of the paragraphs had a significant impact upon success in formulating a literal main idea statement.

All materials were written in an expository style, for pilot studies had indicated that narrative materials evoked divergent rather than the desired convergent responses.

The final scale employed for rating main idea responses was developed after a number of pilot scales had been tried and found to be inadequate. The final version, too, was tried out in a pilot study, and there was consensus among the investigators that it was adequate for the present research task. The final seven point scale included categories ranging from both elements correctly stated to no response. Intermediate ratings on the scale were made on the basis of the generality and relevancy of one or both responses.[1]

PROCEDURE

Two hundred and eighty-eight children were chosen from Grades 1 through 6 in an urban Wisconsin school system to serve as subjects. The sample was drawn from three schools located in diverse but representative socio-economic areas of the city.

Initially, 75 children from each grade level were designated at random. The appropriate classroom teachers were then asked to identify those children who, in their judgment, could read a sample test selection. The assumption was that classroom teachers would be reasonably accurate in making such judgments regarding their pupils' reading ability. From this pool of pupils who were expected to have no difficulty with the mechanics of reading, twenty-four boys and twenty-four girls from each grade level were chosen at random to participate in the study.

---

[1] A complete description of the rating scale appears in the original article.

Pilot studies revealed the need for a brief warm-up task to permit the establishment of rapport between examiner and subject and to establish a set among the subjects to respond in complete sentences. The warm-up task was simply to compose and read back four simple sentences.

The test directions required the subject to read a paragraph silently while thinking about "what all the sentences together say," a phrase intended to direct him toward a synthesis of all the elements present rather than selection of a single specific thought. The subject was permitted to ask for any words which he did not know. Then he was told to "make up just one sentence in your own words that says what all the sentences tell you." The directions were partially repeated between each paragraph.

Within each grade, equal numbers of boys and girls were assigned to read paragraphs of each type and style. Each subject read three test paragraphs, randomly ordered, of a single type and style. Three graduate students, each an active participant in the prior pilot studies and the production of materials, served as examiners. One examiner worked in each of the three schools from which subjects were selected.

The 288 subjects were tested individually in a private room provided by the school. A testing session began with a warm-up task, followed by oral directions given by the examiner. Upon completion of the first paragraph, the subject was asked for his response to the main idea task. The response was written down verbatim by the examiner on a specially prepared answer form. The examiner accepted what the subject said without comment unless there was need for clarification of the referent given—e.g., "What do you mean by 'they'?" The procedure for reading the next two paragraphs was identical. Each paragraph was completed before going on to the next one. The entire task took approximately eight minutes.

Each subject's main idea responses were coded and typed on master sheets to eliminate possible bias in judging. Four judges, each of whom had had experience in developing and working with the Response Scale, scored the 864 responses independently. If at least two judges did not agree, the responses were returned for reconsideration and rescaling by each judge. Final interjudge agreement was .79, which was considered adequate for the requirements of the study.

The mean of the 12 scale values given to the three responses by four judges comprised the subject's final score. That is, each of the four judges rated each subject's response to Paragraphs A, B, and C, and the mean of the resultant 12 ratings was the subject's score. This mean score was used in the analysis of the data.

DESIGN

A $2 \times 2 \times 6$ completely crossed analysis of variance design, which contained 24 cells with 12 subjects in each cell, was used in the study. The three independent variables were: (1) Type of paragraph, where Type I was written at grade level and Type II was written at first grade level in difficulty; (2) Style of paragraph, where Style A required synthesis of the predicate only and Style B required synthesis of both the subject and predicate; and (3) Grade level of the subjects. Although equal numbers of boys and girls served as subjects, sex was not considered as an independent variable in the analysis. This decision was made because preliminary investigations revealed no systematic sex differences in responses.

The dependent variable was the mean response rating for the main idea statements of each subject on a scale that ranged from 0–6.

Results

An analysis of variance on mean response ratings demonstrated a significant ($P < .05$) effect for paragraph type and grade placement. There was no significant effect due to paragraph style nor were any interactions significant. Type II paragraphs (those written at first grade or base level according to the Spache Formula) yielded higher scores (mean = 3.8) than Type I paragraphs (written at each grade level), for which the mean was 3.3.

Mean response score for each grade level is presented in Table 1.

Scheffé post hoc tests revealed that with the exception of the fourth and fifth grade and fifth and sixth grade comparisons, the differences between all other grade level means were significant at the .05 level.

There was no significant relationship between the style of the paragraph and the mean rating of the main idea statements. Therefore, it can be interpreted that the subject's ability to formulate the main idea of a paragraph was not affected by the generality or specificity of the subjects of specific sentences. This was true across grade levels and across types of paragraphs. There was also no significant relationship between the mean ratings of main idea statements and combinations of Type and Style of paragraphs, Type of paragraphs and Grade, Style of paragraphs and Grade, or Type and Style of paragraphs and Grade.

Discussion

As indicated at the outset, the purpose of this study was to examine the ability of pupils in the latter part of grades one through six to synthesize and state the main ideas of brief, carefully controlled paragraphs which were written with one specific but implied main idea. Fortunately, the results of the investigation did permit certain generalizations to be drawn. However, before proceeding to a discussion of the conclusions and implications, three limitations of the study must be presented.

First, the operational definition of a main idea employed during the investigation obviously places certain limitations on the study, since it is only one of a number of definitions that might have been used. For example, the general topic of a paragraph and the title for a paragraph were alternative definitions considered by the investigators. The point is that the results and conclusions of the investigation rest on the definition and one must be aware of the three assumptions inherent to the operational definition used, namely: (1) the optimal main idea statement is a sentence, not a topic or phrase; (2) the optimal main

Table 1

MEAN RATINGS OF MAIN IDEA STATEMENTS ACROSS GRADE LEVELS IRRESPECTIVE OF TYPE OR STYLE OF PARAGRAPHS READ ($N = 48$ AT EACH GRADE)

	Grade levels					
	1	2	3	4	5	6
Mean ratings	2.71	3.12	3.52	3.96	4.05	4.20

idea statement contains the general topic of the passage and the specific restrictions of the passage; (3) the general topic portion of the main idea statement is more important than the specific portion of the main idea statement.

Second, the accepted definition also influenced the development of the main idea rating scale utilized in the study. For example, the general topic portion of the main idea statement was deemed to be more important than the specific portion of the main idea statement. In other words, the investigators made this value judgment which, in turn, influenced the magnitude of the rating any one main idea statement received.

Finally, the paragraphs constructed for the investigation were carefully controlled in terms of content, readability and conceptual structure, and length. Thus, the limitation that the paragraphs were not necessarily representative of reading materials generally available to children existed. Whether generally acceptable "representative" materials can ever be found is, of course, a moot question.

With these limitations in mind several conclusions and implications can be drawn from the results of the investigation:

1. Since the mean ratings of the main idea statements were significantly higher when first grade level paragraphs (Type II) rather than paragraphs at grade level (Type I) were used across grade levels, it would seem that, in general, the easier the materials are in terms of readability, the more adequate children's main idea statements will be. In other words, the shorter the sentences and the easier the words in a reading selection, the less energy the child has to exert in decoding words and eliciting literal meanings and the more energy he can exert in synthesizing the ideas in a selection and inferring the main idea.

The implication seems clear: instructional programs designed to teach children to formulate main ideas should employ very easy materials.

2. The significant differences among grades in mean ratings of main idea statements and the fact that the mean ratings consistently increased in magnitude from grade one through grade six suggests that the ability to formulate main idea statements is developmental in nature. However, the fact that the practical differences in mean ratings were not greater than they were from grade to grade and that even at the sixth grade level the mean rating was not particularly high in terms of the scale used raises questions about the effectiveness of the instruction devoted to the development of this basic comprehension ability during the elementary school years. It would seem, therefore, that pupils should be given practice in inferring main ideas beginning in the primary grades and that such practice should be continued over a period of years.

3. Since the style of the paragraphs utilized did not significantly influence the mean ratings of main idea statements made by subjects in this investigation, while the level of difficulty of the paragraphs did, it seems reasonable to conclude that the semantic structure of the materials is not as crucial to the evaluation of pupils' ability to formulate main ideas as is the number of difficult words and the average sentence length in a selection. This does not mean that further work on the relationship between the semantic structure of materials and the ability of children to state main ideas should not be considered, but it does suggest that the readability level of the materials should be given foremost consideration in studies of this nature.

4. Finally, the fact that there is a

paucity of research dealing with main idea comprehension abilities suggests that what has been done in this investigation should be viewed as an initial attempt in this area. Although the methodology of the study was carefully developed, it undoubtedly can be improved upon in the future. It also seems reasonable to hypothesize that children with different cognitive styles and abilities may perform in different ways on comprehension tasks of this nature and that inquiries devoted to the study of this possible phenomenon may provide a basis for differential instruction in inferring main ideas.

References

Dale, E. and Chall, J. A formula for predicting readability. *Educational Research Bulletin*, January 1948, **27**, 11–20.

Spache, G. A new readability formula for primary grade reading materials. *Elementary School Journal*, March 1953, **53**, 410–13.

Stone, C. R. Measuring difficulty of primary reading material: A constructive criticism of Spache's measure. *Elementary School Journal*, October 1957, **57**, 36–41.

VII

Organization and Sequence

It seems reasonable to assume that the manner in which subject matter is presented to students will make a difference in how well the students learn the material. Instructional materials may be organized in many ways and presented in a wide variety of sequences. Undoubtedly, the optimal organization and sequence (if such a thing exists) for a particular subject matter depends largely on the nature of the task. In this section, papers which are representative of several approaches to the study of organization and sequence factors in instruction will be presented. There will be no attempt at an extensive coverage of such work, however, since approaches to this problem for which a plausible argument could be made are numerous. The reports that follow represent some of those approaches which are currently receiving attention and seem promising.

There are, first of all, some relatively simple organization and sequence techniques which have value. Section III dealt with procedures for shifting stimulus control by means of prompting and fading procedures. Since this material has already been discussed, it will not be repeated here except to note the great importance of sequence in these procedures (e.g., Hively, 1962).

Research on discovery versus expository learning (Section VI) is also relevant here. In the discovery procedure the student is presented with examples from which he is to infer a rule, concept, or principle; while in expository instruction, the student is told the rule before he sees it exemplified. As already noted in Section VI, research on this topic leaves much to be desired, and it remains to be seen which procedure is more effective—if, indeed, either is invariably superior.

A third area of interest is the issue of part versus whole learning. The question is whether it is more effective or efficient to practice a given learning task as a whole or to practice separately various component parts which are later combined to form the whole task. A closely related question concerns the considerations which should go into the determination of the parts of a learning task. Margolius and Sheffield (Chapter 32) have provided some interesting theory and data on this point. They see the determination of parts, or "D-A spans" as they call them, as a compromise between the "natural units" of a task and the amount of material the student is capable of assimilating at a given time. They demonstrate that a complex serial (sequenced) task can be learned more readily by a part method than by a whole method. It should be noted, however, that different results might be obtained with other kinds of tasks. More research is needed on this important issue. The analysis of the task into "demonstration-assimilation span segments" seems most promising. But often a concern for task analysis has been missing in other research on this topic.

Another variable which must be discussed in a consideration of organization and sequence factors in instruction is distributed practice. Research on distributed practice with written materials (e.g., Rothkopf and Coke, 1963) has generally found that spreading out the learning effort facilitates retention. Reynolds and Glaser (Chapter 33) investigated the related phenomenon of spaced review—of spacing practice on parts of the learning task at widely separated intervals throughout the lesson. They compared the learning and retention of groups that received all of the frames on a certain topic in a biology program at one time with groups that received the same material split into three sections and spaced throughout the program. The spaced review groups were superior in both learning and retention. These results have obvious implications for classroom practice.

Gagné (Chapter 34) has proposed that knowledge of subject matter and skills forms a hierarchy. Skills and knowledge lower in the hierarchy must be mastered before higher skills and knowledge can be attained. Gagné advocates a form of task analysis aimed at identifying this hierarchy. The analysis continues until subskills, called *entering behaviors,* are identified which the student can perform without instruction. Instruction then proceeds by building on these entering behaviors, teaching skills and knowledge in the order prescribed by the hierarchy, until the most complex skills and concepts have been mastered.

This conception of knowledge acquisition is intuitively very appealing. Gagné and his associates have provided some supporting data (Gagné and Bassler, 1963; Gagné, 1965). Merrill (Chapter 35), however, in a study designed explicitly to test Gagné's theory of hierarchical organization failed to show an advantage for groups which had mastered each of the subordinate tasks of an imaginary science over groups that had not. Further research is necessary to clarify the applicability of Gagné's promising notions.

Ausubel (1963) has developed a cognitive theory of verbal learning in which, similar to Gagné's position, knowledge is said to be organized into hierarchies. The apex of a hierarchy is occupied by the most "abstract, general, stable, and inclusive ideas." Lower levels are occupied by progressively more detailed, more specific, and less stable ideas. In line with this view of subject matter and cognitive functioning, Ausubel believes that providing "advance organizers"—passages to be read prior to studying new material—helps a student integrate the new material into his existing "cognitive structure." The organizers may compare and contrast the material to be learned with what the student already knows, or they may outline the material in an abstract and general fashion. In the experiment reprinted here, Ausubel (Chapter 36) provides evidence which suggests that organizers do facilitate learning.

One consistent and important finding from laboratory studies of rote learning is that material learned before (proactive interference) and after (retroactive interference) the to-be-remembered material interferes with the recall of that material. Ausubel's finding (Chapter 36) that advance organizers faciliate rather than interfere with learning seems to contradict this finding from the laboratory. Ausubel and his associates (e.g., Ausubel, Stager, and Gaite, 1968) have explicitly investigated interference in meaningful (as opposed to rote) learning, and failed to find any such effect. In experiments they conducted, Entwisle and Huggins (Chapter 37), however, did find proactive and retroactive interference when learners studied one topic and then immediately studied a related topic. Here again we have an issue which needs further investigation. Obviously, interference possibilities, if they exist in school learning, must be considered when one organizes a lesson or series of lessons.

The final paper in this section is by Wayne Lee (Chapter 38). This paper represents one of the few efforts to analyze organizational factors in prose materials. This is a curious state of affairs when one considers that a large part of the knowledge possessed by both children and adults is transmitted by means of prose. English teachers have been telling us for years that clear organization is a prerequisite to effective written communication. Surprisingly, there is little data to support this assertion and even less on just what good prose organization is. Lee's research is a useful start on this very important issue.

References

Ausubel, D. P. *The psychology of meaningful verbal learning.* New York: Grune and Stratton, 1963.

Ausubel, D. P., Stager, M., and Gaite, A. J. H. Retroactive facilitation in meaningful verbal learning. Paper read at the annual convention of the American Educational Research Association, Chicago, Illinois, February 1968.

Gagné, R. M. Some factors in learning nonmetric geometry. Monograph for the Society of Research in Child Development, 1965, **30,** 42–49.

Gagné, R. M. and Bassler, O. C. Study of retention of some topics of elementary nonmetric geometry. *Journal of Educational Psychology,* 1963, **54,** 123–31.

Rothkopf, E. Z. and Coke, E. U. Repetition interval and rehearsal method in learning equivalencies from sentences. *Journal of Verbal Learning and Verbal Behavior,* 1963, **2,** 406–16.

32

Optimum Methods of Combining Practice with Filmed Demonstration in Teaching Complex Response Sequences: Serial Learning of a Mechanical-Assembly Task

GARRY J. MARGOLIUS / *Boston University*

FRED D. SHEFFIELD / *Yale University*

An inherent difficulty in the use of training films is that the learning which occurs while viewing the film is limited to acquisition of perceptual and symbolic responses which must later be translated into overt performance. The learner has a double problem. He must retain the visual and verbal contents of the film, and he must later utilize the new perceptual-symbolic material to guide his overt behavior. When the purpose of the training film is to teach a complex response sequence, such as assembly of a rifle, the training effectiveness of a single filmed demonstration may be fairly limited. The serial learning of the perceptual-symbolic sequence will be attenuated by intra-serial interference, and overt performance will be further attenuated by incomplete transfer—in the actual task situation—of the implicit responses acquired.

Presumably the above difficulties in the use of training films can be offset to

some extent by interspersing overt practice periods in the course of a filmed demonstration. General considerations suggested the concept of a "demonstration-assimilation span" (D-A span), which refers to the amount of demonstration content which the learner can assimilate and translate into overt performance without much loss through interference from other parts of the demonstration and from the disparity between the film situation and the practice situation. General theoretical considerations further suggested the concept of "consolidation" of demonstration material, which here refers to the effects

Reprinted in abridged form with the permission of the authors and the publisher from *Student Response in Programmed Instruction*, Publication 943, Division of Behavioral Sciences, National Academy of Sciences–National Research Council, Washington, D.C., 1961.

of an overt practice—at a time when assimilation of a segment of demonstration material is optimum—in preventing subsequent interference from assimilation of new portions of the demonstration content. It is presumed that practice at overt performance at the end of an appropriately short sequence will "consolidate" the sequence so that it combines by a cross-conditioning mechanism into an organized unit of elements, which elements hang together and are less subject to interference from other elements, past or future. The argument is that even the same element, or a highly similar one, in a different part of the sequence, will interfere less because the individual element has become part of a perceptual pattern and no longer functions as a discrete stimulus or response. Finally, theoretical considerations suggested the concept of "natural units" of the task to be learned. Such units are a function of the particular serial-learning task and would not necessarily correspond with D-A span units. Elements of such units would be expected to be relatively free of intra-serial interference from elements in other units of a complex response sequence.

The purpose of the present research was to test the theoretical expectation that, in the joint use of filmed demonstration and overt practice, the appropriate use of practice periods interspersed through the film would be more effective than the use of practice only at the termination of the filmed demonstration. It was assumed in this research that overt practice adds significantly to the amount of learning obtained from the demonstration, and no control was used to illustrate the fact that demonstration *plus* practice is more effective than demonstration alone. Thus the main question was: Given the use of both demonstration and practice, what is the most effective way of combining the two? The specific context in which

this question was asked was that in which the task involved serial learning of a complex mechanical assembly which could not be acquired from a single filmed demonstration.

The demonstration-practice conditions considered in answering this question were the following:

1. *D-A Span Segment* practice. In this treatment the demonstration was stopped at the end of a given segment of the film and the learners practiced overtly what had been shown during the segment. The segments used had been previously empirically established as approximately one demonstration-assimilation span in length, although the subdivision was partly in terms of natural units.

2. *Larger-Segment* practice. In this treatment adjacent segments used in the first treatment were combined into larger segments and practice was interpolated at the end of each successive *pair* of segments used in the first treatment.

3. *Whole* practice. In this treatment the demonstration was continued through its entirety and practice was given only at the end of each complete showing.

4. *Transition* conditions. In this treatment the first showing utilized D-A span segments exactly as in the first treatment, the second showing utilized Larger-Segment practice exactly as in the second treatment, and the final showing utilized Whole practice exactly as in the third treatment. Thus *transition* was provided from initially smaller segments to the final stage of practicing the entire assembly as a whole.

Purpose

The purpose of this experiment was to compare the four treatments described above. Specifically, the purpose was to intersperse overt practice at the end of each "natural unit" and/or "demonstration-assimilation span" of demonstration material and compare the degree of learning with that produced with an equal amount of overt practice given (1) at the end of larger sub-units of the film, (2) at the end of the entire film, and (3) at the end of units of increasing size, starting with smallest and ending with the entire demonstration. In all four conditions the learners saw the entire demonstration three times and practiced the entire mechanical assembly three times; what was varied was the timing of demonstration and practice used prior to the final test.

Method

DEMONSTRATION AND PRACTICE MATERIALS

A 16-mm. black and white film, 18 minutes in length demonstrated the step-by-step assembly of an automobile ignition distributor. The component parts were introduced in the film as needed, and the correct fitting together of these in a sequential order was depicted. An accompanying narration identified the parts and described the movements necessary to complete the assembly.

A standard automobile distributor of the same model as that depicted in the film demonstration was used for overt practice. The component parts, plus five confusion pieces, were laid out by the experimenter in a standardized pattern on a large white Masonite sheet before each practice period. A screwdriver and tweezers were made available to the learner.

SUBJECTS

Forty male undergraduate students at Boston University served as voluntary subjects. Each subject was assigned to one of four groups. All subjects were paid for the three-hour experimental period. Potential subjects were disqualified in cases of prior knowledge about the automobile distributor.

DESIGN

All subjects viewed the entire film three times and were given an opportunity to practice the assembly in conjunction with each demonstration. At the conclusion of training each subject was asked to assemble the distributor without any further film instruction. This fourth and final assembly was considered a terminal *performance test*.

As already noted, the critical experimental differences among subjects were concerned with the method of interpolating demonstration and practice portions of training. Preliminary study had indicated that the film could be divided into four sections, each roughly approximating a demonstration-assimilation span. The divisions were made in terms of ability to assemble the actual distributor parts after viewing a segment of the film rather than in terms of film footage. The first and last of the four sections selected were judged to be "natural units" of material. The middle two sections together were judged to comprise a "natural unit," but a unit too long and complex to be assimilated in a continuous showing. This middle "natural unit" was therefore subdivided into two D-A span units. The film divisions thus chosen served as the focal points around which the experimental manipulations could occur during training. The four training procedures were differentiated with respect to the number of film sections viewed by the learner before training practice was attempted during each of the three training sessions.

DETAILS OF TRAINING PROCEDURE

1. D-A Segment Method. The subject was seated at a table upon which the distributor parts had previously been placed and covered from view. He was instructed to observe and listen carefully to the material presented in the film, since he would soon be called upon to demonstrate his knowledge. The room light was then lowered and the film projector started. For this group the projector was stopped at the end of the first demonstration session (D1), and the room light was turned up. The subject was then instructed to select the parts necessary to complete the assembly demonstrated thus far, as quickly and accurately as possible. He was reminded of the name of the last piece necessary and the cover was removed from the distributor parts. When the subject indicated that he was finished with his selection, the experimenter recorded both time and errors, corrected the selection if necessary, and then covered the remaining, or non-selected, parts. The subject was further instructed to assemble the correct selection of parts as quickly and as accurately as possible and to notify the experimenter upon completion. While the subject was at work his *temporary* errors—those he made but corrected during the practice period—were recorded by the experimenter. When the subject indicated completion or exceeded the time limit, the practice material was removed and a record was made of *fixed* (uncorrected) errors and assembly time. Each uncorrected faulty response or omission of a part counted as a *fixed* error. Assembly-time score did not include time taken to screw parts together. The experimenter stopped his watch whenever the subject placed the screwdriver in position and started it again when the subject removed the screwdriver, in order to minimize differences due to mechanical aptitude.

Sections 2, 3, and 4 were run in a similar fashion. Before each period of assembly practice, the experimenter corrected any fixed errors in the previous attempt. For example, when the subject was ready to begin the assembly practice of Section 3, he was handed a correct assembly through Sections 1 and 2. He never observed corrections being made, however; he was simply informed at the beginning of the next practice unit that the assembly up to that point was now correct. Following the four film-and-practice periods, the entire procedure was repeated a second and then a third time.

2. *Larger-Segment Method.* This group viewed Sections 1 and 2 of the film as a single unit, followed by practice of both sections; they then viewed sections 3 and 4 as a single unit, followed by practice of both these latter units. In practicing Sections 1 and 2 the subjects were scored for P1 (practice session 1) and P2 separately, and any mistakes in assembly at the end of P1 were corrected before starting P2. The same procedure was used when they practiced P3 and P4. Thus, practice was made identical in form to that used in the D-A Segment method, the difference being that the Larger-Segment group practiced two smaller segments in immediate succession rather than with an interpolated film section. The purpose of this procedure was to make practice (and measurement) conditions identical for both groups, except for the size of the demonstration-practice segment involved. The procedure as described was repeated three times prior to the final test.

3. *Whole Method.* This group viewed the entire film without interruption as a single demonstration unit. They then practiced the entire assembly but, as in the first two groups, they were scored separately for P1, P2, P3, and P4, and any necessary corrections were made at the end of each of these practice sections. This arrangement of demonstration and practice was repeated as

before for a total of three complete demonstration-and-practice periods before the final test.

4. *Transition Method.* This group was also given three complete demonstration-and-practice periods, but these were arranged so that the first period was identical with that of the D-A Segment method, the second period was identical with that of the Larger-Segment method, and the final period was identical with that of the Whole method.

Time limits for both total task and sections of the task were assigned on the basis of pre-test results so that all subjects with minimum knowledge necessary for task completion could easily finish both selection and assembly within the times allotted.

FINAL TEST PROCEDURE

For the final test, the subject was once again presented with the distributor parts and instructed to assemble the complete mechanism without preliminary selection of parts and without any break between units. The experimenter recorded assembly time and errors for each of the four sections separately as before, although the subject proceeded without a break and without any corrections. It should be noted that while the total assembly time for the final test could be determined accurately, the part-times for the separate units were in some cases approximate because of variations introduced by the subjects in the order of assembling the parts.

Results

Figure 1 shows the performance of all four groups on three practice trials and the final test trial. On the practice trials, all of the increases at successive stages of practice were significant ($P < .01$) in each of the four groups. Not only was

there a significant practice (trials) effect, but also a significant difference between groups in that the D-A span and Transition groups performed better than the Larger-Segment group, which in turn performed significantly better than the Whole method group. There was no significant difference between the D-A span and Transition groups. The performance rate data for the final criterion test indicate essentially the same results and relative group performance as on the practice trials. Analyses of error scores also yielded the same results. The D-A span and Transition group performed best and the Whole method group achieved the least, no matter how the data were analyzed.

Interpretation

If one reviews the data for final test performance, it can be seen that the poorest result in terms of performance rate was found with the Whole method of practice. All of the other methods involved some form of practice interspersed through the demonstration. At the most gross level of conclusion, therefore, it would appear that interspersed practice periods can be used to advantage in training films demonstrating complex mechanical assemblies. It should be recalled that time spent in practice was identical for all groups. Thus, the above conclusion does not merely imply that interspersed practice adds to what the film teaches; rather it implies that practice during the film can be made superior to practice at the end of the film. The conclusion applies, of course, only to equally lengthy and complex assembly tasks.

The preferred methods of interspersing practice appear to be either the use of D-A span segments of demonstration and practice or the use of a transition

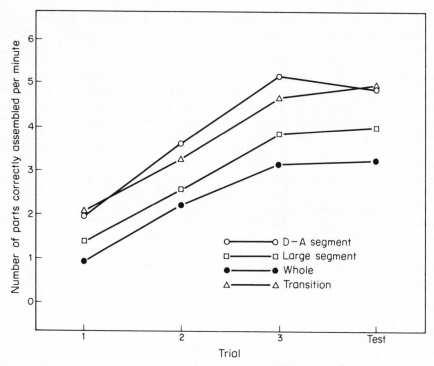

Fig. 1 Average rate of assembly of an automobile ignition distributor for three practice trials and a test trial.

method starting with such units and progressing to successively larger units. Theoretically some form of transition would provide the most effective method of integrating the entire task. In the present research, however, the slight superiority of the Transition method over the D-A span segments on the final test was not at all significant. This may reflect too rapid transition in the Transition method used. Thus, the advantage of consolidation of material is lost if the transition shifts the training procedure too rapidly in the direction of the Whole method of demonstration and practice. Transition should keep pace with consolidation or the gains will be cancelled rather than being additive.

An alternative possible explanation of the fact that the Transition method

did not prove to be superior to the D-A span method is that in the progression to larger segments the larger segments were not combined along lines of natural units. Thus the film had four D-A spans but was judged to have only three natural units, the middle one being two D-A spans in length. In the Transition method, the larger segments used consisted of (a) the first natural unit plus half of the second one (these comprising the first two D-A spans), and (b) the second half of the second natural unit plus the last natural unit (these comprising the last two D-A spans). It may well be that a transition which merely combined the middle two D-A spans into the middle natural unit would have proven a more effective procedure than any of those used in the two experiments.

33

Effects of Repetition and Spaced
Review upon Retention of a Complex
Learning Task

JAMES H. REYNOLDS / *Colgate University*

ROBERT GLASER / *University of Pittsburgh*

Laboratory investigations of overlearning (Krueger, 1929; Postman, 1961) and retroactive inhibition (e.g., Briggs, 1957) have generally shown that retention of paired-associate lists is positively related to degree of original learning. These findings are consonant with most existing learning theories, which assume that the strength of learning—and therefore resistance to forgetting—varies as a function of the number of practice repetitions. In contrast, several early investigations reviewed by Welborn and English (1937) have indicated that retention of meaningful material tends to remain constant regardless of amount of repetition during original learning. Most of these investigations employing meaningful tasks, however, are subject to certain criticisms regarding methodology, primarily with respect to the inadequate control procedures used in presentation of the experimental material and other proactive and retroactive material which might affect retention. Because of such methodological problems, the validity of past results indicating that repetition has little effect upon retention of meaningful tasks has been questioned (e.g., Slamecka & Ceraso, 1960).

One purpose of the research reported here was to evaluate the effect of repetition upon retention of a complex and meaningful learning task using programed instruction as an apparatus for controlling the relevant presentation variables assumed to be related to retention. Through the use of various program sequences, the amount of repetition and the order of presentation of both experimental and interpolated material could be manipulated with considerable precision. At the same time, the

Reprinted with the permission of the senior author and the publisher from *Journal of Educational Psychology*, 1964, Vol. 55, 297–308.

programing technique permitted presentation of the learning task in an environment similar to that in which complex learning often takes place, i.e., in the classroom. Thus the technique provided for evaluation of repetition effects upon retention of meaningful materials learned under classroom conditions, but controlled with respect to relevant presentation variables.

A second problem investigated, using the same programed materials, was the effect of spaced review upon retention of meaningful material. Although periodic review of material previously learned is a prevalent teaching method, little attention has been given to systematic evaluation of its effect upon retention. Distribution of practice studies using lists of paired-associate materials has indicated that temporal factors in presentation have varying and complicated effects upon learning (Underwood, 1961). Typically, however, the designs used in such investigations are not analogous to spacing procedures which are used in reviewing meaningful material, so generalizations from the laboratory to the classroom are difficult to make.

In the present research, an attempt was made to replicate the use of review as employed in the classroom by inserting review sequences into an instructional program at various points following original learning. The retention of groups receiving spaced review was compared with the retention of other program groups which received no spaced review after learning the same tasks. Because the variable studied was one which interacted with the length of the retention interval, comparisons of review and nonreview treatments were made under two conditions: (*a*) retention at equivalent times following the end of original learning, and (*b*) retention when the amount of time following the

last exposure to the experimental material was equivalent for the review and nonreview groups. Results for the first condition, and for the investigation of repetition and spaced review effects upon retention, are described in Experiment I. The second condition under which spaced review effects were further evaluated is presented in Experiment II.

EXPERIMENT I

Method

MATERIALS

Programs. A 1280-frame program, covering the 10 topics in biology outlined in Table 1, was used. Within this program the sixth topic, a 115-frame sequence on mitosis, was selected for experimental variation. The topic introduced 11 new technical terms—mitosis, interphase, prophase, metaphase, anaphase, telophase, spindles, cell plate, indentation, equator, chromosomes—and required the subject to learn their meanings and usage in describing the mitosis process. Using the original 115-frame sequence as a standard, two new sequences were written which taught the same material, but differed from the original and from each other in the frequency with which the technical terms were repeated. To construct the new sequences, the number of stimulus and response repetitions of each of the 11 critical terms in the original sequence (hereafter designated as the 1.0 sequence) were first tabulated. Then a second sequence of frames, similar in content to the 1.0 sequence, but containing just half as many stimulus and response repetitions of each term, was written. Finally a third sequence, also similar to 1.0, but containing 50% more stimulus-response repetitions of each term, was constructed. These new sequences, designated .5 and 1.5, respectively, were 75 frames and 175 frames in length.

By inserting any one of the three experimental sequences (.5, 1.0, 1.5) into the larger program as Topic 6, amount of repetition of the experimental material could be varied while keeping presentation of both prior and subsequent learning materials constant. Column A of Table 1 illustrates the three repetition conditions thus formed. These conditions were designated M-.5, M-1.0, and M-1.5, indicating that the three repetition levels were presented intact as massed (M) practice.

The .5 and 1.0 sequences were also used in constructing two spaced review (R) conditions. To provide for spaced review, two short sections were written; these sequences were 22 and 28 frames in

length and together contained the same number of repetitions of the 11 terms as the .5 sequence. As shown in Column B of Table 1, the review sections were inserted after Topic 7 and Topic 8 (Plant and Animal Reproduction). Thus one review condition (R-1.0), consisting of the .5 sequence and the two review sections, contained the same number of repetitions of the 11 terms as condition M-1.0, but spaced them out over several topics rather than presenting them intact. A second review condition (R-1.5), consisting of the 1.0 sequence plus the review sections, was equivalent in number of repetitions to M-1.5, but they were also distributed over topics rather than massed.

Table 1

TITLE AND ORDER OF BIOLOGY TOPICS PRESENTED TO THREE MASSED REPETITION GROUPS AND TWO SPACED REVIEW GROUPS

Order of topics	A Massed repetition groups (M-.5, M-1.0, M-1.5) [a]	B Spaced review groups (R-1.0, R-1.5)
1	Cells	Cells
2	Protozoa	Protozoa
3	Tissues	Tissues
4	Organs and Systems	Organs and Systems
5	Green Plants	Green Plants
6	Mitosis (.5 or 1.0 or 1.5)	Mitosis (.5 or 1.0)
7	Plant Reproduction (107 frames)	Plant Reproduction (107 frames)
(Review)	—	Review Mitosis (28 frames)
8	Animal Reproduction (217 frames)	Animal Reproduction (217 frames)
(Review)	—	Review Mitosis (22 frames)
9	Classification (165 frames)	Classification (165 frames)
10	Heredity (95 frames)	Heredity (95 frames)

[a] The numbers .5, 1.0, and 1.5 indicate the relative amounts of repetition used in the different experimental versions.

Tests. Measures of unaided recall, aided recall, and recognition of the 11 mitosis terms were used to assess retention. The Unaided Recall Test (22 points) required the subject to describe and illustrate the mitosis process without the aid of external cues. The Aided Recall Test contained 15 incomplete sentences

which required the use of the experimental terms as fill-ins. The Recognition Test was an 18-item multiple-choice measure. Two additional tests, evaluating aided recall and recognition of material from three nonexperimental topics (Cells, Plant Reproduction, and Animal Reproduction), were employed as control measures.

SUBJECTS

A total of 75 junior-high-school students participated in the experiment. Scholastic aptitudes, as measured by the Otis Quick-Scoring Mental Ability Test (Beta), ranged from 100 to 134, with a median IQ of 117. At the time of the experiment, all subjects belonged to one of three classes taking a general science course. None of the subjects had taken previous courses in biology, and none had had previous experience with programed instruction.

DESIGN AND PROCEDURE

Prior to the experiment, the subjects with equivalent intelligence were assigned to one of five groups by a randomized blocks method (Edwards, 1960, Ch. 11). Each group received one of the five experimental conditions. The programs were administered with Min-Max II teaching machines to all groups in 20 consecutive classroom science periods, each period lasting 40 minutes. At the beginning of every period the teacher, who served as the experimenter for all groups, assigned to each group the number of frames that were to be completed in that session. The subjects finishing an assignment early were permitted to use the remainder of the session as a study period, provided they did not study biology. Since the programs contained slightly different numbers of frames because of the experimental variations, daily work assignments to the groups varied from session to session, ranging from assignments of 50 frames to a maximum assignment of 80 frames for any single 40-minute session. By regulating the daily assignments, all of the five groups completed the experimental mitosis section during Sessions 10 and 11, and completed the entire program in the twentieth session.

Before beginning the program, the subjects were given the Recognition Test as a pretest to determine the equivalence of the five groups on prelearning knowledge of mitosis. The first retention testing (T_1) was administered on the 2 days immediately following completion of the program. In T_1, Aided Recall Tests were given first for both the experimental and control material. These measures were followed by the experimental and control Recognition Tests. After a 3-week interval, during which the subjects were not exposed to any of the material learned in the programs, a second retention test (T_2) was administered. T_2 was composed of four separate tests, presented in order of decreasing difficulty. First the Unaided Recall Test was administered, which had not been given at T_1, but was used in T_2 both as a warm-up task and as an additional retention measure; then the Aided Recall (completion) and the Recognition (multiple-choice) Tests of mitosis, and finally the Recognition Test for the control materials, were given. The subjects were unaware that this T_2 battery was to be administered, and all four tests were given in a single session to prevent the possibility of reviewing.

Results

Table 2 summarizes the means and standard deviations of all groups on the pretest and the various measures obtained during T_1 and T_2. Analyses of variance, employing the randomized-blocks technique (Edwards, 1960, Ch. 11), were used to compare the groups on each of these measures. Several subjects were absent at various times during the series of testings. Each absence required that the entire block with which the absent subject was matched be eliminated from the analyses, reducing the size of all groups by one. Fortunately, the absences were distributed over the testing periods in a way that necessitated removal of only one or two blocks of subjects from each of the analyses made. However, it was necessary to remove different blocks on different analyses, so that the group Ns of 13 or 14 that were used in the various analyses did not always represent the same subjects in each analysis.

Table 2

SUMMARY OF MEANS AND STANDARD DEVIATIONS FOR ALL GROUPS
ON PRETEST AND RETENTION TESTS ADMINISTERED AT T_1 AND T_2

Test	Total possible score	Statistic	Group				
			Massed repetition			Spaced review	
			M-.5	M-1.0	M-1.5	R-1.0	R-1.5
Pretest							
Recognition (Mitosis)	18	$\overline{X}$	3.62	2.92	2.54	3.92	2.92
($N = 13$)		s	1.66	1.98	1.76	2.43	2.22
Immediate retention (T_1)							
Aided Recall ($N = 14$)							
Mitosis	15	$\overline{X}$	3.79	5.21	7.57	10.00	9.79
		s	3.49	4.59	5.67	4.76	4.69
Control	39	$\overline{X}$	18.57	17.50	17.79	22.14	19.36
		s	9.15	7.05	9.25	9.85	7.37
Recognition ($N = 13$)							
Mitosis	18	$\overline{X}$	6.00	7.08	8.54	10.00	8.92
		s	4.26	5.22	4.79	5.93	3.66
Control	13	$\overline{X}$	11.31	12.77	12.69	13.08	12.38
		s	3.55	4.17	3.61	3.25	2.47
Delayed retention (T_2)							
Unaided Recall ($N = 14$)							
Mitosis	22	$\overline{X}$	2.93	4.29	3.14	6.57	6.14
		s	3.60	4.92	3.80	4.90	4.87
Aided Recall ($N = 14$)							
Mitosis	15	$\overline{X}$	4.86	6.14	6.71	9.50	10.07
		s	4.45	5.19	5.40	4.77	4.75
Recognition ($N = 14$)							
Mitosis	18	$\overline{X}$	6.79	7.71	8.29	10.50	10.93
		s	4.21	5.92	5.72	6.35	6.08
Control	20	$\overline{X}$	12.29	12.86	12.86	15.00	13.93
		s	3.77	3.51	3.57	2.83	2.62

As can be seen in Table 2, mean scores among the five groups on the pretest ranged from 2.54 to 3.62. An analysis of variance showed that the pretest differences among groups were not significant ($F = 1.22$, $df = 4/64$, $p > .05$). A series of correlated t tests, made for each group on the differences between the Recognition pretest scores and the T_1 Recognition scores, yielded significant t values ranging from 2.34 to 3.84, indicating that the higher mean scores for each group at the time of T_1 were due to the effect of the program treatments rather than chance.

Repetition Effects. The M-.5, M-1.0, and M-1.5 groups received the ex-

perimental T_1 measures of Aided Recall and Recognition on the tenth day following original learning of mitosis. A simple analysis of variance showed no significant differences among the groups on the T_1 Recognition Test ($F = .98$, $df = 2/24$, $p > .05$). For the T_1 Aided Recall Test, however, a significant difference among means was indicated ($F = 4.50$, $df = 2/26$, $p < .025$). Further analysis of the Aided Recall results showed that the M-.5 group mean was significantly lower than the mean for the M-1.5 group ($t = 3.12$, $df = 13$, $p < .01$); but, although there is a regular trend of higher performance with increased repetition, all other mean differences were within chance limits. The results of analyses of variance performed for the T_1 control measures were not significant ($F < 1.00$ and $F = 1.17$ for Aided Recall and Recognition control tests, respectively), implying that the reliable difference obtained for the experimental Aided Recall Test was due to the varying repetition levels received and not to extraexperimental differences among the groups.

The Unaided Recall, Aided Recall, and the experimental and control Recognition Tests were administered at T_2, 21 days following T_1. Analyses of variance comparing the M-.5, M-1.0, and M-1.5 groups on all four T_2 measures yielded F values below 1.00, indicating no significant differences among the repetition levels in retention of either the experimental or the control materials. The significant difference obtained for Aided Recall at time T_1 apparently dissipated between T_1 and T_2, leaving retention equivalent for all three massed repetition groups three weeks after termination of the program.

Effects of Spaced Review. Table 2 shows that the performance of the R-1.0 and R-1.5 groups was generally higher than the M groups on all retention tests administered at T_1 and T_2. Since the R-1.0 and R-1.5 groups received the same T_1 and T_2 measures as were obtained for Groups M-1.0 and M-1.5, these four groups could be compared on all measures in a series of 2×2 analyses of variance to evaluate statistically the effects of two levels of repetition (1.0 and 1.5), two levels of review (R and M), and their interaction.

Results of the factorial analyses of the two experimental and the two control tests administered at T_1 showed that neither the repetition effect nor the interaction between repetition and review was significant for any measure, indicating that the two levels of repetition used had neither a general nor a differential

effect upon retention of the M and R groups.

In comparing the two levels of review, a significant F value of 13.17 ($df = 1/55$, $p < .01$) obtained for the experimental Aided Recall Test indicated that recall of the mitosis material was reliably greater for the R treatment than for M. The difference between M and R treatments on the other experimental test, Recognition, was not significant ($F = 2.31$, $df = 1/51$). On the control Recognition Test, also, no difference between M and R was found ($F < 1.00$); however, a significant difference between the M and R treatments was obtained for the control Aided Recall Test ($F = 4.22$, $df = 1/55$, $p < .05$). This latter finding of a reliable difference on one of the control measures implies that the superior aided recall of the experimental material demonstrated by the R groups at T_1 may have been due to some effect other than the experimental treatment alone.

Turning to the analyses of the data obtained from the M-1.0, M-1.5, R-1.0, and R-1.5 groups at T_2, there were again no significant differences for the repetition effect or the Repetition $\times$ Review interaction on any of the four T_2 tests administered. At this time, performance of the R groups was superior to M on all three of the retention tests of the experimental material; with $df = 1/59$, the F values for the review effect were 7.76 ($p < .01$), 13.15 ($p < .01$), and 4.54 ($p < .05$) for the Unaided Recall, Aided Recall, and Recognition Tests, respectively. As at time T_1, however, R performance was also significantly higher than M on the control test ($F = 5.56$, $df = 1/55$, $p < .05$). Again the control data indicate that the superior retention demonstrated by the R groups on the experimental material may not have been due to the experimental treatment alone.

Delayed Retention. The Aided Recall and Recognition Tests of mitosis and the control Recognition Test were administered to all groups at both T_1 and T_2. Table 2 indicates that many of the T_2 means were slightly higher than the T_1 means obtained for the same group on the same test. Individual t tests between T_1 and T_2 means failed to reveal significant changes over time for any group in either direction. These comparisons, which suggest that no forgetting occurred during the 3-week intertest interval, will be discussed further after the results of the second experiment have been presented.

Discussion

The results from the T_1 and T_2 testings of the M-.5, M-1.0, and M-1.5 repetition groups indicate that stimulus-response repetition differences as large as 200% had only a limited effect upon retention of programed materials after a period of interpolated learning, and that even this limited effect disappeared over a relatively short period of time. Although the general failure to obtain significant repetition effects is contradictory to findings from investigations employing paired-associate lists in transfer designs (e.g., Briggs, 1957), it supports earlier research in retention of meaningful material as a function of repetition (Welborn & English, 1937).

Slamecka and Ceraso (1960, p. 459), in a comprehensive review of research on proactive and retroactive inhibition, have criticized much of the previous research in retention of meaningful material. They list such control problems as whole presentation, unlimited recall times, and group testing and presentation procedures as reasons for the discrepancies found among studies of retention of meaningful and nonmeaningful material. To demonstrate the effects of such design problems, these reviewers cite one study

using meaningful rote material under controlled laboratory conditions which indicated that when appropriate control measures are taken the retention of meaningful material can be shown to vary with repetition in the same way as does retention of unconnected materials. In the present study, group testing and presentation procedures were used intentionally in an effort to replicate the classroom learning environment. However, the use of the programing instrument permitted sequential presentation of the learning task to each subject individually and also controlled the quantity of stimulus presentation and response evocation for all of the materials learned. The partial and transitory effect of repetition obtained under these conditions suggests that, while a relationship between number of stimulus-response repetitions and retention of meaningful material may be demonstrable in the laboratory, the relevance of this relationship in more complex learning situations is limited.

Comparisons of the M and R treatments at T_1 and T_2 indicate that retention was generally superior for the R treatment on both the experimental and the control materials. Since all groups were equivalent in intelligence and pretest knowledge of the experimental material, there is some basis for assuming that spaced review had facilitating effects upon retention of both experimental and control topics. The alternative possibility exists, however, that the groups receiving the R treatment were superior in general knowledge of biology prior to the experiment—or at least in prior knowledge of the control materials, which was not evaluated in the pretest. Such a difference would account for the difference in retention of the control topics and even suggests that the R groups may have had some advantage in retaining the experimental material simply because the other tasks presented were already familiar. This possible influence of pre-experimental differences in general knowledge of the total learning task was evaluated further in the second experiment.

A second problem in interpreting the spaced review results is the discrepancy in length of the interpolated interval elapsing between the last practice frames of the experimental mitosis topic and the retention tests. All subjects receiving the M treatment finished instruction in mitosis at the end of Day 11, while those in the R groups did not receive final review of this material until Day 15. Since retention testing were administered to all groups at the same time relative to the end of the program, the retention intervals for the R treatment were consistently 4 days shorter than for M. This discrepancy was unavoidable, since no single experiment can vary spacing while simultaneously controlling both prior learning and total learning. Therefore, a second experiment evaluating the effect of spaced review was performed, this time controlling amount of prior learning and length of interval between last practice and test, but permitting the total amount of learning material presented to vary.

EXPERIMENT II

The design of Experiment II differed from that of Experiment I in several major respects. First, although groups received either the M or the R treatment in the same manner as previously described, only one level of repetition (1.5) was used. Second, a pretest and additional retention tests of the control materials were administered to evaluate more precisely the effect of spaced review upon retention of the control topics. Third, the R group did not receive a T_1 testing immediately following

completion of the program, but instead received other interpolated tasks before being given T_1. Although this procedure necessarily resulted in the R group receiving more interpolated (and possibly interfering) material than group M, it permitted an equating of the M and R groups with regard to the length of the retention interval elapsing between the last frame of the mitosis material and administration of the retention measures. These changes in design, and several other procedural variations, are described in more detail below.

Table 3

DESCRIPTION OF BIOLOGY PROGRAM PRESENTED TO ALL GROUPS IN EXPERIMENT II

Unit	Topic	Number of frames
1	Introduction to Cell Structure	150
2	The Plastids	74
3	The Nucleus	43
4	The Cytoplasm	74
5	Animal and Plant Cells	31
6	Protozoa	39
7	Tissues, Organs, and Systems	50
8	Green Plants	183
9	Mitosis	115
10	Reproduction of Seed Plants	107
11	Animal Reproduction	217
12	Men in Biology	39
13	Classification of Plants and Animals	123
14	Heredity	99
	Total frames	1344

Method

SUBJECTS

Two intact eighth-grade science classes were selected to participate in the experiment on the basis of the following criteria: neither had been exposed to biology instruction during the school year, neither had had previous familiarity with programed instruction, and the mean IQs of the two groups were equivalent. The classes chosen were from different schools and had different science teachers.

MATERIALS

Prior to Experiment II certain modifications were made in the first five sections of the original biology program in order to make it a more effective instructional tool. Modifications consisted of making minor changes in the wording of certain frames and adding new frames in some cases to clarify difficult sections. The resulting program differed from that used in Experiment I in that it was 64 frames longer (totaling 1,344 frames) and was divided into 14 sections rather than 10. Table 3 summarizes the newer revision, giving the names, order, and sizes of each topic. Since the changes occurred only in control topics, their possible effects upon the data of Experiment II were equivalent for the experimental treatments compared. All programs were administered with Min-Max II teaching machines. The experimental mitosis sequences inserted into the revised program were the same sequences used in Experiment I, and the retention tests were also identical to those previously described.

DESIGN AND PROCEDURE

A massed-learning group (M) received the M-1.5 program described in the first experiment, followed by a T_1 retention test at the end of the program. Because of the increased length of the revised program, the time taken to complete it was 1 day longer than in Experiment I. Consequently, the length of the interpolated learning interval between the last trial of the mitosis topic and T_1 was 10 school days for Group M. An R group was administered the same treatment as described previously for the R-1.5 group, except that the T_1 testing was not given immediately following completion of the program. Instead, Group R received five science periods of teacher instruction in astronomy after finishing the program, and

received the T_1 test in the sixth science period. These interpolated astronomy periods extended the Group R interval between the last review trial of mitosis and T_1 to 10 school days, making it equivalent to the interpolated learning interval of Group M. As in Experiment I, a T_2 retention test was administered to both groups 3 weeks following T_1.

Testing procedures varied slightly from those used in Experiment I so that more information concerning prior knowledge and learning of the control materials could be obtained. The pretest consisted of the Recognition measures for both experimental and control materials, providing an assessment of equivalence of the groups in general knowledge of biology as well as knowledge of mitosis. At both T_1 and T_2 the Aided Recall and the Recognition Tests for the experimental and control topics were administered. As in the first experiment, the Unaided Recall Test of mitosis was given only at T_2, as a warm-up task and an additional retention measure.

Daily administration of the program was accomplished as described for Experiment I. All tests at T_1 and T_2 were administered in one session, without prior warning from the experimenter that they would be given. In the interval between T_1 and T_2 both groups received instruction in science topics unrelated to biology, minimizing the probability of systematic practice and review during the 3-week forgetting period.

Results

Two subjects in Group R and six subjects in Group M failed to complete the entire program and all retention tests because of absence, and were eliminated from the final data. The results for the remaining subjects are summarized in Table 4, including the measures taken for the R and M groups prior to administration of the program, and also at the retention testing intervals which occurred 10 days (T_1) and 31 days (T_2) following the last review trial of the

Table 4

MEANS AND STANDARD DEVIATIONS OF R AND M GROUPS ON ALL
TESTS AND RESULTS OF *t* TESTS FOR DIFFERENCES BETWEEN MEANS

Test	Spaced review (R) (N = 23)		Massed repetition (M) (N = 35)		
	$\overline{X}$	s	X	s	t
Pretests					
IQ	118.74	6.81	119.17	9.98	1.18
Recognition					
Mitosis	2.87	1.49	3.37	1.93	1.05
Control	10.30	2.28	11.31	2.52	1.55
Immediate retention (T_1)					
Aided Recall					
Mitosis	11.00	3.44	8.14	4.41	2.62*
Control	20.30	7.55	20.37	6.39	.04
Recognition					
Mitosis	12.22	4.00	9.23	4.73	2.50*
Control	13.96	2.79	14.91	2.28	1.42
Delayed retention (T_2)					
Unaided Recall					
Mitosis	11.74	4.21	7.00	3.49	4.58***
Aided Recall					
Mitosis	11.13	3.40	8.17	4.71	2.60*
Control	21.52	8.08	21.66	6.09	.75
Recognition					
Mitosis	12.83	4.18	9.34	4.44	3.00**
Control	14.09	2.25	14.17	2.72	.12

Note: $23 + 35 - 2 = 56$ *df.*
  $*p < .02.$
  $**p < .01.$
  $***p < .001.$

mitosis material. Differences between the group means for each measure were evaluated by independent two-tailed *t* tests, and the resulting *t* values are also included in Table 4.

There were no significant differences between group means on any of the pretest measures, indicating that the groups were equivalent in intelligence and also in preprogram knowledge of the experimental and control materials. The means on the Recognition pretest of mitosis are no higher than would be expected from guessing on an 18-item 5-choice multiple-choice test, suggesting that neither group had any knowledge of the mitosis topic prior to taking the program. Control-item means for the

Recognition pretest were above chance limits of guessing, however, reflecting some degree of preprogram knowledge of the control materials.

As shown in Table 4, no significant differences between Group M and Group R were found for any of the control tests at either T_1 or T_2. The two groups, equivalent in pretest performance on the control material and given equivalent presentations of that material during learning, retained their learning to the same degree. On the experimental mitosis materials, however, significant differences were found between the groups on all tests administered at T_1 and T_2. All differences were in the same direction, with Group R demonstrating higher retention performance than Group M regardless of the type of retention tested or the length of the retention interval.

The same Aided Recall and Recognition Tests were administered to both groups at both T_1 and T_2. Inspection of the means shows that for each group the T_2 performance is nearly the same, and in all but one case slightly higher, than performance on the same test at T_1. As in Experiment I, none of the changes are significant in either direction, indicating that neither forgetting nor significant improvement in retention occurred during the T_1–T_2 interval.

Discussion

The consistent superiority of Group R over M in retention of the experimental material, even with length of the forgetting interval between last practice and testing equated, confirms the previously tentative finding that the spacing of review sequences has a facilitating effect upon retention of material learned in a programed sequence. The fact that Group R was exposed to more new material (i.e., the additional astronomy topic presented by the teacher) between the end of the program and T_1 does not detract from the results, since this material, if it had any effect at all upon retention, would presumably serve as additional interference rather than as an aid in retaining the experimental material.

In contrast to Experiment I, no differences between the M and R conditions in retention of control materials were obtained in Experiment II. Two explanations must be considered in accounting for this discrepancy. First, it is possible that the extension of the retention interval in Experiment II to 5 days following the end of the program for the R group caused additional forgetting of the control topics, masking a superior retention of this material that may have existed at a point immediately following the end of the program. An alternative explanation, however, is that the findings obtained for the control material in Experiment I were due simply to unmeasured differences between groups in prior knowledge of the control topics, and that neither the R treatment itself nor the change in retention intervals in Experiment II had any reliable effect upon this material.

Although the present data cannot rule out either of these interpretations, the latter one appears to be more likely. The changes in retention interval did not affect results for the experimental task, so there is little reason to expect that the same change would, in itself, have a significant effect upon the control material. Also, the Experiment II pretest indicated equivalence of groups in prior knowledge of the control topics, and a subsequent equivalence in retention of these topics. These aspects of the data suggest that the spaced review treatment, while producing a significant facilitation in retention of the material that was spaced, had no differential effect upon retention of the accompanying material that was not spaced.

In both experiments, comparisons of the means obtained on the same tests given at the two retention intervals showed no significant forgetting, and in most cases a slight but nonsignificant improvement in performance, over the 3-week interval separating the two retention testings. Two aspects of the testing procedures used may explain the failure to obtain the expected decrease in retention over time. First, it is noted that the initial testing (T_1) occurred several days after the last experimental and control materials were presented for learning, the interim days being used to present other biology topics which were not included in the tests used (e.g., Men in Biology, Classification, Heredity). These interpolated topics may have interfered with an initially high level of learning of the experimental and control topics, causing rapid forgetting to a moderate, but stable, level of retention. Hovland (1951, p. 646) has presented evidence that retention of meaningful material dissipates rapidly following learning, soon reaching a level which is maintained without further retention loss over long periods of time. If such a stable level of retention had already been reached at the time of initial testing, it would be expected that (*a*) performance would not be at ceiling, and (*b*) little further forgetting would occur over the next several weeks. These expectations are substantiated by the data from both experiments. Second, it has been shown that, when identical tests are used at two retention intervals, practice effects tend to carry over from the first testing and elevate performance artificially on the second test (Ammons & Irion, 1954). Either of these explanations, or both, may account for the failure to obtain a decrease in retention performance over the 3-week period separating the two testings.

The combined results of the two experiments have implications for several areas of learning research which may warrant further investigation. Regarding programed instruction, the findings suggest that the often-criticized monotony of repetition found in many early programs may in fact be of little value in enhancing retention and may be profitably replaced by a series of short instructional sequences in several related topics, each interspersed with short reviews of the preceding material. Further research would be required to determine optimal spacing procedures when a number of topics are being taught simultaneously. A second consideration is the extent to which the present findings are generalizable to classroom instructional procedures other than programing. Systematic evaluation of the effects of spaced review under a variety of instructional conditions may indicate that retention is optimized not so much by instructional procedures per se as by temporal conditions employed in their presentation. Finally, the present studies illustrate the utility of programed instruction as a research tool for investigation of learning variables in complex learning situations. By controlling presentation variables systematically, while allowing environmental factors to vary in ways that are often present in complex learning situations, the programing instrument can be useful in investigating variables which may be relevant in the context of meaningful learning environments but have received little attention in the controlled environment of the laboratory.

References

Ammons, A. and Irion, A. L. A note on the Ballard reminiscence phenomenon. *J. Exp. Psychol.*, 1954, **48**, 184–86.

Briggs, G. E. Retroactive inhibition as a function of degree of original and interpolated learning. *J. Exp. Psychol.*, 1957, **53**, 60–67.

Edwards, A. L. *Experimental design in psychological research* (rev. ed.). New York: Holt, Rinehart & Winston, 1960.

Hovland, C. I. Human learning and retention. In S. S. Stevens, ed., *Handbook of experimental psychology*. New York: Wiley, 1951. Pp. 613–89.

Krueger, W. C. F. The effect of overlearning upon retention. *J. Exp. Psychol.*, 1929, **12,** 71–78.

Postman, L. Retention as a function of degree of overlearning. *Science*, 1961, **135,** 666–67.

Slamecka, N. J. and Ceraso, J. Retroactive and proactive inhibition of verbal learning. *Psychol. Bull.*, 1960, **57,** 449–75.

Underwood, B. J. Ten years of massed practice on distributed practice. *Psychol. Rev.*, 1961, **68,** 229–47.

Welborn, E. L. and English, H. Logical learning and retention: A general review of experiments with meaningful verbal materials. *Psychol. Bull.*, 1937, **34,** 1–20.

34

The Acquisition of Knowledge

ROBERT M. GAGNÉ / *Florida State University*

The growing interest in autoinstructional devices and their component learning programs has had the effect of focusing attention on what may be called "productive learning." By this phrase is meant the kind of change in human behavior which permits the individual to perform successfully on an entire *class* of specific tasks, rather than simply on one member of the class. Self-instructional programs are designed to ensure the acquisition of capabilities of performing classes of tasks implied by names like "binary numbers," "musical notation," "solving linear equations" rather than tasks requiring the reproduction of particular responses.

When viewed in this manner, learning programming is not seen simply as a technological development incorporating previously established learning principles, but rather as one particular form of the ordering of stimulus and response events designed to bring about productive learning. It should be possible to study such learning, and the conditions which affect it, by the use of any of a variety of teaching machines, although there are few studies of this sort in the current literature (cf. Lumsdaine & Glaser, 1960). In the laboratory, the usual form taken by studies of productive learning has been primarily that of the effects of instructions and pretraining on problem solving (e.g., Hilgard, Irvine, & Whipple, 1953; Katona, 1940; Maltzman, Eisman, Brooks, & Smith, 1956).

When an individual is subjected to the situation represented by a learning program, his performance may change, and the experimenter then infers that he has acquired a new capability. It would not be adequate to say merely that he

Reprinted with the permission of the author and the publisher from *Psychological Review*, 1962, Vol. 69, 355–65.

has acquired new "responses," since one cannot identify the specific responses involved. (Adding fractions, for example, could be represented by any of an infinite number of distinguishable stimulus situations, and an equal number of responses.) Since we need to have a term by means of which to refer to what is acquired as a result of responding correctly to a learning program, we may as well use the term "knowledge." By definition, "knowledge" is that inferred capability which makes possible the successful performance of a *class of tasks* that could not be performed before the learning was undertaken.

SOME INITIAL OBSERVATIONS

In a previous study of programmed learning (Gagné & Brown, 1961) several kinds of learning programs were used in the attempt to establish the performance, in high school boys, of deriving formulas for the sum of n terms in a number series. Additional observations with this material led us to the following formulation: In productive learning, we are dealing with two major categories of variables. The first of these is knowledge, that is, the capabilities the individual possesses at any given stage in the learning; while the second is instructions, the content of the communications presented within the frames of a learning program.

In considering further the knowledge category, it has been found possible to identify this class of variable more comprehensively in the following way: Beginning with the final task, the question is asked, What kind of capability would an individual have to possess if he were able to perform this task successfully, were we to give him only instructions? The answer to this question, it turns out, identifies a new class of task which appears to have several important characteristics. Although it is conceived as an internal "disposition," it is directly measurable as a performance. Yet it is *not the same* performance as the final task from which it was derived. It is in some sense *simpler*, and it is also *more general*. In other words, it appears that what we have defined by this procedure is an entity of "subordinate knowledge" which is essential to the performance of the more specific final task.

Having done this, it was natural to think next of repeating the procedure with this newly defined entity (task). What would the individual have to know in order to be capable of doing *this* task without undertaking any learning, but given only some instructions? This time it seemed evident that there were two entities of subordinate knowledge which combined in support of the task. Continuing to follow this procedure, we found that what we were defining was a hierarchy of subordinate knowledges, growing increasingly "simple," and at the same time increasingly general as the defining process continued.

By means of this systematic analysis, it was possible to identify nine separate entities of subordinate knowledge, arranged in hierarchical fashion (see Figure 1). Generally stated, our hypothesis was that (*a*) no individual could perform the final task without having these subordinate capabilities (i.e., without being able to perform these simpler and more general tasks); and (*b*) that any superordinate task in the hierarchy could be performed by an individual provided suitable instructions were given, and provided the relevant subordinate knowledges could be recalled by him.

It may be noted that there are some possible resemblances between the entities of such a knowledge hierarchy and the hypothetical constructs described by three other writers. First are the habit-

family hierarchies of Maltzman (1955), which are conceived to mediate problem solving, and are aroused by instructions (Maltzman et al., 1956). The second are the "organizations" proposed by Katona (1940), which are considered to be combined by the learner into new knowledge after receiving certain kinds of instructions, without repetitive practice. The third is Harlow's (1949) concept of learning set. Harlow's monkeys acquired a general capability of successfully performing a class of tasks, such as oddity problems, and accordingly are said to have acquired a learning set. There is also the suggestion in one of Harlow's (Harlow & Harlow, 1949) reports that there may be a hierarchical arrangement of tasks more complex than oddity problems which monkeys can successfully perform. Since we think it important to imply a continuity between the relatively complex performances described here and the simpler ones performed by monkeys, we are inclined to refer to these subordinate capabilities as "learning sets."

Requirements of Theory

If there is to be a theory of productive learning, it evidently must deal with the independent variables that can be identified in the two major categories of instructions and subordinate capabilities, as well as with their interactions, in bringing about changes in human performance.

INSTRUCTIONS

Within a learning program, instructions generally take the form of sentences which communicate something to the learner. It seems possible to think of such "communication" as being carried out with animals lower than man, by means of quite a different set of experimental operations. Because of these communications, the human learner progresses from a point in the learning sequence at which he can perform one set of tasks to a point at which he achieves, for the first time, a higher level learning set (class of tasks). What functions must a theory of knowledge acquisition account for, if it is to encompass the effects of instructions? The following paragraphs will attempt to describe these functions, not necessarily in order of importance.

First, instructions make it possible for the learner to *identify the required terminal performance* (for any given learning set). In educational terms, it might be said that they "define the goal." For example, if the task is adding fractions, it may be necessary for the learner to identify $15\frac{3}{4}$ as an adequate answer, and $6\frac{3}{4}$ as an inadequate one.

Second, instructions bring about proper *identifications of the elements* of the stimulus situation. For example, suppose that problems are to be presented using the word "fraction." The learner must be able to identify $\frac{2}{5}$ as a fraction and .4 as not a fraction. Or, he may have to identify Σ as "sum of," and n as "number." Usually, instructions establish such identifications in a very few repetitions, and sometimes in a single trial. If there are many of them, differentiation may require several repetitions involving contrasting feedback for right and wrong responses.

A third function of instructions is to establish *high recallability* of learning sets. The most obviously manipulable way to do this is by repetition. However, it should be noted that repetition has a particular meaning in this context. It is not exact repetition of a stimulus situation (as in reproductive learning), but rather the presentation of additional examples of a class of tasks. Typically, within a learning program, a task representing a particular learning set is achieved once, for the first time. This may then be followed by instructions which present one or more additional examples of this same class of tasks. "Variety" in such repetition (meaning variety in the stimulus context) may be an important subvariable in affecting recallability. Instructions having the function of establishing high recallability for learning sets may demand "recall," as in the instances cited, or they may on other occasions attempt to achieve this effect by "recognition" (i.e., not requiring the learner to produce an answer).

The fourth function of instructions is perhaps the most interesting from the standpoint of the questions it raises for research. This is the "guidance of thinking," concerning whose operation there is only a small amount of evidence (cf. Duncan, 1959). Once the subordinate learning sets have been recalled, instructions are used to promote their application to (or perhaps "integration into") the performance of a task that is entirely new so far as the learner is concerned. At a minimum, this function of instructions may be provided by a statement like "Now put these ideas together to solve this problem;" possibly this amounts to an attempt to establish a *set*. Beyond this, thinking may be guided by suggestions which progressively limit the range of hypotheses entertained by the learner, in such a way as to decrease the number of incorrect solutions he considers (cf. Gagné & Brown, 1961; Katona, 1940). Within a typical learning program, guidance of thinking is employed after identification of terminal performance and of stimulus elements have been completed, and after high recallability of relevant learning sets has been ensured. In common sense terms, the purpose of these instructions is to

suggest to the learner "how to approach the solution of a new task" without, however, "telling him the answer."

Obviously, much more is needed to be known about the effects of this variable, if indeed it is a single variable. Initially, it might be noted that guidance of thinking can vary in *amount;* that is, one can design a set of instructions which say no more than "now do this new task" (a minimal amount); or, at the other end of the scale, a set of instructions which in effect suggest a step-by-step procedure for using previously acquired learning sets in a new situation.

SUBORDINATE CAPABILITIES: LEARNING SETS

When one begins with the performance of a particular class of tasks as a criterion of terminal behavior, it is possible to identify the subordinate learning sets required by means of the procedure previously described. The question may be stated more exactly as, "What would the individual have to be able to do in order that he can attain successful performance on this task, provided he is given only instructions?" This question is then applied successively to the subordinate classes of tasks identified by the answer. "What he would have to be able to do" is in each case one or more performances which constitute the denotative definitions of learning sets for particular classes of tasks, and totally for the entire knowledge hierarchy.

A theory of knowledge acquisition must propose some manner of functioning for the learning sets in a hierarchy. A good possibility seems to be that they are mediators of positive transfer from lower-level learning sets to higher-level tasks. The hypothesis is proposed that specific transfer from one learning set to another standing above it in the hierarchy will be zero if the lower one cannot be recalled, and will range up to 100% if it can be.

In narrative form, the action of the two classes of variables in the acquisition of knowledge is conceived in the following way. A human learner begins the acquisition of the capability of performing a particular class of tasks with an individual array of relevant learning sets, previously acquired. He then acquires new learning sets at progressively higher levels of the knowledge hierarchy until the final class of tasks is achieved. Attaining each new learning set depends upon a process of positive transfer, which is dependent upon (a) the recall of relevant subordinate learning sets, and upon (b) the effects of instructions.

Experimental Predictions and Results

Using the procedure described, we derived the knowledge hierarchy depicted in Figure 1 for the final task of "deriving formulas for the sum of n terms in number series.

As mentioned previously, it contained nine hypothesized learning sets. (The final row of circled entities will be discussed later.) Each of these subordinate knowledges can be represented as a class of tasks to be performed.

MEASURING INITIAL PATTERNS OF LEARNING SETS

It is predicted that the presence of different patterns of learning sets can be determined for individuals who are unable to perform a final task such as the one under consideration. To test this, we administered a series of test items to a number of ninth-grade boys. These items were presented on 4″ × 6″ cards, and the answers were written on specially prepared answer sheets. This particular method was used in order to make testing continuous with the administration of a learning program to be described hereafter. Each test item was carefully prepared to include instructions having the function of identification of terminal performance and of elements of the stimulus situation.

Beginning with the final task, the items were arranged to be presented in the order I, IIA, IVA, IVA2, IVAB, IIB, IIIB, IVB1, and IVB2. For any given subject, the sequence of testing temporarily stopped at the level at which successful performance was first reached, and a learning program designed to foster achievement at the next higher level (previously failed) was administered. This program and its results will shortly be described. Following this, testing on the remaining learning set tasks was undertaken in the order given. The possibility of effects of the learning program on the performance of these lower-level learning sets (not specifically practiced in the learning) is of course recognized, but not further considered in the present discussion.

A particular time limit was set for each test item, at the expiration of which the item was scored as failed. If a wrong answer was given before this time limit, the subject was told it was wrong, and encouraged to try again; if the correct answer was supplied within the time limit, the item was scored as passed. It is emphasized that these time limits, which were based on preliminary observations on other subjects with these tasks, were *not* designed to put "time pressure" on the subjects, nor did they appear to do so.

The patterns of success achieved on the final task and all subordinate learning set tasks, by all seven subjects, are shown in Table 1. The subjects have been arranged in accordance with their degree of success with all tasks, beginning with one who failed the final task but succeeded at all the rest. Several things are apparent from these data.

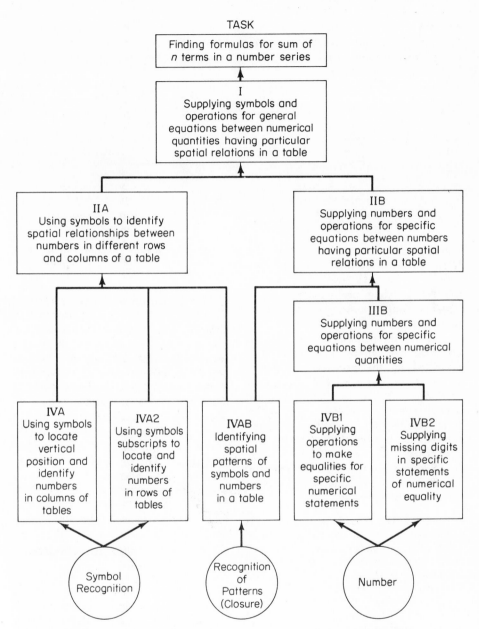

Fig. 1 Hierarchy of knowledge for the task of finding formulas for the sum of *n* terms in a number series.

First of all, it is quite evident that there are quite different "patterns of capability" with which individuals approach the task set by the study. Some are un-able to do a task like IIA (see Figure 1), others to do a task like IIB, which is of course quite different. Still others are unable to do either of these, and in fact

Table 1

PATTERN OF SUCCESS ON LEARNING SET TASKS RELATED TO THE
FINAL NUMBER SERIES TASK FOR SEVEN NINTH GRADE BOYS

Subject	Final	I	IIA	IIB	IIIB	IVA1	IVA2	IVAB	IVB1	IVB2
WW	−	+	+	+	+	+	+	+	+	+
WC	−	+	+	+	+	+	+	+	+	+
PM	−	−	−	+	+	+	+	+	+	+
GR	−	−	−	+	+	+	+	+	+	+
DJ	−	−	−	−	+	+	+	+	+	+
JR	−	−	−	−	−	+	+	+	+	+
RH	−	−	−	−	−	+	+	+	+	+

(The column group is headed *Task*.)

Note: + = Pass; − = Fail.

cannot perform successfully a task like IIIB. All seven of these subjects were able to perform IV-level tasks successfully; although in preliminary observations on similar tasks, we found some ninth-grade boys who could not.

Second, the patterns of pass and fail on these tasks have the relationships predicted by the previous discussion. There are no instances, for example, of an individual who is able to perform what has been identified as a "higher-level" learning set, and who then shows himself to be unable to perform a "lower-level" learning set related to it.

If learning sets are indeed essential for positive transfer, the following consequences should ensue:

1. If a higher-level learning set is passed (+), *all* related lower-level tasks must have been passed (+).
2. If *one or more* lower-level tasks have been failed (−), the related higher-level tasks must be failed (−).
3. If a higher-level task is passed (+), *no* related lower-level task must have been failed (−).
4. If a higher-level task has been failed (−), related lower-level tasks may have been passed (+). The absence of positive transfer in this case would be attributable to a deficiency in instructions, and does not contra-

dict the notion that lower-level sets are essential to the achievement of higher-level ones.

The relationships found to exist in these seven subjects are summarized in Table 2, where each higher-lower-level task relationship possible of testing is listed in the left-hand column. It will be noted that there are several relationships of the type higher (−), lower (+), as listed in Column 5. These provided no test of the hypothesis regarding hierarchical relations among learning sets. The instances in the remaining columns do, however. The + + and − − instances are verifying, whereas + − instances would be nonverifying. As the final column indicates, the percentage of verifying instances is in all cases 100%.

EFFECTS OF LEARNING PROGRAM ADMINISTRATION

If the characteristics of instructions as previously described are correct, it should be possible to construct a learning program which can be begun for each individual at the point of his lowest successful learning set achievement, and bring him to successful achievement of the final class of tasks. Briefly, its method should be to include frames

Table 2

PASS-FAIL RELATIONSHIP BETWEEN RELATED ADJACENT HIGHER- AND LOWER-LEVEL
LEARNING SETS FOR A GROUP OF SEVEN NINTH-GRADE BOYS

	Number of cases with relationship				Test of relationships	
Relationship examined	Higher + Lower +	Higher − Lower −	Higher + Lower −	Higher − Lower +	N (1+2+3)	Proportion (1+2)/ (1+2+3)
Final Task: I	0	6	0	1	6	1.00
I: IIA, IIB	1	5	0	1	6	1.00
IIA: IVA1, IVA2, IVAB	2	0	0	5	2	1.00
IIB: IIIB	3	2	0	2	5	1.00
IIIB: IVAB, IVB1, IVB2	5	0	0	2	5	1.00

Note: + = Pass; − = Fail.

which have the functions of (a) insuring high recallability of relevant learning sets on which achievement has been demonstrated; (b) making possible identifications of expected performance and of new stimuli, for each newly presented task; and (c) guiding thinking so as to suggest proper directions for hypotheses associating subordinate learning sets with each new one.

A program of this sort was administered to each of the seven ninth-grade boys, beginning at the level at which he first attained success on learning set tasks (Table 1). This was done by means of a simple teaching machine consisting of a visible card file clipped to a board mounted at a 40° angle to the learner's table, and containing material typed on 4″ × 6″ cards. The learner wrote his answer to successive frames on a numbered answer sheet, then flipped over the card to see the correct answer on the back. He was instructed that if his answer was wrong, he should flip the card back, and read the frame again until he could "see" what the right answer was.

After completing the instructional portion of the program for each learning set, the learner was again presented with the identical test-item problem he

had tried previously and failed. If he was now able to do it correctly, he was given five additional items of the same sort to perform, and then taken on by instructions to another learning set in either a coordinate or higher-level position in the hierarchy. This process was continued through the performance of the final task.

The data collected in this way yield pass-fail scores on each test item (representing a particular member of a class of tasks) *before* the administration of the learning program, and similar scores on the same item *after* learning. It is recognized that for certain experimental purposes, one would wish to have a different, matched, task for the test given after learning, to control for the effects of "acquaintance" during the first test. Since this study had an exploratory character, such a control was not used this time. However, it should be clearly understood that the first experience with these test items in question, for these subjects, involved only activity terminating in failure to achieve solution. No information about the correct solutions was given.

A striking number of instances of success in achieving correct solutions to learning set tasks was found following learning as compared with before. These results are summarized in Table 3. Although for learning set IIB the percentage of success was only 50% (with two cases), there were two learning sets for which 100% success was achieved, and the percentage for all instances combined was 86%. These results provide additional evidence compatible with the idea of the knowledge hierarchy.

Table 3

NUMBER OF INSTANCES OF PASSING AND FAILING FINAL TASK AND SUBORDINATE LEARNING SET TASKS BEFORE AND AFTER ADMINISTRATION OF AN ADAPTIVE LEARNING PROGRAM, IN A GROUP OF SEVEN NINTH-GRADE BOYS

Task	Number failing before learning	Number of these passing after learning	Percentage success
Final Task	7	6	86
I	5	4	80
II	5	5	100
IIB	2	1	50
IIIB	2	2	100
Total	21	18	86

The learner in such a program does not "practice the final task"; he acquires specifically identified capabilities in a specified order. In as many as six out of seven cases, we were able by this means to bring learners from various levels of competence all the way to final task achievement. (It is perhaps important that the exception was JR, one of two who had most to learn.) Of course, it must be recognized that two separable causes contribute to the effects of the learning program in this study: (a) the correctness of the learning set analysis; and (b) the specific effectiveness of the instructions contained in the learning program.

Implications for Individual Differences Measurement

It is evident that learning sets, as conceived in this paper, operate as "individual differences" variables, which, when suitably manipulated, also become "experimental" variables. There are some additional implications which need to be pointed out regarding the functioning of learning sets in the determination of measured individual differences.

As the process of identification of subordinate learning sets is progressively continued, one arrives at some learning sets which are very simple and general, and likely to be widespread within the population of learners for which the task is designed. Consider, for example, learning set IVB (Figure 1), which is represented by a task such as $4 \times 2 = 5 + ?$ If one makes a further analysis to identify a subordinate learning set for this task, the answer appears to be, "adding, subtracting, multiplying, and dividing one- and two-place numbers." It is interesting to note that this is exactly the task provided by a set of factor reference tests (French, 1954) called Number. In a similar manner, the other two circled entities in the last row of Figure 1 were identified. One is Symbol Recognition (called Associative Memory by the factor researchers), and Recognition of Patterns (called Flexibility of Closure). The implication is, therefore, that these simplest tasks, identified by factor analysis techniques as common to a great variety of human performances, also function as learning sets.

The hypothesis has been proposed that learning sets mediate positive transfer to higher-level tasks. Very often, if not usually, the measurement of transfer of training implies that a second task is learned *more* rapidly when preceded by the learning of an initial task, than when not so preceded. Accordingly, it seems necessary to distinguish between expected correlations of these basic factors (at the bottom of the hierarchy) with rate of attainment of higher-level learning sets on the one hand, and correlations of these same factors with achievement of higher-level learning sets on the other.

The implications of this line of reasoning would seem to be somewhat as follows: Factors which are found by the kind of psychological analysis previously described to lie at the bottom of the knowledge hierarchy should exhibit certain predictable patterns of correlation with higher-level learning sets. They should correlate most highly with rate of attainment of the learning sets in the next higher level to which they are related, and progressively less as one progresses upwards in the hierarchy. The reason for this is simply that the rate of attainment of learning sets in a hierarchy comes to depend to an increasing extent on the learning sets which have just previously been acquired and accordingly to a decreasing extent upon a basic factor or ability. Some analogy may be drawn here with the findings of Fleishman and Hempel (1954) on motor tasks.

The expected relationships between factor test scores and achievement scores (passing or failing learning sets) throughout such hierarchies seem to require a somewhat more complex derivation. First of all, such relationships will depend upon the effectiveness of a learning program, or perhaps on the effectiveness of previous learning. If the learning program is perfectly effective, for example, and if differences in rate of attainment are ignored, everyone will pass all the learning set tasks, and the variance will accordingly be reduced to zero. Under these circumstances, then,

one may expect all correlations with basic factors to be zero. However, one must consider the case in which the learning program is not perfectly effective. In such a case, the probability that an individual will acquire a new learning set, as opposed to not acquiring it, will presumably be increased to the extent that he scores high on tests of related basic abilities. If one continues to collect scores on learning set tasks of both successful achievers and those who fail, the result will presumably be an increasing degree of correlation between basic ability scores and learning set tasks as one progresses upwards in the hierarchy. The reason for this is that the size of the correlation comes to depend more and more upon variance contributed by those individuals who are successful, and less and less on that contributed by those who effectively "drop out."

The difference in expectation between the increasing pattern of correlation with achievement scores, and the decreasing pattern with measures of rate of attainment, is considered to be of rather general importance for the area of individual differences measurement. Confirmatory results have been obtained in a recent study (Gagné & Paradise, 1961) concerned with the class of tasks "solving linear algebraic equations."

Discussion

The general view of productive learning implied in this paper is that it is a matter of transfer of training from component learning sets to a new activity which incorporates these previously acquired capabilities. This new activity so produced is qualitatively different from the tasks which correspond to the "old" learning sets; that is, it must be described by a different set of operations, rather than simply being "more difficult." The characteristics of tasks which make achievement of one class of task the required precursor of achievement in another, and not vice versa, are yet to be discovered. Sufficient examples exist of this phenomenon to convince one of its reality (Gagné, Mayor, Garstens, & Paradise, 1962; Gagné & Paradise, 1961). What remains to be done, presumably, is to begin with extremely simple levels of task, such as discriminations, and investigate transfer of training to tasks of greater and greater degrees of complexity, or perhaps abstractness, thus determining the dimensions which make transfer possible.

The path to research on the characteristics of instructions appears more straightforward, at least at first glance. The establishment of identifications is a matter which has been investigated extensively with the use of paired associates. The employment of instructions for this purpose may need to take into consideration the necessity for learning differentiations among the stimulus items to be identified, as well as other variables suggested by verbal learning studies. The function of inducing high recallability would seem to be a matter related to repetition of learning set tasks, and may in addition be related to time variables such as those involved in distribution of practice. As for guidance of thinking, the distinguishing of this function from others performed by instructions should at least make possible the design of more highly analytical studies than have been possible in the past.

In the meantime, the approach employed in the experiment reported here, of proceeding backwards by analysis of an already existing task, has much to recommend it as a way of understanding the learning of school subjects like mathematics and science, and perhaps others also. Naturally, every human task yields a different hierarchy of learning

sets when this method of analysis is applied. Often, the relationship of higher to lower learning sets is more complex than that exhibited in Figure 1. It should be possible, beginning with any existing class of tasks, to investigate the effects of various instruction variables within the framework of suitably designed learning programs.

The major methodological implication of this paper is to the effect that investigations of productive learning must deal intensively with the kinds of variables usually classified as "individual differences." One cannot depend upon a measurement of *general* proficiency or aptitude to reveal much of the important variability in the capabilities people bring with them to a given task. Consider, for example, the seven ninth-grade boys in our study. Each of them had "had" algebra, and each of them had "had" arithmetic. There was no particularly striking relationship between their ultimate performance and their previous grades in algebra (although there is no doubt some correlation), nor between this performance and "general intelligence." But the measurement of their learning sets, as illustrated in Table 1, revealed a great deal about how they would behave when confronted with the learning program and the final task. For some, instructions had to begin, in effect, "lower down" than for others. Some could do Task 1 right away, while others could not, but could do it equally well provided they learned other things first. The methodological point is simply this: if one wants to investigate the effects of an experimental treatment on the behavior of individuals or groups who start from the same point, he would be well advised to measure and map out for each individual the learning sets relevant to the experimental task. In this way he can have some assurance of the extent to which his subjects are equivalent.

References

Duncan, C. P. Recent research on human problem solving. *Psychol. Bull.*, 1959, **56**, 397–429.

Fleishman, E. A. and Hempel, W. E. Changes in factor structure of a complex psychomotor test as a function of practice. *Psychometrika*, 1954, **19**, 239–52.

French, J. W., ed. *Kit of selected tests for reference aptitude and achievement factors*. Princeton, N.J.: Educational Testing Service, 1954.

Gagné, R. M. and Brown, L. T. Some factors in the programing of conceptual learning. *J. Exp. Psychol.*, 1961, **62**, 313–21.

Gagné, R. M., Mayor, J. R., Garstens, H. L., and Paradise, N. E. Factors in acquiring knowledge of a mathematical task. *Psychol. Monogr.*, 1962, **76** (7, Whole No. 526).

Gagné, R. M. and Paradise, N. E. Abilities and learning sets in knowledge acquisition. *Psychol. Monogr.*, 1961, **75** (14, Whole No. 518).

Harlow, H. F. The formation of learning sets. *Psychol. Rev.*, 1949, **56**, 51–65.

Harlow, H. F. and Harlow, M. K. Learning to think. *Scient. American*, 1949, **181**, 36–39.

Hilgard, E. R., Irvine, R. P., and Whipple, J. E. Rote memorization, understanding, and transfer: An extension of Katona's card-trick experiments. *J. Exp. Psychol.*, 1953, **46**, 288–92.

Katona, G. *Organizing and memorizing*. New York: Columbia Univer. Press, 1940.

Lumsdaine, A. A. and Glaser, R. *Teaching machines and programmed learning*. Washington, D.C.: National Education Association, 1960.

Maltzman, I. Thinking: From a behavioristic point of view. *Psychol. Rev.*, 1955, **62**, 275–86.

Maltzman, I., Eisman, E., Brooks, L. O., and Smith, W. M. Task instructions for anagrams following different task instructions and training. *J. Exp. Psychol.*, 1956, **51**, 418–20.

35

Correction and Review on Successive Parts in Learning a Hierarchical Task

M. DAVID MERRILL / *Stanford University*

Educators often assume that in mastering a hierarchical task (i.e., a task where knowledge of each successive part is a prerequisite to knowledge of the next part) learning and retention are facilitated by mastering each part of the material before proceeding to the succeeding parts.

The intrinsic programing technique of Crowder (1960) and the hierarchical task analysis of Gagné and coworkers (Gagné, 1962, 1965; Gagné, Mayor, Garstens, and Paradise, 1962; Gagné & Paradise, 1961) assume mastery of each part is desirable or essential before proceeding to the next part. Ausubel (1963) hypothesizes that mastery of previous parts in a hierarchical task promotes facilitation in learning subsequent parts.

The purpose of this study is to test this assumption. If it is true, then the following hypotheses should be supported: In a hierarchical learning task:

1. If Part I is mastered, subjects are able to learn Part II faster and with fewer errors than if Part I is not mastered before proceeding to Part II, etc.
2. When the terminal test requires every subject to review previously presented materials until he is able to answer every question correctly, subjects who are required to master each successive part of the task before proceeding take less total time to master the terminal test than subjects who proceed from part to part with no requirement of mastery.
3. Subjects who are required to master each successive part of the task before proceeding retain the material better than subjects who proceed from part to part with no requirement of

Reprinted with the permission of the author and the publisher from *Journal of Educational Psychology*, 1965, Vol. 56 pp. 225–34. The Method and Results sections have been condensed by the editors. Most tables of data have been omitted.

mastery even when the terminal test requires every subject to review previously presented materials until he is able to answer every question correctly.

Method

MATERIALS

Organization. The task used was a complex imaginary science called the Science of Xenograde Systems. This science is a description of a system of satellites that move about a nucleus. The nucleus contains small particles which affect the motion of the satellites. The laws governing the relationships between these particles make up the subject matter of the science. In content and structure, this task is almost identical to many scientific topics taught in school, and yet, because it is imaginary, it is extremely unlikely that any student will already know any of the content.

The terminal task selected was at the level of application (Bloom, 1956) and required the student to: "Generate a Xenograde System given only defining conditions." It consisted of 68 problems which, as a group, required the use of every principle of the science. The student had to choose those principles which were appropriate to a given problem and then use them to solve that problem.

Gagné (1962, 1965) suggested rules for generating a hierarchical structure. Applying such an analysis to the Science of Xenograde Systems yielded the hierarchy illustrated in Figure 1. Each of the boxes represents a single learning set. The boxes are arranged to illustrate their hierarchical relationship. Starting at the top of the diagram, it was necessary to understand the sets at the next level before one could perform the task at the higher level. For example, to be able to generate a Xenograde System one must know how to find *blip* locations and also how to find the *distance* of satellites at a given time.

The knowledge required to learn each set in the hierarchy was classified into five types (Bloom, 1956): Terminology, Specific Facts, Methodology, Conventions, and Principles and Generalizations. In order to evaluate the attainment of the goal, the behavior necessary to demonstrate comprehension and/or application was specified for each learning set. Working from this classification, each of the types of knowledge was made explicit by writing a specific definition or statement for each of the items. This list of statements comprised a condensed summary of all the knowledge necessary to attain the specified terminal behavior.

The learning sets were divided into five lessons and a test section as indicated by the dotted lines in Figure 1. Lesson 1 was an overview of the entire science and served to organize the presentation. Lesson 2 presented the laws that govern the motion of the particles in the nucleus. Lesson 3 presented the laws that govern the motion of the satellites. Lesson 4 presented the laws that govern the interaction between the particles in the nucleus and the satellites, and Lesson 5 presented formulas for finding the exact moment a blip occurred and the exact distance of a satellite under various circumstances. The test section contained 68 questions which, when answered, generated a Xenograde System.

A quiz was given after each lesson. This quiz was constructed to ascertain whether or not the behaviors specified for each learning set had been attained. The questions asked were comprehensive-type questions (Bloom, 1956). There were one or two questions for every learning set in the lesson.

Program. The mode of presentation was branching-type programed instruction. Each of the boxes in the flow diagram in Figure 2 represents a frame of the teaching program. The presentation frames (P) contained a short passage of material and a multiple-choice question concerning the passage. As Figure 2 shows, each frame was reviewed until *S* made the correct response.

The P frames were written from the summary statements and the Bloom classification. Each learning set was presented

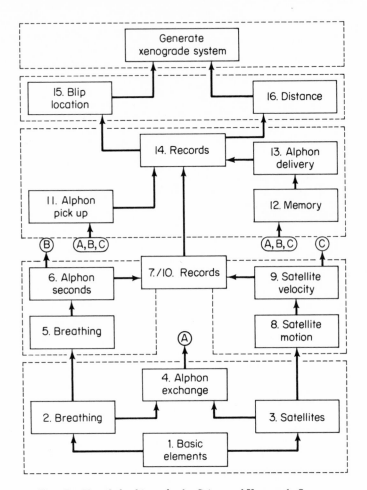

Fig. 1   Knowledge hierarchy for Science of Xenograde Systems.

in one to four P frames depending on the complexity of the principle and the number of terms to be presented. Since the Bloom classification assumes a taxonomy where lower levels are included in higher levels, it was felt that demonstration of comprehension was sufficient to assume recall ability. Therefore, the questions used on the P frames were of the problem-solving type, which required the student to use the principles just presented. The quizzes were also presented in programed form, including review and correction.

The test section was arranged in the same way as the quizzes. On the question frame (Q) there appeared a Xenograde System table which the subject was required to complete. The first frame in the test section had only the initial conditions of the system filled in the table. Each question asked for a single item of information. If the subject responded correctly, he was shown the next Q frame which showed the answer to the last question in the table. If he made an error, he was shown a general review. If he made a second or third error, he was shown the specific review until he responded correctly. By the time he reached Question 68, the entire table appeared correctly filled in.

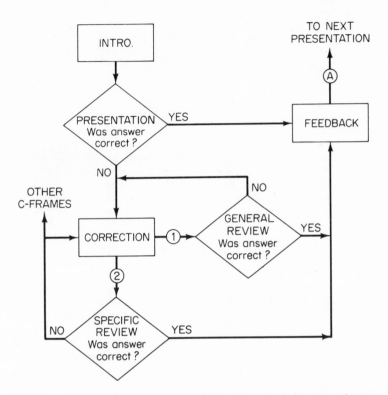

Fig. 2   Flow diagam for program lessons—correction/review procedure.

The lesson quizzes contained four or five answer alternatives to each question; in the test section there were always eight possible answers plus an "I don't know" alternative.

APPARATUS

A complex computer-based teaching-machine system, SOCRATES (System for Organizing Content to Review And Teach Educational Subjects), was used to present the content of the imaginary science to the subjects. The major components of this system are an IBM 1710 control system connected to a number of modified Auto-Tutor Mark II teaching machines. The components of the system are illustrated elsewhere (Merrill, 1964; Stolurow & Davis, 1963). The AutoTutor machines were located in student stations con-

structed from DuKane language-laboratory booths equipped with a special enlarged desk top. . . . This provided room for the AutoTutors as well as for writing space. The learning material was presented to the student by means of a 35-millimeter filmed image projected on a high-contrast rear-projection lenscreen. When directed to do so by the projected material, the student could respond by pushing one of 10 buttons located to the right of the viewing screen.

SUBJECTS

Sixty-two volunteers (25 males and 37 females) were recruited from the undergraduate- and master's-level education courses offered during the 1964 summer session at the University of Illinois. About half of these subjects were required to participate as part of their course assignment. The other participants were solicited by presenting this participation as a means whereby they could learn more about teaching machines, programed instruction, and particularly about computer-based instruction. The mean age of the subjects was 25 years with a standard deviation of 6.5 years. The range was from 17 years to 48 years. Most of the subjects were teachers or public-school administrators and/or in teacher training. There were 21 different subject-matter specialties represented including sciences, languages, mathematics, art, and the social sciences.

DESIGN

Prior to learning the imaginary science, all subjects were given a battery of aptitude tests selected from the *Kit of Reference Tests for Cognitive Factors* (French, Ekstrom, & Price, 1963). The following tests were selected: Locations Test (I–2), Addition Test (N–1), Division Test (N–2), Subtraction and Multiplication Test (N–3), Mathematics Aptitude Test (R–2), and Advanced Vocabulary Test (V–5). The entire battery took 52 minutes plus instruction time. The tests were assembled in a single booklet in the order given above.

The subjects were randomly assigned to one of five experimental groups: Group I received correction and review on lessons and on quizzes; Group II correction and review on lessons but not on quizzes; Group III no correction and review on lessons but only on quizzes; Group IV no correction and review on either lessons or quizzes; and Group V was given only the summary statements (no lessons or quizzes).

Immediately following the presentation of the lessons or summary all groups were presented the test section with the review procedure. Three weeks later they were presented the test section without review.

PROCEDURE

Subjects were first required to come to the laboratory for pretesting. The pretests were given in a single session to groups of subjects varying in size from 1–30. The learning sessions required 6 hours of machine time, which could be in 1-, 2-, or 3-hour sessions depending on the subject's schedule. Subjects were encouraged to schedule their sessions as close together as possible, not to try to learn the entire science in one session, and not to discontinue a session until they had completed the lesson on which they were working. The first few frames of the film instructed the subject in the operation of the machine and pointed out to him the reason for using an imaginary science. Following the introductory material, subjects were presented the lessons and quizzes or the summary and then the test section. Three weeks after completing the learning sessions the subjects returned for the retention session. Between the learning session and the 3-week retention test, most of the subjects attended three lectures. Lecture 1 explained the SOCRATES System and how it operates. Lecture 2 explained the purpose and design of the experiment, and Lecture 3 discussed programed instruction and its future in education.

Results

The groups were compared on each of the six pretest measures, and no significant differences were found. Covariance analysis was used as a means of reducing variance due to individual aptitudes which were thought to be related to the performance variables. The F tests for homogeneity of regression for each of the variables reported indicated that this assumption could not be met. For this reason only the analyses of variance are reported. The two response measures used were Time and Error. These two measures were not significantly correlated.

The first hypothesis specifies that mastery of each lesson should facilitate learning and therefore result in fewer errors and less time to learn on each succeeding lesson. It was assumed that correction/review promotes this mastery. If this hypothesis were to be supported, it would be anticipated that the groups receiving correction/review would make more errors and take more time on each successive lesson. The statistical design for this comparison is a Lindquist (1953) Type III mixed design.

The analysis for Errors and Time on P frames is reported in Table 1. The analyses for time and errors on Q frames were very similar and are therefore not reported.

Table 1

RESULTS OF TYPE III ANALYSIS

Source	P frames	
	Errors	Time
Between		
Lessons (L)	ns	ns
Quizzes (Q)	ns	ns
L × Q	ns	ns
Within		
Tasks (T)[a]	S*	S*
L × T	ns	S**
Q × T	ns	S*
L × T × Q	S*	ns

[a] Tasks are lessons 1–5.
  * $p < .05$.
  ** $p < .01$.

In the main this analysis does not support Hypothesis 1. The three-way interaction ($F = 7.05$) for Errors on P frames reported in Table 1 seems to indicate that subjects in Group III (correction/review on quizzes) do make progressively more errors per frame than groups receiving correction/review on frames (Groups I and II). It was hypothesized that subjects in Group IV (no correction/review) would make progressively more errors than all other groups. This prediction was not supported.

The Time data are in opposition to the hypothesis in that both interactions (Fs = 2.97, 7.33) indicate that receiving correction/review caused subjects to take progressively more time per frame. The measure used for this comparison is time spent only on P frames and does not include time spent on the review frames. This result seems to indicate that rather than facilitating performance, the correction/review procedure used tends to make people more cautious and consequently causes them to spend more time in an effort to get a correct answer and thereby avoid the review material.

Hypothesis 2 suggests that because of the facilitation due to correction/review, Groups I and II would take less total time to complete the entire task than would Groups III and IV, but the results are in direct opposition to the hypothesis. Groups I and II took more time during the learning (time on lessons 1–5, $F = 7.26$); Groups I and II took significantly more total time ($F = 11.92$) than did Groups III and IV; and regardless of the time spent in learning, there is no difference between Groups I–IV in the number of errors made on the test section.

Hypothesis 3, also tested by a two-way analysis of variance design, predicts that those subjects who received correction/review while learning would make fewer errors and take less time on the retention test. The results indicate that those groups which received correction/review on lessons take longer to complete the test ($F = 8.83$), even 3 weeks after learning, than those subjects who received correction/review only on quizzes or not at all. This finding lends support to the indication mentioned earlier that correction/review on lessons tends to teach subjects to be cautious and consequently to proceed more slowly. There is, however, no significant difference in the number of errors.

Group V was a special control group which was included to obtain a measure of the effectiveness of the review material that was used in the lessons. Because this group did not see any of the lessons but was presented only the set of summary statements which were used for the general review in the lessons, their understanding of the material could only be based upon these summary statements and the correction/review procedure common to all groups in the test section. One would anticipate that this group would take longer to complete the test section than the other groups ($F = 9.59$) but that this group would take less time to complete the test section than the time required for other groups to complete lessons 1–5 plus the test section ($F = 12.42$). The comparisons of this control group with the experimental groups indicate that both of these assumptions are true. It would seem logical to assume that this group would also make more errors ($F = 12.33$). The analysis also supports this assumption.

The question as to the effectiveness of this method of instruction cannot be answered without the retention data. Subjects in Group V did not make significantly more errors on the retention test than any of the other groups and they did not take significantly more time. Apparently the summary statements and review technique used in this study were very effective instructional techniques. There is some question as to whether Group V would perform as well in a transfer situation where they would be asked to solve a new Xenograde problem. There were also informal comments from subjects in Group V indicating that this procedure was extremely frustrating to the subjects, but data on attitudes of participants were not gathered systematically. The fact remains, however, that 3 weeks after learning, Group V retained as much as

any group, performed as efficiently as the experimental groups, and, considering total time in learning and testing, represented by far the most efficient procedure.

Discussion

Interpretation of the results obtained in this study depends on a full understanding of the concept of a hierarchical task. The definition given in the introduction of this report involves several distinctions. The first is between a hierarchical task and a hierarchical presentation of that task. A hierarchical task is a logical derivation in which the concepts, principles, and generalizations of the higher levels are combinations, reorganizations, and elaborations of the concepts, principles, and generalizations of the lower levels. The task analysis suggested by Gagné (1962, 1965) and used to organize the Science of Xenograde Systems produces a hierarchical task in this sense. A hierarchical presentation of a task results when Part I is presented to the learner first and each subsequent part then follows on up through the levels of complexity. In this research the presentation was hierarchical to all groups. Group V did not receive the actual lessons, but they were presented the summary which was organized into lessons in a manner parallel to the other groups.

A second distinction which is more crucial to this study than the first and which is implemented by the different treatments for each of the groups is between a presentation in which no attempt is made to have the student master each level before proceeding and a presentation in which an effort is made to ensure that the student understands the material in one level before being allowed to proceed to the next. It is this distinction which was under investigation in this experiment. The results seem to indicate that it is not necessary to master one level before proceeding to the next. In fact, when one tries to ensure mastery by a two-stage correction/review procedure, there actually results an increment in the amount of time a student spends in trying to answer a question. Group 5 represents the extreme case where there is only a minimum of understanding of the various levels before attempting performance at the highest level. On the first presentation of the terminal task the subjects in this group made more errors and took more time than the other groups, but with the correction/review procedure they apparently gained the understanding they missed and were able to perform as well as the other groups on the retention test.

References

Ausubel, D. P. *The psychology of meaningful verbal learning.* New York: Grune & Stratton, 1963.

Bloom, B. S. (ed.), Engelhart, M. D., Furst, E. J., Hill, W. H., and Krathwohl, D. R. *Taxonomy of educational objectives: Handbook I. Cognitive domain.* New York: David McKay, 1956.

Crowder, N. A. Automatic tutoring by intrinsic programming. In A. A. Lumsdaine and R. Glaser, eds., *Teaching machines and programmed learning.* Washington, D.C.: National Education Association, 1960. Pp. 286–98.

French, J. W., Ekstrom, Ruth B., and Price, L. A. *Manual for kit of reference tests for cognitive factors* (rev. ed.). Princeton, N.J.: Educational Testing Service, 1963.

Gagné, R. M. *The conditions of learning.* New York: Holt, 1965.

Gagné, R. M. The acquisition of knowledge. *Psychological Review,* 1962, **69,** 355–65.

Gagné, R. M., Mayor, J. R., Garstens, Helen L., and Paradise, N. E. Factors in acquiring knowledge of a mathematical task. *Psychological Monographs,* 1962, **76** (7, Whole No. 526).

Gagné, R. M. and Paradise, N. E. Abilities and learning sets in knowledge acquisition. *Psychological Monographs,* 1961, **75** (14, Whole No. 518).

Lindquist, E. F. *Design and analysis of experiments in psychology and education.* Boston: Houghton Mifflin, 1953.

Merrill, M. D. Transfer effects within a hierarchical learning task as a function of review and correction on successive parts. Technical Report No. 5, 1964, Training Research Laboratory, University of Illinois, Contract NONR 3985(04), Office of Naval Research.

Stolurow, L. M. and Davis, D. Teaching machines and computer-based systems. Technical Report No. 1, 1963, Training Research Laboratory, University of Illinois, Contract NONR 3985(04), Office of Naval Research.

36

The Role of Discriminability in Meaningful Verbal Learning and Retention

DAVID P. AUSUBEL / *City University of New York*

DONALD FITZGERALD / *University of Melbourne*

In a recent study (Ausubel, 1960), it was shown that introductory material at a high level of abstraction, generality, and inclusiveness (advance organizers) facilitates meaningful verbal learning and retention. By deliberately introducing relevant and appropriately inclusive subsuming concepts into cognitive structure, one provides helpful ideational scaffolding which enhances the incorporability and longevity of the more detailed material in the learning passage.

Advance organizers, however, ordinarily have two distinct functions that correspond in turn to two different aspects of the unfamiliarity of meaningful learning material. Sometimes, as in the above-mentioned experiment, the new material is almost completely unfamiliar in the sense that cognitive structure is barren of even generally related concepts. Under these circumstances the purpose of the organizer is simply to provide ideational anchorage or scaffolding. More typically, however,

the new learning material (e.g., Buddhist doctrines) is a variant of related, previously learned concepts (Christian doctrines) already established in cognitive structure. Here the role of the organizer is not only to provide optimal anchorage at an optimal level of inclusiveness, but also to increase the discriminability of the learning passage from analogous and often conflicting ideas in the learner's cognitive structure.

This second role of organizers is predicated on the assumption that if the distinguishing features of the new learning passage are not originally salient or readily discriminable from established ideas in cognitive structure, they can be adequately represented by the latter for memorial purposes, and hence would not persist as separately identifiable memories in their own right. It is as-

Reprinted with the permission of the senior author and the publisher from *Journal of Educational Psychology*, 1961, Vol. 52, 266–74.

sumed, in other words, that only discriminable categorical variants of previously learned concepts have long-term retention potentialities. Thus, if a *comparative* type of organizer could first delineate clearly, precisely, and explicitly the principal similarities and differences between the new learning passage (Buddhism) and existing, related concepts in cognitive structure (Christianity), it seems reasonable to suppose that the more detailed Buddhist ideas would be grasped later with fewer ambiguities, fewer competing meanings, and fewer misconceptions suggested by the learner's knowledge of Christianity; and that as these clearer, less confused Buddhist meanings interact with analogous Christianity meanings during the retention interval, they would be more likely to retain their identity. In this experiment, therefore, the value of a comparative organizer was tested by contrasting its effects on the retention of a Buddhism learning passage with both those of a nonideational (*historical*) introduction and those of a simple *expository* organizer.

It is hypothesized, first, that to the extent that the organizer is rendered discriminable from related concepts (Christianity) established in cognitive structure, and hence to the extent that it increases the discriminability of the Buddhism learning passage from these Christianity concepts, it facilitates the learning and retention of the new Buddhist ideas. In addition, it is hypothesized, for analogous reasons, that the discriminability (and hence the learning and retention) of the Buddhism passage varies as a function of the clarity and stability of the learner's existing knowledge of Christianity, and that subjects with relatively unclear and unstable concepts of Christianity derive relatively more benefit from the organizers than do subjects with clear and stable concepts in this area of knowledge.

These hypotheses were suggested by the findings of a previous experiment (Ausubel & Blake, 1958) in which the learning and retention of a comparative Buddhism passage were contrasted with that of an expository Buddhism passage. However, for the following reasons, the organizer approach was adopted in this experiment, in perference to manipulating the learning material itself: First, organizers provide advance ideational scaffolding. Second, they provide the learner with a generalized overview of *all* of the major similarities and differences between the two bodies of ideas *before* he encounters the new concepts individually in more detailed and particularized form. Finally, they create an advance set in the learner to perceive similarities and differences, and, by avoiding overly explicit specification, encourage him *actively* to make his own differentiations in terms of his own particular sources of confusion.

The hypotheses advanced in this study apply only to meaningful learning material which, although unfamiliar to subjects, is relatable to long-established and relatively stable concepts in cognitive structure. They do not apply to rote learning, to completely unfamiliar learning material, or to learning tasks that can only be related to unstable or recently learned concepts. The organizers, furthermore, must consist of ideational material (both similarities and differences) at a high level of abstraction, generality, and inclusiveness, rather than constitute a simple summary or a mere listing of specific comparative points.

Method

SUBJECTS

The experimental population consisted of predominantly senior undergraduate students (94 women and 61 men) in six sections of an educational psychology course at the University of Illinois. All subjects were enrolled in one of 10 teacher education curricula at the secondary school level. The experiment was conducted separately in each section as a required laboratory exercise, and was performed during regularly scheduled class hours. In order to maximize ego involvement, subjects were informed that after the data were processed their individual scores, as well as the class results, would be reported to them.

LEARNING PASSAGES, ORGANIZERS, AND MEASURING INSTRUMENTS

The learning material used in this study was a specially prepared 2,500-word passage dealing with Buddhist concepts of God, immortality, soul, faith, salvation, morality, and responsibility. These concepts were elaborated in considerable detail. The passage only presented the significant *ideas* of Buddhism and ignored material on the life of Buddha, the history and geographical distribution of Buddhism, schools of Buddhism, and Buddhist ritual. Flesch analysis of the passage yielded an abstractness score of 19.19 (highly abstract) and a readability score of 42.46 (difficult).

The topic of Buddhism was chosen both because it was explicitly unfamiliar to undergraduate students, and because it dealt with variants of previously learned concepts (i.e., Christian doctrines) generally familiar to all of our subjects and, presumably, reasonably well-established in the cognitive structure of most of them. Both criteria were important since the main purpose of the study was to ascertain whether advance organizers could facilitate the learning and retention of *unfamiliar* meaningful material by increasing the discriminability between the new material and *related* concepts already established in cognitive structure. The use of unfamiliar learning material also made it possible for all subjects to start from approximately the same base line in learning the passage. Empirical confirmation of the

unfamiliarity of the Buddhism material was obtained when a group of comparable subjects, who had not studied the learning passage, made scores which, on the average, were only slightly and not significantly better than chance.

Still another advantage of the Buddhism material inhered in the fact that its learnability was relatively uninfluenced in our population by such factors as sex, field of specialization, and variability in relevant incidental experience. It is true that women subjects made significantly higher scores than men subjects on both the Buddhism and Christianity tests. This superiority, however, was not a function of differential background, interest, or motivation related to sex per se, but reflected significantly superior academic aptitude as measured by verbal score on the School and College Ability Test (SCAT).

Knowledge of the Buddhism material was tested 3 and 10 days after learning, by equivalent forms of a 45-item multiple-choice test with corrected split-half reliabilities of .80 and .79, respectively. The correlation of the 3- and 10-day retention scores was .79. This latter figure indicated both relatively high stability over time, in view of the different (3- versus 10-day) retention abilities involved, as well as a high degree of relationship between the two retention abilities. Test questions covered principles, facts, and applications, and were selected by an item analysis procedure from a larger population of items. Scores on both tests showed a satisfactory range of variability and were distributed normally. Since they were intended as power tests, no time limit was imposed.

Three types of introductory passages were used in this experiment, each about 500 words in length. The *comparative* organizer pointed out explicitly the principal similarities and differences between Buddhist and Christian doctrines. This comparison was presented at a much higher level of abstraction, generality, and inclusiveness than the Buddhism passage itself, and was deliberately designed to increase discriminability between the two sets of concepts. The *expository* organizer, on the other hand, merely presented the principal Buddhist doctrines at a high level of abstraction, generality, and inclusiveness, without making any reference whatsoever to Christianity. It was not explicitly designed to increase discriminability between the two religions, but merely to provide some general ideational scaffolding for the detailed Buddhist material. The *historical* introduction was intended solely as a control treatment. It contained interesting historical and human interest material about Buddha and Buddhism, but neither provided any ideational scaffolding nor attempted to compare Buddhism and Christianity. No information was included in any of the introductory passages that could constitute a direct advantage in answering questions on the Buddhism test.

It was methodologically important to provide an historical introduction for the control group in order that any obtained differences in retention outcomes between experimental (comparative) and control (historical) groups could be attributed to the particular nature of the comparative organizer (i.e., to its enhancing effects on discriminability) rather than to its presence per se. The purpose of exposing another group of subjects to an expository introduction was to determine whether the comparative organizer could increase the discriminability of the learning passage over and above that which could be attributed to the influence of a simple organizer (i.e., to the mere provision of advance ideational scaffolding).

A 36-item multiple-choice test on Christianity was used to measure variability among our subjects with respect to the stability and clarity of those existing (Christianity) concepts within cognitive structure which were analogous to the Buddhism learning material, and hence potentially interfering. Test items were noncontroversial, dealing with Old and New Testaments, church history, and denominational beliefs and differences. The scores on this test were normally distributed and the corrected split-half reliability was .84.

Scores on the verbal portion of the SCAT were available for 65 subjects. This test had been previously administered as part of a battery of entrance examinations for incoming university freshmen.

PROCEDURE

On the first day of experimentation, all subjects took the Christianity test and then (after assignment to a treatment group) studied one of the three kinds of introductions for 8 minutes. Membership in a treatment group (comparative, expository, or historical) was determined by random assignment. The population of each of the three treatment groups was also stratified by sex so that the proportion of men to women subjects would be the same in each group. This was necessary because of the women's significantly higher verbal SCAT scores. It was possible to administer all three treatments simultaneously because they consisted of identical appearing introductory passages (with identical sets of directions), differing only in content.

To equalize the possible effects of prior extended exposure to the Buddhism material, those few subjects (5% of the total) who had taken a course in comparative religion were equally distributed in random fashion, among the three treatment groups. It had also been assumed that random assignment of subjects would render the different treatment groups equivalent with respect to such factors as learning ability and knowledge of Christianity. This assumption was confirmed empirically by the finding that differences between these groups on SCAT and Christianity test scores were negligible.

In order to control for the effects of different instructor, situational, and classroom climate variables in the six sections, students *within each* section were equally divided among the three treatment groups. Since analysis of the data showed that homogeneity of variance prevailed, both on an intersectional as well as an an intergroup basis, for both the Christianity test scores and the two sets of Buddhism test scores, it was considered justifiable to treat the scores of the three treatment groups on each of these instruments as comparable random samples from the same population.

Two days after studying their designated introductions all subjects read and studied the same Buddhism passage for 35 minutes. One form of the Buddhism test was administered to all subjects 3 days later, and an equivalent form of the same test was administered one week after the first test, or 10 days after the learning passage.

A special randomly assigned control group of subjects was constituted out of the six sections, along the same lines described above for the three treatment groups. The procedure followed with this special group was identical with that used for the comparative group except that subjects studied a 1,800-word passage on the endocrinology of human pubescence instead of the Buddhism passage. The purpose of this procedure was to ascertain to what extent mere knowledge of the comparative organizer (without any exposure to the Buddhism learning passage itself) could increase scores on the Buddhism tests beyond chance expectancy.

Results and Discussion

Comparison of corresponding 3- and 10-day means of total treatment groups shows that retention loss during this interval was relatively slight. The loss was greatest in the historical group ($p = .05$), least in the expository group, and intermediate in the comparative group ($p < .10$). This low degree of retention loss is probably attributable both to the negatively accelerated shape of most retention curves, particularly in the case of meaningful material, and to the "rehearsal effect" of the 3-day Buddhism test on the subsequent test of retention. The retention scores of our subjects over the two intervals were highly correlated ($r = .79$).

EFFECT OF ORGANIZERS ON RETENTION

On a 3-day basis, only the comparative organizer was effective in facilitating retention of the Buddhism material. Table 1 shows that the mean retention score of the total comparative group was significantly superior to both that of the historical group ($p = .05$) and that of the expository group ($p = .05$). However, practically all of this obtained difference between the comparative group, on the one hand, and the expository and historical groups, on the other, was derived from the below-median subgroups on the Christianity test. Within these below-median subgroups the differences between the means in question were much greater than the corresponding differences between total treatment groups, and their level of significance was also correspondingly higher ($p = .02$, $p = .005$).

It is apparent, therefore, that although provision of ideational scaffolding in the form of an expository organizer did not enhance retention of the Buddhism passage over a 3-day interval, the combined scaffolding and explicit discriminability effects induced by the comparative organizer did significantly improve retention. The short-term retention loss in the control group was evidently small enough to preclude the possibility of a significant difference in retention attributable to the facilitating effects of a simple expository organizer. It is true that an expository type of organizer significantly increased 3-day retention in an earlier experiment (Ausubel, 1960); but the learning passage used then was more unfamiliar to subjects, and the latter also had the benefit of studying the organizer on two separate occasions.

As hypothesized, subjects with relatively superior knowledge of Christianity derived considerably less benefit from the comparative organizer than did subjects whose knowledge of Christianity was less impressive. This finding was consistent with the self-evident proposition that if discriminability of a learning passage is already high because of endogenous factors within cognitive structure (i.e., because of the clarity and stability of related established knowledge), less scope exists for the potentially facilitating influence of exogenously manipulated factors (i.e., organizers) designed to promote discriminability.

On a 10-day basis, both the comparative and expository total groups were significantly superior to the historical total group in retaining the Buddhism material ($p = .02$, $p = .05$), but the difference between the comparative and expository groups was negligible (see Table 1). As was true of the 3-day scores, however, most of the difference between organizer and control groups was derived from the below-median subgroups on the Christianity test. When the means of just these below-median subgroups were compared, the significance level of the comparative-historical and the expository-historical differences was enchanced ($p = .0025$, $p < .05$), and the difference between the comparative and expository groups was significant at the .10 level.

In comparing the 10- to the 3-day retention data, it appears first, that only over the longer time interval was the natural retention loss sufficiently great to provide scope for the limited facilitating influence of the scaffolding effects available from the expository organizer. Second, although the comparative organizer was not significantly more effective than the expository organizer over the longer interval when the results of all subjects in these groups were considered, there was a suggestive trend in

this direction among the below-median subjects.

One explanation of the relatively small difference in 10-day retention, attributable to the influence of explicit comparison per se, is the possibility that confronting the learner in advance with the major principles of Buddhism in a detail-free context (the expository organizer) *implicitly* increased the discriminability of his Buddhism ideas by enabling him to make his own comparisons with Christianity. Another plausible explanation is that by enhancing retention generally, the rehearsal effect induced by the 3-day Buddhism test had a leveling influence on the relative degree of facilitation that might have been expected from the two kinds of organizers. This interpretation is supported by the erosion of the significant retention difference between the comparative and expository groups from the third to the tenth day.

Table 1

MEAN RETENTION TEST SCORES OF EXPERIMENTAL AND CONTROL GROUPS ON BUDDHISM PASSAGE

	Treatment group		
Knowledge of Christianity	Comparative organizer	Expository organizer	Control (historical)
3-day retention:			
Above-median	23.50	22.50	23.42
Below-median	20.50	17.32	16.52
Total	21.83	19.91	19.97
10-day retention:			
Above-median	21.79	22.27	20.87
Below-median	19.21	17.02	14.40
Total	20.31	19.65	17.63

Note: Chance score on the multiple-choice test of 45 items is 9.0.

The tendency noted above in the 3-day results—for only the below- as opposed to the above-median subgroups on the Christianity test to derive appreciable benefit from the organizers—also appeared in the 10-day data. Thus, in the learning and retention of unfamiliar ideational material that is relatable to established concepts in the learner's cognitive structure, both comparative and expository organizers appear to be effective only in those instances where existing (endogenously determined) discriminability between the two sets of ideas is inadequate as a consequence of the instability or ambiguity of the established concepts.

The special control group which only studied the comparative organizer (without any exposure to the Buddhism passage itself) made a mean score of 13.20 on the 3-day Buddhism test and a mean score of 13.45 on the 10-day test. These scores were significantly greater than the scores of a comparable naive group (which took the Buddhism tests without being exposed to either organizer or learning passage), but were substantially below those of the historical and two organizer groups.

It is quite unlikely, however, that the organizers per se directly furnished pertinent information enabling subjects to obtain higher scores on the Buddhism tests. In the first place, a deliberate effort was made to avoid providing such information in the two organizers. Second, if the organizers themselves had furnished useful information in answering test items, it would be difficult to explain why subjects in the expository group did not make higher scores than subjects in the historical group on the 3-day Buddhism test. Much more credible, therefore, is the explanation that exposure to the comparative organizer merely increased the general sophistication of subjects in the special control group about Buddhist concepts, and thereby helped them to eliminate mis-

leads in the multiple-choice test questions. Thus, they were able to obtain better than chance scores without studying the learning passage itself. But when the learning passage was available (i.e., in the historical and two organizer groups), subjects were neither benefited by the general sophistication they obtained from an ideational organizer, nor handicapped by not possessing such sophistication.

EFFECT OF KNOWLEDGE OF CHRISTIANITY ON RETENTION

The data clearly support the hypothesis that the discriminability of the Buddhism learning material varies as a function of the clarity and stability of the established concepts to which it is related (i.e., Christianity), and hence that Buddhism retention scores are positively correlated with knowledge of Christianity. Table 1 shows that within each treatment group the mean retention score of the above-median group was significantly greater than the mean retention score of the below-median group. For the historical, expository, and comparative groups, these differences were significant at the .0005, .001, and .02 levels, respectively, on the 3-day Buddhism test, and at the .0005, .0005, and .10 levels, respectively, on the 10-day Buddhism test. The same trends are shown by the positive correlations between scores on the Buddhism and Christianity tests (see Table 2).

It is evident, therefore, that the clearer and more stable the subject's knowledge of Christianity was, the more discriminable this knowledge was from Buddhism concepts, and hence the higher the Buddhism retention scores were. And conversely, the less clear and more unstable the subjects' knowledge of Christianity was, the less discriminable it was from Buddhism concepts,

Table 2

CORRELATIONS OF BUDDHISM RETENTION SCORES AND OTHER MEASURES

| | Buddhism retention scores | | | | | |
| | Comparative group | | Expository group | | Historical group | |
Other measures	3-day	10-day	3-day	10-day	3-day	10-day
Christianity scores	.37*	.21	.57**	.42**	.55**	.56**
Verbal ability scores	.62**	.60**	.75**	.79**	.58**	.52*
Christianity scores with verbal ability eliminated	.06	−.07	.40**	.14	.40**	.43**

* Significant at .05 level.
** Significant at .01 level.

and the lower the Buddhism retention scores were.

The data also confirm the hypothesis that organizers (by virtue of their leveling effect on the endogenous discriminability advantage inherent in a clear and stable knowledge of Christianity) reduce the relationship between Christianity knowledge and Buddhism retention scores in proportion to their facilitating effect on retention. The leveling effect of the organizers (particularly the comparative) can be seen in Table 1 by comparing the relative magnitude of the differences between above-median and below-median subgroups in the various treatment groups. For historical, expository, and comparative groups the respective *t* values of these differences were 4.86, 3.43, and 2.24 for the 3-day Buddhism scores, and 4.72, 3.99, and 1.59 for the 10-day Buddhism scores. Correlations between the Buddhism and Christianity scores show the same trend (see Table 2). The correlation between the Christianity and Buddhism scores was higher in the historical than in the comparative group for both the 3-day ($p = .12$) and 10-day ($p = .04$) retention intervals. The almost identical correlations, on the other hand, between Christianity and 3-day Buddhism scores in the expository and historical groups,

reflected the ineffectiveness of the expository organizer in facilitating retention over the 3-day interval.

Because of the positive correlation of .44 ($p < .01$) between Christianity and SCAT scores, however, it was necessary to check the alternative hypothesis that the significantly higher retention scores of subjects in the above-median groups reflect superior verbal ability rather than superior knowledge of Christianity per se (endogenous discriminability). But since the availability of only 65 SCAT scores made it impossible to match for verbal ability those subjects within each treatment group who were above and below the median score on the Christianity test, it was necessary to resort to partial correlation.

The partial correlations between the Buddhism and Christianity scores, with the effect of verbal ability eliminated, are shown for all three groups in Table 2. For the historical group the partial correlations of .40 and .43 (for the 3- and 10-day scores, respectively), although lower than the corresponding simple correlations of .55 and .56 were still significant at the .01 level. Three of the four other partial correlations, however, were negligible and nonsignificant, indicating that the corresponding simple correlations largely reflected the positive relationship between verbal ability and Buddhism retention scores. The intrinsic residual relationship between knowledge of Christianity and retention of the Buddhism material, after the effect of verbal ability was eliminated, was actually close to zero in these instances, because of the leveling influence of the organizers on the endogenous discriminability advantage conferred by superior knowledge of Christianity. The partial correlation between the Christianity and 3-day Buddhism scores remained significant at the .01 level in the expository group, in as much as the expository organizer did not facilitate retention over the 3-day interval.

Intergroup comparison of the partial correlations in Table 2 shows even more clearly than does corresponding comparison of the simple correlations between Buddhism and Christianity scores, that the organizers (in proportion to their facilitating effect on retention) reduced the significant relationship between knowledge of Christianity and retention of the Buddhism material. With the influence of verbal ability eliminated, the partial correlation between Christianity and 3-day Buddhism scores in both the historical and expository groups was significantly higher than in the comparative group ($p = .05$, $p = .05$). The partial correlation between Christianity and 10-day Buddhism scores in the historical group was higher than the corresponding partial correlations in the expository ($p = .08$) and comparative ($p = .01$) groups. In effect then, by being provided with a given type of discriminability aid (organizer), subjects possessing relatively little knowledge of Christianity (and hence little endogenous discriminability) were placed on approximately the same footing with respect to the discriminability variable and its effect on retention, as subjects possessing greater

knowledge of Christianity (and greater endogenous discriminability).

Table 2 also shows that the correlation between verbal ability and Buddhism retention scores in the historical group (where the relationship was not influenced by interaction with organizer effects) was approximately the same as that between Christianity and Buddhism scores. But unlike the latter relationship, which was attenuated by interaction with the organizers, the correlation between verbal ability and Buddhism scores was slightly higher in the comparative than in the historical group, and suggestively but not significantly higher in the expository than in the historical group ($p = .17$, $p = .07$). At the very least, therefore, it is definite that neither organizer detracted from the strong positive relationship between verbal ability and the retention of the Buddhism material; and there was a suggestive tendency for verbal ability to have an even greater impact on the retention of the Buddhism passage when subjects were given the benefit of an expository organizer.

Summary and Conclusions

This experiment was concerned with the role of endogenous and externally manipulated discriminability in the learning and retention of unfamiliar ideational material (Buddhism) that was relatable to previously learned concepts (Christianity) already established in cognitive structure.

The learning task consisted of a 2,500-word passage on the principles of Buddhism. Two days before studying this learning passage, one experimental group studied a 500-word *comparative* organizer explicitly comparing the major ideas of Buddhism and Christianity. Another experimental group studied an *expository* organizer which made no reference to Christianity. A control group studied an *historical* introduction dealing with the history rather than with the ideas of Buddhism. Retention of the Buddhism material was tested 3 and 10 days after the learning session by means of equivalent forms of a multiple-choice test. For purposes of analysis, subjects in the various treatment groups (university undergraduates) were divided into above- and below-median subgroups in terms of their scores on an objective test of Christianity.

Subjects with greater knowledge of Christianity made significantly higher scores on the Buddhism retention test than did subjects with less knowledge of Christianity. This significantly positive relationship between Christianity and Buddhism test scores held up even when the effect of verbal ability was eliminated. Hence the data support the hypothesis that the learning and retention of unfamiliar verbal material varies positively with its discriminability from

related, previously learned concepts established in cognitive structure, and that this endogenously determined discriminability is a function of the clarity and stability of the latter concepts.

On a 3-day basis only the comparative organizer was significantly effective in facilitating the retention of the Buddhism material, but over a 10-day interval both comparative and expository organizers were significantly effective. These facilitating effects of the organizers on retention outcomes, however, only applied to subjects in the below-median subgroups on the Christianity test. Thus in the learning and retention of unfamiliar ideational material that is relatable to established concepts in the learner's cognitive structure, both comparative and expository organizers appear to be effective only in those instances where existing discriminability between the two sets of ideas is inadequate as a consequence of the instability or ambiguity of established concepts.

References

Ausubel, D. P. The use of advance organizers in the learning and retention of meaningful verbal material. *J. Educ. Psychol.*, 1960, **51**, 267–72.

Ausubel, D. P. and Blake, E., Jr. Proactive inhibition in the forgetting of meaningful school material. *J. Educ. Res.*, 1958, **52**, 145–49.

37

Interference in Meaningful Learning

DORIS R. ENTWISLE / *Johns Hopkins University*

W. H. HUGGINS / *Johns Hopkins University*

The theory of transfer of training has been developed mainly from studies using nonsense materials or psychomotor tasks. As is well known, predictions involving meaningful verbal materials are hazardous, and sometimes there is little a priori reason to expect interference rather than facilitation or vice versa. Ausubel (1963) has recently re-emphasized the inappropriateness of extrapolating principles derived from nonsense materials to learning tasks involving meaningful materials.

It appeared to us that theory of electric circuits, as usually taught to *beginning* students in engineering, might be an almost classic example of a classroom learning situation that could produce negative transfer. Because of the difficulty in prediction already mentioned, however, the specific kind of transfer occurring was studied in two experiments, as reported below. Negative transfer was thought likely because circuit theory involves many dual sets of closely related principles. For instance, a circuit may be solved with voltages taken as unknowns *or* with currents taken as unknowns. The rules and procedures in the one method of solution are very similar, but not identical, to the rules and procedures for the other method of solution. An instructor (or text) often treats circuit theory as a set of subunits, each of which has this duality.

Circuit theory is usually presented topic by topic, with the duality in one topic stressed before proceeding to the next topic. Under these conditions, one might anticipate both retroactive and proactive inhibition, because each topic includes two sets of material that are similar and therefore easy to confuse.

Two experiments were carried out

Reprinted with the permission of the senior author and the publisher from *Journal of Educational Psychology*, 1964, Vol. 55, 75–78.

with sophomore students enrolled in the course Introductory Systems and Design at the Johns Hopkins University. Students were assigned by a random procedure to the experimental or control groups independently for each experiment.

Experiment I

METHOD

Subjects. Students in lecture were exposed to definitions of ideal sources, to the three fundamental circuit relations, and to the definitions of elements. Then Experiment I was undertaken. Eighty students were divided into four strata according to mathematical aptitude scores procured from college records. Half of each stratum was randomly assigned to the experimental and control group.

Procedure. The experimental group spent 15 minutes studying voltage principles, and spent the next 15 minutes studying the corresponding current principles.[1] The control group spent 15 minutes studying the same voltage principles being studied by the experimental group, but spent the next 15 minutes studying irrelevant material on computer programing. Then both groups were immediately given a short test on the voltage principles they had studied.

RESULTS

The errors made by the students on the test were subjected to an analysis of variance. The control group made significantly fewer errors ($p < .02$) on the test than the experimental group, with $F = 4.69$ ($df = 1/66$); the respective means were 2.65 errors for the experimental group and 1.62 errors for the control group.

Students who studied voltage prin-

---

[1] Copies of the experimental materials are available from the authors upon request.

ciples and then immediately studied the corresponding current principles retained *less* of what they learned concerning voltage principles than students who spent an equal amount of time studying computer programing.

Experiment II

METHOD

After Experiment I three lectures intervened before Experiment II. In these lectures the topic of branches in a circuit and the corresponding $2b$ equations were presented. At this point the next lecture would have introduced the node-pair and loop methods. The principles of node-pair and loop solutions provided the material for Experiment II.

Subjects. Fifty-four students were ranked in order of mathematical aptitude and successive pairs within this ranking were randomly assigned to the control and experimental groups.

Procedure. It was hypothesized that the experimental group who read material on node-pair solutions and then immediately read the corresponding principles relating to loop solutions would retain less of the node-pair material than the control group. The control group read identical material on node-pair solutions, but afterward read material on matrix theory (irrelevant material). This part of Experiment II exactly replicates Experiment I. Experiment II is more elaborate, however, because proactive inhibition is also investigated.

The posttest used in Experiment II included two subsets of six items each, one set on node-pair and the other set on loop solutions. The two subsets were *exactly* alike in sentence construction and tested dual concepts. For example, two parallel fill-in questions were:

1. The fundamental principle used in writing loop equations is _____.
   Answer: $\Sigma v_k = 0$
2. The fundamental principle used in writing node equations is _____.
   Answer: $\Sigma i_k = 2$

The two subsets of questions were thus exactly equivalent. Also, in the same sense, the readings on node-pair and loop solutions were parallel. For this reason, performance on the two subsets of six items should be the same, unless other factors are at work. The two subsets of six questions were imbedded within a larger set of questions so that the correspondence between them would not be obvious. Each member of a pair was on a separate page, and unrelated questions intervened. Also students were instructed not to return to earlier questions once they had been answered.

Fifteen minutes were spent studying each unit of material, and the test consumed the remainder of a class period.

RESULTS

Errors made by the students on the posttest were subjected to an analysis of variance so that an error-variance estimate could be obtained for testing mean differences in errors made between subtests. The control group made fewer errors on node questions than the experimental group (76 versus 93, respectively), and this difference is statistically significant beyond the .05 level ($t_{52} = 1.83$). Studying loop principles after studying node-pair principles interferes with retention of node-pair principles (retroactive inhibition), and the result of Experiment I is replicated.

The analysis shows, in addition, that learning node principles interfered with subsequent learning of loop principles. The experimental group made more errors on loop principles than the control group made on node principles (101 versus 76; $t_{52} = 2.70$). Since the node and loop materials that were studied and the node and loop subtests were exactly parallel, studying one set of principles for 15 minutes should lead to the same outcome as studying the other set for 15 minutes. But the fact that the experimental group has just previously studied node principles prevents them from

learning as much about loop principles as they should be expected to learn. The control group, with prior time spent in irrelevant activities, made significantly fewer errors after spending the same amount of time studying an equivalent body of material and completing an equivalent test.

The implications of the experiment can best be appreciated by inspection of Table 1 showing the mean number of errors made by both groups on the two equivalent subtests. The standard deviation associated with all these means happens to be .345 and was estimated from a variance analysis appropriate to the split-plot design used in the experiment.[2]

As a matter of fact, it appears that proactive interference was about equal to retroactive interference in this experiment. Thus the interference is double barreled: learning node material first interferes with later assimilation of loop material, and later learning of loop material retroactively interferes with the previously learned node material. The overall decrement is therefore the sum of the decrements for each topic considered separately.

Table 1

MEAN NUMBER OF ERRORS IN TEST IN EXPERIMENT II

Group	Node subtest	Loop subtest	Total test
Experimental[a]	3.44	3.74	7.18
Control[b]	2.81	4.41	7.22

[a] Studied each set of material 15 minutes.
[b] Studied node material only for 15 minutes.

One result in Table 1 deserves emphasis. It will be seen that there is no

---

[2] Complete analysis of variance tables, and associated *t* tests for both experiments appear in Entwisle and Huggins (1963).

difference in total errors made by the experimental and control groups. Since these errors stem from test items relating both to node and loop principles and the control group did not see the material on loops, it appears that 15 minutes spent reading node material leads to about the same increment in learning as 30 minutes spent reading the two interfering sets of material. Thus whatever is learned from reading neutral material represents an additional increment for the control group.

Discussion

These results should be considered in the light of several factors. First, the same general results from two independent experiments leave little doubt that negative transfer can occur in the learning of circuit theory. Second, these experiments were done under the extremely constrained circumstances that go hand in hand with using actual course material and regularly enrolled students. The time limitations are very serious, for it is likely that a certain minimal amount of learning must occur before interference would set in. Third, by the time of the second experiment students had already had considerable exposure to circuit theory. If, as has been shown, the material generates interference, the basal level of interference in all students might be rather high. In this event it would be correspondingly difficult to "add" to the basal interference level enough further interference within the period of a few minutes so that a difference between control and experimental groups could be procured. Also, of

course, some students had considerable knowledge of circuit theory before the course started, and they contribute "noise" to a experiment of this kind.

Consideration of these factors suggests that the interference must be pronounced to appear under such generally adverse conditions. That retroactive inhibition was observed for both node and loop materials and that both retroactive and proactive inhibition were observed confirms one's intuition that these two sets of principles are equally suspect in causing negative transfer. Since the duality inherent in circuit theory is not confined to the particular topics used in these experiments but rather is characteristic of the entire body of theory, we conclude with some confidence that interference of the type demonstrated may be a continual source of difficulty to beginning students.

The experiments reported here should be considered in relation to the enormous effort that is being expended to program course materials. The empirical testing of programed materials on circuit theory would be very unlikely to reveal the problem of interference or to provide a solution for it. That is, the overall organization of programed materials is decreed at the outset, and often follows the conceptual organization of usual texts. Once the basic plan is established, modifications are made within the existing framework. Also, of course, these results add to the rather small amount of experimental knowledge relating to transfer of training for meaningful materials. They indicate that it may be profitable to devote more research attention in this area as Ausubel's (1963) recent book suggests.

References

Ausubel, D. P. *The psychology of meaningful verbal learning.* New York: Grune & Stratton, 1963.

Entwisle, D. R. and Huggins, W. H. Interference in the learning of circuit theory. *Proc. IEEE,* 1963, **51,** 986–90.

38

Supra-Paragraph Prose Structure: Its Specification, Perception, and Effects on Learning

WAYNE LEE / *Bell Telephone Laboratories*

It was the purpose of this report to present some beginning thoughts and experimental results pertaining to an understanding of molar prose structure and the effects such structure has in learning. In particular, the following assertions were experimentally investigated: (1) It is possible to construct different prose passages with essentially the same content, but which differ in level of structure. (2) Subjects can perceive structural differences among such passages. (3) Structural differences affect not only "how much" is learned, but what is learned. (4) Learning at different structural levels will be affected by interactions with mode (auditory or read) and method (part or whole) of presentation.

These assertions were, generally speaking, borne out by the data. In addition, effects of intelligence and the rated interest of different passages were investigated.

"Structure," in the sense intended in this report, does not refer to the way a sentence is constructed; i.e., the report is not concerned with structure as the linguist views it. Structure refers to the way paragraphs are put together to form a passage. It seems reasonable that the way a passage is structured, in the molar sense that will be used henceforth, would affect learning and communication. A passage judged to be poorly organized, or structured, would probably also be judged to be confusing, rambling, not to the point, etc. In addition to these common sense observations, there has been much discussion in the literature of human learning of related ideas. McGeoch and Irion (1952) discuss the importance of such concepts as the unity and meaningfulness of the

Reprinted with the permission of the author and the publisher from *Psychological Reports*, 1965, Vol. 17, 135–44.

material to be learned. Connected prose is presumed to be somewhere on a scale of meaningfulness above syllables and digits, but the relation between prose and poetry on this dimension is unclear. "Meaningful" is used in ways which make it seem to be the same dimension as molar prose structure, except that it extends to smaller units than the paragraph. Although "meaningful" is used in this way, the operational specification is nowhere explained.

Stephen's *Educational Psychology* (1956) pays perhaps as much attention to the question of structure as any text in this area and readily accepts the importance of structure for learning and the importance of making sure the student sees the relationships among parts of the material he is learning. Stephens, however, has found very little evidence to present, and that which is presented is from traditional verbal learning experiments rather than from experiments on prose learning with experimentally varied structure.

Verbal learning theorists have lately demonstrated renewed interest in verbal materials having aspects of prose, e.g., meaning and various kinds of structure in the stimulus material (Deese & Kaufman, 1957; Epstein, 1962; Miller & Selfridge, 1950; Whitman & Garner, 1962). There has also been increasing interest in the structure of the responses (Bousfield, 1953; Tulving, 1962) as an indication of the way information is stored and withdrawn. It is worth considering whether effects found by these authors are related to any effects occurring with prose passages.

UNIT OF ANALYSIS FOR MOLAR STRUCTURE

The unit of analysis to be manipulated in the present study is the paragraph. The manipulations do not alter any paragraph itself, but only the relations of the paragraphs to other paragraphs. It is apparent that "paragraph" is not the neatest sort of unit that one might use. There is no agreement on what a paragraph is, and where one should begin and end. An experimental study of paragraphs would shed some light on how reliable an entity the paragraph is. For the purposes of this study, a "paragraph" is simply a group of sentences which stay together as a unit in the manipulations of the passages. It is the author's belief that, by and large, the same experimental results would obtain, regardless of who did the paragraphing. The important thing is that each sentence has appropriate context; i.e., each sentence has preceding and/or succeeding sentences which are appropriate and which remain the same throughout all experimental manipulations.

SPECIFICATION OF SUPRA-PARAGRAPH PROSE STRUCTURE

Three major aspects seem to enter into the molar specification of prose structure: (a) unity, (b) sequence or order, and (c) hierarchy. Unity means that paragraphs which deal with the same thing should be placed together in the passage. Sequence means that the units (paragraphs) may have a logical or natural ordering relation to one another and that a well-organized passage would have the units in the appropriate sequence. Hierarchy refers to the fact that some ideas are at a higher, more encompassing level than others. This hierarchy is seen whenever a passage is outlined. Ideas in an outline, at Roman I, say, are at a higher level, or encompass the ideas under Roman IA, IB, etc., and these in turn are at a higher, or more encompassing, level than the 1's and 2's under them. Hierarchical organization is, of course, a most important concept nowadays in many fields, including structural linguistics, organization theory, and heuristic problem-solving programming. Some authors have noted that behavior in general seems to be organized in such a manner, and have spoken of the "hierarchical organization of behavior" (Miller, Galanter, & Pribram, 1960, p. 15).

A distinction will be made between *implicit* and *explicit hierarchical structure* in a prose passage. *Implicit hierarchy* refers to the abstract outline-type structure of a passage when this is not made apparent to S. Presenting S an outline of the passage, at least down to the paragraph level, would make the structure *explicit*. Another method was used in this investigation to make the structure explicit, which will be explained below. A passage may have a hierarchical structure, but its psychological effects may depend on this structure's being made explicit.

These three aspects of organization have all been previously noted; the point here is to focus on them together as a starting point in the analysis of molar prose structure. The three aspects are not necessarily independent of one another for all passages, but it seems possible to study their effects separately in many cases. One can consider, for example, an abstract hierarchical structure, which, interpreted, could be a good or a poor outline of a passage. It would be a poor outline if paragraphs grouped together do not belong together; yet, in a sense, there is the same hierarchical structure in both cases. Also, it is possible to have paragraphs collected together properly under a heading, satisfying unity to a degree, even though the paragraphs are not properly ordered with respect to one another. A narrative which has its paragraphs in the proper sequence would necessarily have paragraphs which belong together in some

sense. On the other hand, it is possible to imagine a sequence of units in the correct order, which has no implicit hierarchy or necessarily any unity between succeeding units other than that implied by the order. The alphabet is such a sequence.

The preceding discussion by no means leads to an unambiguous specification of amount of molar structure for a prose passage; it is only meant to be suggestive. The next section will show, however, that these ideas can be used to generate passages which can be assigned ordinal relations of amounts of structure. The experimental results showed that the specification has some validity.

Method

CONSTRUCTION OF MATERIALS

Two passages were each arranged so as to have three levels of structure. The two passages dealt with the same topic, except that one was longer and was used in a second experiment. Each passage concerned disciplinary problems in the Navy and was in the form of a lecture to Naval officer candidates. The material was chosen with the following characteristics in mind: it was expected that it would be of interest to the male students who would receive it; the general subject matter would not be something they would typically have encountered in any direct way; there were no unfamiliar terms or concepts in the passage, so that each paragraph could be meaningfully interpreted by S. Any conclusions from the data should be made with this last point in mind. Material in which concepts are introduced early which are vital for understanding material coming later could be expected to give different results.

The middle level of structure was

prepared by taking the passage in normal order. In general, the middle level of structure, S2, is conceived to be prose material structured much as it would be in an expository passage in a magazine or book, for those materials in which there are no summary-type paragraphs. The low level of structure, S3, was derived from this by randomly ordering the paragraphs and by removing, in some cases, a few transitional words, such as "second" and "therefore," which related the paragraph to the preceding one. Thus, S3 contained substantially the same material as S2, sentence by sentence, except that the paragraphs were in different orders—in one case natural, and in the other case, random. The two passages, the longer and the shorter, were independently randomized.

The high level of structure, S1, was obtained from S2 by adding certain materials designed to make the hierarchy of the passage explicit. This material consisted of (a) an initial paragraph pointing out the main aspects to the passage (there were two main parts for the shorter passage, and three for the longer); (b) a final paragraph of summary and conclusions; (c) main headings in capital letters preceding the main two or three parts of the passage and the final summary, and second order underlined headings preceding the subparts of a main section; and (d) transitional paragraphs, briefly mentioning what was just covered in a section and what material was coming next, to emphasize the structural "joints" of the passage, and to give emphasis to the hierarchy. S1 contained the same paragraphs as S2 and S3 exactly, but, as stated, contained additional material also emphasizing the hierarchy.

The passage for Exp. I contained 16 paragraphs and about 1630 words for S2 and S3. The additional material added for S1 amounted to about 380

words. The passage for Exp. II contained about 2120 words for S2 and S3, and about 510 words more for S1.

The two main aspects of the shorter passage were (a) eliminating potential troublemakers by pre-selection and (b) prevention of misconduct by various means once men had entered the service. The main headings preceding these sections in S1 were PRE-SELECTION and PREVENTION OF MISCONDUCT. The second-order headings under the first section were *Principles of Psychological Testing, Background of Offenders,* and *Paper-and-pencil Testing;* under the second section there were *Special Instructions, Warnings,* and *Helping the Recruit Solve His Problem.* In addition to the above, the longer passage for Exp. II contained a third main section, labeled ONCE TROUBLE OCCURS, and subheadings *Military Law, Good of the Ship and the Navy,* and *Character of the Offender.*

TESTS OF LEARNING

There are several kinds of things *S* might learn from a prose passage. It was hypothesized that the effect of structure level and the interactions with other factors would differ depending on what sort of learning was measured. This assumption proved to be justified.

The first test, T1, was designed to see how well *S* could utilize material from a number of paragraphs and abstract the main ideas presented in the passage. The emphasis in scoring was largely on the number of main points correctly mentioned and very little on detailed elaboration of any one idea. Two such questions were prepared for Exp. I. They were short essay type questions, and *S*s had 4 min. on each. The first question was, "Discuss briefly the possibility of eliminating troublemakers from the Navy by prior selection. What were the main aspects of this problem, as given in the passage? What conclusions were reached, and why?"

The second type of test, T2, was designed to see how much detail could be recalled about material presented in a single paragraph. An example is, "How does the typical AWOLee view the short-range effects of his delinquency and the long-range effects?" In this test, scoring was based on how much detail was recalled about a single point, in contrast to T1, where the number of main points mentioned, each abstracted from many paragraphs, was the criterion. Two minutes were allowed for the short essay answer required. There were six questions in Exp. I and seven in Exp. II.

The third test, T3, was designed to discover how much rote learning had occurred. The idea was to see whether Ss knew word-for-word material from the passage, in contrast to the ideas those words conveyed. This test consisted of two-choice multiple-choice questions. One choice was a sentence taken directly from the passage. The other was a paraphrase of the sentence, giving the same idea in different words. Ss' task was to choose the sentence taken word-for-word from the passage. There were 20 such questions in Exp. I and 26 in Exp. II.

Ss AND EXPERIMENTAL DESIGN

Ss for both experiments were male undergraduate students at Johns Hopkins University, who participated as part of an introductory psychology course requirement.

Exp. I employed a three-factor randomized design. The three factors were structure of the material (three levels), mode of presentation (read or auditory, two levels), and part or whole method of presentation (two levels). The passage was presented twice, and the part-whole factor refers to whether the entire passage was presented completely and then re-presented (whole method), or whether the repetition was given after each paragraph was presented. There were 7 Ss in each of the 12 cells of the design, or 84 Ss altogether. Ss in one cell generally did the experiment as a group. There were not always 7 Ss available in the group, however, so many cells contained Ss from different experimental sessions.

Exp. II was a two-factor randomized design. The two factors were prose structure (three levels) and verbal aptitude score of the College Board SCAT exam (five levels). Exp. II was performed after Exp. I, using a longer passage. With the longer passage, the mode and part-whole factors were no longer feasible within the allotted 1-hr. experimental period. There were 3 Ss in a cell, or 45 altogether. Ss were run in small groups, 3 to 6 in a group. In this case, Ss in a group were from various cells of the design. Ss read the passage once.

INSTRUCTIONS

The instructions began by stating that "This experiment concerns the way in which the construction of a prose passage affects learning." The instructions for Exp. I briefly exhorted Ss to pay close attention to the passage and then explained the method of reading or listening that defined the part or whole method of presentation. The instructions for Exp. II differed from those of Exp. I in that a paragraph was devoted to explaining the kinds of tests that Ss would receive after reading the materials; a special point was made that the thoroughness of the exam would require them to read the passage most carefully. Ss in both experiments were instructed not to go back over the material, except in the manner indicated under the part or whole instructions.

After the presentation, and before the test, a rating of passage interest was requested in Exp. I, and in addition, a rating of how well the passage was structured, or organized, was requested in Exp. II. The ratings were on 9-point scales, and Ss were instructed that the midpoint should represent the typical reading assignment they received in college. Then, before each test was presented, its nature was described briefly, and the time limit for each question was pointed out. Periodically, E would state how much time was left for a question.

Results and Discussion

RATINGS

The only experimental manipulation which affected the interest ratings was the mode of presentation. The auditory mode was judged to be less interesting than the reading mode ($F = 8.2$; $df = 1/72$; $p < .01$); the average ratings were 3.6 and 4.4 out of a possible 9.0, respectively. This difference may be due in part to the rather hurried reading E gave because of time limitations. In any case, this effect will not be of vital concern here. It will not complicate interpretations of the results found on learning, since there was no corresponding main effect of mode for any test of learning. The curious thing is that the ways of structuring the passage and the part-whole method of presentation had no effects on interest, although, as will be shown, they did affect learning.

A structure rating was available only for Exp. II. There was a significant main effect of passage structure on rated structure ($F = 12.3$; $df = 2/30$; $p < .01$). This effect was due to the high rating given S1. It had an average rat-

ing of 7.7 out of a possible 9.0, whereas 5.0 was supposed to be the average rating for typical assigned readings. The ratings of the other two structures averaged 4.9 and 4.4 for S2 and S3, respectively, which did not differ significantly. It appears, then, that S1 was designed in a way that agreed very well with Ss' ideas on what a well-organized passage is like: it has a hierarchy which is carefully made explicit.

It also seems that there is little difference between the perceived organization in the typical assignment in college (which was to be valued 5 on the rating scale) and a passage with randomized paragraphs. This outcome is one that at first is likely to be greeted with considerable astonishment. The reaction probably has merit; the question is, when will and will not paragraph randomization affect perceived structure? The author postulates that the effect of randomization of paragraphs on perceived structure would depend on the extent to which the perceived proper unities and sequences are altered. It may be that in the present passage, no violation of these principles is perceived in S3. All the paragraphs dealt with disciplinary problems in the Navy, and Ss, without explicit help, cannot perceive the way the paragraphs relate. The learning data support this train of thought. Passages in which randomization upsets these principles in a more obvious way can be contrived for a more direct test.

The invariance of perceived structure upon paragraph randomization may turn out to be fairly general. Much of the verbal material dealt with in everyday life is not too different in structure from S3, e.g., conversations and news broadcasts. Yet, would Ss be apt to give a typical conversation or news broadcast a low rating for structure? As long as (a) the immediate context for most sentences is appropriate, (b) all paragraphs deal with somewhat the same topic, (c) there is no strong apparent ordering schema, and (d) the hierarchical structure is not apparent for a type S2 ordering of paragraphs: there seems to be little reason for paragraph sequence to affect perceived structure.

LEARNING

T1 and T2 were each scored by E and by a research assistant. The answer sheets were randomized for each question, with only a random number on each sheet for identification. Each scorer randomized the answer sheets separately, and each decided on the proper pointing system, based on the principles given in the instructions.

The score for S was the sum of the points of the questions in a test. The scores of the two scorers were summed, and an analysis of variance was performed on the scores of each test for each experiment. T3 was scored objectively since it was a multiple-choice test.

Experiment I. The following effects were significant for Exp. I, T1: structure $(F = 12.0; df = 2/72; p < .01)$, structure $\times$ part-whole $(F = 3.7; df = 2/72; p < .05)$. The average percentages of points relative to the maximum allowable for S1, S2, and S3 were 60, 47, and 44%, respectively. Thus it is apparent that S1 accounted for the significant main effect. Since, as previously stated, the content of T1 largely emphasized the kinds of material that were added in forming S1 from S2, nothing of great theoretical interest regarding the effect of structure per se on learning can be made of this. The significant interaction does have theoretical importance, however. The effect means that the direction of the simple main effect for the part-whole factor differed, de-

pending on the level of structure of the material. The whole method was superior only at S1; the part method was superior at the other two levels of structure. The conclusions are that the main ideas of a passage, requiring abstraction from several paragraphs, are learned best if the hierarchy is rather painstakingly pointed out in the passage; that if it is so pointed out, the whole method of presentation gives even further advantage to learning. If the passage is not explicitly structured, the part method is superior. The conclusions apply, it should be emphasized, only to the learning of the main abstract parts of the passage.

The following effect was significant for Exp. I, T2: structure $\times$ mode $(F = 3.88; df = 2/72; p < .05)$. The auditory mode of presentation was superior only at S3, whereas the reading mode was superior at both S2 and S1. This result seems in accordance with the idea of McGeoch and Irion (1952, p. 483): the greater effectiveness of the visual mode, when found, has been thought due to greater clarity of impression and unity, whereas audition centers upon smaller units. This interaction was found only for T2, the test of ability to reproduce detailed knowledge of material from a single paragraph. It should be noted that there was no main effect of structure for learning this detailed within-paragraph material.

In T3 of Exp. I, only the part-whole main effect was significant $(F = 4.2; df = 1/72; p < .05)$. The part method was superior with an average of 78% correct replies, whereas the whole method gave only 73% correct replies.

Experiment II. The following effects were significant for T1: structure main effect $(F = 5.2; df = 2/30; p < .01)$; SCAT level main effect $(F = 5.0; df = 4/30; p < .01)$. The average percentage of the maximum possible points at the structure levels S1, S2, and S3, were 38, 24, and 23, respectively. The same scores for the SCAT levels, from highest to lowest, were 40, 29, 31, 22, and 21.

No absolute comparison of structure percentage scores can be made with Exp. I, since scoring of data from the two experiments was not done at the same time, and one scorer independently generated new criteria between scorings. In addition, a new question was added to T1 in Exp. II, and there is no reason to expect that it should have the same average score as the first two questions. One would expect lower scores in Exp. II, however, since the passage was longer, and Ss were given only one presentation of the material instead of two as in Exp. I. The general trend of results remained the same, however; S1 received a considerably higher average score than S2 and S3, which hardly differed from each other. That S1 should show such a high relative score is not remarkable, as was pointed out, since extra T1-pertinent material was given in S1. It is somewhat curious, however, that S2 and S3, which contained virtually the same material, sentence by sentence, differing only in paragraph order, should not differ in either experiment. This result means that paragraph randomization for the lengths of passages used here, and for the type of material used, does not affect an S's capacity to draw upon material from several paragraphs to abstract out the major sections of the passages.

It is also rather curious that the ratings of how well structured the passages were matched closely the general trend of results for T1 learning; i.e., S1 was rated high in structure, and the main parts were well learned. Both S2 and S3 were rated lower and about the same in structure, and the main parts or outline of the passages were learned less

well and about equally so. This suggests that perceived structure of a passage is closely correlated with the extent to which an S has learned the outline of a passage, provided that an implicit hierarchy is present. There is no such relation with learning on T2 or T3.

There were no significant effects in Exp. II for T2 or T3. This implies that, for the conditions of Exp. II, high verbal intelligence is a measure of the ability of Ss to abstract out the main parts or the outline of the passage, but not of the extent to which Ss absorb the details within paragraphs, nor of the extent to which rote learning is accomplished. Since there was no interaction in T1, this effect of high verbal intelligence exerted itself equally for the randomized passage and for S1. Naturally, Ss with high SCAT scores and the treatment S1 received the highest T1 scores of all.

This result suggests that a covariance analysis of T1 of Exp. I would indicate a strong within-cell correlation between the criterion and SCAT scores. The scores were obtained for the Ss in Exp. I, but no such correlation was found. A considerable number of differences occurred between Exp. I and Exp. II; so it is not possible to pin down why the relation held in one case, but not the other. In one case the passage was presented twice, in the other, once; in one case, half the Ss received auditory presentation, in the other, all Ss read the passage; the nature of the examinations was indicated in the instructions of Exp. II, but not of Exp. I. One thing the difference is *not* due to is the nature of the additional third question in Exp. II. The scores for Exp. II were analyzed using just scores from the same two questions used in Exp. I, but the same general trend of results was apparent in these two questions as in the test as a whole. A reasonable hypothesis seems to be that the effect of SCAT level is present for lower levels of learning that exist when the passage is only presented once.

CONCLUSIONS

The general method outlined for the specification of molar, or supra-paragraph prose structure has received validation. The methods used to give a passage explicit hierarchical structure resulted in a passage rated very high in structure. The effects of two classical verbal learning variables, mode of presentation, and part-whole, were shown to be opposite, depending on the level of structure of the passage. In addition, it was shown that it is important in prose learning studies to take care as to what sort of measure of learning is used; different effects appeared for the three sorts of tests used in this study: (a) main parts, (b) within-paragraph details, and (c) rote. Structure is specifiable and psychologically important at the higher levels of prose organization dealt with in this report.

References

Bousfield, W. A. The occurrence of clustering in the recall of randomly arranged associates. *J. Gen. Psychol.*, 1953, **49**, 229–40.

Deese, J. and Kaufman, R. A. Serial effects in recall of unorganized and sequentially organized verbal material. *J. Exp. Psychol.*, 1957, **54**, 180–87.

Epstein, W. A further study of the influence of syntactical structure on learning. *Amer. J. Psychol.*, 1962, **75**, 121–26.

McGeoch, J. A. and Irion, A. L. *The psychology of human learning* (2nd ed.). London: Longmans, Green, 1952.

Miller, G. A., Galanter, E., and Pribram, K. H. *Plans and the structure of behavior.* New York: Holt, 1960.

Miller, G. A. and Selfridge, J. A. Verbal context and the recall of meaningful material. *Amer. J. Psychol.*, 1950, **63**, 176–85.

Stephens, J. M. *Educational psychology* (rev. ed.). New York: Holt, 1956.

Tulving, E. Subjective organization in free recall of "unrelated" words. *Psychol. Rev.*, 1962, **69**, 344–54.

Whitman, J. R. and Garner, W. R. Free recall learning of visual figures as a function of form of internal structure. *J. Exp. Psychol.*, 1962, **64**, 558–64.

VIII

Evaluation of Instruction

Educational evaluation has often been considered to be equivalent to educational measurement. Within recent years, however, the broader scope of evaluation has been made clear by specialists in the area, most particularly by Michael Scriven in "The Methodology of Evaluation" (1967). Measurement is the assignment of numbers to classes of events, and often it is a part of the methodology of evaluation, but *only* a part. Evaluation is a dual process that includes *both* description and judgment; it is the collection and use of data from many sources on which to base educational decisions. Evaluators make judgments regarding the worth and merit of educational programs; these judgments are based on data—part of which, but *only* a part, is student outcome data. This point is most clearly made by Robert Stake in Chapter 39.

The papers included in this section were selected not only because they represent some of the best thinking on evaluation but also because they represent a variety of approaches. Scriven's paper (1967), although an important one, is not reprinted here because it should be read only *after* one has done considerable reading in the area of evaluation. Stake's paper makes many of the same points as Scriven's and, in addition, presents a clear operational model of educational evaluation. Stake makes the plea that we collect data on three aspects (antecedents, transactions, and outcomes) of four domains (intents, observations, standards, and judgments) in order to make rational, well-based decisions. His model is important in that it demands attention for the multiple aspects of evaluation and is generalizable across situations—from the large national curriculum projects to the single classroom program.

Most classroom teachers are concerned not only with evaluating the learning progress of their students but also with the improvement of course content. Chapter 40 by Cronbach addresses itself to this latter issue. In order to use test data for the improvement of a course, one's primary concern must be with the effects of that course on students. A course, Cronbach insists, should be compared with its objectives and intents, not with other courses. He suggests that one gathers the most data by assessing general, rather than specific, effects and by administering different test items to different students.

Glaser's paper (Chapter 41) has much in common with that of Cronbach: He too is concerned with the construction of tests that provide answers to evaluative questions. Glaser draws the important distinction between criterion-referenced tests (those that measure *degree* of learning) and norm-referenced tests (those primarily designed to discriminate among individuals). When evaluating an educational program, one is primarily interested in discriminating among groups (programs), a purpose for which norm-referenced tests are not designed and should not be used.

Most importantly, perhaps, evaluators need to know *why* programs produce the effects or changes they do, a point vividly expressed by Hastings in Chapter 42. If you know why a lesson fails, you can revise it to make it more successful. And if you know why a lesson succeeds, you may be able to generalize to other lessons. No evaluation effort should stand alone but should contribute to the knowledge and efforts of other curriculum developers and evaluators.

Evaluation should be viewed as a *rational* decision-making process; its methodologies are drawn from many disciplines. Education has become a far too expensive and important enterprise to allow the decisions affecting it to be made on any other than rational grounds. It is the intent of the editors that Section VIII will provide some understanding of such decision-making.

Reference

Scriven, M. The methodology of evaluation. In R. E. Stake, ed., *Perspectives in curriculum evaluation.* Chicago: Rand McNally, 1967.

39

The Countenance of Educational Evaluation

ROBERT E. STAKE / *University of Illinois*

President Johnson, President Conant, Mrs. Hull (Sara's teacher) and Mr. Tykociner (the man next door) are quite alike in the faith they have in education. But they have quite different ideas of what education is. The value they put on education does not reveal their way of evaluating education.

Educators differ among themselves as to both the essence and worth of an educational program. The wide range of evaluation purposes and methods allows each to keep his own perspective. Few see their own programs "in the round," partly because of a parochial approach to evaluation. To understand better his own teaching and to contribute more to the science of teaching, each educator should examine the full countenance of evaluation.

Educational evaluation has its formal and informal sides. Informal evaluation is recognized by its dependence on casual observation, implicit goals, intui-tive norms, and subjective judgment. Perhaps because these are also charac-teristic of day-to-day, personal styles of living, informal evaluation results in perspectives which are seldom ques-tioned. Careful study reveals informal evaluation of education to be of variable quality—sometimes penetrating and in-sightful, sometimes superficial and dis-torted.

Formal evaluation of education is recognized by its dependence on check-lists, structured visitation by peers, con-trolled comparisons, and standardized testing of students. Some of these tech-niques have long histories of successful use. Unfortunately, when planning an evaluation, few educators consider even these four. The more common notion is to evaluate informally: to ask the opin-

Reprinted with the permission of the author and the publisher from *Teachers College Record*, 1967, Vol. 68, 523–40.

ion of the instructor, to ponder the logic of the program, or to consider the reputation of the advocates. Seldom do we find a search for relevant research reports or for behavioral data pertinent to the ultimate curricular decisions.

Dissatisfaction with the formal approach is not without cause. Few highly-relevant, readable research studies can be found. The professional journals are not disposed to publish evaluation studies. Behavioral data are costly, and often do not provide the answers. Too many accreditation-type visitation teams lack special training or even experience in evaluation. Many checklists are ambiguous; some focus too much attention on the physical attributes of a school. Psychometric tests have been developed primarily to differentiate among students at the same point in training rather than to assess the effect of instruction on acquisition of skill and understanding. Today's educator may rely little on formal evaluation because its answers have seldom been answers to questions *he* is asking.

Potential Contributions of Formal Evaluation

The educator's disdain of formal evaluation is due also to his sensitivity to criticism—and his *is* a critical clientele. It is not uncommon for him to draw before him such curtains as "national norm comparisons," "innovation phase," and "academic freedom" to avoid exposure through evaluation. The "politics" of evaluation is an interesting issue in itself, but it is not the issue here. The issue here is the *potential* contribution to education of formal evaluation. Today, educators fail to perceive what formal evaluation could do for them. They should be imploring measurement specialists to develop a methodology that reflects the fullness, the complexity, and the importance of their programs. They are not.

What one finds when he examines formal evaluation activities in education today is too little effort to spell out antecedent conditions and classroom transactions (a few of which visitation teams do record) and too little effort to couple them with the various outcomes (a few of which are portrayed by conventional test scores). Little attempt has been made to measure the match between what an educator intends to do and what he does do. The traditional concern of educational-measurement specialists for reliability of individual-student scores and predictive validity (thoroughly and competently stated in the American Council on Education's 1951 edition of *Educational Measurement*) is a questionable resource. For evaluation of curricula, attention to individual differences among students should give way to attention to the contingencies among background conditions, classroom activities, and scholastic outcomes.

This paper is not about what should be measured or how to measure. It is background for developing an evaluation plan. What and how are decided later. My orientation here is around educational programs rather than educational products. I presume that the value of a product depends on its program of use. The evaluation of a program includes the evaluation of its materials.

The countenance of educational evaluation appears to be changing. On the pages that follow, I will indicate what the countenance can, and perhaps, should be. My attempt here is to introduce a conceptualization of evaluation oriented to the complex and dynamic nature of education, one which gives proper attention to the diverse purposes and judgments of the practitioner.

Much recent concern about curriculum evaluation is attributable to contemporary large-scale curriculum-innovation activities, but the statements in this paper pertain to traditional and new curricula alike. They pertain, for example, to Title I and Title III projects funded under the Elementary and Secondary Education Act of 1966. Statements here are relevant to any curriculum, whether oriented to subject-matter content or to student process, and without regard to whether curriculum is general-purpose, remedial, accelerated, compensatory, or special in any other way.

The purposes and procedures of educational evaluation will vary from instance to instance. What is quite appropriate for one school may be less appropriate for another. Standardized achievement tests here but not there. A great concern for expense there but not over there. How do evaluation purposes and procedures vary? What are the basic characteristics of evaluation activities? They are identified in these pages as the evaluation acts, the data sources, the congruence and contingencies, the standards, and the uses of evaluation. The first distinction to be made will be between description and judgment in evaluation.

The countenance of evaluation beheld by the educator is not the same one beheld by the specialist in evaluation. The specialist sees himself as a "describer," one who describes aptitudes and environments and accomplishments. The teacher and school administrator, on the other hand, expect an evaluator to grade something or someone as to merit. Moreover, they expect that he will judge things against external standards, on criteria perhaps little related to the local school's resources and goals.

Neither sees evaluation broadly enough. *Both* description and judgment are essential—in fact, they are the two basic acts of evaluation. Any individual evaluator may attempt to refrain from judging or from collecting the judgments of others. Any individual evaluator may seek only to bring to light the worth of the program. But their evaluations are incomplete. To be fully understood, the educational program must be fully described and fully judged.

Towards Full Description

The specialist in evaluation seems to be increasing his emphasis on fullness of description. For many years he evaluated primarily by measuring student progress toward academic objectives. These objectives usually were identified with the traditional disciplines, e.g., mathematics, English, and social studies. Achievement tests—standardized or "teacher-made"—were found to be useful in describing the degree to which some curricular objectives are attained by individual students in a particular course. To the early evaluators, and to many others, the countenance of evaluation has been nothing more than the administration and normative interpretation of achievement tests.

In recent years a few evaluators have attempted, in addition, to assess progress of individuals toward certain "interdisciplinary" and "extracurricular" objectives. In their objectives, emphasis has been given to the integration of behavior within an individual; or to the perception of interrelationships among scholastic disciplines; or to the development of habits, skills, and attitudes which permit the individual to be a craftsman or scholar, in or out of school. For the descriptive evaluation of such outcomes, the Eight-Year Study (Smith and Tyler, 1942) has served as one model. The proposed National Assessment Program may be another—this statement appeared in one interim report:

> . . . *all committees worked within the following broad definition of 'national assessment.'*
>
> *1. In order to reflect fairly the aims of education in the U.S., the assessment should consider both traditional and modern curricula, and take into account ALL THE ASPIRATIONS schools have for developing attitudes and motivations as well as knowledge and skills* . . . [*Caps added*] (*ETS Developments, 1965*).

In his paper, "Evaluation for Course Improvement," Lee Cronbach (1963) urged another step: a most generous inclusion of behavioral-science variables in order to examine the possible causes and effects of quality teaching. He proposed that the main objective for evaluation is to uncover durable relationships —those appropriate for guiding future educational programs. To the traditional description of pupil achievement, we add the description of instruction and the description of relationships between them. Like the instructional researcher, the evaluator—as so defined—seeks generalizations about educational practices. Many curriculum project evaluators are adopting this definition of evaluation.

The Role of Judgment

Description is one thing, judgment is another. Most evaluation specialists have chosen not to judge. But in his recent *Methodology of Evaluation* Michael Scriven (1967) has charged evaluators with responsibility for passing upon the merit of an educational practice. (Note that he has urged the evaluator to do what the educator has expected the evaluator to be doing.) Scriven's position is that there is no evaluation until judgment has been passed, and by his reckoning the evaluator is best qualified to judge.

By being well experienced and by becoming well informed in the case at hand in matters of research and educational practice, the evaluator does become at least partially qualified to judge. But is it wise for him to accept this responsibility? Even now when few evaluators expect to judge, educators are reluctant to initiate a formal evaluation. If evaluators were *more* frequently identified with the passing of judgment, with the discrimination among poorer and better programs, and with the awarding of support and censure, their access to data would probably diminish. Evaluators collaborate with other social scientists and behavioral research workers. Those who do not want to judge deplore the acceptance of such responsibility by their associates. They believe that in the eyes of many practitioners, social science and behavioral research will become more suspect than it already is.

Many evaluators feel that they are not capable of perceiving, as they think a judge should, the unidimensional *value* of alternative programs. They anticipate a dilemma such as Curriculum I resulting in three skills and ten understandings and Curriculum II resulting in four skills and eight understandings. They are reluctant to judge that gaining one skill is worth losing two understandings. And, whether through timidity, disinterest, or as a rational choice, the evaluator usually supports "local option," a community's privilege to set its own standards and to be its own judge of the worth of its educational system. He expects that what is good for one community will not necessarily be good for another community, and he does not trust himself to discern what is best for a briefly-known community.

Scriven reminds them that there are

precious few who can judge complex programs, and fewer still who will. Different decisions must be made—P.S.S.C. or Harvard Physics?—and they should not be made on trivial criteria, e.g., mere precedent, mention in the popular press, salesman personality, administrative convenience, or pedagogical myth. Who should judge? The answer comes easily to Scriven partly because he expects little interaction between treatment and learner, i.e., what works best for one learner will work best for others, at least within broad categories. He also expects that where the local good is at odds with the common good, the local good can be shown to be detrimental to the common good, to the end that the doctrine of local option is invalidated. According to Scriven the evaluator must judge.

Whether or not evaluation specialists will accept Scriven's challenge remains to be seen. In any case, it is likely that judgments will become an increasing part of the evaluation report. Evaluators will seek out and record the opinions of persons of special qualification. These opinions, though subjective, can be very useful and can be gathered objectively, independent of the solicitor's opinions. A responsibility for processing judgments is much more acceptable to the evaluation specialist than one for rendering judgments himself.

Taylor and Maguire (1966) have pointed to five groups having important opinions on education: spokesmen for society at large, subject-matter experts, teachers, parents, and the students themselves. Members of these and other groups are judges who should be heard. Superficial polls, letters to the editor, and other incidental judgments are insufficient. An evaluation of a school program should portray the merit and fault perceived by well-identified groups, systematically gathered and processed.

Thus, judgment data and description data are both essential to the evaluation of educational programs.

Data Matrices

In order to evaluate, an educator will gather together certain data. The data are likely to be from several quite different sources, gathered in several quite different ways. Whether the immediate purpose is description or judgment, three bodies of information should be tapped. In the evaluation report it can be helpful to distinguish between *antecedent, transaction,* and *outcome* data.

An antecedent is any condition existing prior to teaching and learning which may relate to outcomes. The status of a student prior to his lesson, e.g., his aptitude, previous experience, interest, and willingness, is a complex antecedent. The programmed-instruction specialist calls some antecedents "entry behaviors." The state accrediting agency emphasizes the investment of community resources. All of these are examples of the antecedents which an evaluator will describe.

Transactions are the countless encounters of students with teacher, student with student, author with reader, parent with counselor—the succession of engagements which comprise the process of education. Examples are the presentation of a film, a class discussion, the working of a homework problem, an explanation on the margin of a term paper, and the administration of a test. Smith and Meux studied such transactions in detail and have provided an 18-category classification system. One very visible emphasis on a particular class of transactions was the National Defense Education Act support of audio-visual media.

Transactions are dynamic whereas

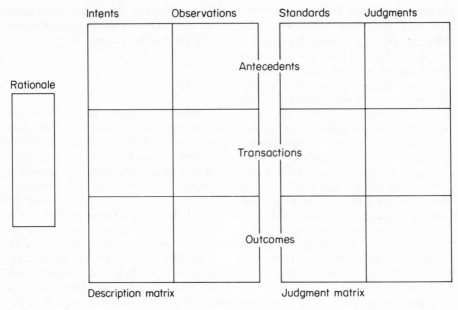

Fig. 1 A layout of statements and data to be collected by the evaluator of an educational program.

antecedents and outcomes are relatively static. The boundaries between them are not clear; e.g., during a transaction we can identify certain outcomes which are feedback antecedents for subsequent learning. These boundaries do not need to be distinct. The categories should be used to stimulate rather than to subdivide our data collection.

Traditionally, most attention in formal evaluation has been given to outcomes—outcomes such as the abilities, achievements, attitudes, and aspirations of students resulting from an educational experience. Outcomes, as a body of information, would include measurements of the impact of instruction on teachers, administrators, councilors, and others. Here too would be data on wear and tear of equipment, effects of the learning environment, cost incurred. Outcomes to be considered in evaluation include not only those that are evident, or even existent, as learning sessions

end, but include applications, transfer, and relearning effects which may not be available for measurement until long after. The description of the outcomes of driver training, for example, could well include reports of accident-avoidance over a lifetime. In short, outcomes are the consequences of educating—immediate and long-range, cognitive and conative, personal and community-wide.

Antecedents, transactions, and outcomes, the elements of evaluation statements, are shown in Figure 1 to have a place in both description and judgment. To fill in these matrices the evaluator will collect judgments (e.g., of community prejudice, of problem solving styles, and of teacher personality) as well as descriptions. In Figure 1 it is also indicated that judgmental statements are classified either as general standards of quality or as judgments specific to the given program. Descriptive data are classified as intents and observations. The evaluator can organize his data-gathering to conform to the format shown in Figure 1.

The evaluator can prepare a record of what educators intend, of what observers perceive, of what patrons generally expect, and of what judges value the immediate program to be. The record may treat antecedents, transactions, and outcomes separately within the four classes identified as *Intents, Observations, Standards,* and *Judgments,* as in Figure 1. The following is an illustration of 12 data, one of which could be recorded in each of the 12 cells, starting with an intended antecedent, and moving down each column until an outcome judgment has been indicated.

Knowing that (1) Chapter XI has been assigned and that he intends (2) to lecture on the topic Wednesday, a professor indicates (3) what the students should be able to do by Friday, partly by writing a quiz on the topic. He observes that (4) some students were absent on Wednesday, that (5) he did not quite complete the lecture because of a lengthy discussion and that (6) on the quiz only about 2/3 of the class seemed to understand a certain major concept. In general, he expects (7) some absences but that the work will be made up by quiz-time; he expects (8) his lectures to be clear enough for perhaps 90 per cent of a class to follow him without difficulty; and he knows that (9) his colleagues expect only about one student in ten to understand thoroughly each major concept in such lessons as these. By his own judgment (10) the reading assignment was not a sufficient background for his lecture; the students commented that (11) the lecture was provocative; and the graduate assistant who read the quiz papers said that (12) a discouragingly large number of students seemed to confuse one major concept for another.

Evaluators and educators do not expect data to be recorded in such detail, even in the distant future. My purpose here was to give twelve examples of data that could be handled by separate cells in the matrices. Next I would like to consider the description data matrix in detail.

Goals and Intents

For many years instructional technologists, test specialists, and others have pleaded for more explicit statement of educational goals. I consider "goals," "objectives," and "intents" to be synonymous. I use the category title *Intents* because many educators now equate "goals" and "objectives" with "intended student outcomes." In this paper Intents includes the planned-for environmental conditions, the planned-for demonstrations, the planned-for coverage of certain subject matter, etc., as well as the planned-for student behavior. To be included in this three-cell column are effects which are desired, those which are hoped for, those which are anticipated, and even those which are feared. This class of data includes goals and plans that others have, especially the students. (It should be noted that it is not the educator's privilege to rule out the study of a variable by saying, "that is not one of our objectives." The evaluator should include both the variable and the negation.) The resulting collection of *Intents* is a priority listing of all that may happen.

The fact that many educators now equate "goals" with "intended student outcomes" is to the credit of the behaviorists, particularly the advocates of programmed instruction. They have brought about a small reform in teaching by emphasizing those specific classroom acts and work exercises which contribute to the refinement of student responses. The A.A.A.S. Science Project, for example, has been successful in developing its curriculum around behavioristic goals (*Science,* 1966). Some curriculum-innovation projects, however, have found the emphasis on behavioral outcomes an obstacle to creative teaching (see Atkin, 1963). The educational evaluator should not list goals only in terms of anticipated student behavior. To *evaluate* an educational program, we must examine what teaching, as well as what learning, is intended. (Many antecedent conditions and teaching transactions can be worded behavioristically, if desired.) How intentions are worded is not a criterion for inclusion. Intents can be the global goals of the Educational Policies Commission or the detailed goals of the programmer (Mager, 1962). Taxonomic, mechanistic, humanistic, even scriptural—any mixture of goal statements is acceptable as part of the evaluation picture.

Many a contemporary evaluator expects trouble when he sets out to record the educator's objectives. Early in the work he urged the educator to declare his objectives so that outcome-testing devices could be built. He finds the educator either reluctant or unable to verbalize objectives. With diligence, if not with pleasure, the evaluator assists with what he presumes to be the educator's job: writing behavioral goals. His presumption is wrong. As Scriven has said, the responsibility for describing curricular objectives is the responsibility of the evaluator. He is the one who is experienced with the language of behaviors, traits, and habits. Just as it is his responsibility to transform the behaviors of a teacher and the responses of a student into data, it is his responsibility to transform the intentions and expectations of an educator into "data." It is necessary for him to continue to ask the educator for statements of intent. He should augment the replies by asking, "Is this another way of saying it?" or

"Is this an instance?" It is not wrong for an evaluator to teach a willing educator about behavioral objectives—they may facilitate the work. It is wrong for him to insist that every educator should use them.

Obtaining authentic statements of intent is a new challenge for the evaluator. The methodology remains to be developed. Let us now shift attention to the second column of the data cells.

Observational Choice

Most of the descriptive data cited early in the previous section are classified as *Observations*. In Figure 1 when he describes surroundings and events and the subsequent consequences, the evaluator[1] is telling of his Observations. Sometimes the evaluator observes these characteristics in a direct and personal way. Sometimes he uses instruments. His instruments include inventory schedules, biographical data sheets, interview routines, checklists, opinionnaires, and all kinds of psychometric tests. The experienced evaluator gives special attention to the measurement of student outcomes, but he does not fail to observe the other outcomes, nor the antecedent conditions and instructional transactions.

Many educators fear that the outside evaluator will not be attentive to the characteristics that the school staff has deemed most important. This sometimes does happen, but evaluators often pay *too much* attention to what they have been urged to look at, and too little attention to other facets. In the matter of selection of variables for evaluation,

---

[1] Here and elsewhere in this paper, for simplicity of presentation, the evaluator and the educator are referred to as two different persons. The educator will often be his own evaluator or a member of the evaluation team.

the evaluator must make a subjective decision. Obviously, he must limit the elements to be studied. He cannot look at all of them. The ones he rules out will be those that he assumes would not contribute to an understanding of the educational activity. He should give primary attention to the variables specifically indicated by the educator's objectives, but he must designate additional variables to be observed. He must search for unwanted side effects and incidental gains. The selection of measuring techniques is an obvious responsibility, but the choice of characteristics to be observed is an equally important and unique contribution of the evaluator.

An evaluation is not complete without a statement of the rationale of the program. It needs to be considered separately, as indicated in Figure 1. Every program has its rationale, though often it is only implicit. The rationale indicates the philosophic background and basic purposes of the program. Its importance to evaluation has been indicated by Berlak (1966). The rationale should provide one basis for evaluating Intents. The evaluator asks himself or other judges whether the plan developed by the educator constitutes a logical step in the implementation of the basic purposes. The rationale also is of value in choosing the reference groups, e.g., merchants, mathematicians, and mathematics educators, which later are to pass judgment on various aspects of the program.

A statement of rationale may be difficult to obtain. Many an effective instructor is less than effective at presenting an educational rationale. If pressed, he may only succeed in saying something the listener wanted said. It is important that the rationale be in his language, a language he is the master of. Suggestions by the evaluator may be an obstacle, becoming accepted because they are attractive rather than because they designate the grounds for what the educator is trying to do.

The judgment matrix needs further explanation, but I am postponing that until after a consideration of the bases for processing descriptive data.

Contingency and Congruence

For any one educational program there are two principal ways of processing descriptive evaluation data: finding the contingencies among antecedents, transactions, and outcomes; and finding the congruence between Intents and Observations. The processing of judgments follows a different model. The first two main columns of the data matrix in Figure 1 contain the descriptive data. The format for processing these data is represented in Figure 2.

The data for a curriculum are *congruent* if what was intended actually happens. To be fully congruent the intended antecedents, transactions, and outcomes would have to come to pass. (This seldom happens—and often should not.) Within one row of the data matrix the evaluator should be able to compare the cells containing Intents and Observations, to note the discrepancies, and to describe the amount of congruence for that row. (Congruence of outcomes has been emphasized in the evaluation model proposed by Taylor and Maguire.) Congruence does not indicate that outcomes are reliable or valid, but that what was intended did occur.

Just as the Gestaltist found more to the whole than the sum of its parts, the evaluator studying variables from any two of the three cells in a column of the data matrix finds more to describe than the variables themselves. The relationships or *contingencies* among the variables deserve additional attention. In the

Descriptive Data

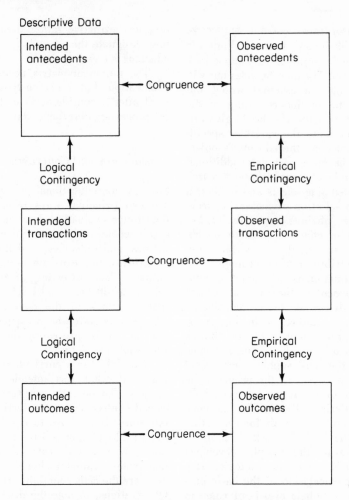

Fig. 2 A representation of the processing of descriptive data.

sense that evaluation is the search for relationships that permit the improvement of education, the evaluator's task is one of identifying outcomes that are contingent upon particular antecedent conditions and instructional transactions.

Lesson planning and curriculum revision through the years have been built upon faith in certain contingencies. Day to day, the master teacher arranges his presentation and selects his input materials to fit his instructional goals. For him the contingencies, in the main, are logical, intuitive, and supported by a history of satisfactions and endorsements. Even the master teacher and certainly less-experienced teachers need to bring their intuited contingencies under the scrutiny of appropriate juries.

As a first step in evaluation it is important just to record them. A film on floodwaters may be scheduled (intended transaction) to expose students to a background to conservation legislation (intended outcome). Of those who know both subject matter and pedagogy, we ask, "Is there a logical connection between this event and this purpose?" If so, a logical contingency exists between these two Intents. The record should show it.

Whenever Intents are evaluated the contingency criterion is one of logic. To test the logic of an educational contingency the evaluators rely on previous experience, perhaps on research experience, with similar observables. No immediate observation of these variables, however, is necessary to test the strength of the contingencies among Intents.

Evaluation of Observation contingencies depends on empirical evidence. To say, "this arithmetic class progressed rapidly because the teacher was somewhat but not too sophisticated in mathematics" demands empirical data, either from within the evaluation or from the research literature (see Bassham, 1962). The usual evaluation of a single program will not alone provide the data necessary for contingency statements. Here too, then, previous experience with similar observables is a basic qualification of the evaluator.

The contingencies and congruences identified by evaluators are subject to judgment by experts and participants just as more unitary descriptive data are. The importance of non-congruence will vary with different viewpoints. The school superintendent and the school counselor may disagree as to the importance of a cancellation of the scheduled lessons on sex hygiene in the health class. As an example of judging contingencies, the degree to which teacher morale is contingent on the length of the school day may be deemed cause enough to abandon an early morning class by one judge and not another. Perceptions of importance of congruence and contingency deserve the evaluator's careful attention.

Standards and Judgments

There is a general agreement that the goal of education is excellence—but how schools and students should excel, and at what sacrifice, will always be debated. Whether goals are local or national, the measurement of excellence requires explicit rather than implicit standards.

Today's educational programs are not subjected to "standard-oriented" evaluation. This is not to say that schools lack in aspiration or accomplishment. It is to say that standards—benchmarks of performance having widespread reference value—are not in common use. Schools across the nation may use the same evaluation checklist[2] but the interpretations of the checklisted data are couched in inexplicit, personal terms. Even in an informal way, no school can evaluate the impact of its program without knowledge of what other schools are doing in pursuit of similar objectives. Unfortunately, many educators are loath to accumulate that knowledge systematically (Hand, 1965; Tyler, 1965).

There is little knowledge anywhere today of the quality of a student's education. School grades are based on the private criteria and standards of the

---

[2] One contemporary checklist is *Evaluative Criteria*, a document published by the National Study of Secondary School Evaluation (1960). It is a commendably thorough list of antecedents and possible transactions, organized mostly by subject-matter offerings. Surely it is valuable as a checklist, identifying neglected areas. Its great value may be a catalyst, hastening the maturity of a developing curriculum. However, it can be of only limited value in *evaluating*, for it guides neither the measurement nor the interpretation of measurement. By intent, it deals with criteria (what variables to consider) and leaves the matter of standards (what ratings to consider as meritorious) to the conjecture of the individual observer.

individual teacher. Most "standardized" test scores tell where an examinee performing "psychometrically useful" tasks stands with regard to a reference group, rather than the level of competence at which he performs essential scholastic tasks. Although most teachers are competent to teach their subject matter and to spot learning difficulties, few have the ability to *describe* a student's command over his intellectual environment. Neither school grades nor standardized test scores nor the candid opinions of teachers are very informative as to the excellence of students.

Even when measurements are effectively interpreted, evaluation is complicated by a multiplicity of standards. Standards vary from student to student, from instructor to instructor, and from reference group to reference group. This is not wrong. In a healthy society, different parties have different standards. Part of the responsibility of evaluation is to make known which standards are held by whom.

It was implied much earlier that it is reasonable to expect change in an educator's *Intents* over a period of time. This is to say that he will change both his criteria and his standards during instruction. While a curriculum is being developed and disseminated, even the major classes of criteria vary. In their analysis of nationwide assimilation of new educational programs, Clark and Guba (1965) identified eight stages of change through which new programs go. For each stage they identified special criteria (each with its own standards) on which the program should be evaluated before it advances to another stage. Each of their criteria deserves elaboration, but here it is merely noted that there are quite different criteria at each successive curriculum-development stage.

Informal evaluation tends to leave criteria unspecified. Formal evaluation is more specific. But it seems the more careful the evaluation, the fewer the criteria; and the more carefully the criteria are specified, the less the concern given to standards of acceptability. It is a great misfortune that the best trained evaluators have been looking at education with a microscope rather than with a panoramic view finder.

There is no clear picture of what any school or any curriculum project is accomplishing today partly because the methodology of processing judgments is inadequate. What little formal evaluation there is is attentive to too few criteria, overly tolerant of implicit standards, and ignores the advantage of relative comparisons. More needs to be said about relative and absolute standards.

Comparing and Judging

There are two bases of judging the characteristics of a program, (1) with respect to absolute standards as reflected by personal judgments and (2) with respect to relative standards as reflected by characteristics of alternate programs. One can evaluate SMSG mathematics with respect to opinions of what a mathematics curriculum should be or with regard to what other mathematics curricula are. The evaluator's comparisons and judgments are symbolized in Figure 3. The upper left matrix represents the data matrix from Figure 2. At the upper right are sets of standards by which a program can be judged in an absolute sense. There are multiple sets because there may be numerous reference groups or points of view. The several matrices at the lower left represent several alternate programs to which the one being evaluated can be compared.

Each set of absolute standards, if formalized, would indicate acceptable and meritorious levels for antecedents,

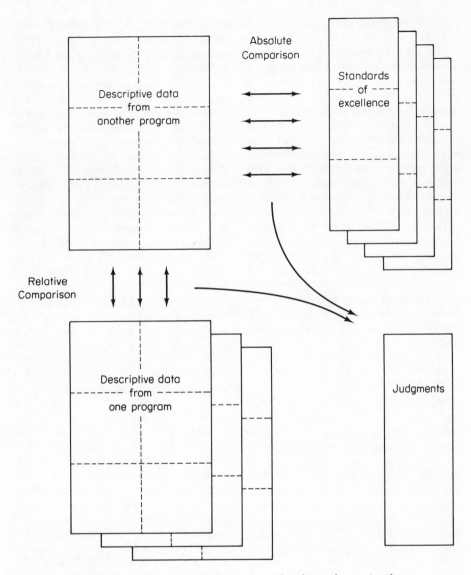

Fig. 3 A representation of the process of judging the merit of an educational program.

transactions, and outcomes. So far I have been talking about setting standards, not about judging. Before making a judgment the evaluator determines whether or not each standard is met. Unavailable standards must be estimated. The judging act itself is deciding which set of standards to heed. More precisely, judging is assigning a weight, an importance, to each set of standards. Rational judgment in educational evaluation is a decision as to how much to pay attention to the standards of each reference group (point of view) in deciding whether or not to take some administrative action.[3]

Relative comparison is accomplished in similar fashion except that the standards are taken from descriptions of other programs. It is hardly a judgmental matter to determine whether one program betters another with regard to a single characteristic, but there are many characteristics and the characteristics are not equally important. The evaluator selects which characteristics to attend to and which reference programs to compare to.

From relative judgment of a program, as well as from absolute judgment, we can obtain an overall or composite rating of merit (perhaps with certain qualifying statements), a rating to be used in making an educational decision. From this final act of judgment a recommendation can be composed.

Absolute and Relative Evaluation

As to which kind of evaluation—absolute or relative—to encourage, Scriven and Cronbach have disagreed. Cronbach (1963) suggests that generalizations to the local-school situation from curriculum-comparing studies are sufficiently hazardous (even when the studies are massive, well-designed, and properly controlled) to make them poor research investments. Moreover, the difference in purpose of the programs being compared is likely to be sufficiently great to render uninterpretable any outcome other than across-the-board superiority of one of them. Expecting that rarely, Cronbach urges fewer comparisons,

more intensive process studies, and more curriculum "case studies" with extensive measurement and thorough description.

Scriven, on the other hand, indicates that what the educator wants to know is whether or not one program is better than another, and that the best way to answer his question is by direct comparison. He points to the difficulty of describing the outcomes of complex learning in explicit terms and with respect to absolute standards, and to the ease of observing relative outcomes from two programs. Whether or not Scriven's prescription is satisfying will probably depend on the client. An educator faced with an adoption decision is more likely to be satisfied, the curriculum innovator and instructional technologist less likely.

One of the major distinctions in evaluation is that which Scriven identifies as *formative* versus *summative* evaluation. His use of the terms relates primarily to the stage of development of curricular material. If material is not yet ready for distribution to classroom teachers, then its evaluation is formative; otherwise it is summative. It is probably more useful to distinguish between evaluation oriented to developer-author-publisher criteria and standards and evaluation oriented to consumer-administrator-teacher criteria and standards. The formative-summative distinction could be so defined, and I will use the terms in that way. The faculty committee facing an adoption choice asks, "Which is best? Which will do the job best?" The course developer, following Cronbach's advice, asks, "How can we teach it better?" (Note that neither are now concerned about the individual student differences.) The evaluator looks at different data and invokes different standards to answer these questions.

The evaluator who assumes respon-

---

[3] Deciding which variables to study and deciding which standards to employ are two essentially subjective commitments in evaluation. Other acts are capable of objective treatment; only these two are beyond the reach of social science methodology.

sibility for summative evaluation—rather than formative evaluation—accepts the responsibility of informing consumers as to the merit of the program. The judgments of Figure 3 are his target. It is likely that he will attempt to describe the school situations in which the procedures or materials may be used. He may see his task as one of indicating the goodness-of-fit of an available curriculum to an existing school program. He must learn whether or not the intended antecedents, transactions, and outcomes for the curriculum are consistent with the resources, standards, and goals of the school. This may require as much attention to the school as to the new curriculum.

The formative evaluator, on the other hand, is more interested in the contingencies indicated in Figure 2. He will look for covariations within the evaluation study, and across studies, as a basis for guiding the development of present or future programs.

For major evaluation activities it is obvious that an individual evaluator will not have the many competencies required. A team of social scientists is needed for many assignments. It is reasonable to suppose that such teams will include specialists in instructional technology, specialists in psychometric testing and scaling, specialists in research design and analysis, and specialists in dissemination of information. Curricular innovation is sure to have deep and widespread effect on our society, and we may include the social anthropologist on some evaluation teams. The economist and philosopher have something to offer. Experts will be needed for the study of values, population surveys, and content-oriented data-reduction techniques.

The educator who has looked disconsolate when scheduled for evaluation will look aghast at the prospect of a team of evaluators invading his school.

How can these evaluators observe or describe the natural state of education when their very presence influences that state? His concern is justified. Measurement activity—just the presence of evaluators—does have a reactive effect on education, sometimes beneficial and sometimes not—but in either case contributing to the atypicality of the sessions. There are specialists, however, who anticipate that evaluation will one day be so skilled that it properly will be considered "unobtrusive measurement" (Webb, *et al.*, 1966).

In conclusion I would remind the reader that one of the largest investments being made in U.S. education today is in the development of new programs. School officials cannot yet revise a curriculum on rational grounds, and the needed evaluation is not under way. What is to be gained from the enormous effort of the innovators of the 1960's if in the 1970's there are no evaluation records? Both the new innovator and the new teacher need to know. Folklore is not a sufficient repository. In our data banks we should document the causes and effects, the congruence of intent and accomplishment, and the panorama of judgments of those concerned. Such records should be kept to promote educational action, not obstruct it. The countenance of evaluation should be one of data gathering that leads to decision-making, not to trouble-making.

Educators should be making their own evaluations more deliberate, more formal. Those who will—whether in their classrooms or on national panels—can hope to clarify their responsibility by answering each of the following questions: (1) Is this evaluation to be primarily descriptive, primarily judgmental, or both descriptive and judgmental? (2) Is this evaluation to emphasize the antecedent conditions, the transactions, or the outcomes alone, or a combination of these, or their functional contingencies? (3) Is this evaluation to indicate the congruence between what is intended and what occurs? (4) Is this evaluation to be undertaken within a single program or as a comparison between two or more curricular programs? (5) Is this evaluation intended more to further the development of curricula or to help choose among available curricula? With these questions answered, the restrictive effects of incomplete guidelines and inappropriate countenances are more easily avoided.

References

American Council on Education. E. F. Lindquist, ed., *Educational measurement.* Washington, D.C., 1951.

Atkin, J. M. Some evaluation problems in a course content improvement project. *Journal of Research in Science Teaching.* 1963, **1**, 129–32.

Bassham, H. Teacher understanding and pupil efficiency in mathematics: A study of relationship. *Arithmetic Teacher*, 1962, **9**, 383–87.

Berlak, H. Comments recorded in *Concepts and structure in the new social science curricula*, Irving Morrissett, ed. Lafayette, Indiana: Social Science Education Consortium, Purdue University, 1966. Pp. 88–89.

Clark, D. L. and Guba, E. G. *An examination of potential change roles in education.* Columbus: The Ohio State University, 1965. (Multilith.)

Cronbach, L. Evaluation for course improvement. *Teachers College Record*, 1963, **64**, 672–83.

Educational Testing Service. A long, hot summer of committee work on national assessment of education. *ETS Developments*, XIII, November 1965.

Gagné, R. M. Elementary science: A new scheme of instruction. *Science*, 1966, **151**, 49–53.

Hand, H. C. National assessment viewed as the camel's nose. *Phi Delta Kappan*, 1965, **47**, 8–12.

Mager, R. F. *Preparing objectives for programmed instruction.* San Francisco: Fearon Publishers, 1962.

Scriven, M. The methodology of evaluation. *AERA monograph series on curriculum evaluation, No. 1.* Chicago: Rand McNally, 1967. Pp. 39–89.

Smith, B. O. and Meux, M. O. *A study of the logic of teaching.* Urbana: Bureau of Educational Research, University of Illinois, n.d.

Smith, E. R. and Tyler, R. W. *Appraising and recording student progress.* New York: Harper and Row, 1942.

Taylor, P. A. and Maguire, T. O. A theoretical evaluation model. *The Manitoba Journal of Educational Research*, 1966, **1**, 12–17.

Tyler, R. W. Assessing the progress of education. *Phi Delta Kappan*, 1965, **47**,13–16.

Webb, E. J., Campbell, D. T., Schwartz, R. D., and Sechrist, L. *Unobtrusive measures: Nonreactive research in the social sciences.* Chicago: Rand McNally, 1966.

40

Evaluation for Course Improvement

LEE J. CRONBACH / *Stanford University*

The national interest in improving education has generated several highly important projects attempting to improve curricula, particularly at the secondary-school level. In conferences of directors of "course content improvement" programs sponsored by the National Science Foundation, questions about evaluation are frequently raised. Those who inquire about evaluation have various motives, ranging from sheer scientific curiosity about classroom events to a desire to assure a sponsor that money has been well spent. While the curriculum developers sincerely wish to use the skills of evaluation specialists, I am not certain that they have a clear picture of what evaluation can do and should try to do. And, on the other hand, I am becoming convinced that some techniques and habits of thought of the evaluation specialist are ill-suited to current curriculum studies. To serve these studies, what philosophy and methods of evaluation are required? And particularly, how must we depart from the familiar doctrines and rituals of the testing game?

Decisions Served by Evaluation

To draw attention to its full range of functions, we may define "evaluation" broadly as the *collection and use of information to make decisions about an educational program.* This program may be a set of instructional materials distributed nationally, the instructional activities of a single school, or the educational experiences of a single pupil. Many types of decisions are to be made, and many varieties of information are useful. It becomes immediately apparent

Reprinted with the permission of the author and the publisher from *Teachers College Record*, 1963, Vol. 64, 672–83.

that evaluation is a diversified activity and that no one set of principles will suffice for all situations. But measurements specialists have so concentrated upon one process—the preparation of pencil-and-paper achievement tests for assigning scores to individual pupils—that the principles pertinent to that process have somehow become enshrined as *the* principles of evaluation. "Tests," we are told, "should fit the content of the curriculum." Also, "only those evaluation procedures should be used that yield reliable scores." These and other hallowed principles are not entirely appropriate to evaluation for course improvement. Before proceeding to support this contention, I wish to distinguish among purposes of evaluation and relate them to historical developments in testing and curriculum making.

We may separate three types of decisions for which evaluation is used:

1. Course improvement: deciding what instructional materials and methods are satisfactory and where change is needed.
2. Decisions about individuals: identifying the needs of the pupil for the sake of planning his instruction, judging pupil merit for purposes of selection and grouping, acquainting the pupil with his own progress and deficiencies.
3. Administrative regulation: judging how good the school system is, how good individual teachers are, etc.

Course improvement is set apart by its broad temporal and geographical reference; it involves the modification of recurrently used materials and methods. Developing a standard exercise to overcome a misunderstanding would be course improvement, but deciding whether a certain pupil should work through that exercise would be an individual decision. Administrative regulation likewise is local in effect, whereas an improvement in a course is likely to be pertinent wherever the course is offered.

It was for the sake of course improvement that systematic evaluation was first introduced. When that famous muckraker Joseph Rice gave the same spelling test in a number of American schools, and so gave the first impetus to the educational testing movement, he was interested in evaluating a curriculum. Crusading against the extended spelling drills that then loomed large in the school schedule—"the spelling grind"—Rice collected evidence of their worthlessness so as to provoke curriculum revision. As the testing movement developed, however, it took on a different function.

The greatest expansion of systematic achievement testing occurred in the 1920's. At that time, the content of any course was taken pretty much as established and beyond criticism save for small shifts of topical emphasis. At the administrator's direction, standard tests covering this curriculum were given to assess the efficiency of the teacher or the school system. Such administrative testing fell into disfavor when used injudiciously and heavyhandedly in the 1920's and 1930's. Administrators and accrediting agencies fell back upon descriptive features of the school program in judging adequacy. Instead of collecting direct evidence of educational impact, they judged schools in terms of size of budget, student-staff ratio, square feet of laboratory space, and the number of advanced credits accumulated by the teacher. This tide, it appears, is about to turn. On many university campuses, administrators wanting to know more about their product are installing "operations research offices." Testing directed toward quality control seems likely to increase in the lower schools as well, as is most forcefully indicated by the state-wide testing just ordered by the California legislature.

After 1930 or thereabouts, tests were given almost exclusively for judgments about individuals: to select students for advanced training, to assign marks within a class, and to diagnose individual competences and deficiencies. For any such decisions, one wants precise and valid comparisons of one individual with other individuals or with a standard. Much of test theory and test technology has been concerned with making measurements precise. Important though precision is for most decisions about individuals, I shall argue that in evaluating courses we need not struggle to obtain precise scores for individuals.

While measurers have been well content with the devices used to make scores precise, they have been less complacent about validity. Prior to 1935 the pupil was examined mostly on factual knowledge and mastery of fundamental skills. Tyler's research and writings of that period developed awareness that higher mental processes are not evoked by simple factual tests, and that instruction that promotes factual knowledge may not promote—indeed, may interfere with—other more important educational outcomes. Tyler, Lindquist, and their students demonstrated that tests can be designed to measure general educational outcomes such as ability to comprehend scientific method. Whereas a student can prepare for a factual test only through a course of study that includes the facts tested, many different courses of study may promote the same *general* understandings and attitudes. In evaluating today's new curricula, it will clearly be important to appraise the student's general educational growth, which curriculum developers say is more important than mastery of the specific lessons presented. Note, for example, that the Bio-

logical Sciences Curriculum Study offers three courses with substantially different "subject matter" as alternative routes to much the same educational ends.

Although some instruments capable of measuring general outcomes were prepared during the 1930's, they were never very widely employed. The prevailing philosophy of the curriculum, particularly among "progressives," called for developing a program to fit local requirements, capitalizing on the capacities and experiences of local pupils. The faith of the 1920's in a "standard" curriculum was replaced by a faith that the best learning experience would result from teacher-pupil planning in each classroom. Since each teacher or each class could choose different content and even different objectives, this philosophy left little place for standard testing.

Many evaluation specialists came to see test development as a strategy for training the teacher in service, so that the process of test making came to be valued more than the test—or the test data—that resulted. The following remarks by Bloom (1961) are representative of a whole school of thought:[1]

The criterion for determining the quality of a school and its educational functions would be the extent to which it achieves the objectives it has set for itself. . . . Our experiences suggest that unless the school has translated the objectives into specific and operational definitions, little is likely to be done about the objectives. They remain pious hopes and platitudes. . . . Participation of the teaching staff in selecting as well as constructing evaluation instruments has resulted in improved instruments on one hand and on the other hand it has resulted in clarifying the ob-

---

[1] Elsewhere, Bloom's paper discusses evaluation for the new curricula. Attention may also be drawn to Tyler's highly pertinent paper (1951).

jectives of instruction and in making them real and meaningful to teachers. . . . When teachers have actively participated in defining objectives and in selecting or constructing evaluation instruments they return to the learning problems with great vigor and remarkable creativity. . . . Teachers who have become committed to a set of educational objectives which they thoroughly understand respond by developing a variety of learning experiences which are as diverse and as complex as the situation requires.

Thus "evaluation" becomes a local, and beneficial, teacher-training activity. The benefit is attributed to thinking about what data to collect. Little is said about the actual use of test results; one has the impression that when test making ends, the test itself is forgotten. Certainly there is little enthusiasm for refining tests so that they can be used in other schools, for to do so would be to rob those teachers of the benefits of working out their own objectives and instruments.

Bloom and Tyler describe both curriculum making and evaluation as integral parts of classroom instruction, which is necessarily decentralized. This outlook is far from that of "course improvement." The current national curriculum studies assume that curriculum making can be centralized. They prepare materials to be used in much the same way by teachers everywhere. It is assumed that having experts draft materials, and revising these after tryout, produces better instructional activities than the local teacher would be likely to devise. In this context it seems wholly appropriate to have most tests prepared by a central staff, and to have results returned to that staff to guide further course improvement.

When evaluation is carried out in the service of course improvement, the chief aim is to ascertain what effects the course has—that is, what changes it produces in pupils. This is not to inquire merely whether the course is effective or ineffective. Outcomes of instruction are multidimensional, and a satisfactory investigation will map out the effects of the course along these dimensions separately. To agglomerate many types of post-course performance into a single score is a mistake, since failure to achieve one objective is masked by success in another direction. Moreover, since a composite score embodies (and usually conceals) judgments about importance of the various outcomes, only a report that treats the outcomes separately can be useful to educators who have different value hierarchies.

The greatest service evaluation can perform is to identify aspects of the course where revision is desirable. Those responsible for developing a course would like to present evidence that their course is effective. They are intrigued by the idea of having an "independent testing agency" render a judgment on their product. But to call in the evaluator only upon the completion of course development, to confirm what has been done, is to offer him a menial role and to make meager use of his services. To be influential in course improvement, evidence must become available midway in curriculum development, not in the home stretch when the developer is naturally reluctant to tear open a supposedly finished body of materials and techniques. Evaluation, used to improve the course while it is still fluid, contributes more to improvement of education than evaluation used to appraise a product already placed on the market.

Insofar as possible, evaluation should be used to understand how the course produces its effects and what parameters influence its effectiveness. It is important to learn, for example, that the outcome of programed instruction depends very much upon the attitude of the teacher; indeed, this may be more important than to learn that on the average such instruction produces slightly better or worse results than conventional instruction.

Hopefully, evaluation studies will go beyond reporting on this or that course, and help us to understand educational learning. Such insight will in the end contribute to the development of all courses rather than just of the course under test. In certain of the new curricula, there are data to suggest that aptitude measures correlate much less with end-of-course achievement than they do with achievement on early units (Ferris, 1962). This finding is not well confirmed, but is highly significant if true. If it is true for the new curricula and only for them, it has one implication; if the same effect appears in traditional courses, it means something else. Either way, it provides food for thought for teachers, counselors, and theorists. Evaluation studies should generate knowledge about the nature of the abilities that constitute educational goals. Twenty years after the Eight-Year Study of the Progressive Education Association, its testing techniques are in good repute, but we still know very little about what these instruments measure. Consider "Applications of Principles in Science." Is this in any sense a unitary ability? Or has the able student only mastered certain principles one by one? Is the ability demonstrated on a test of this sort more prognostic of any later achievement than is factual knowledge? Such questions ought to receive substantial attention, though to the makers of any one course they are of only peripheral interest.

The aim to compare one course with another should not dominate plans for evaluation. To be sure, decision makers have to choose between courses, and any evaluation report will be interpreted in part comparatively. But formally designed experiments pitting one course against another are rarely definitive enough to justify their cost. Differences between average test scores resulting from different courses are usually small, relative to the wide differences among and within classes taking the same course. At best, an experiment never does more than compare the present version of one course with the present version of another. A major effort to bring the losing contender nearer to perfection would be very likely to reverse the verdict of the experiment.

Any failure to equate the classes taking the competing courses will jeopardize the interpretation of an experiment, and such failures are almost inevitable. In testing a drug, we know that valid results cannot be obtained without a double-blind control in which the doses for half the subjects are inert placebos; the placebo and the drug look alike, so that neither doctor nor patient knows who is receiving medication. Without this control the results are useless even when the state of the patient is checked by completely objective indices. In an educational experiment it is difficult to keep pupils unaware that they are an experimental group. And it is quite impossible to neutralize the biases of the teacher as those of the doctor are neutralized in the double-blind design. It is thus never certain whether any observed advantage is attributable to the educational innovation as such, or to the greater energy that teachers and students put forth when a method is fresh and "experimental." Some have contended that any course, even the most excellent, loses much of its potency as soon as success enthrones it as "the traditional method."[2]

Since group comparisons give equivocal results, I believe that a formal study should be designed primarily to determine the post-course performance of a well-described group, with respect to many important objectives and side effects. Ours is a problem like that of the engineer examining a new automobile. He can set himself the task of defining its performance characteristics and its dependability. It would be merely distracting to put his question in the form: "Is this car better or worse than the competing brand?" Moreover, in an experiment where the treatments compared differ in a dozen respects, no understanding is gained from the fact that the experiment shows a numerical advantage in favor of the new course. No one knows which of the ingredients is responsible for the advantage. More analytic experiments are much more useful than field trials applying markedly dissimilar treatments to different groups. Small-scale, well-controlled studies can profitably be used to compare alternative versions of the same course; in such a study the differences between treatments are few enough and well-enough defined that the results have explanatory value.

The three purposes—course improvement, decisions about individuals, and administrative regulation—call for measurement procedures having somewhat different qualities. When a test will be used to make an administrative judgment on the individual teacher, it is necessary to measure thoroughly and with conspicuous fairness; such testing, if it is to cover more than one outcome,

becomes extremely time-consuming. In judging a course, however, one can make satisfactory interpretations from data collected on a sampling basis, with no pretense of measuring thoroughly the accomplishments of any one class. A similar point is to be made about testing for decisions about individuals. A test of individuals must be conspicuously fair, and extensive enough to provide a dependable score for each person. But if the performance will not influence the fate of the individual, we can ask him to perform tasks for which the course has not directly prepared him, and we can use techniques that would be prohibitively expensive if applied in a manner thorough enough to measure each person reliably.

Methods of Evaluation

RANGE OF METHODS

Evaluation is too often visualized as the administration of a formal test, an hour or so in duration, at the close of a course. But there are many other methods for examining pupil performance, and pupil attainment is not the only basis for appraising a course.

It is quite appropriate to ask scholars whether the statements made in the course are consistent with the best contemporary knowledge. This is a sound, even a necessary procedure. One might go on to evaluate the pedagogy of the new course by soliciting opinions, but here there is considerable hazard. If the opinions are based on some preconception about teaching method, the findings will be controversial and very probably misleading. There are no theories of pedagogy so well established that one can say, without tryout, what will prove educative.

One can accept the need for a prag-

---

[2] The interested reader can find further striking parallels between curriculum studies and drug research (see Modell, 1963).

matic test of the curriculum and still employ opinions as a source of evidence. During the tryout stages of curriculum making, one relies heavily on the teachers' reports of pupil accomplishment—"Here they had trouble"; "This they found dull"; "Here they needed only half as many exercises as were provided"; etc. This is behavior observation even though unsystematic, and it is of great value. The reason for shifting to systematic observation is that this is more impartial, more public, and sometimes more penetrating. While I bow to the historian or mathematician as a judge of the technical soundness of course content, I do not agree that the experienced history or mathematics teacher who tries out a course gives the best possible judgment on its effectiveness. Scholars have too often deluded themselves about their effectiveness as teachers—particularly, have too often accepted parroting of words as evidence of insight—for their unaided judgment to be trusted. Systematic observation is costly and introduces some delay between the moment of teaching and the feedback of results. Hence systematic observation will never be the curriculum developer's sole source of evidence. Systematic data collection becomes profitable in the intermediate stages of curriculum development, after the more obvious bugs in early drafts have been dealt with.

The approaches to evaluation include process studies, proficiency measures, attitude measures, and follow-up studies. A process study is concerned with events taking place in the classroom, proficiency and attitude measures with changes observed in pupils, and follow-up studies with the later careers of those who participated in the course. The follow-up study comes closest to observing ultimate educational contributions, but the completion of such a study is so far removed in time from the initial instruction that it is of minor value in improving the course or explaining its effects. The follow-up study differs strikingly from the other types of evaluation study in one respect. I have already expressed the view that evaluation should be primarily concerned with the effects of the course under study rather than with comparisons of courses. That is to say, I would emphasize departures of attained results from the ideal, differences in apparent effectiveness of different parts of the course, and differences from item to item; all these suggest places where the course could be strengthened. But this view cannot be applied to the follow-up study, which appraises effects of the course as a whole and which has very little meaning unless outcomes can be compared with some sort of base rate. Suppose we find that 65 percent of the boys graduating from an experimental curriculum enroll in scientific and technical majors in college. We cannot judge whether this is a high or low figure save by comparing it with the rate among boys who have not had this course. In a follow-up study, it is necessary to obtain data on a control group equated at least crudely to the experimental cases on the obvious demographic variables.

Despite the fact that such groups are hard to equate and that follow-up data do not tell much about how to improve the course, such studies should have a place in research on the new curricula, whose national samples provide unusual opportunity for follow-up that can shed light on important questions. One obvious type of follow-up study traces the student's success in a college course founded upon the high-school course. One may examine the student's grades or ask him what topics in the college course he found himself poorly prepared for. It is hoped that some of the new science and mathematics courses will arouse greater interest than usual among girls; whether this hope is well founded can be checked by finding out what majors and what electives these ex-students pursue in college. Career choices likewise merit attention. Some proponents of the new curricula would like to see a greater flow of talent into basic science as distinct from technology, while others would regard this as potentially disastrous; but no one would regard facts about this flow as lacking significance.

Attitudes are prominent among the outcomes course developers are concerned with. Attitudes are meanings or beliefs, not mere expressions of approval or disapproval. One's attitude toward science includes ideas about the matters on which a scientist can be an authority, about the benefits to be obtained from moon shots and studies of monkey mothers, and about depletion of natural resources. Equally important is the match between self-concept and concept of the field: What roles does science offer a person like me? Would I want to marry a scientist? and so on. Each learning activity also contributes to attitudes that reach far beyond any one subject, such as the pupil's sense of his own competence and desire to learn.

Attitudes can be measured in many ways; the choices revealed in follow-up studies, for example, are pertinent evidence. But measurement usually takes the form of direct or indirect questioning. Interviews, questionnaires, and the like are quite valuable when not trusted blindly. Certainly, we should take seriously any *un*desirable opinion expressed by a substantial proportion of graduates of a course (e.g., the belief that the scientist speaks with peculiar authority on political and ethical questions, or the belief that mathematics is a finished subject rather than a field for current investigation).

Attitude questionnaires have been much criticized because they are subject to distortion, especially where the student hopes to gain by being less than frank. Particularly if the questions are asked in a context far removed from the experimental course, the returns are likely to be trustworthy. Thus a general questionnaire administered through homerooms (or required English courses) may include questions about liking for various subjects and activities; these same questions administered by the mathematics teacher would give much less trustworthy data on attitude toward mathematics. While students may give reports more favorable than their true beliefs, this distortion is not likely to be greater one year than another, or greater among students who take an experimental course than among those who do not. In group averages, many distortions balance out. But questionnaires insufficiently valid for individual testing can be used in evaluating curricula, both because the student has little motive to distort and because the evaluator is comparing averages rather than individuals.

For measuring proficiency, techniques are likewise varied. Standardized tests are useful. But for course evaluation it makes sense to assign *different* questions to different students. Giving each student in a population of 500 the same test of 50 questions will provide far less information to the course developer than drawing for each student 50 questions from a pool of, say, 700. The latter plan determines the mean success of about 75 representative students on every one of the 700 items; the former reports on only 50 items. (See Lord, 1962.) Essay tests and open-ended questions, generally too expensive to use for routine evaluation, can profitably be employed to appraise certain abilities. One can go further and observe individuals or groups as they attack a research problem in the laboratory or work through some other complex problem. Since it is necessary to test only a representative sample of pupils, costs are not as serious a consideration as in routine testing. Additional aspects of proficiency testing will be considered below.

Process measures have especial value in showing how a course can be improved because they examine what happens during instruction. In the development of programed instructional materials, for example, records are collected showing how many pupils miss each item presented; any piling up of errors implies a need for better explanation or a more gradual approach to a difficult topic. Immediately after showing a teaching film, one can interview students, perhaps asking them to describe a still photograph taken from the film. Misleading presentations, ideas given insufficient emphasis, and matters left unclear will be identified by such methods. Similar interviews can disclose what pupils take away from a laboratory activity or a discussion. A process study might turn attention to what the teacher does in the classroom. In those curricula that allow choice of topics, for example, it is worthwhile to find out which topics are chosen and how much time is allotted to each. A log of class activities (preferably recorded by a pupil rather than the teacher) will show which of the techniques suggested in a summer institute are actually adopted, and which form "part of the new course" only in the developer's fantasies.

MEASUREMENT OF PROFICIENCY

I have indicated that I consider item data to be more important than test scores. The total score may give confidence in a curriculum or give rise to discouragement, but it tells very little

about how to produce further improvement. And, as Ferris (1962) has noted, such scores are quite likely to be mis- or overinterpreted. The score on a single item, or on a problem that demands several responses in succession, is more likely than the test score to suggest how to alter the presentation. When we accept item scores as useful, we need no longer think of evaluation as a one-shot, end-of-year operation. Proficiency can be measured at any moment, with particular interest attaching to those items most related to the recent lessons. Other items calling for general abilities can profitably be administered repeatedly during the course (perhaps to different random samples of pupils) so that we can begin to learn when and from what experiences change in these abilities comes.

In course evaluation, we need not be much concerned about making measuring instruments fit the curriculum. However startling this declaration may seem, and however contrary to the principles of evaluation for other purposes, this must be our position if we want to know what changes a course produces in the pupil. An ideal evaluation would include measures of all the types of proficiency that might reasonably be desired in the area in question, not just the selected outcomes to which this curriculum directs substantial attention. If you wish only to know how well a curriculum is achieving *its* objectives, you fit the test to the curriculum; but if you wish to know how well the curriculum is serving the national interest, you measure all outcomes that might be worth striving for. One of the new mathematics courses might disavow any attempt to teach numerical trigonometry, and indeed, might discard nearly all computational work. It is still perfectly reasonable to ask how well graduates of the course can compute and can solve right triangles. Even if the course developers went so far as to contend that computational skill is no proper objective of secondary instruction, they will encounter educators and laymen who do not share their view. If it can be shown that students who come through the new course are fairly proficient in computation despite the lack of direct teaching, the doubters will be reassured. If not, the evidence makes clear how much is being sacrificed. Similarly, when the biologists offer alternative courses emphasizing microbiology and ecology, it is fair to ask how well the graduate of one course can understand issues treated in the other. Ideal evaluation in mathematics will collect evidence on all the abilities toward which a mathematics course might reasonably aim; likewise in biology, English, or any other subject.

Ferris states that the ACS Chemistry Test, however well constructed, is inadequate for evaluating the new CBA and CHEM programs because it does not cover their objectives. One can agree with this without regarding the ACS test as inappropriate to use with these courses. It is important that this test not stand *alone*, as the sole evaluation device. It will tell us something worth knowing, namely, just how much "conventional" knowledge the new curriculum does or does not provide. The curriculum developers deliberately planned to sacrifice some of the conventional attainments and have nothing to fear from this measurement, competently interpreted (particularly if data are examined item by item).

The demand that tests be closely matched to the aims of a course reflects awareness that examinations of the usual sort "determine what is taught." If questions are known in advance, students give more attention to learning their answers than to learning other aspects of the course. This is not necessarily detrimental. Wherever it is critically important to master certain content, the knowledge that it will be tested produces a desirable concentration of effort. On the other hand, learning the answer to a set question is by no means the same as acquiring understanding of whatever topic that question represents. There is therefore a possible advantage in using "secure" tests for course evaluation. Security is achieved only at a price: One must prepare new tests each year, and cannot make before-and-after comparisons with the same items. One would hope that the use of different items with different students, and the fact that there is less incentive to coach when no judgment is to be passed on the pupils and the teachers, would make security a less critical problem.

The distinction between factual tests and tests of higher mental processes, as elaborated, for example, in the *Taxonomy of Educational Objectives*, is of some value in planning tests, although classifying items as measures of knowledge, application, original problem solving, etc., is difficult and often impossible. Whether a given response represents rote recall or reasoning depends upon how the pupil has been taught, not solely upon the question asked. One might, for example, describe a biological environment and ask for predictions regarding the effect of a certain intervention. Students who had never dealt with ecological data would succeed or fail according to their general ability to reason about complex events; those who had studied ecological biology would be more likely to succeed, reasoning from specific principles; and those who had lived in such an ecology or read about it might answer successfully on the basis of memory. We rarely, therefore, will want to test whether a student "knows" or "does not know" certain material. Knowledge is a matter of degree. Two persons may be acquainted with the same facts or principles, but one will be more expert in his understanding, better able to cope with inconsistent data, irrelevant sources of confusion, and apparent exceptions to the principle. To measure intellectual competence is to measure depth, connectedness, and applicability of knowledge.

Too often, test questions are course-specific, stated in such a way that only the person who has been specifically taught to understand what is being asked for can answer the question. Such questions can usually be identified by their use of conventions. Some conventions are commonplace, and we can assume that all the pupils we test will know them. But a biology test that describes a metabolic process with the aid of the $\rightleftharpoons$ symbol presents difficulties for students who can think through the scientific question about equilibrium but are unfamiliar with the symbol. A trigonometry problem that requires use of a trigonometric table is unreasonable, unless we want to test familiarity with the conventional names of functions. The same problem in numerical trigonometry can be cast in a form clear to the average pupil *entering* high school; if necessary, the tables of functions can be presented along with a comprehensible explanation. So stated, the problem becomes course-independent. It is fair to ask whether graduates of the experimental course can solve such problems, not previously encountered, whereas it is pointless to ask whether they can answer questions whose language is strange to them. To be sure, knowledge of a certain terminology is a significant objective of instruction, but for course evaluation, testing of terminology should very likely be separated from testing of other understandings. To appraise understanding of processes and relations, the fair question is one comprehensible to a pupil who has not taken the course. This is not to say that he should know the answer or the procedure to follow in attaining the answer, but he should understand what he is being asked. Such course-independent questions can be used as standard instruments to investigate any instructional program.

Pupils who have not studied a topic will usually be less facile than those who have studied it. Graduates of my hypothetical mathematics course will take longer to solve trigonometry problems than will those who have studied trig. But speed and power should not be confused; in intellectual studies, power is almost always of greatest importance. If the course equips the pupil to deal correctly even though haltingly with a topic not studied, we can expect him to develop facility later when that topic comes before him frequently.

The chief objective in many of the new curricula seems to be to develop aptitude for mastering new materials in the field. A biology course cannot cover all valuable biological content, but it may reasonably aspire to equip the pupil to understand descriptions of unfamiliar organisms, to comprehend a new theory and the reasoning behind it, and to plan an experiment to test a new hypothesis. This is transfer of learning. It has been insufficiently recognized that there are two types of transfer. The two types shade into one another, being arranged on a continuum of immediacy of effect; we can label the more immediate pole applicational transfer, and speak of slower-acting effects as gains in aptitude (cf. Ferguson, 1954).

Nearly all educational research on transfer has tested immediate performance on a partly new task. We teach pupils to solve equations in x, and include in the test equations stated in a or z. We teach the principles of ecological balance by referring to forests, and as a transfer test ask what effect pollution will have on the population of a lake. We describe an experiment not presented in the text, and ask the student to discuss possible interpretations and needed controls. Any of these tests can be administered in a short time. But the more significant type of transfer may be the increased ability to learn in a particular field. There is very likely a considerable difference between the ability to draw conclusions from a neatly finished experiment, and the ability to tease insight out of the disordered and inconsistent observations that come with continuous laboratory work on a problem. The student who masters a good biology course may become better able to comprehend certain types of theory and data, so that he gains more from a subsequent year of study in ethnology; we do not measure this gain by testing his understanding of short passages in ethnology. There has rarely been an appraisal of ability to work through a problem situation or a complex body of knowledge over a period of days or months. Despite the practical difficulties that attend an attempt to measure the effect of a course on a person's subsequent learning, such "learning to learn" is so important that a serious effort should be made to detect such effects and to understand how they may be fostered.

The technique of programed instruction may be adapted to appraise learning ability. One might, for example, test the student's rate of mastery of a self-contained, programed unit on heat, or some other topic not studied. If the program is truly self-contained, every student can master it, but the one with greater scientific comprehension will hopefully make fewer errors and progress faster. The program might be prepared in several logically complete versions, ranging from one with very small "steps" to one with minimal internal redundancy, on the hypothesis that the

better educated student could cope with the less redundant program. Moreover, he might prefer its greater elegance.

Conclusion

Old habits of thought and long-established techniques are poor guides to the evaluation required for course improvement. Traditionally, educational measurement has been chiefly concerned with producing fair and precise scores for comparing individuals. Educational experimentation has been concerned with comparing score averages of competing courses. But course evaluation calls for description of outcomes. This description should be made on the broadest possible scale, even at the sacrifice of superficial fairness and precision.

Course evaluation should ascertain what changes a course produces and should identify aspects of the course that need revision. The outcomes observed should include general outcomes ranging far beyond the content of the curriculum itself: attitudes, career choices, general understandings and intellectual powers, and aptitude for further learning in the field. Analysis of performance on single items or types of problems is more informative than analysis of composite scores. It is not necessary or desirable to give the same test to all pupils; rather, as many questions as possible should be given, each to a different moderate-sized sample of pupils. Costly techniques such as interviews and essay tests can profitably be applied to samples of pupils, whereas testing everyone would be out of the question.

Asking the right questions about educational outcomes can do much to improve educational effectiveness. Even if the right data are collected, evaluation will have contributed too little if it only places a seal of approval on certain courses and casts others into disfavor. Evaluation is a fundamental part of curriculum development, not an appendage.

Its job is to collect facts the course developer can and will use to do a better job, and facts from which a deeper understanding of the educational process will emerge.

References

Bloom, Benjamin S., ed. *Taxonomy of educational objectives.* New York: Longmans, Green, 1956.

Bloom, Benjamin S. Quality control in education. In *Tomorrow's teaching.* Oklahoma City: Frontiers of Science Foundation of Oklahoma, Inc., 1961. Pp. 54–61.

Ferguson, George A. On learning and human ability. *Canadian Journal of Psychology,* 1954, **8,** 95–112.

Ferris, Frederick L., Jr. Testing in the new curriculums: Numerology, "tyranny," or common sense? *School Review,* 1962, **70,** 112–31.

Lord, Frederic M. Estimating norms by item-sampling. *Educational and Psychological Measurement,* 1962, **22,** 259–68.

Modell, Walter. Hazards of new drugs. *Science,* 1963, **139,** 1180–85.

Tyler, Ralph W. The functions of measurement in improving instruction. In E. F. Lindquist, ed., *Educational Measurement.* Washington, D.C.: American Council on Education, 1951. Pp. 47–67.

41

Instructional Technology and the
Measurement of Learning Outcomes:
Some Questions

ROBERT GLASER / *University of Pittsburgh*

Evaluation of the effectiveness of teaching machines and programed learning, and of broadly conceived instructional systems, has raised into prominence a number of questions concerning the nature and properties of measures of student achievement. In the evaluation of instructional systems, the attainment of subject matter knowledge and skill as well as other behavioral outcomes must, of course, be considered, but the remarks in this paper will be restricted primarily to the measurement of subject matter proficiency, as it may be defined by recognized subject matter scholars.

Achievement measurement can be defined as the assessment of terminal or criterion behavior; this involves the determination of the characteristics of student performance with respect to specified standards. Achievement measurement is distinguished from aptitude measurement in that the instruments used to assess achievement are specifi-cally concerned with the characteristics and properties of present performance, with emphasis on the meaningfulness of its content. In contrast, aptitude measures derive their meaning from a demonstrated relationship between present performance and the future attainment of specified knowledge and skill. In certain circumstances, of course, this contrast is not quite so clear, for example, when achievement measures are used as predictor variables.

The scores obtained from an achievement test provide primarily two kinds of information. One is the degree to which the student has attained criterion performance, for example, whether he can satisfactorily prepare an experimental report, or solve certain kinds of word problems in arithmetic.

Reprinted with the permission of the author and the publisher from *American Psychologist*, 1963, Vol. 18, 519–21.

The second type of information that an achievement test score provides is the relative ordering of individuals with respect to their test performance, for example, whether Student A can solve his problems more quickly than Student B. The principal difference between these two kinds of information lies in the standard used as a reference. What I shall call criterion-referenced measures depend upon an absolute standard of quality, while what I term norm-referenced measures depend upon a relative standard. Distinctions between these two kinds of measures have been made previously by others (Flanagan, 1951; Ebel, 1962).

Criterion-Referenced Measures

Underlying the concept of achievement measurement is the notion of a continuum of knowledge acquisition ranging from no proficiency at all to perfect performance. An individual's achievement level falls at some point on this continuum as indicated by the behaviors he displays during testing. The degree to which his achievement resembles desired performance at any specified level is assessed by criterion-referenced measures of achievement or proficiency. The standard against which a student's performance is compared when measured in this manner is the behavior which defines each point along the achievement continuum. The term "criterion," when used in this way, does not necessarily refer to final end-of-course behavior. Criterion levels can be established at any point in instruction where it is necessary to obtain information as to the adequacy of an individual's performance. The point is that the specific behaviors implied at each level of proficiency can be identified and used to describe the specific tasks a student must be capable

of performing before he achieves one of these knowledge levels. It is in this sense that measures of proficiency can be criterion-referenced.

Along such a continuum of attainment, a student's score on a criterion-referenced measure provides explicit information as to what the individual can or cannot do. Criterion-referenced measures indicate the content of the behavioral repertory, and the correspondence between what an individual does and the underlying continuum of achievement. Measures which assess student achievement in terms of a criterion standard thus provide information as to the degree of competence attained by a particular student which is independent of reference to the performance of others.

Norm-Referenced Measures

On the other hand, achievement measures also convey information about the capability of a student compared with the capability of other students. In instances where a student's *relative* standing along the continuum of attainment is the primary purpose of measurement, reference need not be made to criterion behavior. Educational achievement examinations, for example, are administered frequently for the purpose of ordering students in a class or school, rather than for assessing their attainment of specified curriculum objectives. When such norm-referenced measures are used, a particular student's achievement is evaluated in terms of a comparison between his performance and the performance of other members of the group. Such measures need provide little or no information about the degree of proficiency exhibited by the tested behaviors in terms of what the individual can do. They tell that one student is more or less proficient than another, but do not tell how proficient either of them is with respect to the subject matter tasks involved.

In large part, achievement measures currently employed in education are norm referenced. This emphasis upon norm-referenced measures has been brought about by the preoccupation of test theory with aptitude, and with selection and prediction problems; norm-referenced measures are useful for this kind of work in correlational analysis. However, the imposition of this kind of thinking on the purposes of achievement measurement raises some questions, and concern with instructional technology is forcing us toward the kind of information made available by the use of criterion-referenced measures. We need to behaviorally specify minimum levels of performance that describe the least amount of end-of-course competence the student is expected to attain, or that he needs in order to go on to the next course in a sequence. The specification of the characteristics of maximum or optimum achievement after a student has been exposed to the course of instruction poses more difficult problems of criterion delineation.

The Uses of Achievement Measurement

Consider a further point. In the context of the evaluation of instructional systems, achievement tests can be used for two principal purposes. First, performance can be assessed to provide information about the characteristics of an individual's present behavior. Second, achievement can be assessed to provide information about the conditions or instructional treatments which produce that behavior. The primary emphasis of the first use is to discriminate among individuals. Used in the second way, achievement tests are employed to discriminate among treatments, that is, among different instructional procedures by an analysis of *group* differences.

Achievement tests used to provide information about *individual* differences are constructed so as to maximize the discriminations made among people having specified backgrounds and experience. Such tests include items which maximize the likelihood of observing individual differences in performance along various task dimensions; this maximizes the variability of the distribution of scores that are obtained. In practical test construction, the variability of test scores is increased by manipulating the difficulty levels and content of the test items.

On the other hand, achievement tests used primarily to provide information about differences in treatments need to be constructed so as to maximize the discriminations made between *groups* treated differently and to minimize the differences between the individuals in any one group. Such a test will be sensitive to the differences produced by instructional conditions. For example, a test designed to demonstrate the effectiveness of instruction would be constructed so that it was generally difficult for those taking it before training and generally easy after training. The content of the test used to differentiate treatments should be maximally sensitive to the performance changes anticipated from the instructional treatments. In essence, the distinction between achievement tests used to maximize individual differences and tests used to maximize treatment or group differences is established during the selection of test items.

In constructing an achievement test to differentiate among *individuals* at the end of training, it would be possible to begin by obtaining data on a large sample of items relating to curriculum objectives. Item analysis would indicate that some test items were responded to correctly only by some of the individuals in the group, while other items were answered correctly by all members of the group. These latter 1.00 difficulty level items, since they failed to differentiate among individuals, would be eliminated because their only effect would be to add a constant to every score. The items remaining would serve to discriminate among individuals and thus yield a distribution of scores that was as large as possible, considering the number and type of items used.

On the other hand, if this test were constructed for the purpose of observing *group* instead of individual differences, the selection of items would follow a different course. For example, where instruction was the treatment variable involved, it would be desirable to retain test items which were responded to correctly by all members of the post-training group, but which were answered incorrectly by students who had not yet been trained. In a test constructed for the purpose of differentiating groups, items which indicated substantial variability within either the pre- or posttraining group would be undesirable because of the likelihood that they would cloud the effects which might be attributable to the treatment variable.

In brief, items most suitable for measuring individual differences in achievement are those which will differentiate among individuals all exposed to the same treatment variable, while items most suitable for distinguishing between groups are those which are most likely to indicate that a given amount or kind of some instructional treatment was effective. In either case, samples of test items are drawn from a population of items indicating the content of performance; the particular item samples that are drawn, however, are those most useful for the purpose of the kind of measurement being carried out. Hammock (1960) has previously discussed such a difference.

The points indicated above reflect the achievement measurement concerns that have arisen in my own work with instructional technology. There is one further point which must be mentioned, and that is the use of diagnostic achievement tests prior to an instructional course. It appears that, with the necessity for specifying the entering behavior that is required by a student prior to a programed instructional sequence, diagnostic assessment of subject matter competence must take on a more precise function. This raises the problem of developing an improved methodology for diagnostic achievement testing. In this regard, researchers using programed instructional sequences to study learning variables point out that prior testing influences learning, and that this effect must be controlled in determining the specific contribution of programing variables. In an instructional sense, however, the influence and use of pretesting is an important variable for study, since it is not the terminal criterion behavior alone which dictates required instructional manipulations, but the differences between entering and terminal behavior. Furthermore, pretesting of a special kind may contribute to "motivation" by enhancing the value of future responses; there is some indication that this may be brought about by prior familiarity with future response terms (Berlyne, 1960, pp. 296–301) or by permitting some early aided performance of the terminal behavior eventually to be engaged in (Taber, Glaser, & Schaefer, 1963, Ch. 3).

In conclusion, the general point is this. Test development has been dominated by the particular requirements of predictive, correlational aptitude test "theory." Achievement and criterion measurement has attempted frequently to cast itself in this framework. However, many of us are beginning to recognize that the problems of assessing existing levels of competence and achievement and the conditions that produce them require some additional considerations.

References

Berlyne, D. E. *Conflict, arousal, and curiosity.* New York: McGraw-Hill, 1960.

Ebel, R. L. Content standard test scores. *Educ. Psychol. Measmt.,* 1962, **22,** 15–25.

Flanagan, J. C. Units, scores, and norms. In E. T. Lindquist, ed., *Educational measurement.* Washington, D.C.: American Council on Education, 1951. Pp. 695–763.

Glaser, R. and Klaus, D. J. Proficiency measurement: Assessing human performance. In R. Gagné, ed., *Psychological principles in system development.* New York: Holt, Rinehart & Winston, 1962. Pp. 421–27.

Hammock, J. Criterion measures: Instruction vs. selection research. *Amer. Psychologist,* 1960, **15,** 435. (Abstract.)

Taber, J. I., Glaser, R., and Schaefer, H. H. *A guide to the preparation of programmed instructional materials.* Reading, Mass.: Addison-Wesley, 1965.

42

Curriculum Evaluation: The Why of the Outcomes

J. THOMAS HASTINGS / *University of Illinois*

For many years the expression "curriculum evaluation" has tended to mean to most people some sort of use and interpretation of achievement tests. Most assuredly, this is a very real part of the total concept of evaluation, but the thesis of this paper is that the concept must be broadened to include other sorts of ventures besides those of collecting and summarizing the test scores of students who have undergone a particular curricular treatment. The most commonly held idea of the sequence of evaluation endeavors starts with the act of stating the objectives of a set of materials—a full course, a unit of some sort, or a group of several units. This is followed by definition of these objectives in behavioral terms. Next comes the development of items, that is, situations which call for the behavior defined. These items are combined into scorable units; scores are obtained on appropriate samples of youngsters. Then, finally, the sequence ends in attempts to interpret these scores in terms of the extent to which the new materials have developed the behaviors which satisfy the purposes which the innovators had in mind.

A bit of experience in this area on a real job of evaluation will convince anyone that the steps of this total procedure —as simple as they are to state—are laden with problems of several kinds. We have the usual measurement problems of any test construction together with certain special problems of sampling and of the treatment of gain scores. Furthermore, all of this is imbedded in larger tactical problems of deriving the data from ongoing classroom settings. There is no denying the importance of solving these various problems if we are to move forward in evaluation of educational curricula.

Reprinted with the permission of the author and the publisher from *Journal of Educational Measurement*, 1966, Vol. 3, 27–32.

At this point, however, it is important to raise the question of "What are the purposes of evaluation?" in order to lead into the theme that we need a considerably broader attack than is implied by the sequence described in the first paragraph. In curriculum innovation as a real ongoing venture there are *two* general purposes for evaluation. One of these concerns collection of information to be used as feedback to the innovators for further revision of materials and methods. Without such feedback, either the decision to revise or the decision not to revise—and most certainly the decision of how to revise—must be based upon feeling tones and the arguments of personal preference. The second main purpose of evaluation of educational innovation is to provide information as input for decision-making by the schools about adoption of course-content-improvement packages. The extent to which the decision-making system of a school *does not have* empirical data concerning changes in the behavior of students who are undergoing particular curriculum treatments *is* the extent to which the decisions will be based upon such dimensions as glamour, public visibility, political expediency, and personal acquaintance with specific curriculum innovators.

If the educational establishment is to move toward the point of basing decisions about revision and decisions about adoption on educational purpose and outcome, we need far more evaluation data of all kinds than we have had in any instance to date. We do need, however, somewhat different kinds of data for the two purposes I mentioned—revision and adoption.

First, here is a very sketchy description of a hypothetical instance of doing the evaluation job in a superior way using the usual model of test scores. To make the general model an example, the reader should think of the content and grade or age level upon which he can focus most comfortably. This may be a full year's course—such as one of the Biological Sciences Curriculum Study versions or, as will be true if present plans hold, the new High School Geography Project; or the innovation of which you are thinking may consist of units of work which might be inserted at various places in the curriculum—as is true of the School Science Curriculum Project under Salinger's direction and, also, of some of the work in anthropology being carried on at the University of Chicago; or you may have in mind a program of innovation which will cover several years—like the Elementary School Science Project for grades five through eight, which is directed by Atkin, or the Social Science Curriculum Project for grades seven through twelve, which is directed by Leppert. Keep something such as one of these in mind while I give the following description of a *good* "test-centered evaluation." First, let us assume that there are eight definable objectives (we could play the game with three or with twenty-five). These objectives cover such things as knowledge of specific facts and assertions, attitudes toward operations or areas, the development of certain cognitive processes, and the ability to use knowledge in an interpretive fashion. Next, let us assume that we have put each of these objectives in behavioral terms, even to the extent of having two or more kinds of behaviors for each of the objectives. The next assumption is that we have been able to set up two comparable, reliable tests on each of the behaviorally defined objectives and these tests may consist of some paper-and-pencil material, some performance tests, or even some systematically summarized observational data. The two comparable tests are for the purpose of pretesting and posttesting in a design which calls for both immediate learning and for retention. The final assumption is that we now have results in the form of test scores from an appropriate sampling of relevant populations. This allows, if you want it that way, for us to have a sampling from treated groups and a sampling from untreated groups. The point is that there are sets of test scores from relevant samples of youngsters and these scores reflect reasonably well the kinds of behaviors which the curricular materials were intended to develop. These scores can be manipulated statistically in order to draw inferences concerning the extent to which the behaviors have been acquired at the time of use of the curricular materials.

Now let's take a look at what we have in terms of the two purposes mentioned earlier: (1) revision or development of new materials and (2) the adoption of the present materials. In making the adoption-decision we might very easily have sufficient data. The decision to adopt or reject would be based upon the relative values that the school attached to this or that behavior and the extent to which those behaviors were developed.

Now let's look at the curriculum-revision-and-development decision. The data indicate that the new materials meet the criteria on the *average* at such and such a level or with such and such a probability. Shall the innovators try to revise the materials to do a better job? If so, what sorts of revision should they make? I contend that these decisions are of a different sort than those of adoption-decision. The statistical summaries may give us hints that the material did work on this objective but did not work as well with that objective. In any real situation they certainly will tell us that the materials did not work perfectly on any of the objectives.

If we were the innovators, one of the first obvious next moves with the test data would be to pull away from the scores themselves and look more closely for interpretation in the test-item data. From the course-content-improvement standpoint this certainly might help us discover that, although we seem to have done fairly well with this particular attitude, we missed rather dreadfully on that one. Test-item data might tell us that the students acquired certain of the concepts but missed other concepts further than we think should be necessary. The data still help us comparatively little with the question of *how to revise*. What we need are data which throw some light on the "why" of the test results.

This is the point then at which we need information in addition to any of the usual test-information which we might develop. Please understand that this is no assertion that the test-information has been useless. The information from a test-centered evaluation might be all we need for the adoption-rejection decision in the school—and the data would suggest clues to the curriculum builder. The point is that the course-content-improvement innovator needs, deserves, and can get more information than that which is encompassed in tests interpreted through scores or item data. The suggestion is that we should spend considerably more time than we have to date on what may be called instructional research. Perhaps you have a better name for it, but the general nature of the stuff may look a lot like the research on learning which has been going on for years in the psychology laboratories—as a matter of fact, at certain stages in the game it may be difficult to discriminate between standard learning research and instructional research except that in the long run the latter will collect data in an ongoing classroom. For purposes of explication, here are a few examples of the sorts of investigations which could be carried on and which, if carried on, should be of real use to the curriculum innovator in revising his materials.

Easley (1964) and others connected with the Universtiy of Illinois Committee on School Mathematics, under the direction of Max Beberman (1963), have been taking a fresh look at the concept structure of the mathematics material presented to students. They are especially interested in the effects on concept formation and attainment of ordering or sequencing of mathematics exercises. Now concept-formation research has been with us for a long time. Ordinarily the content is color, shape, or number—not real instructional material for the school. Richard C. Anderson (1964) points out, however, in a paper on stimulus sequence and concept learning, that the sequence of stimuli has been treated only incidentally, or at least very rarely, in concept-formation studies. We can be even more certain, however, that the notion of concept sequence has seldom been appropriately studied in the instructional setting of school classrooms using the new curriculum ventures. We certainly have the possibility, however, with the design techniques and the hardware we have at hand today to carry on fairly extensive studies both of sequence of stimuli and of sequence of concepts being developed in units of instructional work. The results of such studies would be important feedback information for decisions about whether or not to revise and in what way to revise new materials which are being tried out. Furthermore, within a given content domain and over some specified age or grade level (or perhaps conditioned by some readiness specification) we might be able to arrive at general rules for the development of new

curricular material which would come closer to the target than would the guesses—reasoned as they are—of the subject-matter specialist or the experienced teacher.

Another example also comes from some work going on in connection with the University of Illinois Committee on School Mathematics. Hiroshi Ikeda (1965) studied the relationship between teacher-held objectives and student achievement. Far too simply stated, the work stems from observations that teachers trained specifically in institutes directed at helping them teach special new mathematics material seem to come out with quite different results. This kind of a fact could have been ascertained from a test-centered evaluation. The point of my argument is that we must go beyond ascertaining that there are differences and inquire into "Why does this difference exist?" Ikeda hypothesized that teachers hold, not necessarily explicitly, somewhat different objectives in their views of the classroom even though they may understand and appreciate the objectives set forth by the authors of the new curriculum materials —and that these "personal" objectives affect student attainment. Such studies could be helpful in locating points for revision of both student and teacher material.

A third example has to do with retention and could be adopted to transfer studies. Retention studies with straight test techniques demand a kind of retention which we think of as *direct recall* of assertions, principles, and perhaps processes. Another kind of retention, however—one which Cronbach (1963) has mentioned—is the type related to savings in learning. The idea is not new— but its application to course-content improvement is. For purposes of this kind of retention we need instructional research which would call for attempts to teach students (or reteach students) material which is based upon material which had been learned previously. By appropriate treatment-nontreatment design and by varying the length of time between the original learning situation and the savings investigation, it should be possible to collect a considerable amount of evidence which would be of real use to the curriculum innovator in revising old materials and developing new. This same general pattern could be used for investigating the savings which would occur in transferring from one domain to another after treatment with different curriculum materials in the same area.

One final type of investigation which would help immeasurably with the development of curriculum materials—and in this case would add valuable information for the adoption-rejection decision in the school—is exemplified by some studies by R. E. Stake and D. D. Sjogren (1964). Without going into detail about their studies, the general import is that they were investigating the relative advantages—for individuals with varying characteristics—of different modes of studying the same materials. If we apply this type of investigation to some of the new curriculum ventures, much more definite statements can be made in answer to the question "For whom are various activity levels effective and what treatments will be most useful for which students?"

Experience says it is important at this point to defend the proposition that such instructional research is a real part of evaluation. Defense may not be necessary for some readers; but others will say, "Why don't you separate the actual curriculum evaluation (the test-centered activities) from what you are calling instructional research, which is a type of investigation educational psychology has been carrying on for years?" First, any investigation that works in the direction of letting us know *why* students learn from this activity better than they do from that activity is by definition part of the input for evaluation decisions of either type. Secondly, the sort of research just described has not been carried on—at least very plentifully—in educational-psychology investigations. Usually such investigations have not been concerned with a particular set of curricular materials. They have been concerned more generally with the concepts of retention, transfer, and concept formation. Such investigations should be centered upon specific curriculum materials. One can visualize the time in the future when a sufficient number of such investigations have been completed across various content areas and with various age levels so that broad principles or generalizations can be made about new materials without having to carry on additional investigations. The effective variables are so plentiful that the day when we can generalize in that fashion is certainly far in the future.

Test-item data and relationships among test scores and subscores would be much more useful, especially to the curriculum innovator, if we were to use techniques of instructional research to attempt to discover answers to the question of "Why do we obtain these outcomes and for whom?" To do the job properly it will be necessary to carry on investigations in a replicative fashion with many different contents and at many different levels. The plea of this paper is simply that all of those involved in curriculum evaluation should attend much more wholeheartedly than they have in the past to instructional research as an important aspect of evaluation.

References

Anderson, R. C. *Stimulus sequence and concept learning (Experiment I).* University of Illinois, Urbana, Ill., 1964. (Mimeo, unpublished.)

Beberman, Max. *Searching for patterns.* University of Illinois Committee on School Mathematics, University of Ill., Urbana, Illinois, 1963. (Mimeo.)

Cronbach, L. J. Course improvement through evaluation. *Teachers College Record,* 1963, **64,** 672–83.

Easley, J. A. Jr. *Features of UICSM Mathematics Project of possible interest to psychologists.* University of Illinois, Urbana, Ill. May 1964. (Ditto.)

Ikeda, Hiroshi. *A factorial study of the relationships between teacher-held objectives and student performance in UICSM high school mathematics.* UICSM Report No. 10. University of Illinois, Urbana, Ill., June 1965.

Stake, R. E. and Sjogren, D. D. *Activity level and learning effectiveness.* Title VII Project No. 753, NDEA Grant 7-37-0220-147. University of Nebraska, Lincoln, Neb., 1964.

Author Index

Adams, M. A., 241
Allen, D. W., 57, 59
Allen, K. E., 180, 183, 184, 189
Alter, M., 120, 130, 174, 178
Ammons, A., 298
Ammons, R. B., 149, 154
Amsel, A., 202, 209
Anderson, B., 122, 130
Anderson, R. C., 75, 76, 107, 111, 112, 113, 117, 163, 382, 384
Angell, D., 125, 130
Angell, G. W., 149, 154
Appel, J. B., 78, 81
Arnstine, D. G., 69, 72
Ashbaugh, W. H., 203, 209
Atkin, J. M., 2, 33, 36, 46, 60, 352, 360
Attneave, F., 258, 262
Austin, G. A., 240, 262
Ausubel, D. P., 8, 10, 265, 269, 279, 280, 312, 319, 320, 321, 329, 330, 333
Ayers, L. P., 47, 53

Bachrach, A. J., 81
Baer, D. M., 183, 184, 188, 189
Barrett, T., 219, 270

Bassham, H., 355, 360
Bassler, O. C., 279, 280
Bathurst, L. H., 257, 262
Beberman, M., 382, 384
Becker, W. C., 81, 82
Bellack, A. A., 4, 5, 10, 12
Berlak, H., 353, 360
Berlyne, D. E., 377, 378
Bernstein, J., 75, 76
Biddle, B. J., 6, 7, 10, 11, 12, 14
Bijou, S. W., 74, 76, 184, 189, 190, 196
Binder, A., 198, 201
Birnbrauer, J. S., 190, 191, 196, 197
Blake, E. Jr., 321, 329
Bloom, B. S., 313, 319, 363, 364, 373
Bolvin, J. O., 11, 14
Bousfield, W. A., 335, 342
Bouthilet, L., 230, 240
Bowen, E., 4, 12
Braden, W., 142, 148
Brawley, E. R., 183, 189
Briggs, G. E., 287, 293, 298
Briggs, L. J., 203, 209
Broadbent, D. E., 258, 262
Brong, C., 85, 93

Subject
Index

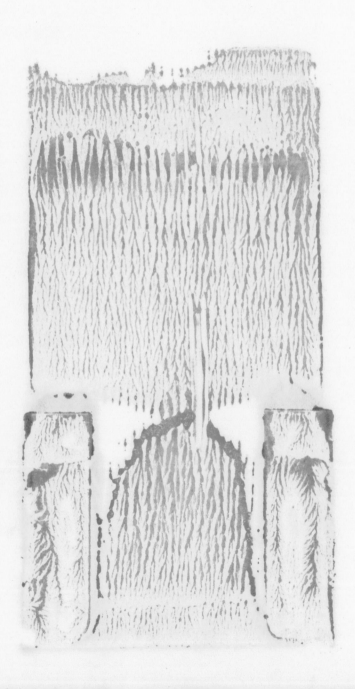